Handbook of Research in International Human Resource Management

LEA'S ORGANIZATION AND MANAGEMENT SERIES

Series Editors
Arthur P. Brief
University of Utah
James P. Walsh
University of Michigan
Associate Series Editor
Sara L. Rynes
University of Iowa

Handbook of Research in
International
Human Resource
Management

Edited by
Michael M. Harris

Lawrence Erlbaum Associates
Taylor & Francis Group

New York   London

Lawrence Erlbaum Associates
Taylor & Francis Group
270 Madison Avenue
New York, NY 10016

Lawrence Erlbaum Associates
Taylor & Francis Group
2 Park Square
Milton Park, Abingdon
Oxon OX14 4RN

© 2008 by Taylor & Francis Group, LLC
Lawrence Erlbaum Associates is an imprint of Taylor & Francis Group, an Informa business

Printed in the United States of America on acid-free paper
10 9 8 7 6 5 4 3 2 1

International Standard Book Number-13: 978-0-8058-4949-3 (Softcover) 978-0-8058-4948-6 (Hardcover)

Library of Congress Cataloging-in-Publication Data

Handbook of research in international human resources / Michael M. Harris, editor.
    p. cm. -- (LEA's organization and management series)
  Includes bibliographical references and index.
  ISBN 978-0-8058-4949-3 (alk. paper) -- ISBN 978-0-8058-4948-6 (alk. paper) -- ISBN
  978-1-4106-1824-5 (alk. paper)
    1. International business enterprises--Personnel management--Handbooks, manuals, etc. 2. International business enterprises--Personnel management. I. Harris, Michael M.

  HF5549.5.E45H363 2007
  658.3--dc22
                                       2007011799

Visit the Taylor & Francis Web site at
http://www.taylorandfrancis.com

and the LEA Web site at
http://www.erlbaum.com

Dedication

This book is dedicated to my wife Pat and our children — Nosson and his wife Ora, David, Rochel, Anne, and Yoni — and our grandchildren Eliyahu Dovid, Zechariah Yosef, and Yitzchak.

Table of Contents

Foreword

In *The World Is Flat*, the Pulitzer prize-winning journalist, Thomas Friedman, describes playing a round of golf in Bangalore, India, in February 2004:

> No one ever gave me directions like this on a golf course before: "Aim at either Microsoft or IBM." I was standing on the first tee at the KGA Golf Club in downtown Bangalore, in southern India, when my playing partner pointed at two shiny glass-and-steel buildings off in the distance ... HP and Texas Instruments had their offices on the back nine. That wasn't all. The tee markers were from Epson, the printer company, and one of our caddies was wearing a hat from 3M. Outside, some of the traffic signs were also sponsored by Texas Instruments, and the Pizza Hut billboard on the way over showed a steaming pizza, under the deadline "Gigabites of Taste!"

In the first chapter alone, Friedman describes how American companies are hiring Indian radiologists to read x-rays taken in the United States, Indian accountants to prepare U.S. taxes, Indian financial journalists to generate earnings reports and conduct basic financial analyses for Bloomberg, and Indian computer experts to talk American consumers through software glitches. What does it take to move from domestic to global manufacturing and service provision? To help organizations make these dramatic kinds of adjustments, what do human resource managers need to know and do?

Some of the HR tasks involved in globalization are much the same as domestic tasks, only more complex. For example, workers must be selected, trained, and compensated in either setting. However, many more uncertainties abound in cross-national settings. Do the same personal traits predict success in different cultures? Can they be assessed via similar methods? How can customer service employees be trained to respond appropriately to the tacit understandings that exist in another culture? Which parts of a job embody strategic knowledge or skills that should not be outsourced, and which represent knowledge or skills that might best be commoditized?

In addition to the greater complexity of such basic HR functions as selection, training, and job design in global settings, there are also questions in areas that many HR managers (and researchers) know little about, such as technology, business strategy, organizational design, organizational change, and international law. Although HR experts should not be expected to have primary responsibility for such areas, there is much that both managers and researchers can do to better advise organizations faced with such daunting challenges.

In the *Handbook of Research in International Human Resource Management*, Michael Harris and other prominent HR researchers address the question of what is known, and not known, about managing people in international settings. After reading the chapters in this volume, one realizes just how many opportunities there are for researchers to provide better guidance to organizations racing to manage in the "flat world" of the twenty-first century. In nearly every functional area of HR, the authors show that there are many questions waiting to be addressed or answered more definitively.

Equally important, this book goes beyond simply reviewing research in the functional areas of HR. For example, Paul Sparrow and Werner Braun situate international HR management (HRM) in the broader context of international business strategy. In addition, David Chan draws on his considerable expertise in both HRM and research methods to alert researchers to important methodological issues in international HR research. Similarly, Robert Gephart and Julia Richardson share their expertise on a set of methodologies—that is, qualitative research strategies—that have been underemployed in human resources research. Making greater use of these methodologies will simultaneously facilitate other objectives, such as tapping the substantial expertise of international HRM practitioners and studying the organizational change processes that inevitably must accompany changes in policies, practices, or procedures. John Lawler, Fred Walumbwa, and Bing Bai discuss aspects of national culture and how they affect the workplace, while Greg Hundley and Pamela Marett describe differences in industrial relations systems and their effects on national economies and workplace relations.

It is an exciting time to get involved in international human resources research. Just as more and more businesses have expanded globally, so more and more business schools have expanded their programs to other continents. As more and more academics teach and get to know managers and academics in other parts of the world, new opportunities for research and consulting collaborations are created. Organizations such as the International Association of Chinese Management Research, InfoHRM, and regional affiliates of the Academy of Management are increasing the number of conferences devoted to international management issues of interest to both academics and practitioners. At this point in time, we have the opportunity to discover, as never before, the extent to which there are certain "universalistic truths" to human behavior. We can also learn the extent to which human skills, abilities, and personalities are malleable in the face of dramatically new stimuli and choices. Harris and the other authors of this handbook help to show us where to begin.

Sara Rynes, Arthur Brief, and James Walsh
Series editors

Acknowledgments

I would like to thank a number of individuals for helping me complete this project. Sara Rynes' help is most appreciated. Sara not only helped convince the publisher of the merits of the book, she was also very helpful in reviewing the chapters, providing comments, and encouraging me to continue when I needed encouragement. She went out of her way to offer help. Anne Duffy was also supportive and provided excellent encouragement as well. Without their ongoing support, this book would not have come to fruition. I would also like to thank the patience of Prudy Taylor Board, project editor. She put up with a major delay that I caused.

Closer to home, Joel Glassman, associate provost for academic affairs, and director, Center for International Studies, along with Keith Womer, dean of the College of Business Administration, both of the University of Missouri-St. Louis, were helpful in providing release time to work on this book. I am most grateful for their assistance in this regard.

Finally, my wife, Pat, has been my life force, enabling me to work on this book. She has practically single-handedly kept me going when life has thrown difficult challenges in my way. Without her presence, I would not have had the desire, let alone the opportunity, to complete this book.

Contributors

Bing Bai
University of Illinois at Urbana-Champaign
Institute of Labor and Industrial Relations
Champaign, Illinois

Caroline Bailey
Queensland University of Technology,
Brisbane, Australia

Allan Bird
College of Business Administration
University of Missouri-St. Louis
St. Louis, Missouri

Werner Braun
Manchester Business School
Booth Street West
Manchester, UK

Jean-Luc Cerdin
ESSEC Business School
Cergy-Pontoise, France

David Chan
National University of Singapore
School of Economics and Social Sciences
Singapore Management University
Singapore

Clive Fletcher
Goldsmiths College, University of London,
  and Personnel Assessment Ltd.
London, UK

Robert P. Gephart, Jr.
Department of Strategic Management
  and Organization
University of Alberta
Edmonton, Canada

Michael Harris
College of Business
University of Missouri-St. Louis
St. Louis, Missouri

Greg Hundley
Krannert Graduate School of Management
Purdue University
West Lafayette, Indiana

John J. Lawler
University of Illinois at Urbana-Champaign
Institute of Labor and Industrial Relations
Champaign, Illinois

Filip Lievens
Department of Personnel Management, Work
  and Organizational Psychology
Ghent University
Ghent, Belgium

Pamela Marett
Sul Ross State University
Alpine, Texas

Jessica R. Mesmer-Magnus
University of North Carolina at Wilmington
601 South College Road
Wilmington, North Carolina

Seungrib Park
Psychology Department
University of Nebraska
Omaha, Nebraska

Julia Richardson
School of Administrative Studies
York University
Atkinson Faculty, Keele Street
Toronto, Canada

Paul Sparrow
Director, Centre for Performance-Led HR
  and Professor of International Human
  Resource Management
Lancaster University Management School
Lancaster, UK

Chockalingam Viswesvaran
Department of Psychology
Florida International University
Miami,
Lancaster University Management School
Lancaster, UK

Fred Ochieng Walumbwa
Department of Management
School of Global Management
 and Leadership
The Arizona State University
Phoenix, Arizona

1 Introduction

Michael M. Harris

CONTENTS

In the last decade or so, there has been a surge of interest in international human resource management (IHRM) issues, as indicated by several updated textbooks in the area, a growth in journals focusing on IHRM issues (e.g., the *International Journal of Human Resource Management*), and a marked increase in international content in major management journals (see Kirkman & Law, 2005). Correspondingly, there has been a rapid increase in the pace of international business. More than ever before, the global business world is interconnected; events in one part of the world (e.g., an explosion in a gas pipeline in the Middle East) have ramifications in other parts of the world (e.g., the Asian stock market). The ability to outsource specific particular functions (e.g., information technology, manufacturing) to other parts of the world means that even the smallest of companies may interact with people in different countries. Clearly, these possibilities lead to greater opportunities, as well as challenges, from a business perspective.

The globalization of business has spawned a number of trends of potential interest for IHRM practitioners. First, the advent of "offshoring," whereby companies in one country send work to be performed in another country, has affected human resource management (HRM) in a variety of ways. For example, from an organizational design perspective, an important question concerns what is the best organizational structure for managing such an arrangement, particularly when workers may be thousands of miles away from the corporate headquarters and when conventional communication methods (e.g., face-to-face discussion) may not be possible on a regular basis. Another question is how best to design a pay-for-performance system for a company where work is performed in another country. Among the many practical questions is the issue of whether workers will even be motivated by whichever pay-for-performance plan is created.

Another important trend is the growing importance of expatriate experience for managerial careers. Over the last few decades, the importance and focus of an expatriate experience appears to have changed. At one time, an expatriate experience may have created more problems than gains for the manager. Today, however, obtaining some kind of international work experience appears to be more critical than ever before (Stroh et al., 2005). It is commonplace for practitioners to assert that having global work experience is essential for a successful career in many fields. In turn, the role of global work experience is likely to change the way in which careers evolve.

From a research perspective, HRM has traditionally had a strong Western orientation. Until recently, most of the scholars in the field have been trained in North American universities and have taken jobs in those universities. Not surprisingly, much of the research published in the mainstream HRM journals, such as the *Academy of Management Journal*, the *Journal of Applied*

Psychology, and *Personnel Psychology*, has been conducted in North American settings, using measures designed and validated in this context. During the last decade, however, there have been some fundamental shifts. More universities in other regions of the world, including the United Kingdom as well as continental Europe, have begun HRM programs. Increasing numbers of scholars from Asia, as well as other areas outside of North America, have begun submitting and publishing IHRM research in mainstream journals. It is clear that we must expand our view of HRM to incorporate a global perspective. This, then, is the purpose of the present volume. Specifically, the aim is to review what is currently known about IHRM, describe what future research questions are important to answer, and in general, provide directions for future IHRM researchers.

The focus of this handbook is on research, not on practice. Although there are practical implications of much of this research, our interest is primarily on describing previous findings, offering new hypotheses, and setting directions for future investigations. In reading the chapters that follow, there are several broad themes that are covered to varying degrees within each chapter. These themes are:

1. Do HR practices, programs, and outcomes differ from country to country? If the answer is yes, why do they differ? Specifically, does culture explain these differences?
2. Is there a "best" set of HR practices and programs that should be implemented internationally?
3. Are our HRM theories broad enough to fit internationally or do we need to develop specific theories for different regions of the world?

I discuss each of these themes in more detail next.

DO HR PRACTICES AND PROGRAMS DIFFER INTERNATIONALLY?

A frequently addressed question in IHRM research is whether HR practices and programs differ from country to country. There are at least two reasons for why this question is commonly addressed. First, in many ways, it is the simplest question to study. At a minimum, all that one needs are data from two countries to offer at least a partial answer to the question. Although there are serious limitations to such a study design (see Chapter 4) and the mere availability of data is not a sufficient reason to conduct a study, there may nevertheless be good reasons to study this question. In particular, determining whether HR practices and programs differ internationally is a precursor to other questions. For example, only if HR practices and programs really differ is it worth asking whether we need to develop specific theories for different regions of the world. The more interesting, and theoretically richer, aspect is the second part of the question—namely, if there are differences in HR programs and practices, why do they exist?

Most of the research in this regard has focused on linking country HR differences to culture. For the most part, the logic here has been that cultures emphasizing collectivism, for example, will prefer compensation rewards that reflect group cohesion, whereas cultures that are predominantly individualistic will emphasize compensation programs that reward individuals. Indeed, examining the relationships between various HR practices and culture appears to have supported these kinds of arguments (e.g., see Chapter 2 on culture).

Quite often, however, this question has not been studied in an ideal way. Instead of obtaining data from a variety of cultures that vary along the spectrum of interest (e.g., individualism/collectivism), researchers have obtained a convenience sample of two countries and compared the results. Any differences are then attributed to the factor of interest (e.g., individualism/collectivism), although there may be other potential explanatory reasons for the differences (see Chapter 4). Thus, there is clearly a need for much more research on the relationship between culture and HR practices, programs, and outcomes.

IS THERE A "BEST" SET OF HR PRACTICES AND PROGRAMS?

Looking over the history of HRM and its related areas, it is safe to say that there has been conflict between the emergence of contingency theories, which assume that "best practices" depend on various contextual factors, and universal theories, which assume that there is a set of "best practices" that apply in virtually all circumstances. In the international context, it might (at least at first blush) seem most reasonable to make an argument for contingency theories, rather than a single universal theory. After all, countries differ widely in terms of history, culture, and traditions. To expect different countries to operate similarly seems simple-minded at best. At the same time, it has been argued that there is a great homogenization going on worldwide; technologies such as the Internet are bringing Western culture throughout the world and are affecting styles, culture, and aspirations, especially among younger generations. In this light, universalistic theories of IHRM do not seem so implausible. Only further research will answer the question as to whether contingency theories or a universalistic theory of "best" HR practices will be sufficient.

Studying whether there is one best set of HRM practices is not a simple task. One approach would involve manipulating conditions such that one group receives a treatment (e.g., pay-for-performance plan X), while another group receives a different treatment (e.g., pay-for-performance plan Y). One would also want to have subjects from many different cultures in each condition to determine whether there is an interaction between treatment condition and culture. Of course, one would also need to control for prior treatment effects. For example, subjects from some cultures may be used to having pay-for-performance plan X, and therefore they have a high comfort level with it. Subjects from other cultures may not have been exposed to this type of plan and therefore will take time to adjust before they reach a comfort level. These and other factors may make it more difficult to truly assess whether there is a "best set" of HRM practices that applies across cultures. Becker and Gerhart's (1996) notion that HR "practices," which seem very different at one level (e.g., a company in one culture uses an individual incentive program, while a company in a different culture uses a group incentive program) may be quite similar at the "architectural" level (e.g., both companies reward employees for performance) may be important here.

These complexities should not be taken, however, as an indicator that a search for the "best set" of HRM practices is misguided or of no value. To the contrary, I believe that the search for a "best set" of HRM practices will help transform our field from an infant science to a well-developed, highly respected science.

ARE OUR HRM THEORIES BROAD ENOUGH TO FIT INTERNATIONALLY?

Finally an important question that must be considered is whether our theories are comprehensive enough to cover HRM on a global basis or whether they need to be modified. There are several possibilities here. One possibility is that all of the relevant variables are included in our theories, but the causal order differs in different cultures; alternatively, some of our theories may need additional variables in order to be applied to other cultures. A third possibility is that we need completely different theories in order to understand HRM programs, practices, and outcomes in different cultures. Again, much more empirical work is needed here to answer this question.

A final comment is in order here. Much of the emphasis on IHRM appears to be on testing for cultural *differences*. As Chan points out in Chapter 4, however, researchers have a tendency to design their studies, and to interpret the results, in ways that will support their assumptions. In a recent review, Ofori-Dankwa and Ricks (2000) asserted that IHRM scholars assume that there will be cultural differences and highlight those findings that show such differences. As a result, they call for more careful analysis and discussion of cross-cultural similarities, as well as differences. We need to be careful to emphasize that there may be similarities across cultures and should be cautious that we do not ignore these similarities when they occur. Of course, apparent similarities may be due to lack of power to find differences, so we must also consider methodological and statistical explanations for apparent similarity as well.

ORGANIZATION OF THE BOOK

The remainder of this volume addresses both research methodology and content-oriented issues. First, Lawler, Walumbwa, and Bai provide an overview of the concept of culture and explain how this construct has been used in previous research. The next two chapters address methodological issues in IHRM. The first of these chapters, by Gephart and Richardson, addresses qualitative research methods and describes various techniques in conducting IHRM research. The next chapter, by Chan, focuses on quantitative research methods, with an emphasis on problems associated with this approach in IHRM research.

Chapter 5, by Sparrow and Braun, addresses macro-level IHRM research. Specifically, they examine strategic IHRM, with an emphasis on the appropriate structure of a global organization and theories concerning the strengths of being a global company. Chapters on employee selection, performance appraisal, and compensation follow next. Chapter 6, on employee selection, by Lievens, addresses questions concerning the relationships between culture and the use of different predictors, reactions to different tests, and whether test validity generalizes across countries and cultures. Fletcher and Bailey's chapter on performance appraisal reviews major theories of performance measurement and offers hypotheses about the relationship between culture and performance appraisal practices. Finally, Harris and Park address compensation in a global context, reporting some well-researched issues, as well as some underresearched areas of compensation.

In Chapter 9, Hundley and Marett address labor relations and unions in a global context. They question the relationship between culture and union-management relations, arguing that there is little reason to assume such a relationship exists. Mesmer-Magnus and Viswesvaran review the literature on expatriates in Chapter 10. They show that while there is a vast literature in this area covering selection, training, and repatriation of expatriates, there are many research questions that remain. Chapter 11, written by Cerdin and Bird, addresses careers. Their chapter offers various models for understanding what constitutes a "career" and both the antecedents and outcomes of having a global career experience. The final chapter in this handbook provides a summary of highlights for each chapter, as well as some suggestions for future research.

REFERENCES

Becker, B., & Gerhart, B. (1996). The impact of human resource management on organizational performance: Progress and prospects. *Academy of Management Journal, 39*, 779–801.

Kirkman, B. L., & Law, K. S. (2005). International management research in AMJ: Our past, present, and future. *Academy of Management Journal, 48*, 377–386.

Ofori-Dankwa, J., & Ricks, D. (2000). Research emphases on cultural differences and/or similarities: Are we asking the right questions? *Journal of International Management, 6*, 173–186.

Stroh, L., Black, J. S., Mendenhall, M. E., & Gregersen, H. B. (2005). *International assignments: An integration of strategy, research, and practice.* Mahwah, NJ: Erlbaum.

2 National Culture and Cultural Effects

John J. Lawler, Fred O. Walumbwa, and Bing Bai

CONTENTS

Several years ago, a major European airline engaged a U.S.-based consultant to help identify ways of enhancing customer service. One recommendation was that flight attendants be trained to smile more at passengers. The union, however, staunchly opposed any such efforts to convert its employees into what it saw as "superficial Americans."

A defining aspect of the Korean workplace is expressed in the Korean term *palli palli*: to work as quickly as possible to accomplish tasks. Korean companies with operations in Thailand soon learned that their Thai employees expected a *cha cha* (Thai for "go slowly") workplace with lots of opportunity for *sanuk* (i.e., fun) during work time. This was a great source of frustration for the expatriate Korean managers.

An American student of one of the authors spent one summer as an intern in the human resources department of a company in East Asia (assigned to a job that only required English). She shared an office with a human resource manager responsible for screening employment applications. The student observed that the manager would spend only a minute or two on each application (though each might contain numerous transcripts, personal statements, award certificates, and letters of recommendation), sorting the documents into "reject" and "interview" piles. Curious as to how the manager could make these decisions so quickly, she learned that he relied almost exclusively on the applicant's photograph, dutifully included in each application, using the principles of *mian xiang* (the Chinese system of face reading) to discern each applicant's character and potential as an employee.

Each of the preceding vignettes illustrates aspects of what we call "culture" and the sorts of conflicts or misunderstandings that it can engender in the cross-national workplace. To the American consultant, the recommendation that the airline's flight attendants project a happier and more lighthearted environment was quite natural; after all, United Airlines' slogan is "Fly the Friendly Skies." Some U.S. airlines in fact evaluate cabin crew by monitoring their smiling behavior and there have been instances of flight attendants being terminated for repeatedly failing to smile a certain proportion of the time while on duty. To Europeans, who American travelers soon learn rarely smile without very good reason, the American preoccupation with feigned happiness is not only superficial but disingenuous. The airline's union felt it was taking a stand against cultural imposition.

Cultural differences are most often illustrated in the United States as conflicts of American culture with that of another country or region. The Korean-Thai example illustrates cultural conflict that is unrelated to American experience. For Americans, East Asians are often all viewed stereotypically as highly focused and work-oriented. Yet as the *palli pallicha-cha* conflict illustrates, there can be substantial cultural variations within this region, with Korea having very much of a "doing" culture and Thailand having much more of a "being" culture. It is also worth noting that the Korean managers described above ultimately learned that the more relaxed work pace in Thailand did not much impact net productivity. Korean workers are often exhausted long before their work shifts end, starting very fast and ending slowly; Thais work at a constant, if generally more relaxed, pace throughout the entire work shift, so that total output of workers in the Thai subsidiaries was not much less than in the Korean plants.

One can imagine the amazement on the part of the intern in the third example, having been trained to rely only on what are viewed as rigorously and scientifically validated selection methods. In the United States, using applicant photographs for screening purposes, or even requesting photographs, is taboo (except, perhaps, for certain kinds of jobs, such as models or actors, where one's appearance is a clear job-related requirement). But there are many parts of the world where fate and the metaphysical are seen to bear heavily on human affairs and thus job candidates can be better assessed through intuitive or spiritual than scientific means. Face reading is but one of many such approaches often encountered in many parts of Asia and that can have implications for the manner in which companies manage human resources. Face reading is used not only to select employees, but to choose business partners, friends, and even marriage partners. In fact, at least some in East Asia have been known to undergo cosmetic surgery to acquire more auspicious features (to fool fate, just as Westerners might do the same to fool the clock).

These anecdotes illustrate aspects of culture and ways in which cultural differences can impact the human resource management (HRM) contexts of globally involved companies. This chapter provides an overview of contemporary theories and research related to cross-national variations in culture and their relationship to issues that might be of concern to the international human resource manager. We consider in turn (a) the meaning and nature of culture, (b) ways of operationalizing culture and characterizing various "cultural syndromes," (c) current research relating to the impact of cultural differences on workplace outcomes, and (d) ways of enhancing cross-cultural research related to international human resource management (IHRM). In our conclusion, we discuss the relevance of the material we have reviewed to the specific managerial concerns of internationally active firms.

CULTURE AS A CONCEPT

As intuitively apparent as the notion of a national culture might be to anyone who has stepped out of his or her home country (or, for that matter, has encountered a visitor from abroad), the concept is not without its critics. There are writers in the IHRM area who are dismissive of "culturalist" explanations of cross-national variations in HR policies and practices. One reason for this may be that culture has often been treated as a residual category, especially in cross-country comparative studies. Earlier research on variations in HR polices and practices would ascribe what could not otherwise be explained in cross-national variation to differences in national culture. This is in many ways comparable to criticisms of personality studies, in which individual behavior not explained by other factors is attributed to a person's "disposition." Although personality at the individual level and culture at the group level are analogous in some ways (in the sense that culture implies something of a group disposition), the concepts are quite distinct. And, as in the case of personality research, there has been extensive theory development and efforts at measuring features of national culture that address the criticism that it is merely a residual category.

ATTRIBUTES OF CULTURE

There are many elements or features of culture as a rigorously defined concept and we look at some of the more important ones here. Perhaps most fundamentally culture is a group-level phenomenon and is defined in terms of the central tendencies of a group with respect to a range of attributes. It is also necessary to differentiate between *objective* and *subjective* culture (Triandis, 1972). Objective culture refers to the outward expressions of group preferences and includes such things as art, clothing, literature, music, food, architecture, language, social arrangements (e.g., organizational structures, family living arrangements), and myths and rituals. Thus, objective culture consists of cultural expressions that can be observed directly and is roughly equivalent to the colloquial use of the term "culture" (as in the statement: "Going to an art exhibit is a cultural experience."). More relevant to our concerns in this chapter is what Triandis termed subjective culture or "a cultural group's characteristic way of perceiving the man-made part of its environment" (p. 4 1972).

Triandis's definition bears similarities to other, related notions of culture, such as Kluckhohn's (1951) definition of culture as "patterned ways of thinking, feeling and reacting, acquired and transmitted mainly by symbols, constituting the distinctive achievements of human groups, including their embodiments in artifacts; the essential core of culture consists of traditional ideas and especially their attached values" (p. 86). Kluckhohn links the objective and subjective elements found in Triandis's definition. Subjective culture relates to the cognitive systems through which the world is perceived and evaluated, especially in relation to the ambiguous and often arbitrary meanings associated with human interaction. Objective culture is the vehicle through which subjective culture is defined, reinforced, and transmitted, especially to the younger generation or those new to the group or society. Thus, the French seek to preserve their secular society and enforce assimilation by banning headscarves for Moslem schoolgirls (as well as the wearing of all other religious symbols in public schools). In contrast, although in the United States any sort of officially sponsored religious activities or displays in public schools is strictly prohibited, the expression of religious beliefs by students through symbols, such as the wearing of a crucifix, a Star of David, or a headscarf, are constitutionally protected and fundamental to American culture. Thus, in contrast to the French government, the U.S. federal government has in fact gone to court to support Moslem schoolgirls who wish to wear headscarves when this practice has been banned by local school districts.

Authoritarian regimes have long recognized the linkages between objective and subjective culture, often regulating and using music, art, literature, and architecture to promote political visions and help maintain control, thus giving rise to the grandiose architectural visions of Albert Speer in Nazi Germany and "socialist realism" as an art form in the Soviet Union. Even in democratic Israel there remains a *de facto* ban on the performance of works by Richard Wagner, as his operas, often glorifying Germanic culture, were utilized by Nazis for ideological purposes (though Wagner himself had died long before Hitler's ascent).

Definitions of culture have been proposed by other authors, such as Hofstede's (1980) notion of culture as the "software of the mind" and in works by Kealey and Ruben (1983); Lytle, Brett, and Shapiro (1999); and Kroeber and Kluckhohn (1963). All of these writers take the position that for groups to function cohesively, there must be shared meanings and interpretations of reality, especially, as we have noted, in ambiguous circumstances. Group members need to understand many things to ensure the functioning and continuity of the group: how power, status, and authority are allocated within the group, the nature of group members' obligations to one another and to those outside the group, what is to be interpreted as beauty and ugliness, what goals in life are to be valued, what is moral and what is immoral behavior. This information is largely imparted through the group's subjective culture, which influences group members' values, beliefs, and ways of perceiving the world. In addition, cultures often include social norms (which might be institutionalized in the form of laws and regulations, as in the case of the French ban on religious symbols in public schools).

Of course, not all aspects of a group member's cognitive system are imparted by culture. There are other influences, including individual experience, upbringing, personality, and perhaps inherent proclivities. There is diversity within cultures, so culture is not a monolithic force, but a central tendency. Culture is a group-level characteristic, but cultural attributes generally have analogous cognitive structures at the individual level. For example, cross-cultural psychologists have identified a variety of personal cultural values, examples of which are idiocentrism and allocentrism (Triandis & Gelfand, 1998). Those who are high on idiocentrism tend to place greatest emphasis on the achievement of personal rather than group goals, while the opposite is true for those scoring high on allocentrism. Mexico, for example, is a collectivist culture, which means that most people are predominantly allocentric, though there are certainly many who are predominantly idiocentric in Mexico as well. Of course, groups can vary in terms of internal cohesiveness; some cultures have little variance among group members, whereas others have very substantial variance.

The most common way of discerning subjective culture for a group is by averaging individual-level measures of relevant cognitive characteristics across members of the group (e.g., Hofstede, 1980). And given what we have said about variability within a cultural group, it is also important to assess the variance in such measures. National cultural norms, such as Hofstede's, are only point estimates and failing to take into account intragroup variation leads to treating all members of a group the same—one of the negative consequences of stereotypical thinking. It would be a mistake to interpret a specific cultural characteristic of a group as merely the average of group member values or beliefs. Culture is the product of the interaction of group members, so although individual values and perceptions help to shape a culture, culture in turn impacts and shapes group members' values and perceptions. Thus, the generation of a culture is an example of the "social construction of reality" that involves the interaction of individual- and group-level phenomena.

Culture is both learned and transgenerational. It is not inherent, but is acquired by group members through group interaction. The transgenerational aspect is important, as culture incorporates much of the knowledge the group needs to thrive, thus must necessarily (and often times formally, as through systems for schooling the young) be passed on to the next generation. Cultural characteristics have staying power and hence a short-term fad is not a cultural characteristic. Many Americans are fond of dogs and keep one as a pet ("man's best friend"); this attachment is probably very much a cultural characteristic (as it is in many other societies, though in some societies dogs are more apt to be seen as a food than a pet [cats also!]). Many years ago, a creative American entrepreneur marketed what were known as "pet rocks"—essentially a small stone in a box that had been provided a name and was supposed to be treated by its owner as a companion, much as a dog or cat (but without all the complications and difficulties). Though a very popular product for a few months (certainly providing empirical support to Barnum's adage regarding the birth frequency of the gullible), this was merely a passing fad that would surely never be viewed as part of American culture in the same way as is the love of dogs (although the propensity to follow this sort of fad might be part of American culture).

Young people often disavow their parent's values, but adopt them as they mature. Most people who went through the "hippie" era during the late 1960s went on to pursue conventional careers, to pay taxes, to worry about their children taking drugs or exhibiting strange behaviors, and perhaps to vote a Republican ticket. Culture most certainly can and does change. For example, Hofstede (1997) argues that economic growth and development tend to transform traditional hierarchical and collectivist cultures into more individualist and egalitarian cultures. The argument is that in less affluent societies, people require a large network of trusted friends and family members for help and protection, particularly in times of economic adversity (which occur with considerable frequency). However, as people become more affluent, as governments establish social welfare systems, and as the demands of industrial development are felt, collective support and extensive interdependence is no longer required. They also become more able to fend for themselves and no longer need to defer to social superiors upon whom they may have depended for various resources. These findings and the logic supporting them are very consistent with sociological theories of modernity—the process of transition from more traditional, largely agrarian societies into industrial and postindustrial societies (Waters, 1995). Theories of modernity stress the emergence of individualism, the supplanting of the extended family by the nuclear family, and the breakdown of ascriptively based social hierarchies.

This process seems to be at work in many parts of East Asia as a consequence of the growth that has occurred there in the past three decades (Ralston, Egri, Stewart, Terpstra, & Kaicheng, 1999). Yet cultures usually change very gradually and the cultural transformation taking place in East Asia would seem to be consistent with this general rule. Some dramatic event, such as the September 11 bombings, might cause a more abrupt shift in culture. Americans are said to have become more collectivist and insular in the wake of September 11, though this might only be a temporary change.

Another important defining characteristic of culture is *tightness* and *looseness* (Triandis, 1995a, 2002). Tight cultures are those in which members of the cultural group feel compelled to conform to cultural standards, whereas loose cultures are those in which standards are not so compelling and those who breach cultural standards are generally forgiven. Japan is often given as the quintessential example of tight culture. As an example, many visitors to Japan (including one of the authors) have experienced being admonished by Japanese fellow pedestrians for crossing a street against a light, though very late at night and with no traffic visible in any direction. There are countless other examples of Japanese conformity to social expectations, including abiding by even the most seemingly insignificant of laws and regulations. The same would be true (perhaps even more so) in Singapore. In contrast, although China is also very much of a collectivist culture, people often find ways of working around laws and regulations, as reflected in the Chinese saying "the mountains are high and the emperor is far away."

Finally, cultural characteristics are often differentiated in terms of whether they are *emic* or *etic*. An etic cultural characteristic is one that is found, though perhaps to varying degrees, across many or most cultures. *Cultural syndromes*, such as individualism/collectivism and uncertainty avoidance, are examples of etic characteristic of national cultures. All national cultures can be defined in terms of the degree to which they are individualistic or collectivist, or degree to which they promote or limit risk-taking behaviors. In contrast, an emic cultural characteristic is one that is specific to a given group (or perhaps a set of closely related groups). Rituals that are unique to a group are often examples of emic cultural characteristics. Many of the activities that surround the celebration of the Fourth of July in the United States, as well as the practice of "sky burial" in Tibet,* are examples

---

* As is so for many Buddhists, Tibetans believe the body should be destroyed at death and not buried. Cremation is the usual way of handling this, but its high altitude means that Tibet has little wood or other naturally occurring material that could be easily spared for cremations. Hence, with some exceptions, Tibetans undergo "sky burial," in which the body is offered to and devoured by vultures as part of the funeral ceremony. To the living, this is intended to reinforce the notion of the impermanence of the body and material things. Though well suited to the needs and resources of Tibetan society, "sky burial" would not likely be an easy means for people in most other cultures to dispose of loved ones.

of emic cultural characteristics. Often the terms describing emic concepts for a particular group will be expressed in words or expressions that are only understood by members of the group. At the societal level, this might include words or expressions that cannot be easily translated into any other language and often can only be fully grasped by native speakers of the language.

CULTURAL DIVERSITY

Much of the earlier cultural literature focused on "culture" as a monolithic construct, generally interpreted in terms of national culture. In fact, individuals are subject to a variety of cultural influences, although the extent of diverse influences may depend upon the nature of the broader society. Considering culture from the perspective of employees in an organization, Punnett and Shenkar (1994) observe that multiple cultures might exist: (a) an overarching organizational culture that influences all employees, (b) unit-specific subcultures that influence only those within particular departments or divisions of the organization, (c) transorganizational cultures that influence members of particular professions or occupations (and cut across organizational boundaries), and (d) supra-organizational cultures that overarch all organizations. Thus, there may be subcultures specific to major units of an organization. However, different types of employees (e.g., engineers, craft workers, accountants, human resource managers) may also be affected by occupational cultures that transcend organizational boundaries. Occupational cultures develop and are reinforced through such mechanisms as common training, membership in professional associations, and off-work interaction with other members of one's occupation or profession. The concept of supra-organizational culture refers primarily to national culture.

Although there may be many cultural influences on a person's life, our focus here is primarily with the notion of national culture, as that is most relevant to the concerns of IHRM. However, "national culture" is itself not so simple a concept. Research dealing with the impact of national culture on work-related behavior, as we review below, often assumes national culture is fixed and invariant within a given country. Yet there might be multiple "microcultures" within a given country. Thus, although we talk about "American culture," there are significant regional variations, so that the cultural characteristics of Midwesterners are seemingly quite different from those of Northeasterners or Californians (although these differences, like regional accents, might seem more apparent to Americans than to those from other countries). Urban and rural cultural differences might be quite pronounced. Population and the geographic dispersion within a country might be important in shaping cultural diversity within a country. However, relatively populous Japan is normally viewed as having a relatively homogeneous culture. Conversely, Singapore, a small island with a population of only a few million, has considerable cultural diversity based on ethnicity, as there are large concentrations of Malays, Indians, and Europeans, as well as the predominant Chinese population. Thus, although Singaporean culture is largely Chinese-based, with strong Confucian influences, understanding behavior both in and outside the workplace requires an appreciation of the other significant culture groups. China and India, the world's two most populous countries, are also quite distinct in terms of intra-country cultural variation. Even though China is culturally diverse in many respects (based on region and to some extent linguistic group), the within-country differences in China are far less than in India, where religious, ethnic, and linguistic differences give rise to a staggering variety of often mutually antagonistic microcultures; hence India's frequent and sometimes violent communal conflicts. The difficulties resulting from merging incompatible cultures into a single nation are evident in the dissolution of the Soviet Union and Yugoslavia, as well as many ongoing conflicts in now independent countries that colonial powers had pieced together from mutually antagonistic tribal groups.

Although cultural diversity within and between countries is a significant issue, an alternative force, especially in this era of globalization, is *cultural convergence*. This is often couched in terms of the "Americanization" or "Westernization" of other cultures, brought about by the widespread dissemination of Western culture through the mass marketing on a global basis of Western products and the Western lifestyle (through music, film, and literature). The spread of English as a global language, especially in business, is another factor seen to promote the erosion of local culture and the emergence of a global popular culture, rooted often in the images if not the substance of American and Western European society. The activities of multinational corporations (MNCs), both in the marketing of products and human resource management in host countries, are viewed as exercises in "cultural imposition." At the extreme, these conflicts are manifested in actions such as Islamic militancy, argued to be the consequence in part of the encroachment of Western culture in traditional Middle Eastern societies.

Although cultural convergence may be linked to the general forces of globalization and the activities of MNCs and powerful Western countries, the relationship here might be more coincidental than causal. The "Americanization" of culture typically involves the transformation of more traditional collectivist and hierarchical cultures into relatively modern individualist and egalitarian cultures. Hofstede (1998) has found that economic development is strongly associated with such cultural changes. For example, as people become more affluent, they are able to act more independently and do not require the support of an extended family or some sort of patron to whom they must be loyal and deferential. Modernity in general, by promoting the growth of democratic institutions and as a consequence of the reorganization of economic activities (away from the interdependence of village life toward more autonomous urban life), encourages individualism and a decrease in what Hofstede terms "power distance" (i.e., social hierarchy). The causal order here is likely bidirectional: growing affluence leads to cultural changes that in turn support further economic development and growth. Thus, the products and ideas marketed by MNCs are probably more (or at least as much) a consequence as a cause of cultural transformation.

CULTURAL SYNDROMES

Our discussion of the basic properties of culture suggests that the concept is complex, especially given the diverse cultural influences that can exist within a society. Thus, to talk in terms of "American culture" or "Brazilian culture" is far too broad and amorphous. As we have already noted, using a country or social group as a proxy for culture is problematic; "culture" reduces to a tautology (we might say Americans act the way they do because of American culture, but then define American culture as the way Americans act). The study of culture, especially the analysis of cross-cultural differences, gained much in the way of scientific credibility when cross-cultural scholars developed and validated measures of cultural traits that could be used to characterize a society. Termed "cultural syndromes," Triandis, Bontempo, Leung, and Hui (1990, p. 302) define these as "shared pattern(s) of beliefs, attitudes, self-definitions, norms, roles, and values organized around a theme." Thus, we think of a national culture as a multifaceted construct formed as a complex of cultural syndromes. And each cultural syndrome can vary along a continuum. National cultures can be compared quantitatively in terms of their similarity and differences along each of several cultural syndromes. This has given rise to the notion of *cultural distance*, in which societies are mapped onto multiple cultural syndromes and compared in terms of their proximity.* This approach also helps us address the problem of national microcultures. For example, we might be able to discern that rural American Southerners are more collectivists than urban dwellers on the East Coast, though the dominant cultures in both areas may be little different in terms of risk aversion or power distance. Although there are a number of approaches to conceptualizing and measuring cultural syndromes, due to space limitation we focus primarily on four of the more widely known and utilized approaches in IHRM, including Hofstede, Triandis, Trompenaars, and House et al.

---

* There are many proximity measures that can be used, though the Euclidean distance measure is most common. In a multidimensional space (in which each dimension represents a cultural attribute), this is calculated for any two countries as the square root of the sum of the squared differences in the values of each country's score along each cultural measure.

HOFSTEDE

Perhaps the best known and most widely utilized typology of cultural syndromes is Hofstede's (1980). Hofstede's groundbreaking multicountry study collected data from more than 70 national subsidiaries of IBM, scattered throughout most regions of the world. This book was updated with extensive references to research spawned by the original work (Hofstede, 2001). Hofstede's data were collected in two waves between 1967 and 1973. For various methodological reasons, the set of countries included in the final analysis was reduced to 40 of this original set, though another 10 countries and 3 geographical regions were later added using data from subsequent work. Hofstede's questionnaire, translated into local languages, contained a variety of items dealing mainly with work-related attitudes. Initially, Hofstede derived four scales, using both theoretical assumptions and empirical methods (e.g., factor analysis): *individualism/collectivism, power distance, uncertainty avoidance,* and *masculinity/femininity.*

Individualism and its converse, *collectivism,* concern the degree to which members of a society tend to see themselves as interdependent with others versus relatively autonomous actors. This cultural dimension is associated with many different characteristic attitudes and values. Collectivists tend to have a strong sense of group identity and sharply distinguish between "in group" and "out group" members, whereas individualists generally have multiple group connections with none being completely dominant. The focal or dominant group of the collectivist might be family, clan or tribe, religion or religious subgroup (e.g., caste in Hinduism), or national identity (as in Japan). Collectivist cultures tend to promote harmony among in-group members, whereas disagreements and overt conflict are more acceptable in individualist cultures. Shame, humiliation, and loss of face are a primary means of enforcing social norms in a collectivist culture, whereas an internal and personal sense of guilt plays a more important role in this respect in individualist cultures. Collectivist cultures endorse particularistic standards in dealing with others. In other words, one is expected to favor those to whom he or she is closest (friends, relatives, classmates) in choices or allocating resources, whereas individualist cultures endorse universal standards. Thus, "nepotism" is often quite acceptable and even considered highly ethical in organizations in collectivist cultures, whereas it would be frowned upon generally in individualist cultures. The Confucian framework defines obligations to others in terms of the closeness of personal relationships, with close family members taking precedence over all others (Scoville, Lawler, & Yi, 2005). One consequence of this is that Western business people often complain about "crony capitalism" in China and many other parts of East Asia, as local companies will often make business decisions based on personal relationships, not objective cost-benefit considerations.

Power distance refers to the tendency of a culture to be hierarchical, with considerable social distance between the high and low ends of the society. In addition, those at the lower end of the power distribution accept and legitimize the control exercised by those at the higher end. That is, not only does power exist, it is not generally challenged or only challenged under extreme circumstances. In traditional Chinese society, the emperor was seen to hold power through the "Mandate of Heaven" and normally as unassailable. However, natural disasters, such as droughts, famine, or earthquakes, as well as man-made disasters, such as the loss of a war, would call the emperor's authority into question, resulting in his displacement by an heir or even the end of a dynasty. In low-power-distance cultures, there may be ongoing competition for power, with those without power hoping to displace those with power.

There are different mechanisms by which hierarchy might be established in high-power-distance cultures. Sometimes power differences are ascriptive, determined by age, gender, or social origins. Thus, in Hinduism, one's caste is determined by birth and cannot be altered. Social mobility only comes by acquiring karma through good deeds in one's current life and hoping for a better "next life." The traditional class system in England was similarly highly ascriptive, with class largely determined by birth. The class system began to erode with the growth of the market economy, as the lower classes could acquire wealth through business activities. But the process took considerable time and elements of class identity still persist (although lower-class deference to the upper classes has largely eroded, so that England is now a low-power-distance culture). Other societies might allocate power and influence by means of merit or achievement. To some extent, Chinese and other Confucian cultures are this way, as there is immense emphasis on educational attainment and becoming a cultivated person or "Confucian gentleman."* In traditional Chinese society, even those of humble origins who studied hard and passed rigorous examinations could move to high-level government positions and might even preempt royal family members in terms of power and influence (though the extent to which this was possible varied historically). Rigorous school admission examinations patterned after this system are still the norm in most parts of East Asia and the traditional examination system for entry into government positions is still in place in Taiwan.† Yet Confucian culture mixes ascriptive and merit-based determinants of hierarchy, as age and gender are still quite important in this respect in most Confucian societies (e.g., China, Taiwan, Japan, Korea, Singapore, and Vietnam).

As we mentioned earlier, collectivist cultures also tend to be high-power-distance cultures. Hwang (2001) for example notes that Confucianism can be summarized in two paramount rules: honor the superior, favor the intimate. The former expresses the strong hierarchical component of Confucian culture, while the latter expresses collectivist particularism. Little wonder that Hofstede found that Confucian societies all tended to score high on collectivism and power distance. In fact, these characteristics would be common to most Asian, African, and Latin American cultures, whereas individualism and lower power distance are characteristic of the United States, Canada, Australia and New Zealand, and much of Europe (even the former socialist countries of Eastern Europe, although the Mediterranean countries of Europe (e.g., Spain, Italy) have more collectivist and higher-power-distance cultures). There are some interesting exceptions to this rule. Israel is a strongly collectivist culture, yet one with low power distance. Conversely, France scores relatively high on power distance (reflected in some of the strong class distinctions that persist), yet is quite individualistic. Thus, French workers may pay deference to their superiors, yet demand respect and independence in return.

Uncertainty avoidance concerns the risk-taking behavior typical of a culture, as well as concern for the absolute. Germany, Japan, and many Arab cultures are all high on uncertainty avoidance. This results in strong social norms and rules, as well as a tendency to view the world in largely "black" or "white" terms. High-uncertainty-avoidance cultures tend to be relatively rigid and less apt to promote innovative behavior, whereas those in low-uncertainly-avoidance cultures are more likely to engage in riskier behaviors. *Masculinity* and its converse *femininity* are related to the extent to which male and female values and social roles are differentiated. In high-masculinity cultures, men and women generally have relatively distinct values. Men place great emphasis on material accomplishment and are expected to be strong and assertive. There may be considerable role differentiation between men and women as well (e.g., men work while women care for the family). In more feminine cultures, nurturing behaviors and a concern with quality of life are widely shared among both men and women (values that are stereotypically viewed as more feminine values).

A fifth cultural dimension was later added to the Hofstede framework, once termed *Confucian dynamism* (because of its importance in differentiating among many Asian cultures and its origins in the efforts of Chinese scholars), it is now, perhaps less colorfully, termed *long-term/short-term orientation*. The short- versus long-term orientation dimension has its origins in research undertaken in Asia by Michael Bond and several Chinese collaborators (Chinese Culture Connection, 1987). However, Hofstede (2001) expanded the concept and extended it beyond Asian cultures. A

---

* Although Confucianism was viewed as antithetical to Maoist thought and suppressed in the People's Republic of China until after the Cultural Revolution, Confucian values have seemingly persisted and there is renewed interest in Confucian philosophy in Mainland China.

† The Examination Yuan, an independent branch of the Taiwanese government, administers rigorous and competitive examinations for most government positions based on a system that existed for perhaps two thousand years in China. This bureau was headed as recently as the 1980s by a direct descendant of Confucius.

long-term orientation is associated with thrift and savings, patience and perseverance, industrious-ness, and an expectation that the best in life will occur in the future as a consequence of persistent effort (values often associated with the most successful economies in East Asia). In cultures with short-term orientations, there is the expectation of relatively immediate results, people tend not to practice thrift and they save little, they value leisure time over work, respect traditions, and are not so concerned with change.

Despite methodological criticisms, Hofstede's research is appealing in that he was able to administer his instrument on comparable samples of workers in many different countries, thus establishing a widely used set of national cultural norms. Indeed, more recent and independent work by other scholars provides support for the validity of Hofstede's scales, such as Schwartz's (1994) study, which identified several cultural dimensions that are closely related to Hofstede's. This is noteworthy, as Schwartz used a different methodology in extracting cultural value dimensions and estimating cultural norms. In addition, this study focused on the education sector rather than the business sector (or a specific company, such as IBM). Finally, as to the criticism that his scales are perhaps out of date as the surveys upon which they were built are nearly 30 years old (raising ques-tions as to whether some national norms may have changed), Hofstede and Peterson (2000) note that the relative standing of cultures on Hofstede's dimensions has been generally stable over time. Hofstede (2001) further contends that culture is a long-term construct that does not quickly change (although there may be short-term fluctuations from norms, societies tend to return to their long-term equilibrium states), that the data used were measured at multiple points in time and items that shifted were excluded, and finally that more recent studies, such as Schwartz (1994), continued to support the general implications of his earlier work.

TRIANDIS

Although Hofstede (1980) conceptualized individualism and collectivism as one bipolar dimension of culture, recent theoretical work suggests that at the personal level, individualist and collectiv-ist orientations can be independent and can coexist to varying degrees (Triandis, 1994, 1995a). In other words, under some circumstances, people may exhibit more collectivist cultural traits, while the same people might, under other circumstances, exhibit more individualist cultural traits. This provides one way of understanding how people can experience diverse cultural influences and respond differently under varying situations. Of course, for culture to mean anything there would necessarily be a dominant set of group values that would influence behavior in most circumstances, a point made by Hofstede (2001). For example, individualism is clearly the dominant cultural value in American society. However, Americans might also harbor collectivist sentiments that will be exhibited in the right setting (e.g., playing in a team sport). It has been argued, for example, that Americans clearly exhibited more collectivist (and atypical) values and behaviors in the period following the September 11 attacks (preferring to spend more time at home with family members, avoiding extensive travel, often displaying the American flag, and engaging in other spontaneous acts of patriotism). Triandis (1995a) sees collectivism and individualism as perhaps the most signifi-cant of dimensions in cross-cultural analysis, as they seem to explain more cross-cultural variation than any other cultural syndrome, though he also incorporates power distance concepts into his notion of individualism and collectivism to form a more complex construct.

Much of the work deriving from Triandis's framework has focused on individual-level cul-tural values (Triandis, 1995a) and thus is distinct from Hofstede's concern with cross-national com-parisons. Triandis and his colleagues (Singelis, Triandis, Bhawuk, & Gelfand, 1995; Triandis & Gelfand, 1998) suggested that the crossing of individualism and collectivism with power distance produces four distinct and independent dimensions: horizontal collectivism (denoted as HC), verti-cal collectivism (VC), horizontal individualism (HI), and vertical individualism (VI), the horizontal and vertical dimensions relating to power distance. Triandis (1995b) differentiates between "same" and "different" notions of self. This is determined by the extent to which one accepts inequality or status differences. The "different self" corresponds to the dimension of verticality and the extent to which a person accepts status differences, whereas the "same self" represents the dimension of horizontality and the extent to which people expect equality and minimal status differences. There is also a distinction between the independent and interdependent selves (Markus & Kitayama, 1991) and is related, respectively, to individualism and collectivism.

The combination of the four types of "self" has received empirical support (Triandis, Chen, & Chan, 1998; Triandis & Gelfand, 1998; Triandis & Bhawuk, 1997; Chen, Meindl, & Hunt, 1997; Singelis et al., 1995; Walumbwa & Lawler, 2003). More specifically, horizontal collectivism (HC) reflects an emphasis on equality and an assumption that all members of the collective are the same. In societies where the HC dimension dominates, such as the Israeli Kibbutz and Eskimo villages, people see themselves as similar to others, and emphasize common goals with others, interdependence, and sociability, but they do not submit easily to authorities (Triandis, 1994, 1995a). In societies where the vertical collectivism (VC) dimension dominates, people see themselves as part of the collective and also accept that there are natural inequalities within the broader society. In VC cultures, such as China and India, people are willing to sacrifice their personal goals for the sake of in-group goals, emphasize integrity among in-group members, and see competition between their in-groups and out-groups as a way of life (Triandis, 1994, 1995a). Equality is stressed by the horizontal individualist (HI), but as a self-reliant individual, rather than as an integrated member of the collective. In HI-dominant cultures, people want to be unique and distinct from groups and are high on self-reliance, but they are not especially interested in becoming distinguished or having high status (Triandis, 1994, 1995a). Australia and Sweden are examples of these sorts of cultures. Finally, with vertical individualism (VI), an acceptance of inequality exists along with an emphasis on individual autonomy. In VI cultures, such as France and the United States, people often want to be distinguished and acquire status, usually in terms of individual competitions with others (Triandis, 1995a).

In addition to providing evidence that individualism and collectivism can be differentiated on vertical and horizontal dimensions, Triandis and his colleagues (Hui, 1988; Triandis, 1995a; Triandis, Bontempo, Villareal, Asai, & Lucca, 1988; Triandis, Chan, Bhawuk, Iwao, & Sinha, 1995) provide evidence that suggest individualism and collectivism can also be viewed as individual personality differences. Specifically, Triandis (2002) argues that individualism and collectivism should be viewed as polythetic constructs because several additional culture-specific attributes define different kinds of individualism or collectivism. At the individual level, these individual cultural predispositions are called idiocentrism and allocentrism (Triandis, Leung, Villareal, & Clack, 1985). Consistent with the definition of collectivism, allocentrics define themselves in terms of the in-groups to which they belong, and in-group harmony is extremely valued (Triandis, 1995a). Because of their socialization processes, the goals of the in-group have primacy over one's personal goals. On the other hand, idiocentrics view the individual as the most basic unit of social perception where individual goals have primacy over in-group goals, and the threshold for in-group confrontation (versus harmony) is lower. This leads idiocentrics to be motivated to satisfy their self-interests and personal goals often at the expense of group interests and goals (Triandis, 1995a). More specifically, whereas allocentrics value and nurture group relationships and define themselves on the basis of their in-group membership (i.e., interdependence), idiocentrics value independence, autonomy, and personal achievement, and place less emphasis on their roles within groups (Markus & Kitayama, 1991). Idiocentrics view the individual as the most basic unit of social perception, where individual goals have primacy over in-group goals and in-group confrontation is acceptable (Triandis, 1995a).

The idea that individualism and collectivism exist at the individual level has received support empirically. Hui (1984) was the first to measure individualism and collectivism at the individual level by creating a 63-item individualism and collectivism scale (INDCOL) and was able to assess an individual's level of individualism and collectivism in the Chinese context (Hui, 1988). Using selected items from Hui (1984), Triandis et al. (1985) established both convergent and discriminant validity of this scale and found allocentrics to be more cooperative and less lonely.

Triandis et al. (1988) examined the structure of idiocentrism and allocentrism and demonstrated that there are similar factor structures of individualism and collectivism at the individual level within the United States, Japan, and Puerto Rico. Trafimow, Triandis, and Goto (1991) found that individuals have access to both idiocentric elements and allocentric elements. Gelfand, Triandis, and Chan (1996) found that idiocentrism and allocentrism are orthogonal at the individual level in the United States. Oishi, Schimmack, Diener, and Sug (1998) provided recent converging evidence of the constructs at the individual level. The authors found that vertical allocentrism was positively correlated with tradition and conformity values, vertical idiocentrism was positively correlated with power and achievement, horizontal allocentrism was positively correlated with benevolence, and horizontal idiocentrism was positively correlated with achievement and self direction. Thus, there appears to be enough evidence supporting the existence of cultural values at the individual level (Triandis & Gelfand, 1998).

TROMPENAARS

Although both Hofstede's and Triandis's cultural dimensions are widely recognized and accepted in the field of IHRM, a more recent description of how cultures differ is provided by Trompenaars and his collaborators (Trompenaars, 1994; Trompenaars & Hampden-Turner, 1998) based on empirical research of more than 15,000 managers from 28 countries, with at least 500 respondents from each country. Building on the work of Parsons (1951) on societal value and relational orientations, Trompenaars and Hampden-Turner (1998) derived seven relationship orientations, along with attitudinal dimensions toward time and the environment, that have considerable implications for IHRM. The seven dimensions include universalism versus particularism, individualism versus communitarianism, neutral culture versus affective culture, specific culture versus diffuse culture, achievement culture versus ascription culture, sequential time orientation versus synchronic time orientation, and inner-directed culture versus outer-directed culture. As noted above, universalism and particularism are subsumed in Hofstede's (1980) individualism-collectivism dimension, though they are treated separately by Trompenaars. Achievement and ascription are not a part of the Hofstede framework directly, though we did note that they are important in differentiating sources of status in higher power-distance cultures. Affective cultures are characterized by strong emotional bonds among group members, whereas neutral cultures are characterized by generally greater emotional distances among group members, except very close friends and family members. Thus, Americans are often seen as "friendly" but emotionally distant, whereas in many Asian and Latin American cultures, people have wide networks of friends with which they share warm emotional relationships. The same distinction would seem to characterize Northern European countries (more emotionally neutral) versus Southern European countries (more affective).

There has been some empirical support for these models (Smith, Dugan, & Trompenaars, 1996). For example, Smith et al. (2002) in a study of 47 countries found that managers in countries characterized by high power distance reported more use of formal rules and procedures set by the organization's top management in handling day-to-day events and that they relied less on their subordinates in dealing with everyday events than do managers from low-power-distance countries.

More important, these cultural dimensions have several implications for IHRM, especially in terms of offering practical suggestions for ways in which MNCs can do business in different cultures. For example, they provide managers with basic tools necessary to analyze the cultures in which they do business and, more important, help managers to understand the complexity in the managing of culturally diverse workforces. As an example, Trompenaars and Hampden-Turner (1998) recommend that when individuals from particularist cultures do business in a universalist culture, they should be prepared for rational and professional arguments. On the other hand, when individuals from universalist cultures do business in particularist cultures, they should be prepared for personal meandering or irrelevancies that seem to go nowhere.

HOUSE ET AL.

The most recent large-scale cross-national study of culture dimensions is found in a multiyear study involving a large number of collaborators headed by Robert House (House, Hanges, Javidan, Dorfman, & Gupta, 2004). Known as the GLOBE Project, House and his associates explored cultural values and practices in 61 nations, with a focus on the linkages between culture and leadership. National cultures were categorized along nine dimensions, based on survey data collected in each of the countries in the study: uncertainty avoidance, power distance, collectivism I (societal collectivism), collectivism II (in-group collectivism), gender egalitarianism, assertiveness, future orientation, performance orientation, and humane orientation. House et al. (2004) further grouped cultures into a set of ten regional clusters, and for each cluster, they develop profiles using all nine globe cultural dimensions for both practices and cultural values.

House and his colleagues' research has important managerial implications. As with other cultural typologies, their cultural profiles provide a convenient way of summarizing intercultural similarities as well as intercultural differences. The regional clusters capture important cultural distinctions both within and among clusters. Moreover, their study involved the largest set of cross-country comparisons of any of the national culture studies. Cultural dimension scores can provide expatriate employees with an initial assessment of the culture and hints on how to behave in that culture. Therefore, the use of these cultural dimensions should be of great help for designing effective managerial systems for employees who work in global environments and reducing expatriate failures and interpersonal conflict based on cultural misunderstanding in multicultural environments in which employees must deal with people of vastly different backgrounds.

CULTURAL EFFECTS IN THE WORKPLACE

Although culture can have a direct impact on a wide range of individual-level, organizational-level, and societal-level outcomes, it often works primarily as a moderator of relationships among other variables. That is, certain effects (e.g., the impact of pay for performance on job satisfaction or organizational commitment) are either accentuated or dampened depending on societal culture or individual cultural values. For example, Walumbwa and Lawler (2003) reported that collectivism moderated the relationship between transformational leadership and work-related attitudes and behaviors. They reported that transformational leadership had a significantly greater impact on work-related outcomes among those scoring high on collectivism than individuals scoring low on collectivism.

Other research concerning the moderating role of culture suggests, for example, that individual cultural values play a critical role on how individuals interpret and react to managerial practices and motivational techniques (Robert, Probst, Martocchio, Drasgow, & Lawler, 2000). Lam, Chen, and Schaubroeck (2002) found that allocentrism and idiocentrism explained how participative decision making and efficacy perceptions interacted to predict performance. Robert and Wasti (2002) found that idiocentrism and allocentrism interacted with organizational individualism to predict work-related attitudes of organizational respect, and satisfaction with promotion, the work itself, coworkers, and supervisors. Walumbwa, Lawler, and Avolio (2005), using data from China, India, Kenya, and the United States, found that the effectiveness of transformational and contingent reward leadership behaviors vary depending upon an individual's level of allocentrism and idiocentrism. Specifically, they found that allocentric workers react more positively in terms of work-related attitudes when they perceive their managers as transformational; idiocentrics react more positively in terms of work-related attitudes when they perceive their managers as displaying contingent reward leadership. More important, these results were stronger in more collectivist societies for allocentrics, suggesting that individual dispositions and societal norms may be contingently, rather than independently, related. Similar interaction effects have also been found between individual cultural dispositions and work-family issues in predicting withdrawal behaviors (Wang, Lawler, Walumbwa, & Shi, 2004). Thus, empirical evidence to date supports the moderating influence of culture both at the higher (i.e., societal) and lower (i.e., individual) levels. Indeed, Lam et al. (2002) and Walumbwa et al. (2005) have argued that national culture and individual cultural values, although cultivated differently in particular societies, have meaningful influences on behavior irrespective of societal boundaries.

There is, in addition to the work we have already considered, a huge literature dealing with the impact of culture and cultural differences on a wide range of specific work-related outcomes at both the individual and higher (e.g., group, societal) levels. Here we are necessarily selective in light of space limitations, focusing on some of the more recent conceptual and empirical literature dealing with the impact of culture on individual-level outcomes most relevant to IHRM concerns. Studies that attempt to identify or give insight into the role of culture are given emphasis. This work helps in understanding such issues as the transferability of a multinational's HR system to another society (and how host-country nationals will respond) and helping expatriate employees understand the cultural differences they will experience in the workplaces and business activities of the countries in which they are to be assigned.

CULTURE AND SELF-IDENTITY

Based on the cultural dimension of individualism-collectivism, various authors (e.g., Bailey, Chen, & Dou, 1997; Markus & Kitayama, 1991; Triandis, 2002) argue that collectivists view the self as interdependent with others and this is accomplished through a proclivity to share resources, whereas individualists view the self as autonomous and independent from groups. Correspondingly, individualists use the individual ("I") as the unit of analysis of social behavior, whereas collectivists use groups ("We"). As we have discussed above, Triandis (1989) uses the terms "idiocentric" and "allocentric" to characterize the essential psychological manifestations of individualist and collectivist cultures. In addition, Erez and Earley (1993) use Triandis's (1989) concept of cultural "tightness" to analyze the different cognitive information-processing styles of self-identity that are identified as self-enhancement, self-efficacy, and self-consistency. The cultural values of a society provide the appropriate frames of reference in evaluating and judging the self in terms of self-enhancement, self-efficacy, and self- consistency. In "tight" cultures, criteria for evaluating and judging are rather narrow in scope compared to "loose" cultures. Thus, tight cultures lead to more rigid and demanding standards of behavior.

CULTURE AND LEADERSHIP

There is overwhelming evidence regarding the linkage between culture and leadership. Schein (1992) argued that culture and leadership are two sides of the same coin and neither can be understood in isolation. In fact, House, Wright, and Aditya (1997) observed that cultural forces affect the kind of leader behavior that is usually accepted, enacted, and effective. To understand the linkage between culture and leadership, two broad questions have been generally addressed in the literature (Avolio, Sosik, Jung, & Berson, 2003; Dickson, Hanges, & Lord, 2001; Walumbwa, 1999; Walumbwa & Lawler, 2003): Are certain leader behaviors and styles culturally universal? Do theories of leadership developed in the Western cultures, and particularly the United States, generalize to other cultural settings?

Dorfman, Howell, Hibino, Lee, Tate, and Bautista (1997) examined the generalizability of six different leadership behaviors and processes in five countries: Japan, the United States, Mexico, South Korea, and Taiwan. Results showed that three leadership behaviors—being charismatic, using contingent reward, and being supportive—had positive impacts across all five cultures, whereas participative, directive, and contingent-punishment leadership behaviors operated as a function of culture. Brodbeck et al. (2000) investigated differences in leadership prototypes across European countries and found that some leadership concepts are culturally endorsed across certain clusters. In the GLOBE Project, Den Hartog, House, Hanges, Ruiz-Quintanilla, and Dorfman (1999) investigated the extent to which attributes of charismatic-transformational leadership are universally endorsed. Results showed that attributes such as being a confidence builder, being motivational, having foresight, being dynamic, planning ahead, and being positive and encouraging were universally endorsed, whereas attributes such as compassion, sincerity, being procedural, enthusiasm, sensitivity, promoting autonomy, and being domineering, among others, vary across cultures. Finally, Smith, Misumi, Tayeb, Peterson, and Bond (1989), using performance-maintenance leadership theory (Misumi & Peterson, 1985), examined the perceptions of electronics plant supervisors in Britain, the United States, Japan, and Hong Kong. They reported that whereas leader consideration behavior was evaluated positively by Japanese followers, the same behavior was evaluated as an invasion of one's privacy in highly individualistic cultures such as the United States. In summary, although there are certain leadership attributes that tend to generalize across cultures (Bass, 1997; Javidan, House, Dorfman, Gupta, & Hanges, 2004; House et al., 2004), there is evidence suggesting a significant relationship between culture and the effectiveness of certain leadership styles (House & Aditya, 1997). Indeed, Javidan et al. (2004) asserted that to the extent that cultures are different, the culturally implicit leadership theory should always be different.

EMPLOYEE PARTICIPATION

Rees and Porter (1998) analyze the relationship between participation and Hofstede's cultural dimensions. Corresponding to Hofstede's five dimensions, employee participation is likely to be more acceptable in low-power-distance cultures, in high-femininity cultures, in low-uncertainty-avoidance cultures, in long-term orientation cultures, and employees are more likely to be integrated into groups and participative mechanisms in collectivistic cultures. Triandis (2002) also indicates that in horizontal collectivist cultures there will be higher levels of group participation, whereas in vertical collectivist cultures decisions will be top down and centralized. Despite such empirical supports, a major limitation of these findings is that a majority of the studies are correlational and involved percept-percept data collection techniques (i.e., data collected from the same source respondents using the same questionnaire at the same time).

MOTIVATION AND DECISION MAKING

Motivation is believed to differ along the individualism-collectivism and horizontal-vertical (i.e., power distance) cultural dimensions. The motivational structure in collectivist cultures reflects receptivity to others, adjustment to the needs of others, and restraint of one's own needs and desires, whereas in individualistic cultures it reflects internal needs, rights, and capacities (Markus & Kitayama, 1991). Triandis (2002) also believes that achievement motivation is socially oriented among collectivists, who will be motivated by goals that are widely accepted by the in-group, whereas motivation is largely a personal matter for individualists, who will be more motivated if they have a hand in shaping goals. Along with the horizontal-vertical cultural dimension, Triandis (2002) argues that horizontal cultures will favor small salary differentials, whereas vertical cultures will tolerate large salary differentials.

Decision making differs along these cultural dimensions as well. In horizontal-individualist cultures, decision making will be individual and leaders will delegate authority, whereas in vertical individualist cultures, decisions will be centralized and top down (Earley & Erez, 1997). Decision making has also been found to differ specifically along the power distance cultural dimension. Brockner et al. (2001) state that people in high-power-distance countries are less likely to expect or want to have input into a decision-making process. The tendency for people to respond more favorably when voice is high rather than low should be less pronounced in a high-power-distance culture than in a low-power-distance culture.

TEAMWORK

Salk and Brannen (2000) argue that nationality affects team members' preferences and work behaviors based on social identity theory (Tajfel & Turner, 1986) and social categorization theory (Turner, 1987). Therefore, national culture should be important in explaining patterns of relationships in a team. A similar argument is presented by Neale and Mindel (1992), who argue that national culture plays a very important role in team building and working in multicultural environments. More detailed analysis can be found in Awasthi, Chow, and Wu (1998), who analyzed individuals' decisions in a team-based work setting based on individualistic and collectivistic cultural dimensions. They found, for example, that individualists significantly change the team orientation of their decisions in response to imposed performance measures and rewards, but a similar impact was not found for collectivists. Earley (1999) investigated the effects of power distance and status characteristics on group efficacy and team performance among senior managers in the United States, England, France, and Thailand. Results showed that high-status members' estimate of efficacy was more strongly related to collective efficacy in higher-power-distance cultures. Sosik and Jung (2002) conducted a longitudinal investigation of the effects of culture using U.S. and Korean students on group characteristics (i.e., functional heterogeneity, preference for teamwork, group potency, outcome expectation) and on performance of work groups performing two decision-making tasks over a 15-week period. Results showed that U.S. students (individualists) reported higher levels of functional heterogeneity and group potency and attained higher levels of group performance than did the Korean students (collectivists).

EMPOWERMENT

Marchese (2001) notes that the outcomes associated with empowerment are quite different across countries based on horizontality-verticality. For example, Robert et al. (2000) discuss the fit of empowerment and national culture based in part on power distance and also on collectivism. They argue that power distance should moderate the relationship between job satisfaction and perceived empowerment. Employees in the United States, Mexico, and Poland were found to have more favorable views of their supervisors when perceived empowerment is high, whereas Indian employees rate their supervisors low when empowerment is high. However, the relationship in Mexico (like India, a high-power-distance country) was weaker than in the United States and Poland (both low-power-distance countries). The reasoning is that workers in higher-power-distance cultures would be less comfortable with acting autonomously and their superiors less supportive of empowerment efforts, thus leading to conflict and tension. Satisfaction with coworkers was shown to have a negative impact on coworker satisfaction in India, the most collectivist of the countries studied. The authors felt that empowerment efforts might have encouraged competitiveness that disrupted well-established interpersonal relationships.

NEGOTIATING STYLE

There is an extensive literature suggesting that national culture has an impact on negotiating behaviors and negotiation processes (e.g., Gulbro & Herbig, 1999; Elahee, Kirby, & Nasif, 2002; Lin & Miler, 2003; Chang, 2003). National culture exerts direct influence on the preferences for negotiation approaches. At the same time, national culture has indirect influences on the choice of negotiation approaches by interacting with relational contexts (Lin & Miler, 2003). Gulbro and Herbig (1999) provide detailed arguments on negotiation in international contexts based on Hofstede's five cultural dimensions. They conclude that those from collectivist cultures will spend more time in the non-task-negotiating activities, in planning before and debriefing after a session, and in positioning during negotiating activities than those from individualist cultures. In addition, those from higher-power-distance cultures will spend less time compromising than those from low-power-distance cultures. Those from more masculine cultures will spend less time in persuasive efforts in dealing with the bargaining counterparts than those from more feminine cultures. Finally, those from high-uncertainty-avoidance cultures will spend more time in agreement. Fu and Yukl (2000) compared the perceived effectiveness of influence tactics in China and the United States. Results showed that American managers rated rational persuasion and exchange as more effective styles compared with Chinese managers.

CONFLICT RESOLUTION

Research suggests there are different levels of conflict avoidance in different national cultures. For instance, Ohbuchi and Takahashi (1994) found that the Japanese are much more likely than the Americans to avoid conflicts. Similarly, Triandis et al. (1988) found that Japanese participants avoid conflict in more situations than American participants. Gabrielidis, Stephan, Ybarra, Dos Santos-Pearson, and Villareal (1997) also propose that collectivists display more concern for others than individualists so that the conflict can be more avoided. These findings, of course, are consistent with the view that collectivist cultures are more apt to emphasize harmonious relations, at least with other in-group members, than individualist cultures.

Different conflict resolution styles can be found across cultural dimensions. Trubinsky, Ting-Toomey, and Lin (1991) compared Taiwan and the United States and found that in conflict situations, Taiwanese are more likely than Americans to use obliging, avoiding, integrating, and compromising styles of conflict resolution, as opposed to a confrontational style. Xie, Song, and Stringfellow (1998) also suggest that collaboration, compromise, and hierarchical conflict resolution methods will be more effective, and competition and accommodation less effective, in cultures with low individualism, high power distance, high uncertainty avoidance, and a long-term orientation than in cultures that score high on the first dimension but low on the last three dimensions.

SUGGESTIONS AND RECOMMENDATIONS FOR FUTURE RESEARCH AND PRACTICE

The research summarized in this chapter raises some pertinent questions, which need be addressed in the journey to better understanding the role of culture in IHRM research and practice.

METHODOLOGICAL ISSUES

Although there are several theoretical models and empirical studies, many studies are beset with a number of methodological and measurement problems. For example, a majority of studies involved the use of small convenience samples and use more qualitative and self-rated survey-based designs, where followers often provide both ratings of their cultural environment and the target variables. The use of a single method of data collection (or self-reported data) raises the possibility of common method and source variance, potentially affecting the resulting pattern of relationships found and raising reliability and validity concerns. However, we should also note that researchers have shown that common method variance is rarely strong enough to invalidate research findings (Crampton & Wagner, 1994; Doty & Glick, 1998). In order to advance our understanding of the role of culture, we recommend that researchers incorporate a number of alternative research designs, including but not limited to experimental designs, longitudinal designs, and use of multiple sources and studies to rule out alternative explanations.

ANALYTICAL STRATEGIES

To identify causal relationships and to control for confounding variables, future research involving cultural differences should incorporate the analyses that make it possible to separate the effects of culture from potential spurious effects. For example, the use of multivariate strategies might be helpful, because culture is a multifaceted construct extrinsically linked to many other variables, including age, education, level of economic development, and sex, among other important variables (Triandis, 1995a).

MEASUREMENT OF CRITERIA

Lack of clear specification of criterion measure used in cross-cultural studies is a serious concern. For example, it is possible that culture may have a different relationship with organizational commitment that focuses on follower affective commitment (e.g., Meyer & Allen, 1991) than organizational commitment that focuses on global organizational commitment (e.g., Mowday, Steers, & Porter, 1979). If this were to be true, it is likely that mixed results may in part be attributed to the use of different measures. However, without knowing what measures were used, it would be difficult to discern the cause of mixed results. In addition to the above, we recommend that future research should consider including other attitudinal outcomes, as well as more objective work performance outcomes that may be more or less affected by culture differences. For example, one could include performance measures that require integrative versus individual efforts to test the moderating effects of cultural values (Walumbwa et al., 2005).

LEVEL OF ANALYSIS

Kozlowski and Klein (2000) have pointed out the importance of specifying the level of analysis at which variables and associations are conceptualized. With respect to cross-cultural research, Peterson and Hunt (1997) noted that there has been insufficient attention by researchers to defining the level of analysis at which cultural differences are investigated, making it difficult to identify the impact associated with cultural differences or at worse where the effects of culture are most noticeable. Future research on cultural differences should incorporate research designs that make it possible to examine the effects of cultures at different levels (e.g., individual, dyads, group and/or organizational levels).

CULTURE MEASURES

Although in the past decade there has been a steady increase in the number of measures that have been developed to assess culture, this tendency is worrisome, at best. Serious questions are being raised regarding the convergent and discriminate validity of the majority of these measures. Gelfand et al. (2004) note that this proliferation of measures has created some confusion, as scholars develop measures that assess different aspects of the culture, using different methodologies, often without making reference to other measurements in the literature. We agree with this assessment. Rather than building on earlier measures, there is a tendency to discount earlier measures for the sake of introducing new measures. Given these numerous measures purporting to measure the same constructs, it is not surprising that confusion and conflicting research findings exist within the literature about the relationships that have been found with expected outcomes (Earley & Gibson, 1998). In future studies, it would be beneficial to conduct construct validation studies that include multiple cultural measures to validate their psychometric adequacy (Gelfand et al., 2004).

CONCLUSIONS

We have considered a range of issues related to national culture as it relates to the concerns of both researchers and practitioners interested in international human resource management. We have focused both on culture as a concept, exploring the definitional issues that arise in understanding national culture, various approaches to assessing national culture, the relationship of national culture to work-related outcomes, and the various methodological and conceptual problems confronting those who study culture. As the literature is truly large, we of necessity have provided a sampling of the issues and relevant literature, concentrating mainly on work published in the past decade or so. This work, then, should be viewed as a broad overview of an immense topic rather than a comprehensive survey of the field as a whole. However, we believe our work reflects the most significant issues in this field and the leading studies.

We have discussed cultural issues in a rather abstract manner. However, we need also look at how cross-national differences impact internationally active firms and highlight those areas of HRM practice in which knowledge of cultural issues is essential. We see three fundamental areas in which these issues are especially relevant to the human resource manager.

First, a multinational company may assign its home-country nationals to other countries, move international employees among countries, and bring employees from international affiliates to work or train in the parent company's home country. Failure to select people with appropriate cross-cultural competencies and to prepare them for such expatriate assignments is apt to result in significant adjustment problems leading to poor performance and outright failure in the international assignment (Shaffer, Harrison, and Gilley, 1999). American MNCs in particular have reportedly suffered from these problems, at least during the period of rapid international expansion that occurred in the 1980s and early 1990s, though the extent to which this ever was or continues to be an American problem has been questioned. Cross-cultural adjustment is multifaceted, involving work adjustment, social adjustment, and adjustment to general living conditions, and failure to adjust along any of these dimensions for the employee or an accompanying family member can have a deleterious impact on the employee's effectiveness in the assignment. Conversely, repatriation to one's home country can produce its own set of cultural difficulties for both the employee and accompanying family members. There is now a substantial literature devoted to understanding and resolving repatriation problems (Adler, 2002; Kraimer, Wayne, & Joworski, 2002).

Second, the types of expatriate assignments are changing. There are many reasons for making an international assignment (and these are not mutually exclusive): to manage the affairs of a foreign subsidiary, to facilitate knowledge or technology transfer, to provide expertise to solve a problem or resolve a crisis in a subsidiary, or to provide a developmental experience in the international arena for a high-potential employee. Given the expense of expatriate assignments, longer-term management-focused expatriate assignments are apparently in decline, though probably not the other types (normally shorter-term). There has been a corresponding increase in intra-organizational networks as a means of facilitating global coordination and control. Cross-national teams are much more common, so employees in different countries must learn how to interact with those of other cultures even though they only occasionally if ever visit a foreign subsidiary. The activities of cross-national teams are often facilitated by sophisticated communications technology, including the Internet and organizational intranets. There is increasing use of terms such as "virtual cross-national teams" to describe this phenomenon (Cunha & Da Cunha, 2001). Increasing numbers of employees find themselves regularly interacting with colleagues from several different cultures simultaneously. They may also interact with customers and business partners from many different countries. Thus, cross-cultural competencies related to international activities are increasingly required of those who do not actually live or work abroad.

Third, MNCs must be concerned about the employment practices and systems used in international affiliates for host-country nationals. Kerr, Harbison, Dunlop, and Myers (1996) first proposed the "convergence hypothesis" to describe what they thought at the time would be a general movement among different employment systems in different parts of the world toward the characteristic approaches of the dominant form of industrial management in the United States and other Western economies. They saw convergence as largely driven by competitive necessity. But subsequent research generally failed to support strong convergence forces (Punnett and Shenkar, 1994). Indeed, the emergence of a strong interest in cultural issues on the part of management scholars was very much driven by the recognition that cultural differences across countries and geographical regions was one major force promoting divergence. Much has been written contrasting national and regional HR systems, with many in-depth country analyses. Schuler, Dowling, and De Cieri

(1993) proposed a theoretical framework describing the conditions under which MNCs may choose to adapt to host-country HR practices versus import home-country or global practices. Although many forces are posited to factor into such choices, the cultural similarities and differences between host- and home-countries are important considerations.

REFERENCES

Adler, N. J. (2002). *International dimensions of organizational behavior* (4th ed.). Cincinnati, OH: South-Western.

Avolio, B. J., Sosik, J. J., Jung, D. I., & Berson, Y. (2003). Leadership models, methods, and Applications. In I. B. Weiner (Ed.), *Handbook of psychology: Industrial and organizational psychology* (pp. 277–307). Hoboken, NJ: John Wiley & Sons.

Awasthi, V. N., Chow, C. W., & Wu, A. (1998). Performance measure and resource expenditure choices in a teamwork environment: The effects of national culture. *Management Accounting Research, 9,* 119–139.

Bailey, J. R., Chen, C. C., & Dou, S. G (1997). Conceptions of self and performance-related feedback in the US, Japan and China. *Journal of International Business Studies, 28,* 605–625.

Bass, B. M. (1997). Does the transactional-transformational leadership paradigm transcend organizational and national boundaries? *American Psychologist, 52,* 130–139.

Brockner, J., Ackerman, G., Greenberg, J., Gelfand, M. J., Francesco, A. M., Chen, Z. X., et al. (2001). Culture and procedural justice: The influence of power distance on reactions to voice. *Journal of Experimental Social Psychology, 37,* 300–315.

Brodbeck, F. C., Frese, M., Akerblom, S., Audia, G., Bakacsi, G., Bendova, H., et al. (2000). Cultural validation of leadership prototypes across 22 European countries. *Journal of Occupational and Organizational Psychology, 73,* 1–29.

Chang, L. C. (2003). An examination of cross-cultural negotiation: Using Hofstede framework. *Journal of American Academy of Business, 2,* 567–570.

Chatman, J. A., & Barsade, S. G. (1995). Personality, organizational culture, and cooperation: Evidence from a business simulation. *Administrative Science Quarterly, 40,* 423–443.

Chen, C. C., Meindl, J. R., & Hunt, R. G. (1997). Testing the effects of vertical and horizontal collectivism: A study of reward allocation preferences in China. *Journal of Cross-Cultural Psychology, 28,* 44–70.

Chinese Culture Connections (1987). Chinese Values and the Search for culture-free dimensions of culture. *Journal of Cross-Cultural Psychology, 18,* 143–164.

Crampton, S. M., & Wagner, J. A., III (1994). Percept-percept in microorganization research: An investigation of prevalence and effect. *Journal of Applied Psychology, 79,* 67–76.

Cunha, M. P. E., & Da Cunha, J. V. (2001). Managing improvisation in cross cultural virtual teams. *International Journal of Cross Cultural Management, 1,* 187–208.

Den Hartog, D., House, R. J., Hanges, P. J., Ruiz-Quintanilla, A., & Dorfman, P. (1999). Culture specific and cross-culturally generalizable implicit leadership theories: Are attributes of charismatic /transformational leadership universally endorsed? *Leadership Quarterly, 10,* 219–257.

Dickson, M. W., Hanges, P. J., & Lord, R. M. (2001). Trends, developments, and gaps in cross-cultural research on leadership. In W. Mobley & M. McCall (Eds.), *Advances in global leadership* (pp. 75–100). Stamford, CT: JAI Press.

Dorfman, P. W, Howell, J. P., Hibino, S., Lee, J. K., Tate, U., & Bautista, A. (1997). Leadership in Western and Asian countries: Communalities and differences in effective leadership processes across cultures. *Leadership Quarterly, 8,* 233–274.

Doty, D. H., & Glick, W. H. (1998). Common method bias: Does common methods variance really bias results? *Organizational Research Methods, 1,* 374–406.

Earley, P. C. (1999). Playing follow the leader: Status-determining traits in relation to collective efficacy across cultures. *Organizational Behavior and Human Decision Processes, 80,* 192–212.

Earley, P. C., & Erez, M. (1997). *New perspectives on international industrial/organizational psychology.* San Francisco, CA: Lexington Press.

Earley, P. C., & Gibson, C. B. (1998). Taking stock in our progress on individualism-collectivism: 100 years of solidarity and community. *Journal of Management, 24,* 265–304.

Elahee, M. N., Kirby, S. L., & Nasif, E. (2002). National culture, trust, and perceptions about ethical behavior in intra- and cross-cultural negotiations: An analysis of NAFTA countries. *Thunderbird International Business Review, 44,* 799–818.

Erez, M., & Earley, P. C. (1993). *Culture, self-identity, and work.* New York: Oxford University Press.

Fu, P. P., & Yukl, G. (2000). Perceived effectiveness of influence tactics in the United States and China. *Leadership Quarterly, 11,* 251–266.

Gabrielidis, C., Stephan, W. G., Ybarra, O., Dos Santos-Pearson, V. M., & Villareal, L. (1997). Preferred styles and conflict resolution: Mexico and the United States. *Journal of Cross-Cultural Psychology, 28,* 661–677.

Gelfand, M. J., Bhawuk, D. P. S., Nishi, L. H., & Bechtold, D. (2004). Individualism and collectivism: Multilevel perspectives and implications for leadership. In R. J. House, P. J. Hanges, M. Javidan, P. W. Dorfman, & V. Gupta (Eds.) *Culture, leadership, and organizations: The GLOBE study of 62 cultures* (pp. 437–512). Thousand Oaks, CA: Sage.

Gelfand, M. J., Triandis, H. C., & Chan, K. S. (1996). Individualism versus collectivism or versus authoritarianism? *European Journal of Social Psychology, 26,* 397–410.

Gulbro, R. D., & Herbig, P. (1999). Cultural differences encountered by firms when negotiating internationally. *Industrial Management + Data Systems, 99,* 47–53.

Hofstede, G. (1980). *Culture's consequences: International differences in work-related values.* Beverly Hills, CA: Sage.

Hofstede, G. (1997). *Cultures and organizations: Software of the mind.* New York: McGraw-Hill.

Hofstede, G. (1998). *Masculinity and femininity: The taboo dimension of national cultures.* Thousand Oaks, CA: Sage.

Hofstede, G. (2001). *Culture's consequences: Comparing values, behaviors, institutions and organizations across nations.* Thousand Oaks, CA: Sage.

Hofstede, G., & Peterson, M. (2000). Culture: National values and organizational practices. In N. Ashkanasy, C. Wilderom, & M. F. Peterson (Eds.), *Handbook of organizational culture and climate.* Thousand Oaks, CA: Sage.

House, R. J., & Aditya, R. (1997). The social scientific study of leadership: Quo vadis? *Journal of Management, 23,* 409–474.

House, R. J., Hanges, P. J., Javidan, M., Dorfman, P. W., & Gupta, V. (2004). *Culture, leadership, and organizations: The GLOBE study of 62 cultures.* Thousand Oaks, CA: Sage.

House, R. J., Wright, N. S., & Aditya, R. N. (1997). Cross-cultural research on organizational leadership: A critical analysis and a proposed theory. In P. C. Earley & M. Erez (Eds.), *New perspectives on international industrial and organizational psychology* (pp. 535–625). San Francisco, CA: Lexington Press.

Hui, C. H. (1984). *Individualism-collectivism: Theory, measurement, and its relation to reward allocation.* —Ph.D. thesis, University of Illinois at Urbana-Champaign.

Hui, C. H. (1988). Measurement of individualism-collectivism. *Journal of Research in Personality, 22,* 17–36.

Hwang, K. K. (2001). The deep structure of Confucianism: A social psychological approach. *Asian Philosophy, 11,* 79–204.

Javidan, M., House, R. J., Dorfman, P. W., Gupta, V., & Hanges, P. J. (2004). Conclusions and future direction. In R. J. House, P. J. Hanges, M. Javidan, P. W. Dorfman, & V. Gupta (Eds.), *Culture, leadership, and organizations: The GLOBE study of 62 cultures* (pp. 723–732). Thousand Oaks, CA: Sage.

Kealey, D. J., & Ruben, B. D. (1983). Cross-cultural personnel selection criteria, issues, and methods. pp. 155–175. In D. Landis & R. W. Brislin (Eds.), *Handbook of intercultural training* (Vol. 1). New York: Pergamon.

Kerr, C., Harbison, F. H., Dunlop, J. T., & Myers, C. A. (1996). Industrialism and industrial man. *International Labour Review, 135,* 383–392.

Kluckhohn, C. (1951). The study of culture. In D. Lerner & H. D. Lassewell (Eds.), *The policy sciences.* (pp. 86–101). Stanford, CA: Stanford University Press.

Kozlowski, S. W. J., & Klein, K. J. (2000). A multilevel approach to theory and research in organizations: Contextual, temporal, and emerging processes. In K. J. Klein & S. W. J. Kozlowski (Eds.), *Multilevel theory, research and methods in organizations: Foundations, extensions, and new directions* (pp. 3–90). San Francisco: Jossey-Bass.

Kraimer, M. L., Wayne, S. J., & Joworski, R. A. (2002). Sources of support and expatriate performance. The mediating role of expatriate adjustment. *Personnel Psychology, 54,* 71-99.

Kroeber, A. L., & Kluckhohn, C. (1963). *Culture: A critical review of concepts and definitions.* New York: Random House.

Lam, S. S. K., Chen, X., & Schaubroeck, J. (2002). Participation decision making and employee performance in different cultures: The moderating effects of allocentrism/idiocentrism and efficacy. *Academy of Management Journal, 45,* 905–914.

Lin, X. H., & Miler, S. J. (2003). Negotiation approaches: Direct and indirect effect of national culture. *International Marketing Review, 20,* 286–304.

Lytle, A. L., Brett, J. M., & Shapiro, D. L. (1999). The strategic use of interests, rights, and power to resolve disputes. *Negotiation Journal, 15,* 31–51.

Marchese, M. C. (2001). Matching management practices to national culture in India, Mexico, Poland, and the U.S. *The Academy of Management Executive, 15,* 130–132.

Markus, H. R., & Kitayama, S. (1991). Culture and self: Implications for cognition, emotion and motivation. *Psychological Review, 98,* 224–253.

Meyer, J. P., & Allen, N. J. (1991). A three-component conceptualization of organizationalcommitment. *Human Resource Management Review, 1,* 61–98.

Misumi, J., & Peterson, M. F. (1985). The performance-maintenance (PM) theory of leadership: Review of a Japanese research program. *Administrative Science Quarterly, 30,* 198–223.

Mowday, R. T., Steers, R. M., & Porter, L. W. (1979). The measurement of organizational commitment. *Journal of Vocational Behavior, 14,* 224–247.

Neale, R., & Mindel, R. (1992). Rigging up multicultural teamworking. *Personnel Management, 24,* 36–39.

Ohbuchi, K., & Takahashi, Y. (1994). Cultural styles of conflict management in Japanese and Americans: Passivity, covertness, and effectiveness of strategies. *Journal of Applied Social Psychology, 24,* 1345–1366.

Oishi, S., Schimmack, U., Diener, E., & Sug, E. M. (1998). The measurement of values and individualism-collectivism. *Personality and Social Psychology Bulletin, 24,* 1177–1189.

Parsons, T. (1951). *The social system.* New York: Free Press.

Peterson, M. F., & Hunt, J. G. (1997). International perspective on international leadership. *Leadership Quarterly*, 8, 203–231.

Punnett, B. J., & Shenkar, O. (1994). International management research: Toward a contingency approach. *Advances in International Comparative Management, 9,* 39–55.

Ralston, D. A., Egri, C. P., Stewart, S., Terpstra, R. H., & Kaicheng, Y. (1999). Doing business in the 21st century with the new generation of Chinese managers: A study of generational shifts in work values in China. *Journal of International Studies, 30*(2), 415–428.

Rees, W. D., & Porter, C. (1998). Employee participation and managerial style (the key variable). *Industrial and Commercial Training, 30,* 165–171.

Robert, C., Probst, T. M., Martocchio, J. J., Drasgow, F., & Lawler, J. J. (2000). Empowerment and continuous improvement in the United States, Mexico, Poland, and India: Predicting fit on the basis of dimensions of power distance and individualism. *Journal of Applied Psychology, 85,* 643–658.

Robert, C., & Wasti, S. A. (2002). Organizational individualism and collectivism: Theoretical development and an empirical test of a measure. *Journal of Management, 28,* 544–566.

Salk, J. E., & Brannen, M. Y. (2000). National culture, networks, and individual influence in a multinational management team. *Academy of Management Journal. 43,* 191–203.

Scoville, J., Lawler, J. J., & Yi. X. (2005). Non-Western ethical thought. In J. Budd & J. Scoville (Eds.), *Ethics of human resources and industrial relations* (pp. 89–113). Champaign, IL: Labor and Employment Relations Association.

Schein, E. H. (1992). *Organizational culture and leadership* (2nd ed.). San Francisco, CA: Jossey-Bass.

Schuler, R. S., Dowling, P. J., & De Cieri, H. C. (1993). An integrative framework of strategic human resource management. *Journal of Management, 19,* 419–459.

Schwartz, S. H. (1994). Beyond individualism and collectivism: New cultural dimensions of values. In U. Kim, H. C. Triandis, C. Kagitcibasi, S.-C. Choi, & G. Yoon (Eds.), *Individualism and collectivism: Theory, method, and applications* (pp. 85–122). Newbury Park, CA: Sage.

Shaffer, M. A., Harrison, D. A., & Gilley, K. M. (1999). Dimensions, determinants, and differences in the expatriate adjustment process. *Journal of International Business Studies, 30,* 557–581.

Singelis, T. M., Triandis, H. C., Bhawuk, D. P. S., & Gelfand, M. J. (1995). Horizontal and vertical dimensions of individualism and collectivism: A theoretical and measurement refinement. *Cross-Cultural Research, 29,* 240–275.

Smith, P. B., Dugan, S., & Trompenaars, F. (1996). National culture and the values of organizational employees: A dimensional analyses across 43 countries. *Journal of Cross-Cultural Psychology, 27*, 231–264.

Smith, P. B., Misumi, J., Tayeb, M., Peterson, M. F., & Bond, M. (1989). On the generality of leadership style measures across cultures. *Journal of Occupational Psychology, 62*, 97–109.

Smith, P. B., Peterson, M. F., Schwartz, S. H., Ahmad, A. H., Akande, D., Anderson, J. A., et al. (2002). Cultural values, sources of guidance and their relevance to managerial behavior—a 47-nation study. *Journal of Cross-Cultural Psychology, 33*, 188–208.

Sosik, J. J., & Jung, D. I. (2002). Work-group characteristics and performance in collectivistic and individualistic cultures. *The Journal of Social Psychology, 142*, 5–23.

Tajfel, H., & Turner, J. C. (1986). The social identity theory of group behavior. In S. Worchel & W. G. Austin (Eds.), *Psychology of intergroup relations* (pp. 7–24). Chicago: Nelson-Hall.

Trafimow, D., Triandis, H. C., & Goto, S. (1991). Some tests of the distinction between the private and collective self. *Journal of Personality and Social Psychology, 60*, 649–655.

Triandis, H. C. (1972*). The analysis of subjective culture.* New York: John Wiley.

Triandis, H. C. (1989). Self and social behavior in differing cultural contexts. *Psychological Review, 96*, 269–289.

Triandis, H. C. (1994). Theoretical and methodological approaches to the study of collectivism and individualism. In U. Kim, H. C. Triandis, C. Kagitcibasi, S.-C. Choi, & G. Yoon (Eds.), *Individualism and collectivism: Theory, method, and applications* (pp. 41–51). Thousand Oaks, CA: Sage.

Triandis, H. C. (1995a). *Individualism and collectivism.* Boulder, CO: Westview Press.

Triandis, H. C. (1995b). *New directions in social psychology.* Boulder, CO: Westview Press.

Triandis, H. C. (2002). Generic individualism and collectivism. In M. J. Gannon & K. L. Newman (Eds.), *Handbook of cross-cultural management* (pp. 16–45). Oxford: Blackwell.

Triandis, H. C., & Bhawuk, D. P. S. (1997). Culture theory and the meaning of relatedness. In P. C. Earley & M. Erez (Eds.), *New perspectives in international/organizational psychology* (pp. 13–52). New York: The New Lexington Free Press.

Triandis, H. C., Bontempo, R., Leung, K., & Hui, C. H. (1990). A method for determining cultural, societal, and personal constructs. *Journal of Cross-Cultural Psychology, 21*, 302–318.

Triandis, H. C., Bontempo, R., Villareal, M. J., Asai, M., & Lucca, N. (1988). Individualism and collectivism: Cross-cultural perspectives on self-in-group relationships. *Journal of Personality and Social Psychology, 54*, 323–338.

Triandis, H. C., Chan, D. K., Bhawuk, D. P. S., Iwao, S., & Sinha, J. B. P. (1995). Multimethod probes of allocentrism and idiocentrism. *International Journal of Psychology, 30*, 461–480.

Triandis, H. C., Chen, X. P., & Chan, D. K-S. (1998). Scenarios for the measurement of collectivism and individualism. *Journal of Cross-Cultural Psychology, 29*, 275–289.

Triandis, H. C., & Gelfand, M. J. (1998). Converging measurement of horizontal and vertical individualism and collectivism. *Journal of Personality and Social Psychology, 30*, 118–128.

Triandis, H. C., Leung, K., Villareal, M., & Clack, F. L. (1985). Allocentrism vs. idiocentrism tendencies: Convergent and discriminant validation. *Journal of Research in Personality, 19*, 395–415.

Trompenaars, F. (1994). *Riding waves of culture.* New York: Irwin.

Trompenaars, F., & Hampden-Turner, C. (1998). *Riding the waves of culture: Understanding cultural diversity in global business* (2nd ed.). New York: McGraw-Hill.

Trubinsky, P., Ting-Toomey, S., & Lin, S. (1991). The influence of individualism-collectivism and self-monitoring on conflict styles. *International Journal of Intercultural Relations, 15*, 65–84.

Turner, J. C. (1987). *Rediscovering the social group.* Oxford: Basil Blackwell.

Walumbwa, F. O. (1999). Rethinking the issues of international technology transfer. *Journal of Technology Studies, 25*, 51–54.

Walumbwa, F. O., & Lawler, J. J. (2003). Building effective organizations: Transformational leadership, collectivist orientation, work-related attitudes, and withdrawal behaviors in three emerging economies. *International Journal of Human Resource Management, 14*, 1083–1101.

Walumbwa, F. O., Lawler, J. J., & Avolio, B. J. (2005). *Leadership, individual differences and work attitudes: A cross-culture investigation* (Working Paper). Tempe: Arizona State University, School of Global Management and Leadership.

Wang, P., Lawler, J. J., Walumbwa, F. O., & Shi, K. (2004). Work-family conflict and organizational withdrawal: The moderating effect of cultural differences. *International Journal of Stress Management*
11(4), 392–412.

Waters, M. (1995). *Globalization*. London: Routledge.

Xie, J. H., Song, X. M., & Stringfellow, A. (1998). Interfunctional conflict, conflict resolution styles, and new
product success: A four-culture comparison. *Management Science, 44*, S192–S206.

3 Qualitative Research Methodologies and International Human Resource Management

Robert P. Gephart, Jr. and Julia Richardson

CONTENTS

Qualitative research methodologies have much to contribute to the development of international human resource management (IHRM). The chapter begins by contextualizing different methods in terms of key intellectual paradigms or worldviews in the field of management. We demonstrate how paradigmatic commitments influence the nature, meaning, and appropriate use of qualitative methods as a research tool. Next, we provide an overview of four general qualitative research methods that are useful to IHRM research—case studies, observational strategies, interviews, and the analysis of documents and artefacts. In this chapter we discuss the advantages and limitations of these methods and describe how they have been implemented in previous IHRM research on important topics in the field. We conclude by noting the potential qualitative methods have to advance the field of IHRM.

THE NATURE AND PURPOSES OF QUALITATIVE RESEARCH

Qualitative research is an "umbrella term covering a wide array of interpretive techniques" (Van Maanen, 1979, p. 520) that draw on a combination of observations, interviews, and documents to describe and understand the actual meanings, human interactions, and processes that are meaningful to members of society. Qualitative research often adopts an interpretive, naturalistic approach to understanding phenomena (Denzin & Lincoln, 1994) aiming towards "thick descriptions" (Geertz, 1973) of the conversations and actions of members of society. It seeks to produce "historically situated tales" that include detailed descriptions of social actors' behaviour at specific times and places along with "reasoned interpretations" of this behaviour (Van Maanen, 1998, p. xi).

Fisher and Hartel (2003) provide a recent IHRM study that demonstrates the general orientation of qualitative research. They used interviews and case studies to examine Thai and Western managers' conceptualizations of intercultural effectiveness. The study also sought to identify the different dimensions of perceived effectiveness demonstrated by Thai and Western managers working in intercultural teams. Rather than trying to generalize from the findings the researchers were trying to develop a more in-depth understanding of each of the cases selected as exemplars of views on intercultural effectiveness. The findings suggested that Western managers believed that it was difficult for them to be effective because Thai culture was ethnocentric and homogeneous. Conversely, Thai managers believed that Western managers' ineffectiveness was due to their failure to understand Thai culture. Further, neither group believed that age, gender, religious affiliation, or nationality impacted cultural effectiveness. Yet, Thai managers believed that racial background could have a significant effect on the extent to which an expatriate manager would be successful. Although proficiency in the host country's language is often seen as important for cultural effectiveness neither Thai nor Western managers believe this to be so because English was the generally accepted language of business in Thailand. Further, Western managers believed that general intercultural experience would support effectiveness. Thai managers did not believe this to be the case because they held the view that Thai culture is unique to Asia so having experience elsewhere would not be helpful.

The nature and advantages of qualitative research are further illustrated by the Hawthorne study (Roesthlisberger & Dickson, 1939)— arguably the most influential behavioral science study ever conducted of a business enterprise (Schwartzman, 1993). This study established important intellectual bases for industrial psychology, organizational studies, and personnel and human resources management. It examined the relationship between fatigue and monotony, and job satisfaction and dissatisfaction, using an experimental methodology that varied working conditions. Researchers monitored workers assembling telephone relays (switches) to understand the impact of illumination on productivity. The experiments produced the puzzling "Hawthorne effect" wherein output rose independently of changes in working conditions and rewards. The researchers hypothesized that "psychological factors" such as researchers paying attention to workers may have been responsible for productivity changes. They then used a qualitative research study that produced detailed information on relationships among workers, and the meaning of work. This study included behavioral observations by a "disinterested spectator" (an observer placed within the group) and interviews by an interviewer who did not enter the observation room (Schwartzman, 1993, p. 9). The simultaneous use of observations and interviews constituted a new method. The Hawthorne research thus became the first organizational research study to employ ethnography to describe "the social organization of an industrial working group" (Chapple, 1993, p. 820 cited in Schwartzman, 1993, p. 9). Its specific value was that it demonstrated the importance of the informal organization—the interpersonal relationships—in controlling worker behavior. It also discovered the impact of informal sanctions, such as "binging" workers, on limiting worker output. These findings clearly suggest that the informal organization could work either for or against formal economic objectives in an organization (Schwartzman, 1993, p. 13).

The Hawthorne study started out testing hypotheses but changed to hypothesis generation (Schwartzman, 1993, p. 16). This demonstrates the value of exploratory qualitative research where research questions and methods evolve during research (Schwartzman, 1993). The richness of the study's data has also allowed other researchers to reinterpret it and develop their own insights.

The Hawthorne study demonstrated several key principles that guide qualitative research (Van Maanen, 1998, p. xi): (a) it used observations and interviews to capture the meanings attributed to specific themes, (b) it used analytic induction to surface insights and hypotheses to account for actual observations, (c) it remained close to data both theoretically and methodologically, and (d) it focused on common work behavior in real work settings. In addition, it shows how broad principles or concepts such as formal and informal organization evolve in particular cases. It also describes how situational details unfold over time and provides insights into organizational and managerial processes.

Qualitative research can be further clarified by distinguishing it from quantitative research. Quantitative research employs the hypothetical deductive model by examining variables, measuring associations among variables, and testing propositions using quantitative (numeric) data and techniques. Qualitative research favors inductive, interpretive work and is often oriented to exploration, discovery, description, and theory building (Van Maanen, 1998, p. xii). For example, a study of interorganizational transfer of research and development (R&D) capabilities in international joint ventures in the Chinese automotive industry (Zhao, Anand, & Mitchell, 2005) used a qualitative case study approach because it sought to "explore new theoretical ground" (p. 135) as opposed to testing existing theory. The researchers drew on field observations and interviews with relevant individuals to understand culturally specific themes of relationship hierarchies and interactions. The researchers also noted that a research instrument such as a questionnaire constructed in developing economies may not be applicable to an emerging business context such as China.

Qualitative research involves both data collection and analysis and each of these processes can be qualitative or quantitative. Qualitative data include words and texts. Qualitative analysis involves interpreting these data, settings, or observations using nonquantitative practices and tools, such as literary tropes or scholarly concepts. Qualitative analysis seeks to create an interpretation of a setting or feature that allows others not present in the setting to gain a deeper understanding of the setting or feature (Feldman, 1995, p. 1). The challenge is to produce an analysis that shows how parts of a culture or phenomenon fit together and influence one another and how similar processes may operate in other settings (Feldman, 1995, p. 2). In contrast, quantitative data are observations that are represented numerically. Quantitative analysis involves coding, counting, and measuring phenomena. There are thus four combinations of data and analysis methods. Quantitative analysis of qualitative data is often mistakenly labelled qualitative research but because it ultimately involves quantification it is primarily quantitative in nature. Quantitative analysis of qualitative data creates many unique methodological challenges that differ from the challenges of qualitatively analysing and interpreting qualitative data. Therefore, in this chapter, qualitative research refers to qualitative analysis of qualitative data. We also examine the quantification of qualitative data that is common in positivist qualitative research as elaborated below.

PARADIGMS AND RESEARCH METHODS

Many aspects of empirical research are shaped by the theoretical paradigm or worldview within which the research is conducted (Gubrium & Holstein, 2000). Thus, qualitative and quantitative research reflect one or more underlying scholarly paradigms. The paradigmatic commitments of research reflect particular assumptions about the nature of reality and the construction of knowledge that permeate the research process as a whole. Before selecting specific methodologies, the researcher must understand the paradigmatic assumptions in their research processes and in the theoretical perspectives they are seeking to advance. This allows for theoretical and methodological consistency. We examine three paradigms that are relevant to IHRM: positivism, interpretivism, and critical postmodern perspectives (Rynes & Gephart, 2004). These paradigms are part of a more extensive set of paradigms in social science and management research today. In actual research studies the paradigms are often interwoven and the boundaries between them are blurred. Hence, the scheme presented here is an analytical tool to highlight their respective central and distinctive features.

POSITIVISM AND POSTPOSITIVISM

Positivism and postpositivism use a realist ontology: both assume an objective world exists that can be represented directly by scientific concepts and propositions (Gephart, 1999, 2004; Guba & Lincoln, 1994; Lincoln & Guba, 2000). They are the perspectives commonly taken with quantitative research measuring variables to test hypotheses and propositions. Positivism presumes that causal, deterministic relationships among variables can be verified, uncovered, and specified in mathematical form. Postpositivism assumes that reality can be known only probabilistically, hence falsification of null hypotheses, not verification of hypotheses, is the key goal of science.

Qualitative research in the positivist tradition tends to make the same assumptions made in quantitative positivism. It focuses on quantifying qualitative data to produce variables that are amenable to quantitative assessment. It also seeks to discover important relationships among variables and to test or falsify them. Knowledge is constituted by verified hypotheses in the case of positivism and by nonfalsifiable hypotheses in the case of postpositivism. Given the focus on testing relationships among variables, positivism and postpositivism emphasize methodological rigor and seek to produce reliable results with demonstrable internal and external validity (Gephart, 1999).

The emphasis on testing, validating, or falsifying relationships among variables can be addressed by use of statistical tests of significance and other quantitative tools. In general, researchers using the positivist approach seek to identify, operationalize, and measure key variables and factual features of these variables, and to compare facts to hypotheses or prior research findings as a means of developing knowledge. However, where qualitative analysis of qualitative data is undertaken for positivist purposes, the lack of explicit methods for establishing associations among variables and for testing or falsifying hypotheses poses a considerable challenge. In general, the positivist view uses research methodologies that seek to describe key variables and facts associated with them.

The positivistic use of qualitative analysis in IHRM research is illustrated by a study of managers' perceptions of commitment in the United Kingdom and Sweden (Singh & Vinnicombe, 2000). The researchers used interviews to elicit managers' accounts of the meanings they attributed to the notion of commitment. These meanings could later be used by quantitative researchers to develop a sense of how the concept might be quantified or operationalized. Similarly, in a study of HRM practices in small and medium-sized enterprises in the United Kingdom (Cassell, Nadin, Gray, & Clegg, 2002), quantitative data collected from a telephone survey were supplemented by unstructured interviews. The qualitative interview data helped researchers interpret the quantitative data by providing a more in-depth understanding of meanings attributed to themes discussed during the survey.

INTERPRETIVE RESEARCH

Interpretive research is fundamentally concerned to understand human meanings and definitions of respective contexts (Schwandt, 1994, p. 18; Rynes & Gephart, 2004). It takes the view that reality is socially constructed (Berger & Luckmann, 1966) and assumes a dialectical process wherein subjective realities and meanings emerge and are shared among social actors. These shared or intersubjective meanings are used to create objective realities, which in turn act back on human subjective meanings. Interpretive research thus assumes an objective reality external to human cognition and examines how features of the objective world are humanly constructed and given meanings that, in turn, influence human actions. This represents a more relativist stance than that adopted by positivist research. For example, a study of the impact of a new governance structure on management practice in a U.K. hospital (Mueller, Harvey, & Howorth, 2003) commenced with the assumption that organizational actors create analytical categories or interpretations of events that are "constitutive of social relations" (Mueller et al., 2003, p. 1977) rather than simply describing them.

The focus on understanding human meanings and divergent views of the world characterizes interpretive research. It seeks to understand the key concepts used by social actors, and their respective meanings. Interpretive concepts are thus constructed by drawing on social actors' first-order or natural meanings. This allows social actors' voices to be heard and reports and analyzes the stories they tell. Its validity is thus based on or reflected in the extent to which researchers have utilized the respective methods as a guide to understanding the views of social actors in a given setting and to enacting normal behavior (passing as normal) in the settings studied (Van Maanen, 1981). A study of strategic choice in managerial practices in subsidiaries of British and German multinational corporations (MNCs) (Geppert, Williams, & Matten, 2003), for example, explored how managers constructed meaning and subsequent business strategy from their respective global and national business contexts. Drawing on a qualitative research approach, it used case studies that involved in-depth interviews with CEOs, managers, works councillors, and union representatives in the lifts and escalators industry. Specifically, it explored how meaning and subsequent strategic behaviour might be linked to either parent MNCs or national institutional contexts. A key finding of the study was that national culture still played an influential role in how managers understood their own business practices and how those practices were later put into action. For example, the German subsidiary of Amy, a major global player in the lifts and escalators industry, reflected a textbook-like German approach to change management, where change was more incremental. By comparison a British subsidiary of the same company reflected more radical approaches. Thus, national work patterns and norms in the respective German and British subsidiaries of MNCs were found to be deeply entrenched rather than giving way to more global patterns. A key point here is that interpretive approaches recognize the social embeddedness of individual actors and the extent to which the emerging meanings and interpretations are connected to their respective social context. Thus, in this particular study, local processes were acknowledged and factored into the research process and the emerging theory.

Interpretive research searches for patterns of meaning then, rather than causal associations among variables. Meaningful and symbolic actions such as conversations are key units of analysis. Multiple or divergent meanings are described in detail and examined for their content and implications. The researcher seeks to understand diversity rather than to reconcile it by distinguishing true meanings from false or biased interpretations. Thus, in cross-cultural studies, the multiple cultures perspective deliberately includes conflicting and contradictory findings as key dimensions of the research process (Sackmann & Phillips, 2004). In studying a strike by flight attendants, for example, Dahler-Larsen (1997), reported how individuals might draw on shifting and sometimes contradictory associations and allegiances to different groups to construe their overall organizational identity. This finding clearly incorporates the conflicts that exist between partial identities as part of social interaction and individual identity. Interpretive research thus provides insights into how variations in meaning and sense making reflect differences in objective realities (Gephart, 1999).

A small number of interpretive studies have been conducted in IHRM research. One example is provided by a case study of mentoring relations in a National Health Service Trust hospital in the United Kingdom (Beech & Brockbank, 1999). The authors used interviews and group discussions as "different ways of accessing the perceptions of the actors involved and to attempt to interpret the meanings and understandings that the actors established" concerning mentoring (Beech & Brockbank, 1999, p. 11). A second example is Richardson and McKenna's (2000) study of expatriation that sought to understand how a group of British faculty interpreted their decision to expatriate and their subsequent experience in light of the current trend towards the internationalization of higher education. The study used unstructured interviews and found that the majority of faculty had taken an overseas position in order to see more of the world or simply to experience adventure or life change. However, in evaluating their experience, career development was a dominant theme—even though this theme had scarcely figured at all in the decision to go overseas.

A third example is a study of repatriated U.S. managers undertaken by Osland (1995), who explored the meanings and interpretations participants ascribed to both their overseas assignment and repatriation to the United States. The research used a survey and in-depth interviews to "really focus on the subjective experience" (Osland, 1995, p. xiii) of participants. The findings of the study suggested that the expatriate assignment might be usefully understood by drawing on the metaphor of a hero's adventure. Specifically, themes including "a call to adventure," heroic challenge, and transformation emerged as important in understanding how participants had experienced the initial expatriate assignment and subsequent return to the United States.

A fourth example is provided by Peltonen (1998), who also investigated expatriation. The objective of the study was to understand the meanings participants attributed to their evolving international career paths. Like Osland (1995), Peltonen (1998) also explored how the meanings attributed to the expatriate experience were connected to personal transformation. Peltonen (1998) thus analysed the discursive patterns that emerged in interviews with engineering personnel in two Finnish organizations. This study found that participants drew on a bureaucratic discourse that "emphasizes continuity between past and present in the form of personal evolution in competence" (Peltonen, 1998, p. 879). Participants didn't necessarily see their overseas position as a promotion, but understood it as an opportunity to advance their skills by experiencing a broader cultural and customer context. They drew on an enterprising discourse (Peltonen, 1998, p. 884) to explain how their experience had been an opportunity for self-actualization.

CRITICAL POSTMODERNISM

Critical postmodernism combines critical perspectives and postmodern scholarship, two somewhat distinct views that have certain similarities that are associated with one another in management and social science research (Rynes & Gephart, 2004). Critical scholarship draws on the works of Karl Marx (e.g. 1990) and includes critical theory developed by the Frankfurt school in Germany and elucidated in the works of Jurgen Habermas (e.g. 1973, 1979) and Claus Offe (1984, 1985). Critical theory examines problems with advanced capitalism that emerge from the basic contradiction of capitalism: the owner of capital has the right to appropriate or "skim" surplus value from labour and to retain it for his or her own use. This contradiction engenders other contradictions and inequalities that are basic to management and labour relations issues. Critical scholarship also includes a diverse set of other critical perspectives, often grounded in Max Weber's (1978) work addressing problematic and irrational aspects of capitalist economic and social behavior.

Critical perspectives assume reality is historically constituted and that emerging structures become taken for granted as "natural" features of the world. Thus, the socially constructed reality is conceived as reified by members and taken for granted as immutably concrete and inevitable. Critical research seeks to make social actors reflexively aware of the implications of reified structures and to dereify the taken-for-granted world, thereby encouraging both critique and emancipation from unwanted structures and inequalities. The validity of critical research is based on the researcher's ability to create the critical reflexivity that comprehends ideology in social structures and transforms repressive structures into democratic structures.

Postmodernism is a social era that comes after modernism. It is a style of intellectual production that assumes signs and symbols are detached from the realities they presumably represent (Jameson, 1979; Gephart, Boje, & Thatchenkery, 1996) and builds on the works of Derrida, Foucault, and Baudrillard and also Fredric Jameson (1979). These scholars were well acquainted with critical thought. Postmodern thought addresses the limits of critical thought related to the logic of advanced capitalism and the relationship of signs to appearances. Moreover, it assumes realities are value-laden and contain contradictions. It also aims to understand how hidden dichotomies

TABLE 3.1
Paradigms and Research Methods

Issue	Positivism and Postpositivism	Interpretive Research	Critical Postmodernism
Nature of reality	Reality exists with immutable truths and facts independent of people	Reality created and recognized as true or factual through interpretive practices	Reality historically produced and recognized as true: reification disguises constructed, contradictory nature of reality and hidden interests that are served
Goals	Prediction and control: explanation	Understanding	Understanding and emancipation
Methodological orientation	Describe true facts, assess variables, test hypotheses	Provides thick descriptions of members' meanings including divergent views	Produces descriptions that show reified structures, false truths and alternatives
Implications	Produce knowledge of "true" variable interrelationships	Produces insights into meaning and sense making	Creates critical reflexivity and social change

of power operate and how social categorization is a mechanism of social control and domination (Gephart, 1999). This aim is commonly undertaken by addressing discourse—spoken and written language use (Fairclough, 1992)—in conversations, stories, and texts. Discourse analysis reveals hidden structures of domination and opens spaces for less exploitative communicative behavior. The validity or quality of postmodern scholarship is, therefore, based on its ability to influence readers' views of the world. In general, it employs a variety of discourse analysis and narrative analysis methodologies (Boje, 2001; Riessman, 1993) to uncover and displace hidden ideological aspects and bases of human communication.

The critical perspective is illustrated by Graham (1995), who examined how the Japanese model of lean production work functioned in the Subaru-Isuzu manufacturing facility in Lafayette, Indiana. Graham worked for several months at the manufacturing facility and collected field note data by engaging in covert participant observation of production line work. The study found that the Japanese management model eliminated many of the more serious risks and dangers of assembly line work but created new risks and impacts due to recurrent increases in the speed of the manufacturing process. Demands placed on workers to physically adapt to accommodate the line led to repetitive motion based injuries.

This discussion shows that each paradigm has distinctive assumptions about the world, particular goals, and hence specific methodological needs and orientations. The features of each paradigm are summarized in Table 3.1.

Although a given methodology may be used by any of the paradigms, the actual nature, form, and purposes of its use will vary depending on the respective paradigm. For example, positivism and postpositivist research use qualitative methods to uncover facts to test or falsify hypotheses. A key methodological problem is differentiating true features of the world disclosed in data from false or biased descriptions. Interpretive research uses qualitative methods to uncover meanings, including different meanings held by different groups, so as to provide insights into how people describe and interpret their world(s). A key methodological problem is capturing members' meanings and ensuring all important groups or people are included in the research. Critical postmodern research uses qualitative methods to examine discourse and to uncover evidence of reified structures and hidden contradictions, and alternative interpretations. A key methodological problem is probing beneath superficial interpretations and understandings disclosed in members' statements and documents to uncover reified structures and to show how these structures were produced and how they could be changed.

DATA COLLECTION AND ANALYSIS STRATEGIES

Positivistic research tends to be composed and described in terms of discrete and separate stages. A literature review is completed, research questions or hypotheses are formulated, and appropriate methods of measurement and statistical analysis of variables are specified in advance of data collection and analysis. In contrast, the qualitative research process is open, flexible, and emergent (Van Maanen, 1998). Thus, it may lack discrete stages and may use multiple methods in an overlapping way. Questions may change over the course of research as new topics surface, and methods may also change. Similarly, data collection and analysis may overlap and occur together. For example, the multiple cultures approach to studying cross-cultural issues in IHRM examines the dynamic interplay between different levels of culture, for example, organizational versus national culture, by adopting a "bricolage" approach where research methodologies evolve according to the respective research questions (Sackmann, 1997).

This section describes four general qualitative research methods and specific forms that may be especially useful for IHRM research: case studies, observational methods, interviewing, including focus groups, and analysis of documents and artefacts. These methods generally integrate approaches to data collection with approaches to qualitative analysis of data. Here, we present these methods separately but in actual research studies multiple methods are often used.

THE CASE STUDY METHOD

The case study is a research strategy (Hartley, 1994) describing a single event or unit of analysis determined by the researcher (Rynes & Gephart, 2004). Case studies can be qualitative, quantitative, or a combination of the two. A qualitative case study aims to describe a particular phenomenon and how it changed over time in a specific context, emphasizing processes that underlie the phenomenon and respective changes. For example, Doorewaard, Van Hootegem, and Huys (2002) used interviews with HRM staff and line management and documentary analysis to provide a case description of the processes of team responsibility structure and performance in an organization in the Netherlands.

There are a number of traditions in the use of case studies, including the Chicago school of sociology focusing on professions and occupations, and anthropological case studies of aboriginal groups (Hamel, Dufour, & Fortin, 1993). Case studies allow the researcher to contextualize phenomena (Yin, 1981) providing in-depth understanding and insight into their multiple dimensions. They can be developed in an emergent manner and theory can be used before, during, or after the case is described. They can also support development of robust and conceptually relevant theory by drawing on diverse data sources and addressing multiple aspects of a case over time.

A useful example of a case study in IHRM research is provided by Lam's (2003) study of organizational learning in multinationals. Two U.S. and two Japanese R&D laboratories located in the United Kingdom were compared to explore potential differences between how U.S. and Japanese multinational enterprises (MNEs) managed their global R&D networks (Lam, 2003). To develop the case study, the researcher drew on interviews with relevant organizational personnel, including senior managers; technical staff; HR managers; and academics in partner universities (Lam, 2003). In this research, the case study approach facilitated a deeper understanding of the different relationships with home country headquarters and host country actors and institutions. The study found that Japanese laboratories tended to have less independence and closer connections with home country headquarters. In contrast the U.S. laboratories reflected coordinated autonomy.

The research introduced above demonstrates that case studies offer considerable potential in the field of IHRM. They are especially useful and appropriate where the researcher seeks insights into discrete or explicit phenomena that change over time, where detailed descriptions of the phenomenon are needed, where multiple data sources are available over time, and where process questions or issues require investigation. Case studies can be undertaken in an open, inductive, and exploratory manner. They could also be used to test theory, but given their focused nature, they may be useful primarily for simple tests of theories rather than complex assessments.

OBSERVATIONAL METHODS

Observational methods involve direct observation of phenomena and compilation of a record of observations. Two general observational methods are addressed below: participant observation and ethnography. In addition, we discuss the grounded theory development process here because it is often used with observational or ethnographic data.

Participant Observation

This method includes social interaction with subjects, direct observation of relevant events, formal and informal interviewing, counting, collection of documents, and flexibility in designing and implementing a study (McCall and Simmons, 1969, p. 1). Participant observers often join the group to study its members and use their subjective experiences of group membership as important data. It is useful for observing actual human actions in real contexts and for uncovering and describing members' actual meanings and statements.

There are several important factors to consider in undertaking participant observation (Baker, 1988, p. 231). First, one needs to understand the settings in which behavior occurs. The researcher must observe particular phenomena including verbal and nonverbal behavior and their respective settings. Second, the role of the observer is important. It can vary from full participant to full observer (Baker, 1988, p. 237). In addition, observations may be conducted covertly or overtly, hence researchers must decide whether they will reveal their research identity to participants who are observed (Sharpe, 2002). Overt research is more readily justified in ethical terms. Covert research minimizes the impact of researcher demand effects on participants because they are unaware they are being observed. For example, Melville Dalton used covert observation in his classic study of managerial behavior because he had noted that when other researchers formally approach management for research support "higher managers set the scene and limit the inquiry to specific areas" (1959, p. 275). Third, preparation and access are important.

The researcher must prepare for entry into the field by examining external sources, such as books that describe the context, for example, training programs for expatriate managers, as well as internal sources, that is, information gathered from informants. Researchers must consider the process of entry into the field when they are strangers to those they are observing and when they need to negotiate access to undertake observations. Gaining access to certain groups, such as corporate boards, for example, may be particularly difficult (Le Blanc, 2003). Finally, data collection in participant observation generally involves creating field notes—recording observations. Most notes are written or at least "worked up" after leaving the field. Analysis of field notes generally involves looking for repeated patterns and common themes, as well as deviant or unusual cases (Baker, 1988, pp. 243–244).

Participant observation has been used extensively in management and HRM research. An important example of participant observation research is Barker's study (1993) of self-managing teams, which found that self-managed teams were subject to even stronger controls than bureaucratically managed teams. The self-managing teams used concertive control techniques enacted by workers themselves to control the actions of team members.

Ethnography

This is a form of participant observation that uses direct engagement and interaction with people to understand culture from "the native's point of view" (Malinowski, 1922, p. 25 cited in Schwartzman, 1993, p. 1). It is the trademark of cultural anthropology (Schwartzman, 1993) that seeks to understand another way of life from the perspective of the situated individual (Spradley, 1979). It is "the work of describing a culture" (Spradley, 1979, p. 3) where culture is defined as the acquired knowledge that people use to interpret experience and generate social behavior (Spradley, 1979, p. 5). To achieve insights into cultural features, ethnography emphasizes "thick descriptions" (Geertz, 1973) of behavior in actual contexts using multiple methods and extended involvement in a culture over time. This approach facilitates learning about culture in several ways. First, it examines cultural knowledge, behavior, and artefacts that participants share and use to interpret experiences in a group (Schwartzman, 1993, p. 4). Second, it examines ideas and practices that cultural members take for granted but that influence how their lives evolve in organizational contexts (Schwartzman, 1993). Third, it examines what people say and do, thus providing an understanding of how everyday routines constitute and reconstitute organizational and social structures.

Ethnography in IHRM research is illustrated by Sharpe's (1997) study of team working and managerial control in a Japanese manufacturing subsidiary in the United Kingdom. Sharpe (1997) selected ethnography in order to participate in the routines, rituals, and practices as a member of the shop floor. Sharpe (1997) believed that in using ethnographic and observational methods, she would be able to construct a "richer, reflexive understanding of social processes and dynamics" (p. 230) by actually interacting with the actors and processes that were the focus of her study. Entry to the shop floor was gained by being taken on as a shop floor worker for a period of 15 months. The senior director of the organization and a "gatekeeper," who were both aware of her identity, introduced her to members of the organization as a student working as part of a job placement. Sharpe then rotated between different teams to gain a broader understanding of different team contexts within the organization as a whole. She also conducted interviews with senior managers, supervisors, and team leaders. The findings of the study reported that HRM strategies, use of technology, and other organizational themes shaped subsequent teamwork. For example a team operating in a non-unionized greenfield site appeared to be more homogeneous where workers developed a network of social relationships and interactions outside the work context. Thus, observational methods enabled Sharpe to explore the cultural knowledge of shop floor workers and the interaction that occurred between workers by observing and taking part in those activities. She was also able to observe and experience how participants reacted to attempts to control their behavior and the emerging behavioral outcomes.

A second tradition of ethnography is critical ethnography. Whereas conventional ethnographers display meanings by interpreting them (Thomas, 1993), critical ethnography is a style of ethnography that exhibits a political purpose. It involves a reflective process of selecting from conceptual alternatives and undertaking value-laden judgments of meaning and method to challenge research, policy, and other human activities. Critical ethnographers address an audience on behalf of their subjects as a means of empowering those subjects (Thomas, 1993, p. 4) and attempting to use knowledge for social change. The core of this approach is the study of the processes of domestication and social entrapment by which people come to accept and take for granted their life conditions. Thus, critical ethnography commences from the standpoint that domestication leads to uncritical acceptance of ideological predilections and bases of social life.

Grounded Theory

Grounded theory is an important analytical methodology developed in participant observation undertaken in the interpretive tradition (Glaser & Strauss, 1967). Grounded theory is often based on the analysis of meanings produced in real-life contexts and recorded in field notes and documents collected during participant observation research (Gephart, 2003). It is now widely employed in all three paradigms (above) and with all of the data collection methods discussed in this chapter. We discuss grounded theory at this point because of its origins in observational methods.

Grounded theory calls for the "discovery of theory from data" using inductive procedures (Glaser & Strauss, 1967). Yet, it was also developed to provide a way of grounding grand theories and connecting them to specific contexts and issues (Glaser & Strauss, 1967). It emerged as a critique of a priori or ungrounded theory that is created in abstract spaces and typically imposed on data. It is discovery-oriented and inductive, in contrast to the testing and deductively oriented nature of positivist research and seeks to link abstract theories and concepts to actual patterns of behavior and meaning observed in actual settings. This is achieved by developing or surfacing theory based on observations and past research (Glaser & Strauss, 1967; Gephart, 2003).

Grounded theorizing involves four stages: comparing incidents applicable to each category, integrating the categories and properties, delimiting the theory, and writing the theory (Glaser & Strauss, 1967, p. 105). These stages rely on two important features of grounded theorizing: theoretical sampling and the constant comparative analysis of data (Glaser & Strauss, 1967; Strauss & Corbin, 1990, 1994; Charmaz, 2000; Locke, 2001). *Theoretical sampling* "is the process of data collection for generating theory whereby the analyst jointly collects, codes and analyzes his [or her] data and decides what data to collect next" (Glaser & Strauss, 1967, p. 45). Data collection is thereby "controlled by the emerging theory" (Glaser & Strauss, 1967, p. 45). Initially, one has a general theoretical perspective and a general subject or problem area and perhaps some initial concepts. As data emerge, additional slices of data and groups of people are selected based on theoretical purposes and relevance for developing emergent categories (Glaser & Strauss, 1967, p. 48). Groups or slices of data are selected that have important similarities and differences with key categories being investigated. Selection ceases when theoretical saturation occurs; that is, at the point where no new data are emerging to develop properties of a conceptual category, such as the category of "social loss" of dying patients that Glaser and Strauss (1967) discuss. The *constant comparative method of analysis* generates theory more systematically by using explicit coding and analytical procedures to examine and highlight distinctive conceptual features of observations (Glaser & Strauss, 1967, p. 102). It is intended to generate and plausibly suggest many categories, properties, and hypotheses. This contrasts with analytic induction that is concerned to generate and prove "an integrated, limited, precise and universally applicable theory" (Glaser & Strauss, 1967, p. 104).

Handsen and Khanweiler's (1997) study of the beliefs and perspectives of a group of top business executives illustrates aspects of theoretical sampling. The study specifically aimed to explore the consistency of belief systems within specific groups and across industry fields. Maintaining consistency with their theoretical approach, the researchers selected their sample in order to study the nature and consistency of participants' beliefs systems across industry lines. Thus, organizations and individuals were targeted to explore themes relating to size, technology, market position, reputation, and variation in context as theoretical categories. The final sample of organizations included Delta Airlines, Coca-Cola Inc., Marriott Corporation, Equifax, and Xerox. The sample of individuals included chief executive officers and managers within two reporting levels of the CEO to allow the researchers to examine themes relating to individual status. Reflecting their interest in functional area they also included participants from general management, marketing, finance, sales, human resources, and journalism.

Peltonen's (1998) study of Finnish engineers and managers illustrates the use of constant comparative analysis. Participants' accounts were analysed and compared with one another to explore the patterns or structures used to explicate their respective careers. Analysis suggested that three structures were used to discuss careers: a bureaucratic discourse, an occupational discourse, and an enterprise discourse. Peltonen (1998) then argues for a more discursive understanding of expatriation as embedded in stories told about the expatriate career cycle.

INTERVIEWS AND FOCUS GROUPS

Interviews are perhaps the most widely used data collection strategy in management and the social sciences—they have been used in over 90% of social science research studies (Briggs, 1986, cited in Holstein & Gubrium, 1995). Thus, they are explored in some detail here. Focus groups will also be addressed here because they are group interviews. Commencing with a definition, interviews are situated, face-to-face interactions wherein a researcher poses questions to a subject who replies to the questions (Rynes & Gephart, 2004). The responses may then be recorded verbatim or summarized. At a more general level, interviews are often distinguished on the basis of formality and structure. Structured interviews draw on a preestablished interview schedule or statement of questions and are commonly used in positivist research. Unstructured interviews have much less structure, although general topics or issues to be addressed may be formulated in advance in the form of an agenda. Unstructured interviews are common in interpretive and critical postmodern research. Methodologists (Holstein & Gubrium, 1995) have also distinguished between the conventional approach to interviews, and "active" interviews that include the life story interview, ethnographic interviews, and the long interview. We discuss the conventional approach and then address active forms of interviewing.

Conventional Interviews

Conventional interviews—or more properly the conventional view of interviews—use a positivist ontology to search for "true facts" and the subjective feelings that subjects have for those facts (Holstein & Gubrium, 1995). The subject is conceived as a vessel-of-answers, that is, a reporter of truths they have witnessed. The interviewer is conceived as a disinterested catalyst (Holstein & Gubrium, 1995, p. 38) who triggers subjects' responses.

From this view, the interview is a conversation that is neutral and concern is directed to detecting sources of bias, where subjects must be selected according to how much they know about the research topic. Thus, a sample is developed by identifying a target population then locating the most knowledgeable members of the population. The focus of conventional interviews is the meaning that is produced concerning the research topic. Data collected are the contents of the interview responses, that is, what was said. Analysis involves systematically grouping or summarizing answers provided during interviews. It also seeks to provide a coherent organizing framework that explains aspects of the world respondents portray (Holstein & Gubrium, 1995, p. 79). Truth is based on the correspondence between what lies in the subject qua vessel and objective answers. To that extent, the conventional interview is concerned with reliability, or, whether the subject provides the same answers to the same questions administered over time. Validity, defined as providing the right or correct answers, is also a concern. The conventional interview is especially useful for generating straightforward behavioral and demographic information, especially information about well-defined and familiar categories (Holstein & Gubrium, 1995, p. 73). For example, Cassell et al. (2002) used a conventional interview approach involving telephone interviews and in depth, face-to-face interviews to investigate HRM practices used by small and medium-sized enterprises, the specific characteristics of those practices, and their subsequent effectiveness. This interview methodology thus provided a means to assess the factual aspects of HRM practices in small to medium-sized organizations. The results of the study reflected considerable variability in practices used.

Khatri and Budhwar's (2002) study of strategic HR issues in Singapore provides a further example of conventional interviews. Semi-structured interviews were conducted with CEOs, senior or line managers, and HR managers in nine companies in electronics and machinery and equipment industries. Participants were given an "interview questionnaire" illustrating the questions to be asked. The interviews posed questions about the history of the respective organizations, decision-making events, and interviewees' personal history in the organization. A key finding of the study was that a combination of senior management "enlightenment" (Khatri & Budhwar, 2002, p. 166) and level of HR competency determined the organizational status and role of the HR function.

Further, four types of HR strategy were identified: informal and not communicated, informal and communicated, formal but not communicated, and formal and communicated.

Active Interviews

The "active" approach to interviews (Holstein & Gubrium, 1995) is common in interpretive and critical postmodern research using active interviewing, ethnographic interviews, and/or the long interview to understand informants' conceptions of culture (Spradley, 1979; McCracken, 1988). The active approach assumes the interview is an active rather than passive process. The interviewer and subject—termed "informant"—co-construct and negotiate interview responses (Holstein & Gubrium, 1995). Thus, the active interview captures the discursive, interactional, meaning-making process (Holstein & Gubrium, 1995, p. 78). The focus of interviews in this conception of research is the production of meaning and the practices that produce meaning, as well as the meaning produced. That is, the focus is on how and what the subject and interviewer produce and convey given the interpretive circumstances at hand. Subjects are conceived, therefore, as active producers and narrators of experiential knowledge who are selected based on the researcher's decision about whose voices will be heard and whose voices will be silenced if people are perceived by the researcher in particular ways (Holstein & Gubrium, 1995, p. 27). Thus, theoretical sampling (Glaser & Strauss, 1967) is used to select subjects. Data are analysed to show reality construction practices and the subjective meanings conveyed (Holstein & Gubrium, 1995, p. 79). The goal is to show the coproduction of meaning in the interview and how what is said relates to the experiences and lives being studied.

For example, Richardson and McKenna (2000) employed active interviewing to explore how British faculty interpreted their experience of expatriation. This approach allowed interviewees to explicate their interpretation in their own voice, supported by interaction with the interviewer. Thus, the interview was the locus of interaction and dialogue which facilitated the desired insight into the meanings attached to the expatriate experience more broadly defined.

In this form of interview, reliability of knowledge is not expected because of differences in circumstances of production—no two settings are the same. Validity is not located in correspondence between claims and objective evidence, but derives from respondents' ability to convey situated realities. The active approach to interviewing is especially appropriate when the researcher is interested in subjective interpretations or processes of interpretation.

The Life Story Interview

The life story interview is a method for gathering information on the subjective essence of a person's life (Atkinson, 1998, p. 3). It in an active form of interviewing that seeks to produce a narrative of one person's experience of life, highlighting important aspects. The goal is for the interviewer to elicit a life story that is told as completely and honestly as possible, given constraints of what is remembered and what the teller wants others to know (Atkinson, 1998, p. 8). Thus, "the ability to be humane, empathic, sensitive, and understanding" (Atkinson, 1998, p. 28) takes on more importance than in other types of interviews. The storyteller's interests, rights, and privacy also need to be considered and safeguarded above all else (Atkinson, 1998, p. 37).

The life story interview uses primarily open-ended questions. Thus, in the context of IHRM research, a number of work life and related life issues could be addressed (Atkinson, 1998, pp. 43–53), including cultural settings and traditions related to work, views of work, historical events, retirement, major life or work life themes, and important work experiences. It is, therefore, a unique personal encounter between the researcher and storyteller. Traditional research criteria, including reliability and validity are not the most appropriate evaluative standards (Atkinson, 1998, p. 59) because interpretation of life story data is highly subjective. More appropriate criteria are internal consistency, that is, the consistency or lack of contradictions in the interview; corroboration of the life story by the storyteller at the time she or he reads the transcribed and/or analysed story; and the persuasiveness of the story in terms of its reasonableness and ability to convince others. Further, the life story interview aims to gain insights into the important personal experiences and lives of a small number of individuals who are considered to be important or interesting to the researcher (Atkinson, 1998). Thus, the life story interview is more appropriate for gaining insights into a wide range of personal experiences than for testing, elaborating, or assessing theory.

The Ethnographic Interview

The ethnographic interview is a second active approach to interviewing. Its main aim is to gain insights into the dimensions of a given culture and how members experience them. The subject is considered an informant, that is, a native speaker engaged by the researcher to communicate in their own language (Spradley, 1979, p. 25). Informants provide a model for the ethnographer to imitate and are, therefore, a source of information and teaching. Thus, ethnographers and informants collaborate to produce a cultural description in the interview (Spradley, 1979).

Ethnographic interviews differ from conventional interviews (Spradley, 1979, p. 30) because they explore what informants know about a culture that the researcher can learn, in contrast to conventional interviews, which are based on what the researcher knows about a problem that the subject can verify or explain. More explicitly, the ethnographic interview is concerned to uncover concepts that the informant uses to classify experience. It investigates how informants define concepts and seeks to uncover folk theories informants use to explain their experiences. Finally, the ethnographic interviewer is concerned to translate informants' cultural knowledge into cultural descriptions that colleagues will understand. Conventional interviews interpret and report data in the language of colleagues.

Spradley (1979) outlines a developmental research sequence that describes the process of doing ethnography and ethnographic analysis. Steps 1 to 3 are to identify and interview the informant, then to create an ethnographic record or field notes of the interview. In step 4, one does the initial interviews using descriptive questions that ask the informant to describe or construe settings of interest to the researcher (Spradley, 1979, pp. 85–86). For example, grand tour questions request an overview of a domain such as "Could you describe the place you work?" Step 5 is to review field notes to search for cultural symbols or entities and relationships between them (Spradley, 1979, p. 94). In step 6 one does a domain analysis that involves a search for larger units of cultural knowledge, for example, on-the-job training is one potential cultural domain. In step 7 one asks structural questions about features of a given domain. Step 8 involves a taxonomic analysis that examines the domain's internal structure and, where appropriate, contrasts its elements. Step 9 involves asking contrast questions about how one feature differs from others. Step 10 enacts a componential analysis by systematically searching for attributes or components of meaning associated with cultural symbols, for example, exploring differences between on-the-job and formal training. Step 11 involves discovery of cultural themes. A theme is defined as a postulate or position that often controls behavior or components of meaning associated with cultural symbols (Spradley, 1979, p. 185). Theme analysis involves a search for the relationships among domains and how they are linked to culture as a whole, for example, an analysis of job training that locates on-the-job and formal training in relation to other types of training and other aspects of work life. Step 12 is writing the ethnography, which includes six levels of statements in order of descending generality, from universal statements to specific incident statements (Spradley, 1979, pp. 208–211).

The ethnographic interview is appropriate where the researcher seeks insights into cultural issues in order to understand what informants or cultural members know about phenomena—members' concepts and folk theories, especially where there is need to understand culture and to explain it to cultural outsiders.

The Long Interview

The long interview is an extended form of the structured interview that employs demographic, factual questions and open-ended questions. It uses a structured questionnaire, administered in a face-to-face setting, that produces a "focused, rapid and highly intensive interview process" (McCracken, 1988, p. 7) designed as an efficient and streamlined inquiry process to "take us into the mental world of the individual" (McCracken, 1988, p. 9). Thus, it seeks to accomplish certain objectives of field research without requiring prolonged involvement and is concerned with cultural categories and shared meanings rather than affective states.

There are four general steps to the long interview (McCracken, 1988). Because the interviewer uses a questionnaire, these steps are generally relevant to design and analysis of qualitative questionnaires, although we do not discuss questionnaires further in this chapter. First, in order to design the interview or questionnaire, a review of analytical categories found in the respective literature is conducted. Second, the researcher reviews the features or categories of the culture to be studied, so they can also be addressed in the interview and questionnaire design. This involves familiarizing oneself with the culture by identifying cultural categories and relationships not identified in the literature. It also provides a basis for defamiliarization or distancing the researcher from the setting because it sensitizes him or her to what is known about the culture and allows insights into what is not known. The third step is the discovery of cultural categories in data by constructing the interview questionnaire and undertaking the interview. The interview opens with biographical questions and continues with open-ended questions that relate to phenomena of interest. To allow the respondents to tell their own stories, the investigator plays an unobtrusive role where questions are posed in a nondirective manner. Questions should not supply the terms or bases for answers. Rather, they should prompt respondents to elaborate important responses where they emerge. The fourth step is analysis and discovery of analytic categories. The goal of analysis is to determine the "categories, relationships and assumptions" (McCracken, 1988, p. 42) that inform the respondent's view of the world in general and the specific topic of interest. There are five steps to the analysis process. Each utterance in the interview (or questionnaire response) is examined on its own terms. Next, observations are developed based on individual data segments or utterances, then in relation to the full transcript, and finally in relation to past literature and the cultural review. Then, one investigates connections among the second level observations, relating them to the literature and cultural reviews. Finally, analysis determines inter-theme consistency and contradictions by scrutinizing observations from the first three steps. Patterns and themes from all interviews are then subjected to a final process of analysis.

The long interview is a useful way to gain insights into workplace cultures and cultural issues in the workplace, hence it is of particular use in the field of IHRM. It is especially appropriate where the researcher needs to accomplish cultural descriptions but lacks the time, resources, or access to participate deeply and extensively in groups that are of interest. Second, the long interview is useful where the investigator has some prior understanding of the culture or group being studied but where this familiarity needs to be overcome so that critical reflections are possible (McCracken, 1988, p. 65). Third, the long interview is useful where research requires rich and abundant but manageable data. Fourth, the long interview is appropriate where research seeks to provide important insights from a limited number of informants rather than a large sample. Finally, the long interview is useful as a way of exploring key issues or themes in some detail. A study of the belief systems of top executive managers (Handsen & Khanweiler, 1997) illustrates some of the main themes in long interviews. Informants in this study were asked to relate stories from their experience in their respective organizations using imagery. This imagery was conceived as "symbolic, rule-governed, and visually represents cultural requirements for meaning and order" (Handsen & Khanweiler, 1997). To that extent, the objective of accessing the mental world of the individual (McCracken, 1988, p. 9) was further supported. Triangulation was also implemented by examining the psychological features in the stories told, sorting and analyzing emerging themes and then testing whether they were related to demographic variables. The findings of the study suggested that top executive culture is action-oriented, valuing risk taking, financial knowledge, flexibility, and team orientation. Themes relating to trust, control, and change also emerged as important.

Focus Groups

A focus group is a technique for collecting data on a topic determined in advance by a researcher who assumes the role of moderator in a specified group discussion (Morgan, 1997, p. 2). The researcher provides the focus, the group provides data. Thus, the researcher relies on interactions between group members, based on topics supplied by the researcher, to provide information on phenomena of interest. A study exploring macro-level influences on the work–family interface in China, Hong Kong, Mexico, Singapore, and the United States (Joplin, Shaffer, Francesco, & Lau, 2003) illustrates the use of focus groups. In this study specific a priori questions were constructed along with specific lines of questioning to allow the research objectives to be achieved across all countries. The study also used public data to supplement the focus group data. One key finding was that in societies where macro-environmental changes run counter to cultural values, individuals experience more stress with respect to conflict in relationships between work and family relationships. However, the researchers note this finding should be taken in the context of culture as a dynamic process.

Focus groups have been used in at least three different ways (Morgan, 1997). First, they can be used as a self-contained method and the principal source of data where research goals are consistent with the data that focus groups can provide (Morgan, 1997, p. 3). Second, they can be used to supplement other research methods and are often used as a preliminary source of data collection in quantitative research seeking to generate survey questions. They are especially useful for identifying characteristics of domains that need to be measured, and providing item wordings for survey questions (Morgan, 1997, p. 25). For example, Connell and coworkers (Connell, Ferres, & Travaglione, 2003) drew on data collected from focus groups and a survey questionnaire to develop an in-depth understanding of trust in manager–subordinate relationships in a large Australian organization. This study was undertaken because an annual staff survey for the organization had suggested that trust in managers was very low. The study showed that focus groups can be used subsequent to quantitative research to develop a deeper understanding of the quantitative results. Third, focus groups can be used in multi-method research to generate data that complements other techniques such as participant observation or interviews.

Korabik and Lero's research illustrates the use of focus groups in multi-method IHRM research (Korabik & Lero, 2003). The researchers undertook an international study of the work–family interface in ten different countries. Data collected from focus groups in each of the countries were supplemented by a social policy analysis and a quantitative survey to provide data that were both qualitative and quantitative, both emic and etic, and both micro- and macro-level in nature (Korabik & Lero, 2003, p. 289). Focus groups helped to identify key themes relating to the work–family interface in each of the respective countries. Data collected from the focus groups suggested new variables, such as coping strategies, which had not been identified previously. The data were especially useful in identifying culturally specific themes, such as the role of extended family in the work–family interface. The second component of the study was policy analysis, which developed a macro-analysis of the work–family interface in terms of its connections to society more generally, for example, policies and programs that affect gender roles and family income, etc. The quantitative survey was the third component of the study. Focus group data were used to inform the survey and the survey was administered to a large population—200 males and 200 females in dual career couples. The survey stage allowed a meso- and micro-level understanding of the research topic.

Morgan (1997, p. 34) suggests several rules of thumb for conducting focus groups: they should be homogeneous in composition, they should use a structured format, they should include 6 to 10 participants, and one should use 3 to 5 groups per project. Although these rules present a useful guide, the extent to which they can be applied depends very much on the research context. For example, Korabik and Lero's (2003) research used groups comprised of five women. They introduced an element of diversity by including women with work and family demands. They also used two focus groups in each of the ten countries.

There are a number of advantages to using focus groups (Morgan, 1997, pp. 8–12). First, one can observe a large amount of interaction on a topic in a limited time. Second, the researcher has control over the discussion. Third, access to groups is often more readily acquired than with other methods such as direct observation. Fourth, focus groups can produce data on phenomena that are hard to observe directly, such as attitudes and decision making. Fifth, they provide direct evidence about similarities and differences in participants' opinions and experiences. Sixth, they support unstructured discussions and allow groups to take control of the discussion. Finally, focus groups can generate richer and more voluminous data on topics about which individuals may have little to say.

Like all methodologies, focus groups present potential challenges and limitations. First, it is often difficult to find strangers among homogeneous groups and strangers may not communicate well with one another. Also, in focus groups the concern is to minimize sampling bias rather than enhancing generalization (Morgan, 1997, p. 35) so participants need to be selected with care. In addition, the structure of the group will necessarily vary in terms of question specificity and the role of the moderator. Unstructured groups are useful where one wishes to learn something from the group (Morgan, 1997, p. 39) whereas structured groups are useful where there is a clear, preexisting agenda for research (Morgan, 1997, p. 40). A further limitation is that focus groups are unnatural settings where data may be restricted to verbal data and self-report data and there are a limited variety of interactions. Thus, they are not appropriate where one seeks to directly observe naturally occurring behavior or behavior that is not likely to occur in the focus group, or where there are many barriers to interaction on a topic. There is also less control over, and information generated about, each individual in the group. In some instances focus groups require tradeoffs between free-flowing discussions and researcher controls that keep groups on topic. Further, the group context may influence what is said and groups tend to conform to one another, thus limiting variation, or to become polarized. On the other hand individual and group interviews may produce differing results because the contexts differ. Additionally, because the group is driven by the researcher's interests, there is uncertainty about the accuracy of data provided.

ANALYZING DOCUMENTS AND ARTEFACTS

Analysis of documents and artefacts is the final general method discussed in this chapter. Documents and artefacts are physically enduring forms of data that provide mute evidence (Hodder, 1994, p. 393) about IHRM phenomena. They are mute because they have no inherent meaning: their meaning emerges from writing and reading the documents and from discussing and thinking about artefacts. Further, documents and artefacts can be separated from their authors, producers, or users by time and space, which prevents interaction with those who might otherwise provide an insiders' perspective. They thus commonly need to be interpreted by researchers without the benefit of indigenous commentary. In addition, social actors may not be able to provide reasons or interpretations for related physical materials such as modes of dress.

The characteristics of documents and artefacts lead to special problems for qualitative research (Hodder, 1994). First, records must be distinguished from documents (Hodder, 1994). Records such as a marriage certificate attest to a formal or official transaction and reflect the power of the state and its technologies. They may have local uses that differ from official uses and access to certain records may be restricted by laws related to privacy, confidentiality, and anonymity. Documents are texts prepared for personal reasons and may be more easily accessible but may require more contextual interpretation.

Procedures for interpreting documents and artefacts do not differ greatly from the procedures used to interpret materials collected in case studies, observational studies, and interviews (Hodder, 1994, p. 400). The special problem is to situate materials within contexts and to explore how contexts influence interpretation. In general, analysis involves three hermeneutical procedures.

First, the researcher needs to identify the contexts within which materials have similar meanings. Second, similarities and differences must be recognized. Third, the researcher needs to evaluate or confirm the relevance of theories to the documents or artefacts. Confirmation is often based on coherence—whether or not parts of an explanation are contradictory and whether conclusions follow from given premises. Correspondence could be assessed statistically or by the number of cases accounted for by theory. Two other criteria for determining confirmation are the fruitfulness of theory or data to open new lines of inquiry and the reproducibility of results—whether or not people with different views come to the same results (Hodder, 1994, p. 401).

There are several advantages to analysis of documents and artefacts. First, access can be relatively easy and costs may be low. Second, information in specific documents and records may differ—or not be available—from other sources. Third, materials such as texts endure over time and provide historical insight into phenomena. The major limitation of analysis of documents, records, and artefacts is that meaning does not reside in the materials themselves but is produced by reading, discussing, and using the materials (Hodder, 1994, p. 394), hence the analyst needs to understand the materials in the contexts in which they originated.

Documents, records, and artefacts are often used in positivist research as a means to produce quantitative data from textual or qualitative materials and to test hypotheses. Records are often treated as objective evidence of official transactions whereas documents and artefacts are treated as objective traces of subjective and objective processes. Positivistic uses of these materials aim to uncover the facts disclosed in the documents and compare them to the facts anticipated by theories, concepts, and hypotheses, usually through coding and counting. Computer-aided textual analysis may produce qualitative and numerical results from textual data (Kelle, 1995), which can help advance positivistic qualitative research that is concerned to code textual data and to quantify key features of texts. A study of the implementation of personal medical services (PMS) in the United Kingdom illustrates a positivist approach to documentary analysis (Allgar, Leese, Heywood, & Walker, 2001). This study examined contracts and interim local evaluation reports of pilots for PMS, which were set up to encourage using salaried doctors and practice-based contracts. Each of the pilots provided their contracts and first year local evaluation reports for examination by the researchers. The researchers then developed a content analysis framework to "enable systematic and objective identification of specified characteristics within the documents" (2001, p. 300). Moreover, a specific set of rules and criteria were utilized to develop categories for quantitative comparison between pilots. These categories related to themes such as evaluation, monitoring, objectives, and specification of services to be provided.

Interpretive research using documents, records, and artefacts seeks to understand what these materials mean to social actors, how they were created and given meaning, and the implications these meanings hold for workplace interactions. Interpretive research can be advanced by employing textual analysis strategies that use ideas from hermeneutics and literary criticism (Hararri, 1979; Culler, 1981) to understand important features of documents, records, and texts. Narrative analysis (Boje, 2001; Riessman, 1993) that examines the structural and literary features of stories and texts is also a useful approach to interpreting texts and artefacts. In this view, narrative analysis involves analysts' interpretations of how protagonists in stories and other communication genres interpret phenomena (Riessman, 1993, p. 5). Narratives inform us about past actions and also provide insights into how individuals understand those actions (Riessman, 1993, p. 19). A U.K. study of internal newspapers in four major banks illustrates an interpretive approach to documentary analysis (Hughes, 2000). Discourse analysis was employed because the study aimed to understand how change within the banks was represented by senior managers in their communications about change. The researcher drew on Potter and Wetherell's (1987) recommendation to focus on the variation between communications and how the communications were constructed in terms of language, syntax, and other linguistic features. Analysis suggested a rhetoric characterized by four main themes: the challenge of change, that change is constant, the need for coherence, and that change should be understand in relation to both the external and internal context.

Semiotics can also be used to interpret material culture (Manning, 1988; Gottdeiner, 1995). This is a mode of knowledge for understanding the world as a system of relations whose basic unit is the sign (Gottdeiner, 1995, p. 4). It studies the nature of representation where the sign is conceived as detached from what it signifies and assumes that meaning is created through the double character of signs. Signs have both denotative or explicit meanings and connotative or implicit meanings (Feldman, 1995, p. 4). Thus meaning emerges diachronically from the unfolding chain of words where each word conveys meanings in terms of its location (Gottdeiner, 1995, p. 6). And meaning emerges paradigmatically because each word implies absent but associated words (Gottdeiner, 1995, p. 6). It uncovers meanings that are based in each axis and also explores how meaning is created by differences in these aspects of signs.

Critical postmodern research has begun to utilize rhetorical analysis of texts (Simons, 1989), including deconstructionist techniques, to understand how texts persuade readers about the truthfulness of their claims (Booth, 1983; McCloskey, 1985; Gephart, 1988). Rhetorical analysis shows that overt, ideological features are present in texts and that texts are powerful effects that incorporate institutional logical and ideologies (Brown, 2000). Deconstructionism looks for multiple meanings implicit in a text, conversation, or event (Riessman, 1993, p. 5). It locates the dominant ideology in a text or conversation and uncovers alternative frames to interpret it. It examines taken-for-granted categories such as dichotomies and also the silences or gaps in texts and conversation that support dominant ideologies. Thus, it uses disruptions to reveal other possible meanings and to show that the dominant ideology is unstable. A study of media texts on cross-border acquisitions exemplifies the use of rhetorical analysis as a research methodology (Tienari, Vaara, & Bjorkman, 2003). It analyzed articles published in leading newspapers in Norway, Sweden, and Finland. Specific attention was given to rationalistic and nationalistic discourses and how they were employed in portraying a given acquisition. For example, in Norway nationalistic discourse was used to draw attention to the potential risks of increasing foreign ownership of local business. In contrast, acquisition of a Norwegian bank was presented as a "battle between Norwegians and Swedes" (Tienari et al., 2003, p. 384).

The analysis of documents using textual analysis strategies including narrative analysis, rhetorical analysis, and deconstruction can be illustrated through research on worker safety in the oil and gas industry in Canada (Gephart, 1992, 1993, 1997). This research sought to understand the role of sense making in oil and gas accidents. It used transcripts and observations of regulatory agency hearings into accidents as a means for collecting data. To understand the accidents and the sense making that occurred during subsequent hearings, the researcher extracted and analyzed key narratives from the hearing transcripts to understand the claims and counter claims of hearing participants. The analysis showed that key personnel told different stories during testimony and narrated their experiences of the events in question differently. Further, the stories told by one group about the causes of an accident were often countered or undermined by stories told by another group. Detailed textual analysis of inquiry documents revealed that the government regulatory agency controlled testimony both explicitly and implicitly in ways that distorted the evident logic used by workers both on site during leaks and in the hearing context. In essence, the research used documentary materials to show how regulatory agency communication transformed the logic reflected in stories told by workers into a top-down logic that was acceptable to and consistent with the logic used by regulatory agencies. This transformation or distortion of communication was used by the regulatory agency to privilege its logics and its views and to show that workers and the foreman on site during an accident were responsible for the accident, which killed two people including the foreman and seriously burned three other workers.

DISCUSSION

Researchers undertaking a research project need to address a number of methodological issues and concerns. This chapter has emphasized the importance of creating consistency between the paradigmatic and theoretical assumptions underlying research, including assumptions about reality,

TABLE 3.2
Features of Methods

Method and Key Source	Advantages	Limits
Case study (Hartley, 1994)	Provides thick descriptions of events unfolding over time Useful for theory building Useful in exploratory research	Can be costly and time consuming
Participant observation (McCall & Simmons, 1969)	Allows detailed observations of actual activities and settings Allows researcher participation and experiences of settings Allows flexible pursuit of data and topics	Time consuming Problems in gaining access Development of comprehensive analysis can be difficult
Traditional interviews (Holstein & Gubrium, 1995)	Produce straightforward (factual) information on observable and reportable themes Allow exploration of well-developed concepts or hypotheses Useful in confirmatory research and theory testing	Not well suited to exploratory research or development of new concepts Require formal planning of questions, preselection of subjects, and scheduling of interviews
Active interviews (Holstein & Gubrium, 1995)	Capture interactive and constructive nature of interviews Allow examination of meaning-making processes	Not oriented to collection of "factual" information nor to conventional reliability and validity concerns
Ethnographic interviews (Spradley, 1979)	Allow flexible and informal interview formats Allow detailed exploration of individuals' conceptions of culture Support cross-cultural research	Need to develop relationships with informants and gain access to setting Not highly conducive to production of standardized, comparative information
Long interviews (McCracken, 1988)	Allow rapid and efficient access to cultural themes and issues Produce abundant and rich data	Require development of detailed and standardized questions Conducting interviews may be demanding
Focus groups (Morgan, 1997)	Can be used as self-contained method or in conjunction with other methods Allow observation of participants' interactions about a topic Can produce useful data on hard-to-observe phenomena, e.g., attitudes, opinions, and perspectives	Topic must be determined in advance May be difficult to recruit appropriate participants Require researcher or assistant to moderate discussion Do not capture naturally occurring behavior
Document and artifact analysis (Hodder, 1994)	Many documents are readily accessible and low in cost Documents endure over time and provide historical insights	Difficult to access confidential documents Documents must often be interpreted without knowledge of meanings of creators

the relationship of data to reality, and the methods used to implement the research. Positivistic research assumes data reflect or mirror the world directly, the data are factual, and methods can be used to assess facts and test hypotheses or theories. Interpretive research assumes data represent the world but that data are produced and mediated by interpretive practices. Data that provide "thick descriptions" (Geertz, 1973) of events and meanings are needed, and interpretive research seeks often to engage in exploration, discovery, and theory building given the open and emergent nature of reality. Critical postmodern research assumes reality is often hidden by political interests. Data that display ideologically interpreted realities are sought and methods are used to uncover deeper levels of reality.

The development of theoretical and methodological consistency is the outcome of how methods are used more than which methods are used, because most of the methods can be used in different paradigms or theories. Table 3.2 indicates key advantages and disadvantages of the major methods discussed in this chapter. For purposes of simplicity, ethnography is represented under ethnographic interviewing and grounded theory is omitted because it can be employed with any of the methods noted above. This table is intended to assist readers in selecting methods and addressing the important issues that emerge in the process of undertaking qualitative research. It should also help the reader to create consistency between the scholarly worldview they take and the methods they adopt.

CONCLUSION

Qualitative research methods are useful and important for IHRM research. This chapter suggests that the primary qualitative methods have all been used in IHRM and HRM research but that their uses are often limited. Fully developed applications of key methodologies are not common. Further, most of the uses of methods employ positivistic assumptions and often transform the methods or use them in ways that reflect positivist and not interpretive or critical postmodern assumptions, even when this research is explicitly claimed to use an interpretive or critical postmodern perspective. Thus, IHRM research can be advanced by more effective implementation and use of qualitative research methods. And it can also be advanced by more extensive uses of interpretive and critical postmodern perspectives.

ACKNOWLEDGMENTS

We wish to thank Eleanor Cohen for assistance in preparing this manuscript. Thanks also to Michael Harris for helpful suggestions for improving this chapter.

REFERENCES

Allgar, V., Leese, B., Heywood, P., & Walker, R. (2001). First wave PMS pilots: A critical analysis of documentation. Journal of Management in Medicine, 15, 299–312.

Atkinson, R. (1998). *The life story interview*. Thousand Oaks, CA: Sage.

Baker, T. (1988). *Doing social research*. New York: McGraw-Hill.

Barker, J. R. (1993). Tightening the iron cage: Concertive control in self-managing teams. *Administrative Science Quarterly, 38*, 408–437.

Beech, N., & Brockbank, A. (1999). Power/knowledge and psychosocial dynamics in mentoring. *Management Learning, 30(1)*, 7–27.

Berger, P., & Luckmann, T. L. (1966). *The social construction of reality: A treatise in the sociology of knowledge*. New York: Anchor Books.

Boje, D. (2001). *Narrative methods for organizational and communication research*. Thousand Oaks, CA: Sage.

Booth, W. (1983). *The rhetoric of fiction*. Chicago: University of Chicago Press.

Brown, A. D. (2000). Making sense of inquiry sensemaking. *Journal of Management Studies, 37*, 45–76.

Cassell, C., Nadin, S., Gray, M., & Clegg, C. (2002). Exploring human resource management practices in small and medium sized enterprises. *Personnel Review, 31(5/6)*, 671–695.

Charmaz, K. (2000). Grounded theory: Objectivist and constructivist methods. In N. K. Denzin & Y. S. Lincoln (Eds.), *Handbook of qualitative research* (2nd ed., pp. 509–535). Thousand Oaks, CA: Sage.

Connell, J., Ferres, N., & Travaglione, T. (2003). Engendering trust in manager-subordinate relationships: Predictors and outcomes. *Personnel Review, 32*, 569–590.

Culler, J. (1981). *The pursuit of signs: Semiotics, literature and deconstruction.* Ithaca, NY: Cornell University Press.

Dahler-Larsen, P. (1997). Organizational identity as a "crowded category": A case of multiple and quickly shifting "we" typifications. In S. A. Sackmann (Ed.), *Cultural complexity in organizations* (pp. 367–389). Thousand Oaks, CA: Sage.

Dalton, M. (1959). *Men who manage.* New York, Wiley.

Doorewaard, H., Van Hootegem, G., & Huys, R. (2002). Team responsibility structure and team performance. *Personnel Review, 31(3),* 356–372.

Fairclough, N. (1992). *Discourse and social change.* Cambridge, U.K.: Polity Press.

Feldman, M. (1995). *Strategies for interpreting qualitative data.* Thousand Oaks, CA: Sage.

Fisher, G. B., & Hartel, C. E. J. (2003). Cross-cultural effectiveness of Western expatriate-Thai client interactions: Lessons learned for IHRM research and theory. *Cross Cultural Management, 10,* 4–28.

Geertz, C. (1973). *The interpretation of cultures.* London: Fontana Press.

Gephart, R. P. (1988). *Ethnostatistics: Qualitative foundations for quantitative research.* Thousand Oaks, CA: Sage.

Gephart, R. P. (1992). Sensemaking, communicative distortion, and the logic of public inquiry legitimation. *Industrial Crisis Quarterly, 6,* 115–135.

Gephart, R. P. (1993). The textual approach: Risk and blame in disaster sensemaking. *Academy of Management Journal, 36,* 1465–1514.

Gephart, R. P. (1997). Hazardous measures: An interpretive textual analysis of quantitative sensemaking during crises. *Journal of Organizational Behavior, 18,* 583–622.

Gephart, R. P. (1999). *Paradigms and research methods.* (Research Methods Forum, 4). Retrieved from www.aom.pace.edu/rmd/1999_RMD_Forum_Paradigms_and_Research_Methods.htm

Gephart, R. P., Boje, D., & Thatchenkery, T. (1996). Postmodern management and the coming crises of organizational analysis. In D. Boje, R. Gephart, & T. Thatchenkery (Eds.), *Postmodern management and organizational theory* (pp. 1–18). Thousand Oaks, CA: Sage.

Gephart, R. P. (2003). Grounded theory and the integration or qualitative and quantitative research. *Multilevel Issues in Organizational Behavior and Strategy, 2,* 113–125.

Geppert, M., Williams, K., & Matten, D. (2003). The social construction of contextual rationalities in MNCs: An Anglo-German comparison of subsidiary choice. *Journal of Management Studies, 40,* 617–641.

Glaser, B., & Strauss, A. (1967). *The discovery of grounded theory.* Chicago: Aldine Press.

Graham, L. (1995). *On the line at Subaru-Isuzu: The Japanese model and the American worker.* Ithaca, NY: ILR Press.

Gottdeiner, M. (1995). *Postmodern semiotics.* Oxford, U.K.: Blackwell.

Guba, E. G., & Lincoln, Y. S. (1994). Competing paradigms in qualitative research. In N. K. Denzin & Y. S. Lincoln (Eds.), *Handbook of qualitative research* (2nd ed., pp. 105–117). Thousand Oaks, CA: Sage.

Gubrium, J. F., & Holstein, J. A. (1997). *The new language of qualitative method,* New York, Oxford University Press.

Habermas, J. (1973). *Legitimation crisis.* Boston: Beacon Press.

Habermas, J. (1979). *Communication and the evolution of society.* Boston: Beacon Press.

Hamel, J., Dufour, S., & Fortin, D. (1993). *Case study methods.* Thousand Oaks, CA: Sage.

Handsen, C. D., & Khanweiler, W. M. (1997). Executive managers: Cultural expectations through stories about work. *Journal of Applied Management Studies, 6,* 117–139.

Hararri, J. V. (1979). *Textual strategies: Perspectives in post-structuralist criticism.* Ithaca, NY: Cornell University Press.

Hartley, J. F. (1994). Case studies in organizational research. In C. Cassell & G. Symon (Eds.), *Qualitative methods in organizational research* (pp. 208–229). London: Sage.

Hodder, I. (1994). The interpretation of documents and material culture. In N. K. Denzin & Y. S. Lincoln (Eds.), *Handbook of qualitative research* (2nd ed., pp. 393–402). Thousand Oaks, CA: Sage.

Holstein, J. A., & Gubrium, J. F. (1995). *The active interview.* Thousand Oaks, CA: Sage.

Hughes, M. (2000). Potential, procedures and pitfalls of analysing internal newspapers. *Corporate Communications, 5,* 19–28.

Jameson, F. (1979). *Postmodernism, or, the cultural logic of advanced capitalism.* Durham, NC: Duke University Press.

Joplin, J. R. W., Shaffer, M. A., Francesco, A. M., & Lau, T. (2003). The macro-environment and work-family conflict. *International Journal of Cross Cultural Management, 3,* 305–328.

Kelle, U. (1995). Introduction: An overview of computer-aided methods in qualitative research. In U. Kelle (Ed.), *Computer-aided qualitative data analysis* (pp. 158–166). Newbury Park, CA: Sage.

Khatri, N., & Budhwar, P. S. (2002). A study of strategic HR issues in an Asian context. *Personnel Review, 31,* 166–189.

Korabik, K., & Lero, D. S. (2003). A multi-level approach to cross cultural work-family research. *International Journal of Cross Cultural Management, 3,* 289–303.

Lam, A. (2003). Organizational learning in multinationals: R & D networks of Japanese and U.S. MNEs in the U.K. *Journal of Management Studies, 40,* 673–703.

Le Blanc, R. (2003). Boards of directors: An inside view. Schulich School of Business. Toronto: York University.

Locke, K. (2001). *Grounded theory in management research.* Thousand Oaks, CA: Sage.

Lincoln, Y. S., & Guba, E. G. (2000). Paradigmatic controversies, contradictions and emerging confluences. In N. K. Denzin & Y. S. Lincoln (Eds.), *Handbook of qualitative research* (2nd ed., pp. 163–188). Thousand Oaks, CA: Sage.

Manning, P. (1988). *Semiotics and fieldwork.* Thousand Oaks, CA: Sage.

Marx, K. (1990). *Capital: A critique of political economy.* London: Penguin.

McCall, G. J., & Simmons, J. L. (1969). The nature of participant observation. In G. J. McCall & J. L. Simmons (Eds.), *Issues in participant observation: A text and reader* (pp. 1–5). Reading, MA: Addison-Wesley.

McCloskey, D. L. (1985). *The rhetoric of economics.* Madison: University of Wisconsin Press.

McCracken, G. (1988). *The long interview.* Thousand Oaks, CA: Sage.

Morgan, D. L. (1997). *Focus groups as qualitative research.* Thousand Oaks, CA: Sage.

Mueller, F., Harvey, C., & Howorth, C. (2003). The contestation of archetypes: Negotiating scripts in a U.K. hospital trust board. *Journal of Management Studies, 40,* 1971–1995.

Offe, C. (1984). *Contradictions of the welfare state.* Cambridge, MA: MIT Press.

Offe, C. (1985). *Disorganized capitalism: Contemporary transformations of work and politics.* Cambridge, U.K.: Polity Press.

Osland, J. S. (1995). *The adventure of working abroad.* San Francisco: Jossey-Bass.

Peltonen, T. (1998). Narrative construction of expatriate experience and career cycle: Discursive patterns in Finnish stories of international career. *International Journal of Human Resource Management 9,* 875–891.

Potter, J., & Wetherell, M. (1987). Discourse and social psychology: Beyond attitudes and behaviour. London: Sage.

Richardson, J., & McKenna, S. D. (2000). Metaphorical "types" and human resource management: Self-selecting expatriates. *Industrial and Commercial Training, 32 (6),* 209–218.

Riessman, C. K. (1993). *Narrative analysis.* Thousand Oaks, CA: Sage.

Roesthlisberger, F. J. and Dickson, W. J. (1939). *Management of the worker.* Cambridge, MA: Harvard University Press.

Rynes, S. & Gephart, R. P. (2004). "From the editors: Qualitative research and the *Academy of Management Journal,*" *Academy of Management Journal, 47,* 454–463.

Sackmann, S. A. (1997). *Cultural complexity in organizations: Inherent contrasts and contradictions.* Newbury Park, CA: Sage.

Sackmann, S. A., & Phillips, M. E. (2004). Contextual influences on culture research. *International Journal of Cross Cultural Management, 4,* 370–390.

Schwandt, T. (1994). Constructivist, interpretivist approaches to human inquiry. In N. K. Lincoln & Y. S. Lincoln (Eds.), *Handbook of qualitative research* (2nd ed., pp. 118–137). Thousand Oaks, CA: Sage.

Schwartzman, H. (1993). *Ethnography in organizations.* Thousand Oaks, CA: Sage.

Sharpe, D. R. (1997). Managerial control strategies and subcultural processes: On the shop floor in a Japanese manufacturing organization in the United Kingdom. In S. A. Sackmann (Ed.), *Cultural complexity in organizations* (pp. 228–249). Thousand Oaks, CA: Sage.

Sharpe, D. R. (2002). "Teamworking and managerial control within a Japanese manufacturing subsidiary in the UK." *Personnel Reveiw 31*(3): 267–283.

Simons, H. W. (1989). *Rhetoric in the human sciences.* Thousand Oaks, CA: Sage.

Singh, V., & Vinnicombe, S. (2000). What does "commitment" really mean?: Views of U.K. and Swedish engineering managers. *Personnel Review, 29(2),* 228–256.

Spradley, J. P. (1979). *The ethnographic interview.* New York: Holt, Rinehart and Winston.

Strauss, A., & Corbin, J. (1990). *Basics of qualitative research: Grounded theory procedures and techniques.* Newbury Park, CA: Sage.

Strauss, A., & Corbin, J. (1994). Grounded theory methodology: an overview. In N. K. Denzin & Y. S. Lincoln (Eds.), *Handbook of qualitative research* (1st ed., pp. 273–285). Thousand Oaks, CA: Sage.

Thomas, J. (1993). *Doing critical ethnography.* Thousand Oaks, CA: Sage.

Tienari, J., Vaara, E., & Bjorkman, I. (2003). Global capitalism meets national spirit: Discourses in media texts on a cross-border acquisition. *Journal of Management Inquiry, 12:* 377–393.

Van Maanen, J. (1979). Reclaiming qualitative methods for organizational research: A preface. *Administrative Science Quarterly, 24(4),* 520–526.

Van Maanen, J. (1981). Fieldwork on the beat: An informal introduction to organizational ethnography. Paper presented at the Workshop on Innovations in Methodology for Organizational Research, Center for Creative Leadership, Greensboro, NC, March, 1981.

Van Maanen, J. (1998). Different strokes: Qualitative research in the *Administrative Science Quarterly* from 1956 to 1996. In J. Van Maanen (Ed.), *Qualitative studies of organizations* (pp. ix–xxxii). Thousand Oaks, CA: Sage.

Weber, M. (1978). *Economy and society: An outline of interpretive sociology.* Edited by G. Roth & C. Wittich. Berkeley, CA: University of California Press.

Yin, R. K. (1981). The case study crisis: Some answers. *Administrative Science Quarterly, 26,* 58–65.

Zhao, Z., Anand, J., & Mitchell, W. (2005). A dual networks perspective on inter-organizational transfer of R & D capabilities: International joint ventures in the Chinese automotive industry. *Journal of Management Studies, 42,* 128–160.

4 Methodological Issues in International Human Resource Management Research

David Chan

CONTENTS

Research methodology includes study design and procedures, measurement, and data analysis. The adequacy of the research methodology in a study is judged in terms of the soundness of its logical linkages with the substantive inferences made on the basis of the findings obtained. The fundamental issues in research methodology, which are explicated in textbooks on research methods and statistics, are familiar to experienced empirical researchers and form the cornerstone of their training. However, in addition to these fundamental issues, researchers in international human resource management (IHRM) have to deal with issues of methods, measurement, and data analysis that are either specific or especially relevant to cross-cultural research. Be it in the area of recruitment, selection, training, compensation, or performance appraisal, both new and experienced researchers in IHRM are confronted with a variety of methodological challenges when they conduct cross-cultural organizational studies. When these methodological issues are not adequately addressed, several critical consequences follow. At best, the research questions that can be asked or answered are unnecessarily constrained. At worse, the inferences drawn from the study findings are invalid and misleading.

With increased globalization of organizations, there is an increased proliferation of research in IHRM. However, understanding and addressing methodological issues in IHRM research are

TABLE 4.1

Major Methodological Issues Affecting Substantive Inferences in International Human Resource Management Research

Issue 1:	Explicating the nature of the research question
Issue 2:	Selecting appropriate designs, methods, and sampling
Issue 3:	Developing appropriate measurement
Issue 4:	Performing appropriate data analyses

critical and must take priority over the rush to embrace IHRM studies and the associated findings. Clearly, we need to increase our research database with valid empirical studies in IHRM if we hope to provide an evidentiary basis for IHRM practices that are scientifically defensible. Together with adequate conceptualization, adequate research methodology helps build the foundation for conducting valid IHRM studies.

In the last two decades, there have been significant advances in methodological scholarship that are directly relevant to cross-cultural research. This is particularly true in the field of measurement and data analysis, such as advances in measurement invariance of item responses between groups as well as across time (e.g., Chan, 1998a, 2000; Vandenberg & Lance, 2000). Unfortunately, it is not evident that these advances are readily translated into implementation of IHRM research. Although it is true that more recent advances in methodology will necessarily take some time to translate into implementation of substantive research, I suspect that a major obstacle is the lack of nontechnical and integrative introductions that serve as effective interface between the technical writings in the methodological literature and IHRM researchers who may not be methodological or quantitative experts.

This chapter attempts to partly fill this gap by providing an interface as such. To do this, four major methodological issues that affect substantive inferences in IHRM research, as shown in Table 4.1, will be examined in detail. The chapter's focus is on the logical foundations and potential pitfalls associated with each methodological issue for drawing inferences about different aspects of the substantive research question in an empirical study in IHRM. In the interest of space, only the basic logic of each methodological issue and the features necessary for understanding its relationship with specific aspects of substantive inference are presented. More details of each methodological issue, such as technical information on a specific data analytic technique, are readily available in the relevant literature and some are listed in the references of this chapter.

EXPLICATING THE NATURE OF THE RESEARCH QUESTION

As empirical researchers, we have all been taught that the first step in a study is to formulate the research question. The research question is more fundamental and critical than merely being the first step in a logical sequence of stepwise procedures in the study. Specifically, the research question drives the relative importance of the various methodological issues and provides the basis for determining how we should or could address a specific methodological issue. The nature of the research question guides and therefore helps evaluate our methodological approaches and decisions concerning the empirical study. Basic issues concerning the importance of the research question in a cross-cultural study have been discussed fairly extensively by researchers (e.g., Gelfand, Raver, & Ehrharts, 2002; Triandis, 1994; Van de Vijer & Leung, 1997). Rather than repeating or elaborating these issues here, I will highlight a few "meta-issues" concerning the formulation and importance of the research question with the focus on IHRM studies. These issues may be categorized in terms of three types of distinction, namely, the distinction between descriptive and explanatory questions, the distinction between culture universality and culture specificity, and the distinction between emic and etic approaches.

In any cross-cultural study, the dominant approach adopted may be descriptive or explanatory in nature. In descriptive research, the study describes the pattern of observed results in each culture and compares them to highlight the similarities or differences across the cultures examined. In explanatory research, the study explains observed or predicted similarities and differences in criterion variables across cultures by specifying and appealing to causal or antecedent variables that purportedly influence the criterion variables. Strictly speaking, the large majority of the published studies in cross-cultural research, based on their study design and nature of data and findings, are descriptive in nature even though the discussions in the articles often contain explanatory statements. This is understandable especially in new areas of research where an exploratory approach is inevitable. After all, we need to first describe and compare, before we can explain cultural differences or similarities in and predict or prescribe IHRM actions in different cultures. But because the ultimate goal in IHRM research is often to explain, control, predict, or prescribe, we need to be accurate in our descriptions and comparisons. To be accurate, we need explicit and testable hypotheses (on patterns of similarities or differences across cultures), adequate measurement and data analyses, and valid interpretations of results, so that methodological rigor is critical to both descriptive and explanatory studies in IHRM research. But descriptive and explanatory questions often have different methodological implications as well. For example, although correlational and naturalistic group comparison study designs are typical and often adequate for its purpose in addressing descriptive research questions, they tend to be problematic for addressing explanatory research questions, which are more adequately examined using experimental study designs. For practical reasons, experimental designs are often not possible in explanatory research in IHRM, which typically relies on cross-sectional correlational data and at best naturalistic longitudinal panel data. Hence, careful attention needs to be paid to a variety of methodological issues (as elaborated in this chapter) to ensure sound linkages connecting explanatory inferences to design, measurement, data analysis, and results. Also, attempts to make explanatory inferences from cross-sectional correlational data or naturalistic longitudinal panel data often require moving beyond simple bivariate correlation analyses or comparisons of (culture) group means to employ more sophisticated data analytic techniques, such as mediation analysis, structural equation modeling, and growth curve analyses.

Another important distinction in IHRM research questions concerns the meta-theoretical goal or assumption of the research question in terms of culture universality versus culture specificity. In other words, the research question asked may assume or attempt to show that the phenomenon or relationship under investigation is equally or similarly applicable across the different cultures of interest (i.e., culture universality) or systematically differ in substantive ways across them (i.e., culture specificity). The distinction has implications for how we conduct the IHRM study, including methodological considerations. For example, if culture universality is the goal or the assumption underlying the research question, then the pertinent design, measurement, and study logistic issues to be considered are those that would increase the validity or appropriateness of the methods for demonstrating robustness/generalizability of findings or applicability of findings across cultures. In this sense, multiple cultures are treated simply as multiple samples and not very different in essence from other multiple operationalizations when seeking to demonstrate generalizability across multiple measures and measurement occasions. In other words, we want to ensure that the findings that we obtain in one measurement (i.e., from one culture sample) are not due to chance factors, and we want to demonstrate reliability of findings via consistency across multiple measurements (i.e., multiple culture samples). From this perspective, substantive cultural differences are not denied but they are not considered as relevant to the findings or theory that the researcher seeks to support. Here, the objective of the analyses performed on the cross-cultural data is to establish measurement invariance in responses or equality of direction and magnitude of parameter estimates associated with corresponding relationships involving (presumably) identical variables across cultures.

On the other hand, from the perspective of cultural specificity, the phenomenon of interest is considered inextricably tied to the culture sample and context of the study. In this sense, culture samples are not treated as multiple operationalizations to demonstrate generalizability. Instead, culture samples constitute a moderator variable that affects the magnitude, direction, or even meaning of the relationships involving the focal variables representing the phenomenon under study. That is, any substantive statements or conclusions about the phenomenon based solely on the specific findings of only one culture sample is potentially misleading. When culture specificity is the goal or assumption, then the objective is to demonstrate the lack of measurement invariance of responses or differences in direction/magnitude of relationships involving apparently identical variables across cultures.

One challenge for IHRM researchers is to recognize that their particular meta-theoretical goal or assumption of the research question (the belief in culture universality versus culture specificity) is no gospel truth and requires empirical evidence for support. In practice, researchers may be misled by their confirmatory bias in culture sampling, treatment of data, data analysis decisions, and interpretations of findings. For example, a researcher who uncritically assumes the truth of culture universality may dismiss observed differences across cultures as error variances and therefore minimize these differences through decisions in culture sampling (e.g., including only cultures that are similar in many respects), data coding that involves subjective judgments (e.g., collapsing raw rating scores for Culture A but not for Culture B because the researchers assumes that Culture A has larger variance in ratings simply because of higher error variance), or data interpretation (e.g., interpreting all residual variance as random error variance without considering the possibility of systematic error variance due to omission of relevant culture variables). Clearly, the reverse may also happen. A researcher who uncritically assumes the truth of culture specificity may treat any observed differences across cultures as true variances and therefore attempt to attribute these differences to substantive culture differences when they may in fact be simply due to random error variances.

Finally, much has been written in the cross-cultural psychology literature about the etic–emic distinction in approach to cross-cultural studies. This distinction is related to the distinction between culture universality and specificity, but it is more fundamental because it refers to a paradigmatic difference in the approach adopted by cross-cultural studies to address research questions. Etic and emic approaches adopt different assumptions and often implementations concerning theory development and, sometimes, theory testing, including measurement, data analysis, and inferences. Etic approaches assume that the cultural context of the cognitive sources of theory formulation and hypothesis generation is irrelevant because the theory and hypotheses are about human attitudes and behaviors that are applicable to all people across cultures. In addition, conceptual definitions of the focal constructs are not and cannot be culture-dependent. That is, the focal constructs are commensurate across cultures so that cultures can be meaningfully and directly compared in terms of their mean levels (or variance depending on the research question) on the same construct. In the etic approach, it is perfectly acceptable to adopt or adapt (through translation or minimal changes to item wording) a measure (e.g., a questionnaire) developed in one culture and apply it to another culture to measure the same focal constructs across cultures. The issues of importance for researchers using the etic approach are "technical" in nature, such as ensuring cross-cultural applicability through the use of adequate translation and back-translation techniques. For example, researchers adopting the etic approach would consider it possible to make meaningful and direct cross-cultural comparisons of scores on dimensions of fairness perceptions (because they argue that the conceptual definitions of these dimensions are not culture-specific), so long as care is taken to ensure that technical issues of measurement and use, such as validity of translation, are adequately addressed. Emic approaches, however, are very different. Emic approaches assume that theory formulation and hypotheses are inextricably tied to the cultural context in question. Conceptual definitions of focal constructs are meaningful only when explicated in reference to the specific cultural context because the essence of the construct is indigenous to the culture. It follows logically that adopting or adapting (with minor modifications) the definitions or measurement of constructs from one culture to apply to another constitutes inadequate methodology. Strictly speaking, the term "cross-culture comparison" is not meaningful for emic proponents because the constructs are incommensurate across cultures. For example, researchers adopting the emic approach would argue that the meaning and implications of the same leadership behaviors may vary qualitatively across cultures such that it is inappropriate and indeed misleading to make cross-cultural comparisons of scores on dimensions of fairness perceptions (because they argue that the conceptual definitions of these dimensions are inherently culture-specific). For emic proponents, "cultural psychology" (as opposed to "cross-cultural psychology") is a more adequate term to describe their field. Although etic and emic approaches are ideal types in the sense that virtually all IHRM studies probably have elements of each approach to varying degrees, the distinction helps us understand and clarify assumptions, decisions, and conflicting findings in IHRM studies.

To summarize, my basic point in the above discussion on the nature of the research question in terms of the three types of distinctions is that research methodology is inextricably linked with theory and conceptualization about the phenomenon and constructs of interest. In the remainder of this chapter, I demonstrate some of these linkages by addressing specific methodological issues. For ease of presentation, these issues are classified into various categories corresponding to the following sections as they appear in the chapter: selecting appropriate study designs, methods of data collection and sampling procedures, developing appropriate measurement, and performing appropriate data analyses. These categories of issues differ in their specific concerns but they all share the goal of making appropriate inferences from the cross-cultural data obtained in an IHRM study. The chapter ends with an overview of the advanced issues in research methodology in IHRM and suggestions for further reading.

SELECTING APPROPRIATE DESIGNS, METHODS, AND SAMPLING

The specific research question provides the conceptual basis to select the appropriate study design, method of data collection, and sampling procedure. From the viewpoint of scientific defensibility, the choice and adequacy of the design, method, and sampling must be evaluated in terms of the extent to which the design/method/procedure will logically result in the type of data that can be used to make valid inferences directly related to answering the specific research question. This requires us to be knowledgeable of the validity implications of specific study designs, methods of data collection, and sampling procedures. In practice, however, nonscientific considerations, such as resources, cost, timeline, and sociopolitical factors are important criteria for evaluating the feasibility of a choice and hence they directly affect the final selection of study design, method of data collection, and sampling procedure. This is why actual studies are never perfect even if we know all the scientific (i.e., validity) implications of each design, method, and sampling procedure with respect to the specific research question, because nonscientific considerations are always factored into the implementation of the study. This section highlights important validity implications and practical considerations associated with the selection of study designs, methods of data collection, and sampling procedures, with an emphasis on features directly relevant or unique to IHRM studies.

SELECTION OF STUDY DESIGN

An appropriate study design is one that allows valid inferences to be made from the findings, and these inferences have direct bearing on the research question that the study attempts to answer. Hence, it is important to consider the selection of study design in some detail in this chapter.

Because validity refers to the inferences made, there is no study design that is inherently valid or invalid without relating it to the research question. In IHRM research, the additional and unique aspect of design selection concerns the appropriateness of the design to the cultures under investigation with respect to the research question asked. If the design is not appropriate to one or more cultures under investigation, then the inferences made from the findings are likely to be invalid or at least alternative hypotheses consistent with the findings obtained cannot be ruled out. For example, individuals from some cultures may have experiences and values that are inconsistent with a specific research design or method of data collection. Laboratory experiments that require participants to imagine that they are in specific positions (e.g., a manager) may be more difficult for some cultures than others. For example, in cultures with highly rigid authority structures or low social-economic mobility, participants from lower power or socioeconomic positions may find it more difficult to imagine themselves in higher positions compared to their counterparts in cultures with less rigid structures or higher mobility.

The inconsistency between cultural experiences/values and study design/method may even apply to the individual self-report survey method, which is probably the most widely used design in IHRM studies. In support of this point, Gelfand et al. (2002) cited an unpublished study by Moshinsky (2000), which reported that Russian participants discussed the questions and arrived at a consensus decision to provide the same response even though they had been explicitly instructed to independently complete the individual self-report survey. Although this does not imply that the survey method should not be used with Russian participants, it does illustrate the importance of taking into account the experiences and values of a culture under investigation, which may not always match the assumptions of the study design or method, and the need to adapt the original design or method if necessary and possible.

It is beyond the scope of this chapter to discuss specific designs. Instead, I will focus on some general issues relevant to selecting designs from two broad categories, namely, experimental versus correlational research. Experimental research refers to studies conducted under controlled conditions, in which the independent variables are manipulated. Strictly speaking, culture will not be the independent variable because it is not possible to experimentally manipulate culture. Instead, the independent and dependent variables represent the focal constructs in the IHRM study and cultures represent the contexts across which the treatment effects are tested for invariance. The invariance concern here may be replicability (if the researcher hypothesizes that the treatment effect generalizes across the cultures) or substantive differences (if the researcher hypothesize that the treatment effect is moderated by culture). For example, a researcher may, in each culture under study, manipulate procedural rule violation in a personnel selection system to examine its effect on procedural justice perceptions.

In correlational research, the "independent" (or more accurately, predictor) variables are measured rather than manipulated. The "dependent" (or more accurately, criterion) variables are the outcome variables that we are interested in explaining or predicting. The vast majority of IHRM studies are correlational research consisting of surveys administered to relevant samples from the cultures under study. Similar to treatment effects in experimental studies, the predictor–criterion relationships in correlational studies may be examined across cultures for replicability or substantive differences.

Conceptually, the experimental–correlational distinction and the laboratory-field distinction are orthogonal. The experimental–correlational distinction refers to study design, whereas the laboratory–field distinction refers to study setting, although most studies conducted in laboratory settings have employed experimental designs and most studies conducted in field settings have employed correlational designs.

The strengths and weaknesses of correlational field studies and experimental laboratory studies have been well discussed in organizational psychology and will not be repeated here. As noted by Gilliland and Chan (2001), much of the discussions can be summarized in the tension between internal and external validity. Specifically, critics of experimental laboratory studies often argued that the controlled but contrived situations examined in the studies lack external validity. For example, these critics would argue that college sophomores' justice perceptions in a contrived experimental setting provide little, if any, information on actual employees' justice perceptions in the actual organizational setting because the two settings differ greatly on a wide variety of subject and situational variables that are potential influences on justice perceptions. For IHRM research, these critics might add the argument that the same experimental setting may be more contrived in one culture than another, thereby creating differential external validity across cultures. On the other hand, critics of correlational field studies often argue that the realistic but uncontrolled situations examined in the studies lack internal validity. According to these critics, the uncontrolled nature of the correlational field study prevents us from ruling out the multitude of alternative plausible explanations of the results obtained. For example, if we find a positive correlation between justice perception and organizational commitment, how do we decide which one of the following is true: justice perception causes commitment, commitment causes justice perception, a reciprocal causation exists between justice perception and commitment, or justice perception and commitment are spuriously associated because both are caused by a third variable (e.g., negative affectivity)? For IHRM studies, these critics might add the argument that the uncontrolled environment of correlational field studies brings with it a host of potentially relevant cultural difference variables that vastly increased the number of alternative plausible explanations, making any unambiguous or confident interpretations of results virtually impossible.

Both experimental laboratory studies and correlational field studies are needed as they complement each other to advance IHRM research. The limitations of experimental laboratory research are often addressed by the strengths of correlational field research and vice versa. The question is not if we should conduct experimental laboratory studies in IHRM research but when. When the research question is to test some casual hypothesis involving two or more variables, then the experimental design and controlled setting in laboratory research allow the collection of the relevant data by examining effects attributable to the manipulated independent variable representing the hypothesized cause. On the other hand, when the research question is to assess an association between two or more variables as it occurs in actual organizational settings, then the naturalistic setting employed in correlational field research allows the collection of the relevant data by examining the associations in realistic contexts.

I believe that a program of research in IHRM that would truly advance the study of the phenomenon of interest is one that employs both experimental laboratory studies and correlational field studies in a complementary fashion. Experimental studies conducted in laboratory settings establish causal relationships, and correlational studies in field settings generalize the laboratory findings to naturalistic settings. When variables can be readily manipulated and their effects examined with high internal validity and, even better, also high external validity, then there is little reason to not consider using experiments in laboratory studies to achieve more rigorous inferences. On the other hand, some variables can only be studied by correlational field studies because it is not possible to experimentally manipulate them in a laboratory setting for ethical or practical reasons. Field studies also help identify relevant variables to be included and generate causal hypotheses to be tested in laboratory studies. Laboratory and field studies ask converging questions of the phenomenon of interest and their findings could provide convergent evidence. Greenberg's program of research on justice-based accounts of theft and performance appraisals exemplifies this integrative approach to laboratory and field studies. He used a technique (laboratory or field study) whenever it allowed him to build on his earlier work. For example, he used a laboratory study (Greenberg, 1993) to follow up his field study (Greenberg, 1990) on theft because the former allowed him to control key variables that were impossible to control in the field. He also used surveys in the field setting (Greenberg, 1986) as well as laboratory experiments (Greenberg, 1987) to obtain convergent evidence for his justice-based accounts of performance appraisals.

In IHRM research, there has been an over reliance on correlational field studies. In part, this may have limited theory development, scientific defensibility of research inferences, and the practical conclusions that can be drawn from the research. For example, whereas correlational studies can show that perceptions of justice are correlated with organizational commitment, they cannot lead to the recommendation that improving justice within an organization will improve employee commitment. This latter conclusion requires a field experiment. Field experiments, when adequately conducted, provide a promising way to study justice because they have more realism over laboratory experiments (hence increasing external validity) and more control over correlational field studies (hence increasing internal validity). Unfortunately, only a few studies conducted in field settings have employed quasi-experimental or experimental designs to examine phenomena of interest relevant to HRM (e.g., Greenberg, 1990).

We should also avoid confusing the experiment–correlation distinction or the laboratory–field distinction with the simulation–actual experience distinction. The simulation–actual experience distinction refers to the meaning that participants ascribe to their experience in the study and the fidelity of the experience in representing the actual context to which the researcher intends to generalize the study results. In a simulation, participants undergo experiences or task conditions that the researcher hopes are psychologically very similar, if not equivalent, to those actual experiences or conditions in organizations. Although laboratory experiments are largely simulations, they can vary considerably in fidelity. Fidelity refers to the degree of similarity between the key dimensions of the simulation and the actual experience or situation in the target domain. Consider the example of compensation fairness research. A laboratory experiment in which participants are asked to indicate their distributive justice perceptions after reading written scenarios of either equitable or negatively inequitable rewards is likely to have substantially lower fidelity than one in which participants were asked to indicate their justice perceptions after actually being paid either equitably or negatively inequitably for their task performance in the study. There is no general answer to the question of which specific dimensions of fidelity should be maximized. However, the purpose of a simulation suggests that we should always identify dimensions according to the theory driving the research question and the constructs of interest. A useful rule of thumb is to ask whether or not the participant in the simulation attributes the same meaning to the variables of interest as the participant would in the actual experience or conditions that the simulation is intended to represent (Berkowitz & Donnerstein, 1982). As noted above, IHRM researchers should be particularly sensitive to cultural differences in the mapping of meanings between simulation and actual experiences.

SELECTION OF METHOD OF DATA COLLECTION

Study design (i.e., experimental versus correlational) and setting (laboratory versus field) are both distinct from the specific method of data collection employed in the study (e.g., behavioral observations, verbal protocols, surveys, interviews). For example, an experimental laboratory study may include a self-report questionnaire that is no different in format from the survey used typically in correlational field research to collect data on the dependent measure, manipulation check for the independent variable, or covariate measure. Conversely, a correlational field study may include behavioral observations or cognitive measures such as implicit association tests and knowledge structure elicitation procedures, which are methods of data collection used typically in experimental laboratory research. Isolating the method of data collection from study design and setting is important because it has implications for measurement, data analysis, and inferential issues. For example, if self-report questionnaires are used to collect dependent measure data in an experimental laboratory study, then the researcher still has to deal with measurement issues such as reliability and response sets (e.g., social desirability), analysis issues such as correction for measurement error and range restriction, and inferential issues such as the construct validity of the questionnaire responses. These important issues are sometimes wrongly assumed to be irrelevant to experimental laboratory research.

The most common method of data collection in IHRM research (and probably in cross-cultural psychology as well) is the self-report questionnaire method where items are grouped into scales measuring a variety of constructs in various domains, such as abilities, personality, values, attitudes, and workplace perceptions. The potential problems associated with the use of self-report questionnaires in cross-cultural research (which includes IHRM research) are well documented in the literature and will not be repeated here (for details, see Gelfand et al., 2002; Van de Vijer & Leung, 1997). Many of these cross-cultural study problems, such as inequivalence of meaning of test content, differential familiarity with the response format and test method in general, differences in motivation, and differences in response sets, are in fact not unique to the self-report question-naire method. For example, other methods of data collection, such as the face-to-face interview, the telephone interview, behavioral observations such as assessment centers, and various forms of work simulations, are also susceptible to problems of construct inequivalence of test content and differences in familiarity or response sets.

The above problems associated with cultural differences in reactions to the use of a data collection method are essentially a construct contamination problem. That is, the observed differences in scores across cultures, which are meant to reflect only true substantive cultural differences and random error variances, are contaminated with unintended constructs associated with the test method. I have argued that the basic problem underlying the unintended effects of choice of data collection method on validity and interpretation of findings is the failure to make a clear distinction between test method (method of data collection) and test content or construct. Before deciding on a method of data collection, it is critical to ask if the method, when applied to a particular sample and in a particular context, is in fact contributing systematically to the observed variance of test scores over and above the contribution from the true (intended) test construct variance. This method variance needs to be isolated from the intended test construct variance. When observed variance is not decomposed into method variance and construct variance, any direct comparisons of observed scores across cultures is problematic to the extent that application of the same method to different cultures has in fact contributed to observed differences across cultures. Note that the separation of method and construct is often not easy. For details of the method–construct distinction and examples of the conceptual, measurement, and data analysis issues involved, see Chan (2001) and Chan and Schmitt (1997; 2005).

In many IHRM studies, the choice of data collection method is driven primarily by practical and logistical concerns. Cultures may react differently to the same method of data collection and the nature and extent of method variance is dependent on the method and cultures in question. Because method variance affects the meaning of observed score differences across cultures and therefore the interpretation of these differences, it is important that IHRM researchers acquire a better under standing of the method–construct distinction and the specific method variance problems associated with data collection methods and specific cultures. The issue is increasingly relevant and new knowledge of these problems is needed with the increased popularity of novel methods of data collection, such as the situational judgment test method (paper-and-pencil and video-based), conditional reasoning tests, and Web-based surveys.

To summarize, when selecting the study design as well as method of data collection in IHRM research, we need to pay much attention (and probably more than we do currently) to cultural differences in appropriateness of the design or method. This brings us to the fundamental issue concerning the relevant cultural dimensions that matter to the research question and cultural differences on each dimension among the cultures selected for the study. Clearly, the nature and number of cultural dimensions affect the procedure for sampling cultures, which in turn affects the type and extent of observed cultural differences. In addition, and often neglected, the within-culture differences on focal constructs are equally important but for different reasons. Hence, we next turn our attention to the selection of appropriate procedure, focusing on sampling cultures and sampling within cultures.

SELECTION OF SAMPLING PROCEDURE

Despite the importance of appropriate sampling in IHRM research, dedicated discussion on the theory and practice of sampling is virtually absent in the IHRM literature. Sampling issues in IHRM can be divided into two broad categories. The first category is concerned with sampling cultures and is focused on identifying and selecting the specific cultures to be involved in the IHRM study. The second is concerned with sampling within cultures and is focused on the validity of specific methods for determining the cases to constitute the sample within a given culture in the IHRM study. At the abstract and fundamental level, the same theories, principles, and technical properties of sampling underline both categories of sampling issues (i.e., sampling cultures and sampling within cultures) of sampling issues. Rather than discussing the fundamentals of sampling theories, principles, and techniques that are widely available in textbooks on sampling or social surveys, I will highlight several important sampling issues that affect the conduct of IHRM research and the interpretation of its findings.

The validity issues in sampling are best summarized by the notion of representativeness of the study's sample with respect to the target population about which the inferences are made. The inferences are concerned with answers to the research question. Hence, the specific research question and the characteristics of the target population together form the basis on which the appropriateness of a sampling procedure is evaluated. In the case of sampling cultures, we are concerned with which cultures to include in the IHRM study. The research question and the target population create constraints that restrict or help delimit the appropriate "pool" of cultures in the world to select from. This pool constitutes the sampling frame or the enumerated list of cultures from which the actual sample of cultures will be drawn for the study. Consider a study in which the research question is to test the universality (i.e., generalizability across cultures) of the hypothesis that conscientiousness (a personality construct) positively predicts job performance. As explained earlier in the chapter, the nature of this research question would treat cultures as multiple samples to test for generalizations of findings. Hence, the pool of cultures constituting the sampling frame should consist of numerous cultures representing different regions throughout the world. This will ensure that a random and representative sampling of cultures from the pool would provide a sufficiently wide range of cultures to be included in the study to examine the robustness of the conscientiousness–performance relationships across widely different cultural contexts. Consider another study in which the research question is to examine the possibility that cultures differing along the individualism–collectivism dimension would systematically differ in the extent to which a new compensation system that violates the principle of individual merit would lead to negative procedural justice perceptions. With respect to sampling of cultures, this study should ensure that cultures selected for inclusion differ sufficiently on the individualism–collectivism dimension so that the variation of the selected cultures' scores on the individualism–collectivism dimension is *representative* of the corresponding variation in the population of cultures of interest. A wide and representative variation will avoid methodological problems associated with range restriction that might lead to ambiguous or even misleading interpretations of findings.

One problem in the sampling of cultures concerns the frequent use of only two countries in the IHRM study. In addition to the likely problems of insufficient variation and lack of representativeness associated with the use of only two countries, there is often a problem of confounding of culture and language. When two countries differ in both culture and language, any observed difference in results between the countries per se may be attributable to differences in culture, language, or both. Without an appropriate sample of several cultures that allows culture and language to be unconfounded, it is not possible to isolate variance and between-countries differences due to culture versus language. In an IHRM study examining the measurement equivalence of survey item responses, Ryan, Chan, Ployhart, and Slade (1999) demonstrated how a careful sampling of countries can provide the necessary data to isolate these effects. Note that the issue here is not about the relationship between culture and language. Rather, it is about the methodological problem of failure to separate (naturalistically through sampling of countries and not artificially through manipulation of measures such as language of the survey questionnaire) culture and language effects in the analysis of data and interpretation of results.

Sampling within cultures is as important as sampling of cultures. Clearly, the adequacy of a sample of cultures selected for the study is affected by the adequacy of the sampling within each selected culture. The critical issue is that the sampling within a culture should be representative of that culture, not only in terms of respondent populations but also in terms of the relevant dimensions and contexts of interest. For example, a study of cross-cultural differences or similarities in reactions to promotion tests in law enforcement agencies should ensure that the law enforcement agencies sampled within each culture are representative (rather than unique or atypical) of that culture in terms of the type of tests being used, as well as other relevant contextual variables, such as the length of time that the test has been in use. Valid comparisons of findings across cultures are not possible when the method of sampling within cultures differed in systematic ways across cultures such that it led to differences in representativeness among the culture samples. An adequate IHRM study requires the researcher to explicate the within-culture sampling criteria and ensure that they are consistently implemented in each culture. Unfortunately, implementation often deviates from the intended or planned sampling procedures because of practical considerations or simply a lack of standardization in implementation of sampling procedure across cultures due to poor logistic coordination. Ideally, before any variation in implementation is allowed, the researcher should ensure that the variation is not a threat to validity or the threat can be removed or minimized through adaptation of the data collection procedures or appropriate data analysis (e.g., controlling extraneous differences as a statistical covariate). When implementation differences or problems occurred, the variations should be noted and taken into account when analyzing data and interpreting results.

Sampling of cultures and sampling within cultures are both critical issues that have not been given sufficient attention in cross-cultural studies in general and IHRM research in particular. The central idea in both types of sampling is that the sampling procedure should result in a representative sample so that valid inferences as intended by the purpose of the study can be made. The explicit specification of the research question and the proper definition of the target population and context of interest are both critical because they determine the extent to which the resulting sample is considered representative.

DEVELOPING APPROPRIATE MEASUREMENT

Developing appropriate measurement is a critical part of adequate research methodology. As empirical scientists, IHRM researchers are aware that the phenomena of interest in their studies are often concerned with relationships between predictor and criterion constructs (e.g., conscientiousness and job performance) that are not directly observable but are measured imperfectly using observable indicators. The imperfect measurement of intended constructs is the reason for the importance of two fundamental psychometric concepts in determining the appropriateness of a measure or measurement occasion. These are the familiar concepts of reliability and validity. Detailed discussions of these two concepts are readily available in any textbook on testing and research methodology. I will only summarize the essentials of the two concepts to relate them to IHRM research and provide the psychometric basis for discussing measurement issues involving translation, response scale formats, and response sets.

RELIABILITY AND VALIDITY

An important issue in the interpretation of internal consistency, reliability concerns the number of items on a measure (i.e., test length) and the dimensionality of the measure (i.e., how many distinct constructs are assessed by the measure). All other things being equal, the longer the measure (i.e., more items), the more reliable (in terms of internal consistency) the measure will be. This is partly because of item content sampling. With a larger sample (more items) of the content domain of the target construct, we get a more consistent and adequate measure. It is possible to estimate the effect that shortening or lengthening a measure will have on the reliability coefficient using the Spearman-Brown formula. We should note the implications of the relationship between length of a measure and its reliability. First, when we compare two measures of very disparate length, it will not be surprising if they differ substantially in reliability. This problem is often ignored when researchers remove a few items from a measure developed in one culture and apply the shortened measure to another culture due to inappropriate or irrelevant content of these few items in the second culture.

All other things equal, we would expect the reliability coefficient of the shortened measure in the second culture to be lower than that of the original (longer) measure in the first culture. But the two cultures may in fact differ in the extent of random errors due to a host of differences in sample characteristics, administration settings, and other contextual variables. Hence, these differences and differences in test length are confounded as sources of differential reliability across cultures. Second, blindly adding items to a measure in an atheoretical fashion will also increase a measure's reliability but it should not be done. This problem is often not appreciated by many researchers. Internal consistency estimate of reliability presupposes (assumes) unidimensionality in the measure (i.e., that the measure assesses one and only one unitary construct)—it does not prove unidimensionality. It is possible to have a multidimensional measure (measuring several distinct constructs), which has a high internal consistency reliability estimate simply because of the large number of items. The resulting high reliability for the measure is not meaningful. In this case, one should be clear what items are measuring what constructs (i.e., group items into scales measuring constructs) and compute internal consistency reliability estimate for each unidimensional (single-construct) scale.

The magnitude of a reliability coefficient is dependent on the sample on which the coefficient is computed. Because reliability coefficient is essentially a correlation coefficient, its magnitude is similarly affected by range restriction in the observed measure. Hence, we should not take the reliability estimates reported in one culture for granted when using the measure in another culture. We should examine the original culture sample on which the reliability was computed to see if the sample variability on the variable of interest is comparable to the variability of our target culture sample. This is why it is important that studies should always report the reliability of the measure used (computed on the study samples) even if the measure is an established one with reliability information reported in test manuals.

The validity of a measure refers to the accuracy of the inferences made from the test scores. The validity of a measure is not some inherent property of the measure. In fact, there is no such thing as the validity of a measure in the abstract, without reference to the purpose or use of the measure. Statements about a measure's validity should relate to the validity of particular interpretations or types of decisions made from the scores on the measure. Interpretations and decisions do not occur in a vacuum. That is, they occur in particular contexts. It is important to be explicit about the substantive context in question. For example, a cognitive ability test (e.g., Wonderlic Personnel Test) may discriminate well for the general English-speaking population but not too well for university graduates.

We often speak of three different types of validation efforts. Note that they are not different types of validity. Rather, they are different strategies or types of efforts with a common ultimate goal—to establish the accuracy of the inferences made from test scores. The three types of validation efforts are content validation, criterion-related validation, and construct validation. Although we speak of three types of validation efforts, they are actually all aspects of construct validation. Content validity, which is concerned with the adequacy of item content sampling from the content domain of the target construct, usually refers to questions concerning the adequacy of development of the measure. Because construct validity refers to the extent to which the measure captures what it intends to measure, the more representative the content sampling is in development of the measure, the more construct valid the measure will be (i.e., the more the measure captures the essence or core substantive components of the target construct). Because of cultural differences in interpretations or meanings of specific behaviors or attitudes, the same item content may differ across cultures in the extent to which it is representative of the content domain of the same target construct. Criterion-related validity refers to the extent to which the measure predicts (i.e., correlates with) some external variable or construct that is distinct from the measure's intended construct. Some evidence of criterion-related validity might be considered as evidence of construct validity. To establish criterion-related validity, we obviously need criterion measures to represent the criterion construct(s). Criterion measures needed for criterion-related validity must have content validity. Construct validity is most often empirically demonstrated by confirming predictions in relationships among various measures that are content-valid. The confirmation of predicted relationships proceeds by criterion-related validation.

The role of theory is fundamental in the validation of a measure. In construct validation of a measure, we often use theory to locate the test construct in a nomological network of constructs, which forms the conceptual basis for the criterion-related validation. Even in trying to establish content validity in construction of the measure, we have some theory of what constitute relevant or core aspects of the target construct. In other words, rational judgment is involved in all three types of validation efforts. In content validation, there are judgments about relevant or representative behaviors that form the core aspects of the content domain, which refers to an infinitely large repertoire of behaviors. In criterion-related validation, there are judgments about the relevance of the criterion (criteria) selected. In construct validation, there are judgments concerning the evidence to assemble and the relationships to investigate. The relationship between theory and validation is reciprocal. Theory is needed to guide validation and validity evidence provides empirical support for the theory being tested.

LANGUAGE DIFFERENCES AND TRANSLATING QUESTIONNAIRES

Often, a questionnaire established in one culture is in a language different from the language of the target culture in which the researcher intends to apply the questionnaire. In such situations, the primary measurement issues revolve around the validity of the translation. That is, is there translation equivalence such that the translated questionnaire faithfully reproduces all the semantic content associated with the wording of the items on the original questionnaire? The widely accepted practice to maximize translation equivalence is via the process of blind back-translation (Brislin, Lonner, & Thorndike, 1973). In this process, a translator translates the measure from the original language to the target language. A different translator who has not seen the measure in its original language then translates the measure back to the original language. This back-translated version is compared with the original version for discrepancies and all three versions (original, translated, back-translated) are then discussed to arrive at a consensus version between the two translators. Ideally, a third person proficient in both languages who did not participate in the translation or back-translation process should also join the consensus discussion to offer additional and independent views.

Two points about language differences and translation are noteworthy for IHRM research. First, as noted in the preceding section, culture and language translation differences may be confounded if we do not have a sufficient number of relevant countries to isolate these differences (Ryan et al., 1999). Second, translation equivalence contributes to but does not necessarily imply construct equivalence. It appears that many IHRM researchers (and other cross-cultural researchers) are not fully cognizant of this distinction in equivalence, since they often explicitly or implicitly conclude that construct equivalence exists solely on the basis of a purportedly successful back-translation process (i.e., a consensus achieved between translators). Translation equivalence does not equate with construct equivalence because the former focuses on cross-cultural identity in semantic content of item wording, whereas the latter is concerned with the cross-cultural identity in meanings that respondents associate the item content with and interpretations that they make from these meanings. The same semantic content may evoke different conceptual frames of reference, meanings, and interpretations across cultures. For example, the same semantic content of an item referring to the proactive behavior of speaking up in disagreement with the supervisor may be construed by respondents as moral courage, participatory decision making, initiative, impulsivity, or disrespect for authority, depending on the cultural context and norms for interpreting the meaning of the behavior. Specifically, construct equivalence is about whether or not the same construct is being assessed by the same measure across cultures and the extent to which the construct (if same across cultures) is assessed with the same precision (see measurement invariance analysis in the section on Developing Appropriate Data Analyses below). Establishing construct equivalence is essentially a construct validation effort to gather evidence to support the accuracy of inferences made concerning constructs on the basis of the scores on the measures. Viewed in this light, translation equivalence may be seen as one type of preliminary evidence and more direct convergent validity evidence is needed in the construct validation process to establish construct equivalence across cultures. For example, we could perform measurement invariance analyses or compare criterion-related validities across cultures to establish relational equivalence (i.e., cross-cultural identity in direction and magnitude of relationship between the target construct and the same established criterion construct).

RESPONSE SCALE FORMATS AND RESPONSE SETS

One measurement issue that researchers often debate about is the optimal number of scale points on the rating scale that respondents are asked to use to rate items. There should be enough scale points to capture psychologically real distinctions in ratings and also to avoid artifactually imposing a range restriction problem on the data. On the other hand, the number of scale points must not be so numerous that the level of refinement exceeds psychologically real distinctions and introduces additional random measurement error due to differences in ratings that occurred due to chance and not true differences in construct values. Because the level of psychologically real distinctions is likely to depend on the nature of the construct, the item content, and the respondent characteristics, it is unlikely that there is a single ideal number of scale points for all measures, although there is a general consensus among studies (see Krosnick & Fabrigar, 1997) examining the effects of number of scale points on reliability and validity that scale points ranging from five to seven usually provide "optimal" distinctions. We are in need of studies that directly examine if there are cultural differences in the number of response scale points that is optimal for the same given construct and identify the factors contributing to such differences. Such studies are critical because cultural differences in optimal number of scale points, if they exist for a given construct but are not taken into account, would lead to misleading inferences drawn from the results when the same response scale format is used across the relevant cultures.

Another category of issues in item responses relates to cultural differences in response sets (or response styles). A response set refers to a systematic way of responding to items that distorts the observed score as an accurate indication of the true value on the measure's intended construct. By definition, a response set produces systematic error variance in the observed scores and therefore reduces construct validity by increasing construct contamination (i.e., the measure in fact assesses an unintended construct in addition to or instead of the intended construct).

One response set is the tendency to use only specific parts of the response scale regardless of the item content. It is often claimed that cultures in Asia (e.g., China) are more likely than cultures in the West (e.g., the United States) to use the midpoint or the middle region of the response scale (e.g., Lee & Green, 1991). This culture-specific response tendency to use the middle rather than the ends of the rating scales, if it in fact exists, will introduce contamination in the culture sample exhibiting the response set. The contamination in turn leads to problems in interpreting observed culture group differences in means or variances because true construct differences and response set differences are confounded. It is noteworthy that the nature or the cause of the purported central tendency response set among Asian cultures has never been explicitly investigated. Such studies are useful because they would increase our understanding of the response set so that we can decide how to interpret it and take it into account when analyzing results. For example, it is possible that the response set may reflect some more deep-rooted worldview associated with the culture rather than a mere artefact due to a response style to appear moderate in attitude. In this regard, the research by Nisbett (2003) concerning the thought systems of East Asians versus Westerners provides a useful point of departure for theorizing substantive differences that may underlie cultural differences in response sets.

Another important response style that researchers have been preoccupied with is social desirability responding, which is probably the response set that has received the most attention in research. Ganster, Hennessey, and Luthans (1983, p. 322) defined social desirability as the "tendency for an individual to present him or herself, in test-taking situations, in a way that makes the person look positive with regard to culturally derived norms and standards." Paulhus (1984, 1986) distinguished between two types of social desirability responding, namely, impression management and self-deception. Impression management refers to the conscious and deliberate effort to create a specific effect desired by the respondent. Because such responding is typically done to deliberately create a positive evaluation of the respondent by inflating responses relative to the true score, it is aptly described as "faking good." Self-deception, on the other hand, refers to positively biased responding that the respondent actually believes to be true. This response process is often linked to such self-concepts or related notions as self-esteem, self-image, and defense mechanisms. When investigating social desirability as a response set, the common (often implicit) assumption is that it indicates individual differences in the propensity for "faking good," that is, impression management.

Similar to the central tendency response set, social desirability responding introduces construct contamination and creates difficulties in direct comparisons of results across cultures when cultures differ in the response set. In addition, differential social desirability responding across cultures creates difficulties in interpretations because the response set contributes artefactual covariance between substantive constructs assessed by self-report measures. The majority of the research on social desirability responding is focused on how the response set may be detected, the susceptibility of different measures to the response set, and the extent to which the response set affects construct and criterion-related validity of the measures. Surprisingly, studies on cultural differences in social desirability responding and the factors explaining these differences are virtually absent. Research in this direction is certainly needed given the almost exclusive use of self-report measures in IHRM research, and if social desirability is indeed ubiquitous in self-report measures as commonly asserted.

PERFORMING APPROPRIATE DATA ANALYSES

As noted throughout this chapter, the discussions on various methodological issues in cross-cultural research tend to revolve around the central issue concerning the notion of construct equivalence across cultures. This issue, in my opinion, has been and will continue to be the primary driver of fruitful studies in IHRM research and it constitutes one of the primary conceptual bases for evaluating the methodological adequacy of IHRM studies. Although the centrality of construct equivalence has been emphasized in the cross-cultural research literature as early as more than three decades ago (e.g., Berry, 1969), it is only relatively recently that methodological advances in measurement invariance analyses of responses across groups and over time have provided us systematic and rigorous procedures to directly examine substantive research questions, test assumptions, and address issues related to construct equivalence. Details and debates about the technical aspects of measurement invariance analyses are beyond the scope of this chapter (for review, see Chan, 1998a, 2000; Vandenberg & Lance, 2000). This section will summarize the basic logic of measurement invariance and also discuss several issues associated with other data analytic techniques.

MEASUREMENT INVARIANCE

To appreciate the importance of measurement invariance analysis, consider the fact that virtually all areas of IHRM research make direct comparisons between two or more cultures in their responses to the same set of items/measures. On the basis of absolute differences in the scores on the measurement scale, substantive inferences are made about between-culture group differences in the level of the construct purportedly represented by the items/measures. The validity of these inferences is dependent on the often untested assumption that, across culture groups, the same items/measures are measuring the same construct and measuring it with the same precision. When this assumption of measurement invariance is in fact violated, absolute differences in scores between culture groups, and therefore inferences based on these differences, are likely to be misleading or not meaningful.

Hence, measurement invariance is often a statistical hurdle that should be cleared before making direct between-culture group comparisons of scores. On the other hand, measurement invariance or lack thereof may also reflect or represent substantive between-culture group differences that are of theoretical interest.

Currently, measurement invariance analysis is most commonly performed using multiple-group confirmatory factor analysis (MG-CFA). MG-CFA allows us to establish whether the same factor structure holds (applies) across multiple samples (groups). The MG-CFA approach, which estimates parameters in the multiple groups simultaneously, allows us to systematically test hypotheses about the invariance (equivalence) of factor loadings, factor variances-covariances, and unique error terms for a given model across independent samples or groups. Usually, the measurement concern in the MG-CFA analysis is in measurement invariance; that is, the hypothesis that the numbers (responses) in the different groups have the same meaning.

The assessment of measurement invariance across groups proceeds in the following manner (the discussion assumes basic familiarity with the CFA technique). Suppose we have two culture groups. In the first step, the hypothesis that is tested is that factor loadings are equal across the two culture groups. That is, the test here is about whether, for both Culture A and Culture B, the same indicators tap the same factors to the same extent. To do this, a model that allows the factor loadings to be freely estimated across culture groups is fitted to the groups simultaneously. Next, a second and more constrained (i.e., higher model degrees of freedom) model in which the factor loadings for identical indicators are constrained to be equal across groups is fitted to the data. Note that this second model is nested under the first model because we can obtain the second model simply by fixing a free parameter in the first model (conversely, obtaining the first model simply by freeing a fixed parameter in the second model). Because of this nested relationship, we can test the statistical difference in the (necessary) reduction in model fit when we move from the first model (i.e., the free loadings model, which is less constrained or more complex) to the second model (i.e., the equal loadings model, which is more constrained or simpler). A nonsignificant reduction in model fit indicates equality of factor loadings across groups and, in most substantive research, is often taken as evidence of measurement invariance (a fundamental type of factorial invariance) across groups so that direct comparisons of culture group differences is possible.

Equality of factor loadings is not the only available standard for measurement invariance. More stringent standards for measurement invariance would require, in addition to equality of factor loadings, that there are equality of error variances corresponding to identical indicators or equality of factor variances and covariances. The logic and procedure for testing such equality is the same as before. Two points are noteworthy. First, the comparison of error variances and comparison of factor variance-covariance can proceed meaningfully only when equality of factor loadings has been established. Second, these more stringent standards are extremely demanding, and most researchers recognize that it is unrealistic to expect such extreme invariance to hold in actual data except in highly contrived situations such as groups formed via random assignment.

Sometimes we hope to find differences rather than establish equality in the parameters of interest (i.e., factor loadings, error variances, or factor variances-covariances) when making the between-group comparisons. For example, we may have a theory that the same measure does not have construct equivalence across two cultures. This theory would lead to the research hypothesis that factor loadings (and maybe even factor pattern) are different across the culture groups. Alternatively, we may hypothesize that the same constructs are being tapped by the same measure in both cultures but that the constructs are more highly correlated in one culture than in the other (for some theoretical reasons). Here we would hope to find equality of factor loadings but difference (i.e., lack of invariance) in factor variances-covariances.

The MG-CFA approach to measurement invariance analysis is often a precursor analysis (for testing the measurement model) in what is called multiple-group structural equation modeling in which the interest is in modeling between-group differences/similarities in causal relationships among constructs taking into account measurement properties.

The MG-CFA approach can also be extended to apply to tests of measurement invariance of responses across time (i.e., in longitudinal studies where the same measure is administered to the same individuals on two or more occasions) using what is known as longitudinal CFA (LCFA). Other extensions include means and covariance analyses (MACS), multiple-indicator latent growth modeling. The logic of measurement invariance analysis using MG-CFA can be used to model between-groups or within-group across time differences in parameters that represent substantive differences, changes, or processes. The logic of differential item functioning and different construals of type of change (e.g., alpha, beta, gamma change; nine fundamental questions of change, see Chan, 1998a) provide the basis for specifying, testing, and interpreting these substantive measurement invariance models. For details on these extensions, see Chan (1998a, 2000, 2002a, 2002b), Chan and Schmitt (2000), and Chan, Ramey, Ramey, and Schmitt (2000).

OTHER DATA ANALYTIC TECHNIQUES

Because textbook discussions on data analytic techniques typically do not relate the techniques to cross-cultural research, this section illustrates how established techniques may be applied to address cross-cultural questions.

The nature of the research question in the IHRM study, the study design, and the nature of the data obtained should drive the choice of statistical technique for data analysis. The most commonly asked IHRM question is probably a direct comparison of the group mean differences on the focal variable across two or more culture groups. Assuming we have a continuous variable, the appropriate techniques to use are the independent-samples t-test (for two groups) or one-way ANOVA. Note, however, that the appropriate use of these mean comparison techniques and indeed many other statistical techniques (including all techniques discussed below in this section) for direct comparisons of absolute scores across cultures assumes construct equivalence and measurement invariance of responses across culture groups. In addition, the use of these techniques tends to assume an etic rather than an emic paradigm because it is the former but not the latter that would assume and argue for construct equivalence and measurement invariance. However, regardless if one assumes an etic or emic approach, measurement invariance analysis may be performed to test the hypothesis of construct equivalence.

In direct comparisons of culture group mean scores, culture group membership is treated as the "independent variable" (but not in the strict sense of an experimental design where the independent variable is manipulated with random assignment to conditions) or more accurately the predictor variable, and the analysis is focused on the "main effect" of group membership or bivariate predictive relationship between group membership and scores on the focal variable. But culture could also be treated as a moderator variable. Specifically, this pertains to a moderator hypothesis that predicts the direction or magnitude of the relationship between a predictor X and a criterion Y varies across cultures. For example, one could hypothesize that the negative relationship between the extent of violation of a procedural justice rule (e.g., explanation of rationale for a decision) on employee fairness perceptions is stronger for an individualistic culture than a collectivistic culture. Another example is the moderator hypothesis that predicts employee's proactive personality predicts their job performance ratings positively in one culture but negatively in another culture. In these moderator hypotheses, culture is coded as group membership (Z) and its moderator effect on the X-Y relationship may be tested by performing a hierarchical regression analysis to test the statistical significance and amount of incremental variance in the criterion variable (Y) accounted for by the XZ interaction term over and above the variance accounted for jointly by X and Z representing the two main effects.

When there are more than two culture groups, it is still possible to test for culture moderator effects using regression analysis by appropriately coding the culture group membership variable. Alternatively, a more powerful and flexible analysis may be performed using multiple-group structural equation modeling (MG-SEM). In this analysis, the X-Y relationship is estimated in a model for each culture simultaneously and relevant nested multiple-group model comparisons (similar in logic to the MG-CFA described earlier) can be made to test for the equality or difference in the parameter estimates associated with the X-Y relationship. The MG-SEM analysis is a powerful method because it allows the researcher to compare any model of substantive relationships across cultures to see if the same model or different models apply across cultures and, if different models apply, the nature of the cross-cultural differences (i.e., magnitude, direction, and type of relationship linking variables in the model).

Often, culture group membership is a proxy variable for some psychological variable that is hypothesized to affect the criterion variable. In other words, the cultural difference on the criterion variable is in fact a mediation relationship where culture group membership affects the mediator variable, which in turn affects the criterion variable. For example, a researcher may expect individualistic and collectivistic cultures to differ in work-group cohesion because he or she hypothesizes that culture group membership (individualistic versus collectivistic) affects organizational citizenship behavior (e.g., altruism), which in turn affects work-group cohesion. This mediation hypothesis can be directly tested using mediation regression analysis. If there are several mediators postulated, either along the same causal chain or via independent paths, the multiple and complex mediations can be more rigorously tested using SEM analyses. It is also possible to test if mediations involving the focal variables differ (in magnitude, direction, type) across cultures by treating culture groups as distinct groups to be modeled in a MG-SEM analysis with the relevant nested multiple-group model comparisons.

ADVANCED ISSUES AND SUGGESTED FURTHER READINGS

There are several advanced issues in research methodology that are relevant to IHRM but are beyond the scope of this introductory and nontechnical chapter. This section highlights two categories of issues that have gained much attention recently and suggests readings for the interested reader to pursue further. The first category of issues concerns longitudinal modeling. First, longitudinal study designs are important because they aid in causal inferences, and this is especially important given that IHRM research cannot manipulate culture group membership in a true experimental design and cross-sectional study designs are highly limited in establishing causality. Second, many phenomena of interest in IHRM research involve changes and processes that unfold in various ways over time and different fundamental questions may be asked about different aspects of these temporal changes. Examples of these questions include cross-cultural differences in the nature of the change trajectory of a quantitative variable or the manner in which a quantitative variable changes over time. General issues in research methodology concerning longitudinal modeling are discussed in Chan (2002b). Fundamental questions on different aspects of changes over time in cross-cultural organizational research are discussed in Chan (2002c).

Another category of issues that have gained much attention recently concerns the hierarchical structure of the multilevel data inherent in IHRM datasets. In a hierarchical data structure, units of observation at one level of analysis (e.g., individuals) are nested (grouped) within units at a high level of analysis (e.g., cultures). There are many complexities inherent in multilevel research, including problems in validation of multilevel constructs, decomposition of sources of variance in responses, and the associated issues of multilevel measurement and data analysis. For example, to clarify conceptualizations and decide on measurements or operationalizations of similar constructs at multiple levels, we need to formulate and apply appropriate composition models. Composition models specify the functional relationships among phenomena or constructs at different levels of analysis that reference essentially the same content but that are qualitatively different at different levels. Specifying functional relationships between constructs at different levels provides a systematic framework for mapping the transformation across levels. Chan (1998b) proposed a typology of composition models that helps the researcher derive explicit transformation relationships that provide conceptual precision in the target construct, which in turn aids in the derivation of test implications for hypothesis testing. For a summary of the basic issues of conceptualization, measurement, data analysis, and inferences in multilevel research, see Chan (2005).

CONCLUSION

This chapter has adopted a more conceptual view of methodological issues than is usual in IHRM research by emphasizing fundamental issues of construct validity and appropriate inferences, as opposed to the traditional discussions on specific IHRM research methods and techniques. Table 4.2 provides a summary of the major issues discussed in the chapter, including some examples of practical implications for IHRM researchers, most of which have been discussed in this chapter.

TABLE 4.2
Major Issues and Examples of Practical Implications for International Human Resource Management Researchers

Major Issues	Examples of Practical Implications for Researchers
Explicating the nature of the research question	
(a) Descriptive versus explanatory questions	Naturalistic group comparison study designs may be adequate for addressing descriptive questions but problematic for addressing explanatory questions.
	To make explanatory inferences from cross-sectional correlational data or naturalistic longitudinal panel data, move beyond simple bivariate correlation analyses or comparisons of (culture) group means to employ more sophisticated and appropriate data analytic techniques.
(b) Culture universality versus specificity	Gather empirical support as opposed to assuming, without testing, the truth of culture universality or specificity. Avoid confirmatory bias due to untested assumption when sampling cultures, processing data, making decisions on data analysis, and interpreting findings. Need to identify what constitutes true variance, systematic error variance, and random error variance.
	If culture universality is the goal or assumption underlying the research question, ensure that the design, measurement, and study logistics will increase the validity or appropriateness of the methods for demonstrating robustness of findings or applicability of findings across cultures. Treat multiple cultures as multiple samples to demonstrate generalizability. Perform analyses on the cross-cultural data to establish measurement invariance in responses or equality of direction and magnitude of parameter estimates associated with corresponding relationships involving (presumably) identical variables across cultures.
	If culture specificity is the goal or assumption underlying the research question, consider the phenomenon of interest as inextricably tied to the culture sample and context of the study. Do not treat culture samples as multiple operationalizations to demonstrate generalizability, but treat them as constituting a moderator variable, which affects the magnitude, direction, or even meaning of the relationships involving the focal variables representing the phenomenon under study. Perform analyses on the cross-cultural data to demonstrate the lack of measurement invariance of responses or differences in direction/magnitude of relationships involving apparently identical variables across cultures.
(c) Etic versus emic approaches	Ensure that theory development and testing (measurement, data analysis, inferences) are consistent with the approach (etic versus emic) adopted.
	In etic approach, it is meaningful to make cross-cultural comparisons of scores (e.g., mean, variance) on the same construct. Ensure technical issues (e.g., translation) are adequately addressed when making comparisons.
	In emic approach, do not apply the definitions or measurement of constructs from one culture to another. Constructs are meaningfully defined and measured only when they are explicated in reference to the specific cultural context, and the essence of the construct is indigenous to the specific culture.

(Continued)

TABLE 4.2 (Continued)
Major Issues and Examples of Practical Implications for International Human Resource Management Researchers

Major Issues	Examples of Practical Implications for Researchers
Selecting appropriate designs, methods, and sampling	
(a) Selection of study design	Examine validity of study design in relation to the research question.
	Examine appropriateness of study design to each culture under investigation and explicate (if any) alternative hypotheses or interpretation of findings due to differential appropriateness of design across cultures.
	Examine strengths and weaknesses of correlational field studies and experimental laboratory studies to decide when to adopt which study design. Ideally, study a phenomenon of interest by developing a program of research that employs both correlational field studies and experimental laboratory studies in a complementary fashion.
	Consider the use of adequate field experiments, which have more realism over laboratory experiments (hence increasing external validity) and more control over correlational field studies (hence increasing internal validity).
	In studies that simulate situations or task conditions, maximize fidelity of the experience in representing the actual context to which study results are intended to generalize. Be sensitive to cultural differences in the mapping of meanings between simulation and actual experiences.
(b) Selection of method of data collection	Distinguish method of data collection from study design in order to identify relevant issues relating to measurement, data analysis, and inferences.
	Identify possible cultural differences in reactions to the use of a data collection method. The extent of popularity or novelty of a method is likely to vary across cultures.
	Make a clear distinction between test method (method of data collection) and test content or construct, to avoid contaminating cultural differences in test scores with unintended constructs associated with the test method. Decompose the observed variance in test scores into method variance and construct variance.
(c) Selection of sampling procedure	Evaluate validity issues in sampling in terms of the representativeness of the study's sample with respect to the target population about which the inferences are made. Use both the research question and the characteristics of the target population as the basis to evaluate the appropriateness of a sampling procedure.
	When testing hypotheses that assume culture universality, delimit an appropriate pool of numerous cultures representing different regions of the world to form the sampling frame. Ensure random and representative sampling of cultures from the pool to provide a sufficiently wide range of cultures in order to examine robustness of hypothesis across widely different cultural contexts. When testing for cultural differences on a dimension, ensure that cultures selected for inclusion differ sufficiently on the dimension so that the variation of the selected cultures' scores is representative of the corresponding variation in the population of cultures of interest.
	Note inferential problems associated with studies that compared only two countries, especially when the two countries differ in both culture and language.
	The adequacy of a sample of cultures selected for the cross-cultural study is affected by the adequacy of the sampling within each selected culture. Sampling within a culture should be representative of that culture in terms of respondent populations as well as the relevant dimensions and contexts of interest. Explicate the within-culture sampling criteria and ensure that they are consistently implemented in each culture. Note any implementation differences or problems and take them into account when analyzing data and interpreting results.

TABLE 4.2 (Continued)
Major Issues and Examples of Practical Implications for International Human Resource Management Researchers

Major Issues	Examples of Practical Implications for Researchers
Developing appropriate measurement	
(a) Reliability and validity	Maximize reliability and validity when measuring focal constructs.
(b) Language differences and translating questionnaires	Ensure translation equivalence (e.g., via blind back-translation) so that translated questionnaire reproduces all the semantic content associated with the wording of the items on the original questionnaire.
	Note that translation equivalence contributes to but does not necessarily imply construct equivalence. It is possible that the same semantic content (i.e., translation equivalence established) evokes different conceptual frames of reference, meanings, and interpretations across cultures (i.e., lack of construct equivalence). Hence, treat translation equivalence as one type of preliminary evidence and gather more convergent validity evidence in the construct validation process to establish construct equivalence across cultures.
(c) Response scale formats and response sets	Have enough scale points to capture psychologically real distinctions in ratings and to avoid artifactually imposing a range restriction problem on the data, but not so numerous that the level of refinement exceeds psychologically real distinctions and introduces additional random measurement error. The level of psychologically real distinctions (and hence optimal scale points) is dependent on the nature of the construct, although there is some consensus that five to seven scale points usually provide optimal distinctions.
	Identify possible cultural differences in tendency to use specific parts of the response scale regardless of the item content, and separate these differences from substantive differences in the focal construct when developing measures, analyzing data, and interpreting results.
	Identify possible cultural differences in social desirability responding in terms of impression management or self-deception, and separate these differences from substantive differences in the focal construct when developing measures, analyzing data, and interpreting results.
Performing appropriate data analyses	
(a) Measurement invariance	Distinguish between situations in which measurement invariance is a statistical hurdle that should be cleared before making direct between-culture group comparisons of scores and situations in which measurement invariance or lack thereof represents substantive between-culture group similarities or differences that are of theoretical interest.
	Apply appropriate data analytic techniques (e.g., multiple-group confirmatory factor analyses) to test explicit hypotheses about specific types of measurement invariance or lack thereof.
(b) Data analytic techniques	Ensure the choice of data analytic technique is driven by the research question, study design, and nature of the data obtained.
Advanced Issues	
(a) Longitudinal modeling	Where feasible, employ appropriate longitudinal study designs to aid causal inferences or examine changes and processes that unfold in various ways over time.
(b) Multilevel data	Apply relevant composition models and appropriate multilevel data analytic techniques to address issues associated with the hierarchical structure of multilevel data.

Understanding and applying the methodological principles underlying valid and useful IHRM research are more basic than technical knowledge of specific research methods. In addition, it should be evident from reading this chapter that no one specific method or technique is inherently better than others in IHRM research. Complementary methods are needed to produce integrative programs of research that will advance the field of IHRM. Hence, there is a need to better understand how we may integrate correlational and experimental designs, laboratory and field research, quantitative and qualitative approaches, multiple methods of data collection, and different data analytic techniques with different statistical assumptions. Such methodological integration will allow us to obtain triangulation of methods and approaches and achieve convergent validity in substantive inferences in IHRM research.

REFERENCES

Berkowitz, L., & Donnerstein, E. (1982). External validity is more than skin deep: Some answers to criticisms of laboratory experiments. *American Psychologist, 37,* 245–257.

Berry, J.W. (1969). On cross-cultural comparability. *International Journal of Psychology, 4,* 119–128.

Brislin, R. W., Lonner, W., & Thorndike, R. M. (1973). *Cross-cultural research methods.* New York: Wiley.

Chan, D. (1998a). The conceptualization and analysis of change over time: An integrative approach incorporating longitudinal means and covariance structures analysis (LMACS) and multiple indicator latent growth modeling (MLGM). *Organizational Research Methods, 1,* 421–483.

Chan, D. (1998b). Functional relations among constructs in the same content domain at different levels of analysis: A typology of composition models. *Journal of Applied Psychology, 83,* 234–246.

Chan, D. (2000). Detection of differential item functioning on the Kirton Adaption-Innovation Inventory using multiple-group mean and covariance structures analysis. *Multivariate Behavioral Research, 35,* 169–199.

Chan, D. (2001). Modeling method effects of positive affectivity, negative affectivity, and impression management in self reports of work attitudes. *Human Performance, 14,* 77–96.

Chan, D. (2002a). Latent growth modeling. In F. Drasgow & N. Schmitt (Eds.), *Measuring and analyzing behavior in organizations: Advances in measurement and data analysis* (pp. 302–349). San Francisco: Jossey-Bass.

Chan, D. (2002b). Longitudinal modeling. In S. Rogelberg (Ed.), *Handbook of research methods in industrial and organizational psychology* (pp. 412–430). Oxford: Blackwell.

Chan, D. (2002c). Questions about change over time in cross-cultural organizational research. *Asia Pacific Journal of Management, 19,* 449–457.

Chan, D. (2005). Multilevel research. In F. T. L. Leong & J. T. Austin (Eds.), *The psychology research handbook* (2nd ed. pp. 401–418). Thousand Oaks, CA: Sage.

Chan, D., Ramey, S., Ramey, C., & Schmitt, N. (2000). Modeling intraindividual changes in children's social skills at home and at school: A multivariate latent growth approach to understanding between-settings differences in children's social skills development. *Multivariate Behavioral Research, 35,* 365–396.

Chan, D., & Schmitt, N. (1997). Video-based versus paper-and-pencil method of assessment in situational judgment tests: Subgroup differences in test performance and face validity perceptions. *Journal of Applied Psychology, 82,* 143–159.

Chan, D., & Schmitt, N. (2000). Interindividual differences in intraindividual changes in proactivity during organizational entry: A latent growth modeling approach to understanding newcomer adaptation. *Journal of Applied Psychology, 85,* 190–210.

Chan, D., & Schmitt, N. (2005). Situational judgment tests. In A. Evers, O. Smit-Voskuijl, & N. Anderson (Eds.), *Handbook of personnel selection* (p. 219–242). Oxford, UK: Blackwell Publishers, Inc.

Ganster, D., Hennessey, H., & Luthans, F. (1983). Social desirability response effects: Three alternative models. *Academy of Management Journal, 26,* 321–331.

Gelfand, M. J., Raver, J. L., & Ehrharts, K. H. (2002). Methodological issues in cross-cultural organizational research. In S. G. Rogelberg (Ed.), *Handbook of research methods in industrial and organizational psychology* (pp. 216–246). Malden, MA: Blackwell Publishers.

Gilliland, S. W., & Chan, D. (2001). Justice in organizations: Theory, methods, and applications. In N. Anderson, D. S. Ones, H. K. Sinangil, & C. Viswesvaran (Eds.), *Handbook of industrial, work, and organizational psychology* (pp. 143–165). Thousand Oaks, CA: Sage.

Greenberg, J. (1986). Determinants of perceived fairness of performance evaluations. *Journal of Applied Psychology, 71,* 340–342.

Greenberg, J. (1987). Using diaries to promote procedural justice in performance appraisals. *Social Justice Research, 1,* 219–234.

Greenberg, J. (1990). Employee theft as a reaction to underpayment inequity: The hidden cost of pay cuts. *Journal of Applied Psychology, 75,* 561–568.

Greenberg, J. (1993). Stealing in the name of justice. *Organizational Behavior and Human Decision Processes, 54,* 81–103.

Krosnick, E. S, & Fabrigar, L. R. (1997). Designing rating scales for effective measurement in surveys. In L. Lyberg, P. Biemer, M. Collins, E. De Leeuw, C. Dippo, N. Schwarz, & D. Trewin (Eds.), *Survey measurement and process quality* (pp. 141–164). New York: Wiley.

Lee, C., & Green, R. T. (1991). Cross-cultural examination of the Fishbein behavioral intentions model. *Journal of International Business Studies, 22,* 289–305.

Moshinsky, D. (2000). *Acculturation gap and grandparents' perceptions of their grandchildren in families of refugees from the former Soviet Union.* Unpublished undergraduate honor's thesis, University of Maryland, College Park.

Nisbett, R. E. (2003). *The geography of thought: How Asians and Westerners think differently and why.* London: Nicholas Brealey Publishing.

Paulhus, D. L. (1984). Two-component models of socially desirable responding. *Journal of Personality and Social Psychology, 46,* 598–609.

Paulhus, D. L. (1986). Self-deception and impression management in test responses. In A. Angleitner & J. S. Wiggens (Eds.), *Personality measurement via questionnaires: Current issues in theory and measurement* (pp. 143–165). Berlin: Springer-Verlag.

Ryan, A. M., Chan, D., Ployhart, R., & Slade, L. A. (1999). Employee attitude surveys in a multinational organization: Considering language and culture in assessing measurement equivalence. *Personnel Psychology, 52,* 37–58.

Triandis, H. C. (1994). Cross-cultural industrial and organizational psychology. In H. C. Triandis, M. D. Dunnette, and L. M. Hough (eEds.), *Handbook of industrial and organizational psychology* (Vol. 4, pp. 103–172). Palo Alto, CA: Consulting Psychologists Press.

Vandenberg, R. J., & Lance, C. E. (2000). A review and synthesis of the measurement invariance literature: Suggestions, practices, and recommendations for organizational research. *Organizational Research Methods, 3,* 4–69.

Van de Vijer, F., & Leung, K. (1997). *Methods and data analysis for cross-cultural research.* Thousand Oaks, CA: Sage.

5 Human Resource Strategy in the International Context

Paul R. Sparrow and Werner Braun

CONTENTS

In this chapter we address three questions central to the field of strategic international human resource management (SIHRM):

1. *What* are the main SIHRM strategy models and concepts?
2. Should a firm's strategy help decide their HR processes in other cultures?
3. *Do* HR strategies developed in western countries in reality apply to other cultures?

    In this opening section we address the first question by concentrating on what is known so far in this area, including empirical research and the main conceptual models that have been proposed. Human resource management (HRM) is a relatively new term even in Western society: it is said to have evolved in its best known form in the United States and arrived in the mid-1980s in the United Kingdom and much of Europe. HRM evolved as a concept in the 1980s clearly differentiating itself from the study and discipline of personnel administration and personnel management (Staehle, 1994; Storey, 1995). HRM introduces a view of people as resources that have strategic importance for the creation of competitive advantages for an organization. HRM, furthermore, seeks an "internal fit" among the HRM functional areas (e.g. in the form of consistent "bundles" of HRM policies and practices) (Tichy, Fombrun, & Devanna, 1982; Schuler & Rogovsky, 1998) and an "external fit" between such HRM "bundles" of policies and practices and the corporation's strategy (Tichy et al., 1982; Schuler & Jackson, 1987; Schuler, Jackson, & Storey, 2001), as well as its external environment (Beer, Spector, Lawrence, Mills, & Walton, 1985). HRM also introduces a change in perspective by involving top management in the HRM responsibility (Staehle, 1994) and proposes a shift of competences away from the central personnel departments back into line management in order to enhance the strategic integration (Wächter, 1987; Storey, 1995). In terms of outcomes, HRM does not merely seek the employees' compliance with rules and regulations of the organization or administrative efficiency, standard performance, and cost minimization (Guest, 1991). The HRM outcome goals are rather a high employee commitment, and high quality and highly flexible staff (Guest, 1997). Storey (1995, p. 5) defines HRM as "a distinctive approach to employment management which seeks to achieve competitive advantage through the strategic deployment of a highly committed and capable workforce, using an integrated array of cultural, structural and personnel techniques."

In an international context we have seen the development of the field of SIHRM. This has been defined as "human resource management issues, functions and policies and practices that result from the strategic activities of multinational enterprises and that impact on the international concerns and goals of those enterprises" (Schuler, Dowling, & DeCieri, 1993). In contrast to comparative HRM, SIHRM essentially focuses on strategic HRM in multinational corporations (MNCs) and recognizes the importance of linking HRM policies and practices with organizational strategies of the MNC (for example Adler & Ghadar, 1990, 1993; Milliman, Von Glinow, & Nathan, 1991; Taylor, Beechler, & Napier, 1996). The SIHRM literature reflects the growing importance of MNCs and the influence of complex global strategic business decisions on the HRM activities of MNCs (Ferner, 1994; DeCieri & Dowling, 1997; DeCieri, Cox, & Fenwick, 2001; Schuler, Budhwar, & Florkowski, 2002; Schuler & Jackson, 2005). At a conceptual level, SIHRM frameworks have considered an increasing amount of independent variables as influencing factors on the IHRM activities of the MNC over the last decades (Perlmutter, 1969; Perlmutter & Heenan, 1974; Adler, 1991; Adler & Ghadar, 1990, 1993; Milliman et al., 1991; Schuler et al., 1993; Taylor et al., 1996; Schuler & Jackson, 2005). It is the recognition of this variety of influencing factors that leads to a heightened complexity in the perception of relationships between an MNC and its IHRM activities, and which makes the subject important and relevant for research (Schuler et al., 2002; Schuler & Jackson, 2005).

CONCEPTS UNDERPINNING SIHRM

Before detailing the main strands of theoretical thought we draw attention to some fundamental principles that have shaped thinking in the area. Theoretical frameworks in SIHRM have been—and still are—influenced by three developments that emerged in broad historical sequence:

1. Early attention to life-cycle models based on the concept of fit between HRM and (a) progressive stages of the attitude of management at headquarters to international operations; (b) product life cycles; or (c) organizational life cycles.
2. Subsequent development of ideas about organizational design and the process through which strategy and structure can be matched, or ideal MNCs be created.
3. Development of integrative contingency frameworks premised on the need to both integrate and differentiate HRM policies.

Next we explain the influence that each of these developments has had. Having explained these influences we go on to outline four different theoretical underpinnings of the literature.

LIFE-CYCLE MODELS

The early attention to life-cycle models reflected the need for strategic fit between HRM policies and practices and various ways of classifying the evolution of the firm, while the later development of broader contingency frameworks merely expanded the complexity of the "fit" equation. One of the earliest set of studies to leave a strong mark on future SIHRM frameworks was by Perlmutter (1969) and Perlmutter and Heenan (1974). These studies suggested that staffing decisions within

MNCs were a consequence of a progressive series of attitudes of the management at headquarters. With slight variations their differentiation among four distinct attitudes (ethnocentrism, polycentrism, regiocentrism, and geocentrism) can be found throughout much of the theoretical SIHRM literature (see for example, Adler & Ghadar, 1993; Dowling, Schuler, & Welch, 1994; Kamoche, 1996).

Proponents of life-cycle models argue that there is a link between the variation in MNC HRM policies and practices and either the product life cycles in companies or the organizational life cycle in these organizations. For Adler and Ghadar (1990, 1993) the different internationalization strategies of an MNC and the corresponding HRM strategies (expressed by different degrees of integration and differentiation of practice) are related to internationalization phases dependent on the organization's product life cycles with a "fit" required between the HRM system and these cycles. Milliman et al. (1991) extended the model by Adler and Ghadar (1990) principally by looking at organizational life cycles rather than product life cycles. They argued that product life cycles are difficult to apply to MNCs because in many sectors (for example, high technology industries) products have a short life cycle and in any event typically MNCs have multiple products each at different stages of their life cycle. Drawing upon work by Miller and Friesen (1980, 1984) that differentiates between four stages of organizational development (birth, growth, maturity, and revival) they outlined phases of organization initiation, functional growth, controlled growth, and strategic integration. In each of these organizational development stages different levels of external fit (between HRM activities and the MNC business context) and internal fit (between the different HRM functional areas) are necessary. Consequently human resource flexibility becomes central to effective internationalization, and is dependent upon the capacity of HRM to facilitate the ability of the organization to adapt to changing demands both from within the MNC or the MNC's context both effectively and in a timely manner (Milliman et al., 1991).

Life-cycle models can be criticized on three main grounds:

1. They focus on only one independent variable (i.e., the product life cycle or the organizational life cycle) and do not take further influencing variables into consideration. While large diversified MNCs are typically dealing with multiple product life cycles simultaneously, in practice they are also confronted with a wide range of other endogenous and exogenous factors influencing their IHRM policies and practice design.
2. The exact description of a product or organizational life cycle can only be given post hoc which means that such models only have descriptive value rather than predictive qualities.
3. They fall short of discussing *how* an MNC can implement varying international policies and practices while also accounting for the contingencies of multiple host countries.

ORGANIZATION DESIGN MODELS

The second development to influence the literature has been the advent of organization design models. The challenge of considering *how* an MNC can best implement international policies and practices was taken up broadly when attention was directed to organization design and the match between strategy and structure. Many of these assumptions about organization design in MNCs are in turn driven by information-processing theory, a basic assumption of which is that organizations are open social systems that are exposed to both external and internal sources of uncertainty (defined as the difference between information possessed and information required to complete a task). MNCs need to develop information-processing mechanisms capable of dealing with this uncertainty (Galbraith, 1973, 1977; Tushman & Nadler, 1978; Egelhoff, 1991). Information processing in organizations is generally defined as including the gathering of data, the processing and transformation of data into information, and the communication and storage of information in the organization (Tushman & Nadler, 1978; Egelhoff, 1991). According to this perspective, effective organizations are those that create a "fit" between their information-processing capacities and the information-processing requirements determined by such factors as their strategy, task characteristics, interunit interdependence, and their organizational environment.

Applying this perspective to MNCs, Egelhoff (1991) argues that such organizations are large and complex and have very high information-processing requirements, especially if they are pursuing a transnational strategy that requires a reciprocal interdependence between affiliates and headquarters. Information-processing requirements are also high in MNCs because of their focus on flexible, people-based coordination and control mechanisms. Galbraith (1973, p. 15) differentiates between different organizational design features all holding different levels of information-processing capacity (in increasing order): rules and programs; hierarchical referral; goal-setting; vertical information systems; and lateral relations. The higher the information-processing requirement, the more organizations will steer towards the application of lateral relations, such as direct contact between individuals, liaison roles, task forces, teams, and matrix designs (Egelhoff, 1991). MNCs therefore frequently reach the limits of their information-processing capacity.

Egelhoff (1999) went on to differentiate between two perspectives of the MNC that came to dominate thinking about strategy: (a) *Traditional equilibrium models*, dominant in the 1970s and early 1980s, grounded in an industrial organization perspective and epitomized by the early strategy-structure models of Chandler (1962) and Stopford and Wells (1972), as well as the models of the process school of strategy (Prahalad, 1975) and a Porterian view of international strategy (Porter, 1986). (b) "*New change models*," appearing towards the late 1980s, grounded in such theoretical perspectives as the resource-based or knowledge-based view of the firm and seen in the work of Bartlett and Ghoshal (1989) and Hedlund (1986, 1993).

We now discuss the more recent development of new change models. Whereas the early strategy-structure models make a distinction between different structural and strategic MNC orientations depending on certain contingent factors, the new change models formulated an "ideal-type" MNC organizational structure and strategy (Egelhoff, 1999; Harzing, 1999). Some of the most noted examples of these new change models include:

- The heterarchy (Hedlund, 1986)
- Paradigm S (Perlmutter and Trist, 1986)
- The transnational (Bartlett and Ghoshal, 1989)
- The horizontal organization (White and Poynter, 1990)

Among these models, Bartlett and Ghoshal's (1989) concept of the transnational as well as Hedlund's (1986) heterarchy can be regarded as the most influential in the area of strategic management as well as organizational behaviour (Harzing, 1999). The development of these ideal-type MNC organizational structures can be linked to a general evolution of research into MNCs. Birkinshaw and Morrison (1995) noted that research into the MNC evolved in two critical directions during the mid-eighties: a shift away from seeing the MNC as a monolithic entity best viewed from a headquarters perspective toward an emphasis on the MNC affiliate as a unit of analysis (see also Gupta & Govindarajan, 1991; Wolf, 1997); a challenge of the old standing assumptions of equilibrium and "fit" between a firm's strategy, structure, and environment by introducing assumptions of permanently changing business environments that would require equally fast changing organizational responses.

Some important concepts continue to influence the field today as a result of discussion of ideal structures, notably the need to create a matrix in the mind of managers. The ideal-type models suggest that adjustment is handled out of the same organizational design. They also began to change many assumptions about HR strategy. Organizational change cannot occur within conditions of equilibrium. Consequently Egelhoff (1999) asserts that in these models there is no attempt to make the organizational design dependent on variations in strategy and the environment. Moreover, under the assumption of an unpredictable, frequent, and continuous change of strategic and environmental factors, they promoted the idea that the competitive advantage of an MNC cannot reside in any one operation or country and therefore the strategic importance of the affiliates worldwide and their employees is emphasized (see for example Bartlett & Ghoshal, 1986). Consequently, organizational solutions to solve the simultaneous requirements of global integration and local responsiveness (the integration–differentiation dilemma) are less structure-based but rely instead on more informal, people-based coordination and control mechanisms (Roth, Schweiger, & Morrison, 1991). Hence, the solution is seen in creating a "matrix in the minds" of MNC managers (Bartlett & Ghoshal, 1989, 1990).

Given the need to create a matrix in the mind, the emphasis shifted to creating shared values through a corporate culture (Hedlund, 1986; Bartlett & Ghoshal, 1989; White and Poynter, 1990), a normative control system (Hedlund, 1986), the creation of an organizational context (Doz & Prahalad, 1981), and an input-control system (Hamilton & Kashlak, 1999). As Harzing (1999) points out, it is evident that this heightens the role of HRM within MNCs, as companies will increasingly depend on:

- The socialization of employees to ensure that employees share organizational values and goals and are socialized into a common organizational culture (see for example, Edström & Galbraith, 1977a, 1977b, 1978; Ouchi, 1977, 1979, 1980; Mintzberg, 1979, 1983; Child, 1984; Baliga & Jaeger, 1984; Kenter, 1985; Pucik & Katz, 1986; Bartlett & Ghoshal, 1989; Martinez & Jarillo, 1989; Hennart, 1991; Evans, Pucik, & Barsoux, 2002).
- Informal, lateral, or horizontal exchange of information, which includes mutual adjustment, informal communication, and coordination by feedback (see for example, March & Simon, 1958; Thompson, 1967; Lawrence & Lorsch, 1967; Mintzberg, 1979, 1983; Martinez & Jarillo, 1989; Evans et al., 2002).
- Formalized lateral or cross-departmental relations. These include (temporarily) formalized ways to exchange information, such as task forces, cross-functional teams, and integrative departments (see for example Lawrence & Lorsch, 1967; Galbraith, 1973; Martinez & Jarillo, 1989; Evans et al., 2002).

In addition to influencing the field through the idea of creating a matrix in the mind, organization design models have influenced our ideas on how MNCs build capability. It would be fair to say then that until very recently the international management literature adopted a fairly traditional stance to the building of such capabilities within MNCs. The vast majority of models of organizational design and internationalization suggested a clear sequence of evolutionary stages through which the organization has to evolve. A sequence of stages of organization design—variously called international, multinational, global, and transnational/network/heterarchy—has been outlined (Bartlett & Ghoshal, 1989), which suggests a pattern can be found in the way in which the internationalization process has to be managed. In general, the organization structure has to respond to a series of strains that are faced, such as the challenges of growth, increased geographical spread, and the need for improved control and coordination across business units. Organizations have to build capability in each stage sequentially in order to maintain integrated standards for some business lines but remain locally responsive in others (Hamel & Prahalad, 1985; Yip, 1992; Ashkenas, Ulrich, Jick, & Kerr, 1995). Some firms might develop through the various phases rapidly, and might be able to accelerate the process through acquisitions, but any attempt to leapfrog over intermediate steps is generally considered to result in dysfunctions.

Reflecting this view, there has been considerable research examining the role of HRM within MNCs pursuing a global/transnational SIHRM orientation (DeCieri & Dowling, 1997; Egelhoff, 1999; DeCieri et al., 2001; Schuler et al., 2002; Schuler & Jackson, 2005). Similarly, attention has been given to MNC structural attempts to facilitate global/transnational SIHRM orientations, such as an examination of the role of regional headquarters (Daniels, 1986, 1987; Schütte, 1996, 1998).

However, there are two pressing research questions that need to be addressed today: can we accelerate the pace at which organizations progress through the constituent phases? Must organizations really work through each phase in a linear sequence to build organizational capability or can new organizational forms short-circuit the process? In relation to the latter question, the assumption of linear and broadly sequential phases of organizational development no longer seems to fit the modern business environment in which there are many organizations (not necessarily MNCs of course) that begin life as global start-ups, without having to evolve through a series of levels of HRM flexibility and fit (Parker, 1998). Moreover, in relation to SIHRM practices, Braun and Warner (2002) note that many specifications are prescriptive and not based on any evidence that tests effectiveness. Examples in the "global" (Adler & Ghadar, 1990) or the "strategic integration" (Milliman et al., 1991) phases are the discussion of necessary SIHRM policies and practices such as recruiting globally irrespective of nationality, making international assignments and mobility a key for advancement into top management positions, appraising for and rewarding cross-cultural adjustment skills and mobility, and introducing global rewards structures. Research needs to ascertain whether this is a mere catalogue of prescriptive measures, and also provide contextual insight into the workability and effectiveness of such policies.

CONTINGENCY MODELS

The third development to influence the literature has been the development of contingency models. In response to this need for greater sophistication, we have seen the specification of complex contingent relationships. In this last section on general influences we trace the roots of ideas about integration, differentiation, responsiveness, and the transmission of strategic HR capabilities. The field has moved rapidly in recent years in the direction of uniting various theoretical perspectives and identifying a multitude of influencing independent variables, resulting in a number of contingency models (see for example Schuler et al., 1993; Taylor et al., 1996; DeCieri & Dowling, 1998; Schuler et al., 2002). These contingency frameworks are now very elaborate and include an extensive array of independent variables. Common, however, to all these frameworks is the influence of the integration–differentiation concept by Lawrence and Lorsch (1967) as well as the integration–responsiveness (IR) model by Prahalad and Doz (1987). In other words, an MNC's perceived need for integration and control on the one hand and the perceived need for local responsiveness on the other provide a core influence for their choice of SIHRM policies and practices. Schuler and colleagues (Schuler et al., 1993, 2002) refer to this dual need by emphasizing two strategic MNC components: the MNC's interunit linkages, representing the need for integration and control; and the MNC's internal operations, representing the need for local sensitivity.

The dual need for integration and for local responsiveness reflects the fact that MNCs are geographically dispersed and goal-disparate organizations, which need to be coordinated or integrated in some form and to some degree. Ideally this integration is achieved with attention to being globally competitive, efficient, responsive, and flexible to local needs and conditions, as well as being able to transfer learning across units (Bartlett & Ghoshal, 1989). Reflecting the increasing awareness of important explanatory variables, Schuler et al. (1993, 2002) and Dowling, Welch, and Schuler (1998) differentiate between two sets of factors: exogenous (growing by successive additions to the outside) and endogenous (increasing by internal growth and formed within). These influence the strategic HRM components and the IHRM policy and practice decisions. Exogenous factors include industry characteristics; country/regional characteristics (Schuler et al., 1993); country culture (Schuler et al., 2002); and interorganizational networks (DeCieri & Dowling, 1998; Dowling et al., 1998). Endogenous factors include the organizational structure of the MNC (international structure, intra-organizational networks, mechanisms of coordination); international entry mode (DeCieri & Dowling, 1998; Dowling et al., 1998); headquarters international orientation; competitive strategy (corporate-level, business-level strategy); experience in managing international operations (Schuler et al., 1993); and organizational and industry life cycle.

The more recent contingency model by Taylor et al. (1996) develops the work of Schuler et al. (1993) by shifting the perspective towards factors at *three different organizational levels*: corporate level; affiliate level; and individual employee groups. At each level different independent variables are considered to influence the IHRM policies and practice design. In their contingency model they asked "why should firms want to export their HRM system in the first place?" Their work therefore has relevance to the second of our core questions: *should* a firm's strategy help decide their HR processes in other cultures? They explained the circumstances under which strategic HR capabilities are *considered to be generalizable* and capable of transmission or diffusion from the parent organization to affiliates. They argue that different levels of integration and responsiveness within an MNC's IHRM policies and practices are affected by an overall "strategic international HRM (SIHRM) *system orientation*" and the degree of similarity of affiliates' HRM systems to the parent company's HRM system at the corporate level as well as at an affiliate level (p. 717, see also Rosenzweig & Nohria, 1994; Hannon, Huang, & Jaw, 1995; Lu & Björkman, 1997). Two factors shape an organization's SIHRM orientation: whether the parent company actually has a global (as opposed to multidomestic) strategy; and top management believe that the HRM capability of the organization is a source of strategic advantage.

They further considered that there are three orientations (adapted forms of the categorization by Perlmutter, 1969) that result from the answers to these questions as the organization develops, the first of which results from a multidomestic strategy and the second and third from a global strategy. The SIHRM orientations are:

1. *Exportive (ethnocentric)* (a wholesale transfer of HRM policies and practices successful in the parent organization to affiliates).
2. *Adaptive (polycentric)* (the creation of HRM systems with a maximum of adaptation to the local context and conditions).
3. *Integrative (geocentric)* (transfer best practice from wherever it might be found among affiliates in the organization).

These levels of similarity in systems at the subsidiary level are in turn influenced by four contingent factors, such as the strategic role of the subsidiary, whether the site is greenfield or an acquisition, and the cultural distance and legal distance between the parent and subsidiary.

Taylor et al.'s (1996) framework is, however, driven by the assumption that MNCs should develop an *integrative* approach to HRM, sharing best practices from all parts of the organization to create a worldwide system. The focus of the framework is on the need to create global integration—a geocentric orientation—yet they note that the mechanisms to identify and transfer best-HRM practice are *generally not in place in most MNCs.*

We make one final observation on the influence exerted by contingency models before analyzing the four main theoretical perspectives. The contingency frameworks by Schuler et al. (1993) and Taylor et al. (1996) have received praise as they have unified various theoretical perspectives and captured a wide array of independent variables influencing the design of IHRM policies and practices. There are also three criticisms of these models (Weber, Festing, Dowling, & Schuler, 1998):

1. The accumulation of independent variables makes these integrative frameworks increasingly untestable.
2. The "independence" of a number of variables in the frameworks may be questioned. Just taking one example, Porter's (1986) work assumes that industry characteristics and competitive strategy influence one another.
3. Despite the large number of independent variables, existing contingency models still only explain a small part of the overall variance found in HRM policies and practices between MNCs operating in varying contexts. Context and institutional pressures are more complex than even these models assume.

There are then a series of research questions in relation to contingency models. Given the limited variation explained by studies, are there situations in which an integrative approach to HRM globally is wholly *undesirable*, and so, what? Some elements of an HRM system might be required to converge (follow a geocentric path) while other elements may be allowed to remain different. Which elements should converge, why and under what circumstances?

Criticisms aside, the arrival of the integrative theoretical frameworks by Schuler et al. (1993) and Taylor et al. (1996) demonstrates that the field is drawing increasingly on theoretical perspectives from a variety of disciplines, such as sociology, economics, management, and psychology. Each theory has explained some organizational behavior, but in so doing conveys different assumptions about the level and cause of influencing factors in the decision-making process of organizations (for an overview of these issues see Wright & McMahan, 1992; Schuler & Jackson, 1995; Schuler, 2000a, 2000b; Schuler & Jackson, 2005; Fenton-O'Creevy, Gooderham, & Nordhaug, 2005).

THEORETICAL UNDERPINNINGS IN THE SIHRM LITERATURE

Having explained how the three developments of life cycle, organization design, and contingency models have influenced thinking, in this second part of the chapter we consider the question *should* a firm's strategy help decide its HR processes in other cultures? We noted that Taylor et al's (1996) work touches on this question, but to answer this question we move into a discussion of some key theories. It is not possible to discuss exhaustively all the theoretical perspectives connected with the SIHRM field in this chapter, but we provide a brief outline of what we see as the four main perspectives:

1. Resource dependence theory
2. Resource-based view of the firm
3. Knowledge-based view of the firm and organizational learning theory
4. Relational and social capital theory

We leave discussion of a fifth theory, institutional theory, which asks "*do* HR strategies developed in Western countries in reality apply to other cultures?" to our treatment of this question in the final section of the chapter. However, let us return to the question of *should* the strategy help decide the HR processes across countries.

RESOURCE DEPENDENCE THEORY

The first of the four theoretical perspectives that answer the question of "should" is the resource dependence model (Pfeffer & Salancik, 1978; Pfeffer & Moore, 1980; Pfeffer & Cohen, 1984; Pfeffer & Davis-Blake, 1987). This focuses predominantly on power relationships and resource exchanges between an organization and its constituency. From this perspective, organizational decision making is not seen as an outcome of strategic choice. Rather, the theory assumes that all organizations depend on a flow of valuable resources (e.g. money, technology, management expertise) into the organization in order to continue functioning. An MNC affiliate may have more or less dependence and power, as these resources are controlled by various actors, internal to the MNC (e.g. parent company or regional operations) or external to it (e.g. government institutions).

The ability to exercise control over any of these valued resources provides the actor with an important source of power. The higher the scarcity of the valued resource, the more the power of the entity that controls that resource increases (Wright & McMahan, 1992). If external parties control vital resources, an organization is vulnerable and will strive to acquire control in order to minimize its dependence (DeCieri & Dowling, 1998). Pfeffer and Salancik (1978) and Scott (1987) argue that organizations can attempt to reduce this dependency through buffering (e.g. internalizing control by coding of inputs for the production process, or stockpiling), as well as using bridging strategies (e.g., bargaining for more independence, co-optation, joint ventures, or the absorption of resource holders). The theory has been tested empirically through the work of authors such as Pfeffer and Moore (1980), Pfeffer and Cohen (1984), and Pfeffer and Davis-Blake (1987).

This resource dependence perspective is one of the main theoretical perspectives in the more recent integrative SIHRM frameworks (see Schuler et al., 1993; Taylor et al., 1996) discussed earlier and has also helped to explain some of the empirical findings by Rosenzweig and Nohria (1994), Hannon et al. (1995), and Lu and Björkman (1997).

RESOURCE-BASED VIEWS OF THE FIRM

The second theoretical perspective that answers the "should" question is the resource-based view (RBV) of the firm. Wright and Snell and various colleagues argue that this view has emerged as perhaps the most predominant theoretical perspective (Wright, Dunford, & Snell, 2001; Morris, Snell, & Wright, 2006). They feel that it is particularly attractive to SIHRM researchers because it focuses on the execution of various strategies and draws attention to the potential value of a firm's internal asset stocks in this task. As seen earlier in the chapter, SIHRM contingency frameworks have introduced the RBV perspective in connection with top management attitudes regarding the transfer of HRM policies and practices abroad (Taylor et al., 1996).

The idea of looking at firms as a broader set of resources goes back to the work of Penrose (1959). The RBV sees the firm not through its activities in the product market but as a unique bundle of tangible and intangible resources (Wernerfelt, 1984). Whereas the economic perspective views resources as immediately accessible on factor markets (which effectively eliminates firm resource heterogeneity and immobility as a possible competitive advantage), in contrast, the RBV perspective stresses the inherent immobility of valuable factors of production and the time and cost required to accumulate those resources (Peteraf, 1993). Firms are idiosyncratic. Throughout their history they accumulate different physical assets and acquire different intangible organizational assets of tacit learning and dynamic routines (Collis, 1991). Imitation of these assets is only possible if firms go through the same process of irreversible investment or learning (Barney, 1989; Dierickx & Cool, 1989). Historical evolution of a firm in practice constrains its strategic choice and so affects market outcomes. On the other hand, complex social phenomena can be a source of sustainable competitive advantage and will affect organization structure independently of strategic choice (Barney, 1991).

Barney (1991) and similarly Peteraf (1993) argue that in order for firm resources to hold the potential of sustained competitive advantage they must be:

- Valuable, that is, the resource exploits opportunities or neutralizes threats in a firm's environment
- Rare among a firm's current and potential competitors
- Imperfectly imitable, that is, other firms do not possess the same resources and cannot obtain them easily
- Nonsubstitutable with strategically equivalent resources (Ghemawat, 1986; Rumelt, 1987; Dierickx & Cool, 1989; Peteraf, 1993)

The RBV perspective has been discussed in connection with HRM for some time (see Schuler & MacMillan, 1984; Wright & McMahan, 1992; Wright, McMahan, & McWilliams, 1994) and considerable tacit knowledge is considered to reside within the whole HRM system (Lado & Wilson, 1994; Huselid, 1995). However, RBV theories of the firm also present the clearest argument as to *why* firms must transfer capabilities globally. Morris, Snell, and Wright (2006) argue that because MNCs operate in multiple environments they possess variations in both their people (reflecting the skill sets created by national business systems) and in their practices (which reflect local requirements, laws, and cultures). They benefit from a global workforce both by capitalizing on the superior skills that can be found by accessing global labor pools, and by exploiting the cultural synergies of a diverse workforce. SIHRM practices can contribute to the effective management of a firm's employees by enabling such outcomes. This variation is also a potential source of advantage at a local level. In discussing the transfer of HR best practice on a global basis, strategists argue that in a competitive marketplace the act of integrating disparate sources of knowledge within the bounds of the organization becomes a source of advantage (Grant, 1996). Indeed, one of the basic premises of internationalization research is that in order to succeed internationally a firm has to possess some highly advantageous, but intangible, knowledge-based asset.

Ghoshal and Bartlett (1988), Bartlett and Ghoshal (1997), and Nohria and Ghoshal (1997) argue that it is the utilization of organizational capabilities worldwide that provides MNCs with an important source of competitive advantage. The term organizational capability has been developed by both Ulrich (1987) in the HR field and Prahalad and Doz (1987) in the strategy field. As a concept it combines ideas from the fields of management of change, organizational design, and leadership. Ulrich and Lake (1990) argued that organizational capability was about competing "from the inside out." Organizational capability therefore focuses on the ability of a firm's internal processes, systems, and management practices to meet customer needs and to direct both the skills and efforts of employees towards achieving the goals of the organization.

This collection of capabilities reflects things such as a firm's "key success factors," "culture," "brand," "shared-mindset," or "processes" (Ulrich & Lake, 1990; Lawler, 1997) and they reflect "… a firm's capacity to deploy resources, usually in combination, applying organizational processes to effect a desired end" (De Saá-Pérez & García-Falcón, 2002, p. 124). International expansion is only possible when firms can transfer their distinctive knowledge-assets abroad into new international markets (Dunning, 1993; Caves, 1996). If one chooses to follow this logic, then if there is any strategic advantage to be found in a firm's HRM capability (its philosophy, policies, and practices) then this HR capability itself must also be transferred into different geographies around the world.

The capability to effect internal cross-border transfers of HRM practice (along with the knowledge needed to link this practice into local organizational effectiveness) becomes a core competence (Flood, Ramamoorthy, & Liu, 2003). With regard to the question of whether firms should transfer their HRM systems, when organizations globalize they must (Stonehouse, Hamill, Campbell, & Purdie, 2000):

- Learn how best to coordinate and deploy their various capabilities and exploit them in a large number of countries and markets
- Identify new resources in untapped markets that will strengthen their existing core competences
- Enhance existing competences by reconfiguring value-adding activities across a wider geography or range of operations

The RBV of the firm has been questioned more of late. Despite discussion of learning and knowledge transfer within the context of the RBV of the firm, until recently this perspective tended to emphasize the *role of the corporate center in MNCs,* which is generally assumed to be one of shaping the strategic direction of the organization and designing the strategic change programs pursued in the subsidiaries. The immobility in practice of many people and HRM practices also presents a challenge to the RBV of the firm. Ideas from this theory have to be combined with those from other perspectives to deal with the problem of stickiness in knowledge transfer. Though resources can provide a global advantage to the MNC as a whole, this is only *if* the knowledge, skills, and capabilities can be leveraged appropriately. We must draw upon organization learning perspectives, given that knowledge processes inside MNCs are central to the transfer of capability (Foss & Pedersen, 2004; Morris et al., 2006). Attention also has to be given to the mechanisms that explain why such *mutual* transfer of capability is beneficial to the organization, and how it actually happens (Collis, 1991; Hedlund & Ridderstråle, 1997; Kogut, 1997). There are a series of research questions in relation to the RBV:

- Specifically how do the following mechanisms develop the business and technological skills associated with mutual transfer of capabilities? International diversification into multiple markets, collaborating with organizations that have mutually complementary competences (for example through joint ventures), emphasizing strategic leadership roles for national subsidiaries, gaining access to foreign-based clusters of excellence, and building internal centers of excellence based on global best practice.

- Why must the organizational capabilities associated with strategic goals such as meeting customer needs be constituted in the same way in different international components of the firm?
- What does the pursuit of organizational capability mean for the design of IHRM functions and role of business partners? Do these issues make any difference to organizational effectiveness?

Organizational Learning and Knowledge-Based Views of the Firm

The RBV of the firm is then still very influential, but a third theoretical perspective has also found much favor. Given the focus on knowledge transfer, organizational learning and knowledge-based views of the firm have come to influence progressively the field of SIHRM. Although certainly related to the RBV perspective, the knowledge-based view focuses more explicitly on tacit knowledge (as a resource). It is argued that the process of globalization that results from the transfer of such knowledge-based capabilities leads to some organizations building a superior "knowledge transfer capacity." There is as yet little confirmed empirical examination of this, but it is considered to involve two mutually reinforcing capabilities (Martin & Salomon, 2003): (a) The ability of a firm (or business unit) to articulate the uses of its own knowledge, assess the needs and capabilities of the main recipients for the knowledge, and transmit knowledge so it can be used in another location ("source transfer capacity"); and (b) the ability of the transferee to assimilate and retain information from a willing source, that is, evaluate external knowledge, take in all its detail, and modify or create organizational procedures to accommodate the new knowledge ("recipient transfer capacity").

In practice, two positions have been taken on the transfer of knowledge and capabilities within MNCs (Tallman & Fladmoe-Lindquist, 2002): the *capability-recognizing* perspective notes that although MNCs do possess unique knowledge-based resources, these are typically treated as being home-country based or belonging to central corporate functions and top teams, there to be disseminated on a need-to-know basis; and the *capability-driven* perspective (also called the *dynamic capability* perspective), which is concerned with a much wider process of building, protecting, and exploiting mutual capabilities (Teece, Pisano, & Shuen, 1997). In this context, across geographies "the world becomes an important source for new knowledge as well as new markets" (Tallman & Fladmoe-Lindquist, 2002, p. 116).

With regard to the question of whether firms should transfer HR systems, it is argued that by deploying these resources and progressively integrating them into the most value-adding activities, then the organization can build a series of capabilities (such as industry-specific skills, relationships, and organizational knowledge). The organizational learning literature, which probably has had the biggest influence on SIHRM frameworks—such as the one by Schuler et al. (1993)—stresses the effect that time and experience have on organizational learning (for example, Levitt & March, 1988; March & Olsen, 1988; Cohen & Levinthal, 1989, 1990; Barkema, Shenkar, Vermeulen, & Bell, 1997; for a critique of such approaches see Prange, 1999). The focus on learning has brought two concepts into the international management field: absorptive capacity and progressing organizational simplicity. We explain the relevance of each.

According to these authors, prior learning facilitates the learning and application of new related knowledge. Prior related knowledge confers an ability to recognize the value of new information, assimilate it, and apply it to new ends (Cohen & Levinthal, 1989, 1990). These abilities collectively constitute what Cohen and Levinthal (1990) call a firm's "absorptive capacity." This capacity increases incrementally as a function of the previous experiences of the firm and its learning processes (Barkema et al., 1997). March and Olsen (1988) describe the learning cycle as a stimulus-response system in which individuals' actions result in organizational actions, which evoke environmental responses. The latter are reported back to the organizations, where they affect individuals' cognition and preferences and influence their future actions. Levitt and March (1988) view organizational learning as routine-based, history-dependent, and target-oriented. Organizations are seen as learning by encoding inferences from history into routines (e.g. forms, rules, procedures) that guide behavior. In this way, learning can take place independently from individual actors through such processes as socialization, education, and imitation. Knowledge transfer and integration is, however, only facilitated when respective parties have the absorptive capacity or prior experience necessary to understand related ideas (Szulanski, 1996; Tsai, 2002). Groups with large amounts of international experience are more likely to integrate knowledge from other parts of the organization than those that do not (Morris et al., 2006).

Minbaeva, Pedersen, Björkman, Fey, and Park (2003) asked whether absorptive capacity *can be enhanced* by MNCs? What managerial actions are the most important? They argued that the actions reside largely within employees in terms of their abilities and motivations. In international joint ventures, for example, a series of managerial challenges, including differences in organizational culture and managerial style, the need to absorb new product lines, and varying dominant logics, all have to be managed (Vermeulen & Barkema, 2001). Success depends upon processes of organizational learning (and effective knowledge creation, acquisition, and transfer between partners) (Barkema, Bell, & Pennings, 1996; Glaister & Buckley, 1996; Inkpen, 1996; Pilkington, 1996; Schuler, 2001; Schuler & Jackson, 2001; Schuler, Jackson, & Luo, 2003; Schuler & Tarique, 2006).

The second concept that organizational learning theory has brought to the field is that of progressing organizational simplicity. This concept has also been used to explain the (natural) negative forces that exist inside organizations, whereby repeated use of a knowledge base can lead to the tendency of organizations to become rigid, narrow, and simple (Miller, 1993). It has been applied to cross-border alliances by Vermeulen and Barkema (2001). Progressing organizational simplicity posits that firms are inclined to implement habitual ways of organizing and managing (Hedberg, 1981; Levinthal & March, 1993), concentrate on those aspects of their repertoire that appeared most successful in old situations, replicate them and transfer them into the new subsidiary, and install the same sets of technical systems, competitive actions, and organization designs. This increasing routinization, dominance of previous expansion strategies, and resulting narrowness of mental models pervading an internationalization strategy can lead to a failure to perceive and respond to important stimuli (Miller & Chen, 1996; Miller, Droge, & Vickery, 1997; Miller, Lant, Milliken, & Korn, 1996).

There is a counterargument to this hypothesis. This considers that cross-border alliances can in practice act as powerful catalysts of global knowledge management. Vermeulen and Barkema (2001) drew attention to some of the positive (from a knowledge management perspective) forces at play and examined the proposition that acquisitions might actually revitalize the organization, through exposure to manageable levels of shock, leading to superior long-term survival. They looked at the expansion patterns of 25 of the largest Dutch nonfinancial firms (excluding Royal Dutch Shell, Unilever, Philips, and Akzo) over a period of three decades, and studied survival rates and increases in the viability of subsequent ventures. Firms that expanded through greenfield investments (setting up a subsidiary from scratch) did not exploit their knowledge base as effectively as those that expanded through acquisition (the takeover of an existing company).

Organizational learning gains might therefore outstrip short-term downsides to acquisitions, especially where differences between managerial teams create the opportunity for synergies and learning (Krishnan, Miller, & Judge, 1997), or when added value is created through processes of corporate renewal (Haspeslagh & Jemison, 1991). Barkema and Vermeulen (1998) believe that acquisitions bring powerful forces of cognitive change because they:

- Engender conflicts that serve to unfreeze cognitive maps, structures, and processes
- Preserve healthy levels of doubt, diversity, and debate
- Increase the cognitive abilities of organization members

- Create new knowledge from the combination of existing forms of knowledge
- Infuse unique knowledge and inculcate practices that lead to the creation of new knowledge

There are a series of research questions that should be investigated in relation to progressing organizational simplicity. The above discussion of competing views on the organizational learning effects of cross-border acquisitions presents a series of testable propositions that should in the future be investigated. The key questions that must now be asked are:

- How might these forces of cognitive change (be it individual or collective) be engendered?
- What form must global knowledge management take in such situations?
- What can organizations do to help ensure some of the more positive learning outcomes?
- What learning can be influenced by global HR functions?

At a managerial level research should actually test whether the five cognitive changes that Barkema and Vermeulen (1998) specify do actually result from acquisitions. Moreover, a series of HRM practices are considered to be central to the management of these dominant logics, and the necessary migration of knowledge, knowledge appreciation, and subsequent practice of "knowledgeable action" (Iles & Yolles, 2002).

There have been some recent attempts to specify the contribution that HRM makes to global knowledge-management processes. In the context of the debate around knowledge transfer, Jackson, Hitt, and DeNisi (2003) have discussed some of the requirements for HR systems that enhance an organization's capability to gain and use its knowledge resources, identifying generic HR practices associated with four primary tasks of encouraging knowledge-based competition behaviors (as applied to acquiring, creating, sharing, applying, and updating knowledge), ensuring the associated competencies, providing motivation to engage in such behaviors, and providing opportunities through job and organizational design. They argued that we need to understand the combined effects of all elements of this system.

Finally, Sparrow (2006) has examined how each of five main forms of global knowledge management: (a) centers of excellence, (b) managing systems and technology-driven approaches to global knowledge management systems, (c) capitalizing on expatriate advise networks, (d) coordinating international management teams, and (e) developing communities of practice or global expertise networks contribute to three knowledge-based capabilities of:

1. Knowledge acquisition and creation (generation of new knowledge fundamental to the long-term viability of the enterprise).
2. Knowledge capture and storage (creation of an inventory of knowledge so the organization knows what knowledge it possesses, and where it resides; and the maintenance of current knowledge in usable form so that it remains valuable).
3. Knowledge diffusion and transfer (subsequent mobilization and flow of knowledge within the organization that creates knowledge-based value).

The research questions that emerge are too numerous to relay here, but it is useful to note that he lists a series of outcomes that (in theory) should result for each capability from each knowledge management form and a series of propositions that need testing and validation, and argues that we also need to test whether the prescribed HRM roles in fact take place, and if so, whether they are associated with producing the outcomes.

RELATIONAL AND SOCIAL CAPITAL THEORIES

In this section on theoretical underpinnings of the field we now move to the fourth key perspective, which arises from relational and social capital theories. Organizational learning theories have then provided us with a much greater focus on the "how" of internationalization processes. This focus on the how now also has been aided through reference to work on various forms of capital. We concentrate here on relational and social capital theory. Both the internal and external contexts for global firms within which knowledge has to be transferred have changed markedly in recent years. As Buckley and Ghauri (2004, p. 83) note: "...The process of globalization is ... not only reorganising power at world level but also at national and subnational levels. As domestic firms move part of their production to other countries, technology, knowledge and capital become more important." Externally, we can look to the impact of e-commerce and more flexible networks of organizations. Decision makers in MNCs now face far more complex strategic options as a consequence of e-commerce and management through networks.

One response to the renewed complexity and opportunities has been the development of *business networks*. These networks might be built around groups of independent firms or neighboring firms in regional industrial clusters or districts (Best, 1990; Rugman, Cruz, & Verbecke, 1995). It is argued that internal changes, such as more transparent internal transfer pricing arrangements or service level agreements, have brought internal prices more in line with external prices, and have allowed divisional managers to bypass weak or incompetent sections of the company and develop supply or production arrangements that service these broader cross-business networks. In relation to the question of whether firms should transfer HR systems globally, then the answer is yes, *if* HR system convergence is an antidote to incompetence.

Therefore, the literature on interorganizational trust has much relevance to the study of global organizations. Recently this literature has begun to give more attention to the role of what is termed *relational capital* (Chen, Chen, & Ku, 2004). Relational capital is primarily concerned with business networks and the interfirm relationships that exist within these networks. It concerns the sets of interdependent business relationships upon which repeated business transactions are based and thereby includes the goodwill and trust that exist between a firm and its customers, suppliers, partners, government agencies, research institutions, and so forth. Again, with regard to the question of whether firms should transfer HR systems globally, competitive advantage is assumed to result from this form of capital primarily for four reasons.

1. Knowledge sharing across these relational networks is considered to reduce the cost of transactions between network members, and thereby facilitate value creation and innovation (Tsai & Ghoshal, 1998).
2. Firms can access and deploy their existing capabilities in ways that help them seek new markets, resources, efficiencies, and assets (Kale, Singh, & Perlmutter, 2000; Dunning, 2002).
3. The social networks inherent in the relationships affect the rate of creation of interfirm linkages within the MNC, improving its ability to align its organizational design with its global strategy (Tsai, 2000).
4. The ability of partners to absorb and learn from each other at more equal rates is facilitated, thereby extending the life cycle of arrangements such as joint ventures (Lane & Lubatkin, 1998; Yli-Renko, Autio, & Sapienza, 2001).

These assumed benefits all need testing. The underlying research question is as follows. In the context of international management, does knowledge about the relational capital inherent in local linkages determine the benefits (or otherwise) that an MNC might derive from its foreign investments? We might expect the trust that exists in business networks to be beneficial either because the other parties genuinely care about a "trustor's" welfare, or it might exist from a more self-interested view (Saparito, Chen, & Sapienza, 2004). These different motivations should influence the ability to share and create knowledge within the network. Despite the growth of technology, face-to-face contacts with foreign partners are still crucial in cultivating trust, providing access to the flow of information within the network, and providing the opportunity to create new relationships (Dyer & Chu, 2000). Nonetheless, brokering knowledge *across* these organizational boundaries and relational networks, and processes of reciprocal interfirm learning, have become a central feature of competitive strategy (Lubatkin, Florin, & Lane, 2001).

Social capital is related to but different from relational capital. It concerns "the good-will that is engendered by the fabric of social relations and that can be mobilized to facilitate action" (Adler & Kwon, 2002, p. 17) and is defined as "the sum of the resources, actual or virtual, that accrue to an individual or group by virtue of possessing a durable network of more or less institutionalised relationships of mutual acceptance or recognition" (Bourdieu & Wacquant, 1992, p. 119). Social capital theory has mainly been the preserve of economists and sociologists but the value of goodwill in broader terms means that organizational theorists now recognize the relevance of this social structure and the social ties it brings in relation to a wide range of work issues. It is considered to make the achievement of certain ends that would not be attainable in its absence possible. The management of social capital has become viewed as a critical business competence. Whereas human capital theory assumes that people, groups, or organizations do better (i.e., receive higher returns for their efforts) because of their personal traits and characteristics, social capital theory assumes that they do better because they are better "connected." This "connection" may be realized in the form of trust, obligation, or dependency. Certain network structures, or certain locations in this set of exchange relationships, become an asset in their own right, and it is this asset that is the social capital.

Lengnick-Hall and Lengnick-Hall (2006) define social capital in the international context as "the intangible resource of structural connections, interpersonal interactions, and cognitive understanding that enables a firm to (a) capitalize on diversity and (b) reconcile differences." They argue that these two capabilities help international organizations manage the tension between pressures toward integration on a global scale versus local adaptation, and to cope with the challenges arising from diverse national values, economic systems, and workplace conditions, but point out that we now need more research in an international context to examine and understand social capital in an international context. Their work can be used to generate a series of research questions:

- Does dependence upon individuals in "structural holes" (see below) really result in a weakened competitive position and poorer strategic execution?
- How does top management social capital facilitate and constrain strategic choice and execution?
- With what other attributes must social capital be combined in order to lead to the creation of a global mindset?
- Which specific IHRM policies and practices shape the structural, relationship, and cognitive elements of social capital, and consequently how do these policies influence an MNC's ability to learn and exploit what it knows despite cultural differences and geographic distance?

Again, these propositions now need to be tested empirically.

The management literature has long pointed to the role of international managers and expatriates as information brokers. Their brokerage opportunities exist in relation to participation in, and control of, information diffusion (Burt, 1992, 2000). Central to this process is the concept of "structural holes" (holes in the social structure of a network that might not reflect a total unawareness of the other parties but do reflect a lack of attention to them). Structural holes are implicit in the boundaries between cohorts of employees, teams, divisions, and between firms. Individuals, units, or organizations that have relationships that span these holes can create a competitive advantage depending on the nature of their brokerage. Holes act as buffers, with people on either side of the hole circulating in different flows of information. They therefore offer an opportunity to broker the flow of information between people and to control the projects that bring people together from opposite sides of the hole. The research questions that emerge from recent discussion from a special capital perspective should be as follows.

- Which particular social capital structures are associated with greater role effectiveness for international managers, and in what ways?

- Is social capital separate from human capital or are there particular skills and competencies that help build social capital?
- What is the role of HR processes in building, protecting, and capitalizing on social capital?

Summarizing the situation with regard to this fourth area of theory it would be fair to say that, to date, in the international context what we have is theoretical frameworks only. Moreover, in any empirical testing it is difficult to divorce some aspects of social capital from the discussion of organizational learning above. Hansen (2002) argues that social networks provide a conduit for the sharing of knowledge because they inform network members about the existence, location, and significance of new knowledge; create a more heterogeneous base of information and knowledge to draw from; and offer different reference points for members to make comparisons and explore new ideas. Consequently, social networks play an important role in knowledge creation (Morris et al., 2006) and form a circulation system that carries information and ideas to those who need it, when they need it (Lengnick-Hall & Lengnick-Hall, 2006). Similarly, Kostova and Roth (2003) have combined ideas from organizational learning and social capital theories by proposing a contingency perspective that specifies the level of social capital needed in MNCs based upon different types of interdependencies between headquarters and foreign subunits. "Simple interdependence" requires a few easily specified points of interaction supported by readily codifiable exchanges, whereas "complex interdependence" requires many points of interaction and exchanges are not easily codifiable. Therefore, as the degree and complexity of interdependence between headquarters and foreign subunits increase, higher levels of social capital are required. Relating back to the discussion of organizational designs, they predict that the level of social capital required will be highest for transnationals, followed by international MNCs, then global MNCs.

DO HR STRATEGY THEORIES DEVELOPED IN WESTERN COUNTRIES APPLY TO OTHER CULTURES? (OR, HOW CAN HRM STRATEGIES BE MADE TO APPLY IN DIFFERENT CULTURES?)

We now move to the third and final section of the chapter, which asks whether HRM strategies can be made to apply in different cultures. In the context of European HRM, Sparrow and Hiltrop (1997) noted three areas of insight and knowledge that HR professionals need. These concern the range of factors that engender distinctive national and local solutions to HRM issues; the strategic pressures that make these national models more receptive to change and development; and the firm-level processes through which such change and development in actual HRM practice will be delivered. Knowledge about the first area by proxy helps answer the question of whether HR strategy theories developed in western countries *do* actually apply to other cultures, and how HR strategies may be made to apply better in different cultures. This knowledge has largely been produced by the comparative HR researchers. This field has traditionally incorporated a country comparison perspective and asks questions such as (Pieper, 1990; Brewster, Tregaskis, Hegewisch, & Mayne, 1996): How is HRM structured in individual countries? What strategies are discussed? What is actually put into practice? What are the main differences and similarities? To what extent are HR policies influenced by national factors such as culture, government policy, and educational systems? A review of the field is well beyond the scope of this chapter, but readers should consider the work on:

- The culture-bound versus the culture-specific thesis (see for example Harbison & Myers, 1959; Kerr, Dunlop, Harbison, & Myers, 1960; Hickson, Hinings, McMillan, & Schwitter, 1974; Neghandi, 1974; Child & Kieser, 1979; Maurice, Sorge, & Warner, 1980; Child, 1981; Birnbaum & Wong, 1985; Whitley, 1992, 1999; Staehle, 1994; Redding, 1994; Begin, 1997).
- Which HRM practices are more or less culture sensitive (see for example Laurent, 1986, Van Dijk, 1990, Poole, 1990, Kanungo & Jaeger, 1990; Rosenzweig & Nohria, 1994; Lu & Björkman, 1997).

- Empirical examination of patterns of convergence or not in HRM (see for example, Brewster, Mayrhofer, & Morley, 2004).

The main conclusion of course is that the answer to the first part of the question—do HR strategies developed in Western countries apply to other counteries—is clearly no. Therefore, attention is turned to the second part of the question, that is, can HRM strategies be made to apply (better) in other cultures? We concentrate attention on institutional theory and what it has to say about the question. As the fields of international HRM and comparative HRM have begun to combine (under pressures for MNCs to work through partnerships, and to localize their management—and consequently to understand how HRM operates in different national contexts) we have seen an infusion of work to the international HRM field from studies that address these questions from the perspective of institutional theory. This work has been reviewed recently by Björkman (2006). He points out that until the early 1990s little reference to this approach could be found, excepting perhaps work on: (a) examination of the HRM practices found in foreign-owned subsidiaries of MNCs in terms of their degree of global "integration" or MNC "standardization" versus local "responsiveness" or "local adaptation." Empirical studies usually ask subsidiary managers to estimate the extent to which the HRM practices resemble those of local firms and the MNC parent organization, respectively (for example, Rosenzweig & Nohria, 1994; Hannon et al., 1995; Björkman & Lu, 2001; Rosenzweig, 2006). (b) Second, the approach has been used in comparative studies of HRM practices across countries (for example, Gooderham, Nordhaug, & Ringdal, 1999).

Institutional theory developed from the work of Berger and Luckman (1967), who focused on the "taken-for-granted" character of social reality in social institutions (e.g. religion, work, family, politics) and explained how such realities are created and institutionalized through processes such as typification and habitualization. Further theoretical developments (DiMaggio & Powell, 1983; Meyer & Rowan, 1977) focused on the nature and differentiation of a variety of institutional processes within organizations. An underlying assumption is that organizational structures increasingly arise as a reflection of rationalized institutional rules (Meyer & Rowan, 1977) and from "myths" of their institutional environment (DiMaggio & Powell, 1983). Structures are not really determined by an organization's work activities, and the demands made by competition and the needs for efficiency, as much as we might believe (DiMaggio & Powell, 1983). In this sense, institutional theory again promotes a perspective in which organizational decision making is not seen as an outcome from strategic choice. Similar to the buffering and bridging strategies developed by proponents of the resource dependence perspective, efforts have been made to highlight the strategic behaviors that organizations may employ in direct response to institutional processes (see for example, Oliver, 1991; Scott, 1995).

DiMaggio and Powell (1983) described isomorphic processes (the creation of similarity in unrelated forms) that are exerted by external "institutional agencies" in an organizational field (defined as those in an aggregate set of organizations that constitute a recognized area of institutional life). They differentiated three isomorphic pulls:

1. Coercive, that is, pulls resulting from pressures of external institutions such as the state, legal environment, and cultural expectations of societies.
2. Mimetic, that is, organizations modeling themselves on other organizations in their "field" as a standard response to uncertainty (triggered for example through employee transfers or explicitly through agencies such as consultancies).
3. Normative, that is, pulls resulting from the professionalization of functions and individuals (for example through educational institutions or practice dissemination by professional networks).

Therefore, institutional theory soon began to also focus on the role of agencies from within an organization (Scott, 1987; Scott & Meyer, 1989). Scott (1983, p. 16) noted that "the beliefs, norms, rules, and understandings are not just 'out there' but additionally 'in here'." The environment is considered to enter the organization through processes of "imposition," "acquisition," and "authorization" (Scott, 1987). Pulls that emphasize the role of internal agents from within the organization (Scott & Meyer, 1989; Westney, 1993) include:

- "Inducement" of organizational structure (where an organization that lacks power to impose patterns on other organizations instead offers inducements such as funding or certification).
- "Incorporation" (where organizations come to replicate salient aspects of environmental differentiation in their own structure).
- "Bypassing" (where institutionalized and shared values can substitute for formal structure).
- "Imprinting" (where an organizational form retains some of the patterns institutionalized at the time its industry was founded—though this may result from influences of both external and internal agencies).

The theory has left a strong mark on conceptual work in the area of SIHRM (see Westney, 1993; Wright & McMahan, 1992). From an empirical perspective Björkman (2006) also draws attention to the evidence that MNCs from different countries differ systematically in their overseas operations (for example, Yuen & Hui, 1993; Rosenzweig & Nohria, 1994; Guest & Hoque, 1996; Bae, Chen, & Lawler, 1998; Muller, 1998; Björkman & Lu, 2001; Faulkner, Pitkethy, & Child, 2002). Certainly, the current consensus is that firms are not as global or international as is often assumed and a clear country-of-origin effect is still evident. U.S. MNCs, for example, tend to be more centralized and formalized than others in their management of HRM issues, ranging from pay systems through to collective bargaining and union recognition. They tend to innovate more and import leading-edge practices from other nation-states. Japanese MNCs on the other hand have been at the forefront of work organization innovations through lean production, but expect their subsidiaries abroad to fit in with this approach. Even though standard worldwide policies and formal systems are not as apparent as in U.S. MNCs, there is stronger centralized direction and ethnocentric attitudes. In short, "MNCs, far from being stateless organizations operating independent of national borders in some purified realm of global economic competition, continue to have their assets, sales, work-force ownership and control highly concentrated in the country where their corporate headquarters are located" (Ferner & Quintanilla, 1998, p. 710).

However, institutional theory does not just play a role in explaining the continuance of many comparative differences in HRM systems. It also has much to say about the key role of the global HR function in facilitating the transfer of *core processes and management practices*. Institutional theory asks whether this transfer is easy to engineer and automatic and, indeed, can it actually be managed? It has gained much recent support in addressing these questions (Fenton-O'Creevy, 2003, Kostova, 1999; Martin & Beaumont, 2001). We know that global strategies are characterized by particularly intense levels of uncertainty (Weick & Van Orden, 1990). Efforts at globalization within organizations are consequently hampered by problems of information overload (see the section on organization design), managerial complexity in the form of numerous conflicts or paradoxes ("domestic myopia" or only seeing things from within the mindset of the headquarters), and differences in national culture ("expanded socio-cognitive diversity") (Sanders & Carpenter, 1998). Managers in foreign subsidiaries become frustrated with requests to implement "yet another program" from headquarters and may—by intention or not—end up implementing one thing while reporting another.

Therefore, we must consider models that outline *how* transnational transfer of organizational practices can happen successfully. How might an outsider make a judgment that an HRM practice has successfully transferred or not? By thinking about successful transfer of managerial practice as "the degree of institutionalization of the practice at the recipient unit" (Kostova, 1999, p. 311). Convergence of practice ranges from simple implementation to evidence of *internalization*. Internalization should be measured by two things: (a) *Implementation*—following of rules implied by the practice and reflection of these rules in objective behaviors and actions. Diffusion of sets of rules to subsidiary employees seen in, and measured by, the actions of employees. (b) *Internalization of these rules by subsidiary employees*—ability to make sense of and attribute meaning to these rules in the same way as achieved by host-country or headquarters employees, and the ability to infuse the practice with value. The ways in which recipient unit employees attach meaning to the practice is reflected in three psychological states: *practice commitment* (the relative strength of an employee's identification and involvement with the practice); *practice satisfaction* (a positive attitude toward the practice); and *psychological ownership* (the extent to which employees claim that it is their practice).

Kostova (1999) argues that ideas will only transfer successfully internationally if they can be embedded into three contexts (social, organizational, and relational). Kostova and Roth (2002) found support for this model when they examined the transfer of quality practices within an MNC to 104 locations in 10 countries through questionnaires given to 534 managerial informants and 3,238 employees. They made a distinction between *ceremonial* or purely formal adoption and more *substantive* adoption of practices. Kostova and Roth's (2002) model of factors that determine the transfer of best practice is consistent with two important theoretical perspectives. First, it fits the strategic process perspective on the management of change (evidenced in the work of Pettigrew, 1995) in that it points out that international HR professionals have to make the socio-cultural, organizational, and relational contexts more "receptive to change." International HR functions can influence the second and third of these contexts, if not the first. Second, it fits the business system and comparative literature in that it demonstrates the need for international HR professionals to understand how local practice is embedded in a complex set of relationships between national market structures, ways of organizing firms, and authority systems.

However, Martin and Beaumont (2001, p. 1238) note that Kostova's model "has usefully identified measures for evaluating the extent of institutionalization [but] … is relatively silent on the process by which such states might be achieved." Reflecting these criticisms, Björkman (2005) notes that institutional theorists remind us that organizations imitate each other in situations of uncertainty. He argues therefore that researchers should now study *macro- and meso-level processes of institutionalization* to examine, for example, the diffusion of "high performance" work/HRM practices, the HR scorecard, the outsourcing of HRM tasks, and the structure and roles of the HR department in the MNC.

Martin and Beaumont (2001), however, would argue that any model of HR change in MNCs must also incorporate an understanding of the ways in which managers create such "strategic discourses" (Barry & Elmes, 1997; Ford & Ford, 1995). International HR practitioners have to "habitualize" other parts of the organization to the new strategy, make the messages for change more objective as they are shared among employees, and ensure that the messages become "sedimented" into the organization. Martin and Beaumont (2001) also note the importance of the process of "design influence" exerted from the center over local HR practice—exerted either as the direct source of innovation or by tacitly structuring the agenda in terms of what might be deemed acceptable in subsidiaries. This strategic influence role has also been examined by Napier, Tibau, Jenssens, and Pilenzo (1995). It includes being " the change agent of corporate culture; the top management team's symbolic 'communicator' to other levels of the organization; senior managers' mediator in development/career planning opportunities; and the corporate top management team's and particularly the CEO's reliable internal informal advisor" (Novicevic & Harvey, 2001, p. 1252).

Some researchers have considered specifically how MNCs develop organizational capability and consider that it is created out of the international networking at individual and functional levels that surrounds building research and development or production centers, logistic networks, or indeed HR systems and processes on a global scale, and the conduct of these activities in global contexts (see for example, Collis, 1991; Fladmoe-Linquist & Tallman, 1994; Hedlund & Ridderstråe, 1997; Kogut, 1997; Tallman & Fladmoe-Lindquist, 2002). In order to understand how organizations develop, manage, and deploy such capabilities to support their business strategy

(Montealegre, 2002) we generally have to conduct longitudinal studies. In doing so, Sparrow, Brewster, and Harris (2004) and Brewster, Sparrow, and Harris (2005) apply a dynamic capability perspective to the field of SIHRM. They drew three key conclusions about the role of the HR function in international firms. First, the future of the global HR function will be both heavily dependent upon and will be shaped by the globalizing activity of two contiguous functions: information systems and marketing or corporate communications. Second, it is clear that the added value of the HR function in an international firm lies in its ability to manage the delicate balance between overall coordinated systems and sensitivity to local needs, including cultural differences, in a way that aligns with both business needs and senior management philosophy. Third, it is clear that there is a distinction to be made now between international HRM and global HRM. Traditionally, international HRM has been about managing an international workforce—the expatriates, frequent commuters, cross-cultural team members, and specialists involved in international knowledge transfer. Global HRM is not simply about covering these staff around the world. It concerns managing SIHRM activities through the application of global rule-sets that carry meaning across cultures.

CONCLUSIONS

A large amount of the SIHRM literature focuses on the challenge for MNCs in coping with complex cultural, geographical, and institutional pressures. As the chapter has made clear, the adoption of any one theoretical approach often appears somewhat dogmatic. In recent years then, there has been a process of increasing transfusion of theoretical ideas across the perspectives discussed in order to better understand organizational behavior. We are seeing some convergence and synthesis of ideas between different combinations of the theories covered in this chapter. For example, the need to combine insights from institutional theory, knowledge-based theories of the firm, and social capital theory can be seen in recent models of MNC's center–subsidiary relationships based on the "knowledge leveraging" perspective of Grant, Almeida, and Song (2000). This perspective appreciates that knowledge is created in many sites and functions and is accessed in many locations. It argues that "the movement of knowledge between different geographical locations is central [to the process of adding value in knowledge development]" (Grant et al., 2000, pp. 115–116). Kostova and Roth's work (2002), though conducted mainly from an institutional theory perspective, concluded that successful practice adoption is largely dependent upon relationships based on trust and shared identity, requiring insights from social capital theory. In relation to the study of MNCs, social capital has been defined as the knowledge that is embedded within social networks (Nahapiet & Ghoshal, 1998). Others are drawing links between knowledge-based theories and social capital theories. Knowledge flows are now understood to be multidirectional, unplanned, and emergent (Iles & Yolles, 2002). Knowledge flows can be understood through theories of tacit knowledge spread within top management teams through "advice networks" (Athanassiou & Nigh, 2000); social capital theory and the resources that accrue to international managers as a consequence of their boundary spanning roles (Kostova & Roth, 2003); and the application of knowledge transfer theory to the topic of expatriation (Bonache & Brewster, 2001).

Similarly, by integrating some organizational learning perspectives with resource-based views of the firm, Morris et al. (2006) argue that as MNCs "struggle to create and integrate practices across borders, they are faced with unique challenges that either push for global efficiency or local responsiveness. These challenges open the discussion for ways to actually manage both the creation and integration of knowledge on a global scale" (p. 444). They have drawn attention to two competitive capabilities: knowledge creation and knowledge integration at the local level. They also touch upon some institutional theory, by reference to Youndt, Subramaniam, and Snell's (2004) discussion of organizational capital, which they consider to be knowledge and experiences that have become institutionalized and codified such that they reside within an organization. They also note that trust provides the motive for actors in the system of an MNC to interact with others, while shared identity provides an overlapping understanding of what is important to share. Perhaps the most striking of the challenges that they argue remain to be addressed, however, is the need to understand what the economic benefits (or rents) of the adoption of an integrated set of global HR practices actually are, and to examine how such integration creates a source of sustainable competitive advantage.

In other chapters in this volume some attention is given to the geographical coverage and origin of much academic work. This question is less relevant to a chapter on theory, but we would make a general observation. Clearly, most of the theorizing is based on Anglo-Saxon models of management, and even where there has been empirical testing it tends to have been on U.S. multinational enterprises. It is also worth noting that U.S. researchers have favored the RBV, whereas European researchers have been more attracted of late to both institutional theory and to some degree organizational learning perspectives. Certainly the comparative HR field, not featured in this chapter, is dominated by non-U.S. researchers, perhaps not surprisingly. The field does now appear to be mature enough to combine these perspectives.

We make one final observation about the level of analysis that needs to be adopted in SIHRM research if it is to respond to this challenge. In addition to understanding what happens at the level of the firm in its totality—the traditional focus of many SIHRM researchers—we need to better understand how organizations enhance the ability of specific functions to perform globally. Many researchers argue that globalization within organizations is driven by what happens within business functions as they seek to coordinate (develop linkages between geographically dispersed units of a function) and control (regulate functional activities to align them with the expectations set in targets) their activities across borders (Kim, Park, & Prescott, 2003). As Malbright (1995, p. 119) pointed out, "globalization occurs at the level of the function, rather than the firm." This observation has been reinforced by the longitudinal studies of Sparrow et al. (2004). However, the problem is that the HR function is not one that can be considered, currently, as being highly globalized. Indeed, a range of researchers have found that other departments are much more globalized (Hansen, Nohria, & Tierney, 1999; Kim et al., 2003; Yip, 1992). If other functional activities are being better connected across geographical borders through flows of information that are intended to enhance levels of innovation and learning, then the HR functions that service them are themselves going to be forced to become more globalized but in a piecemeal and reactive manner. Clearly more attention needs now to be devoted to understanding the ways in which the HR function itself contributes effectively to the process of globalization.

REFERENCES

Adler, N. J. (1991). International dimensions of organizational behavior (2nd ed.). Boston: PWS-Kent.

Adler, N. J., & Ghadar, F. (1990). Strategic human resource management: A global perspective. In R. Pieper (Ed.), *Human resource management: An international comparison* (pp. 235–260). Berlin: de Gruyter.

Adler, N. J., & Ghadar, F. (1993). A strategic approach to international human resources management. In D. Wong-Rieger & F. Rieger (Eds.), *International management research* (pp. 136–161). Berlin: de Gruyter.

Adler, P. S., & Kwon, S.-W. (2002). Social capital: prospects for a new concept. *Academy of Management Review, 27*(1), 17–40.

Ashkenas, R., Ulrich, D., Jick, T., & Kerr, S. (1995). *The boundaryless organization*. San Francisco, CA: Jossey-Bass.

Athanassiou, N., & Nigh, D. (2000). Internationalization, tacit knowledge and the top management teams of MNCs. *Journal of International Business Studies, 31*(3), 471–488.

Bae, J., Chen, S.-J., & Lawler, J. L. (1998). Variations in human resource management in Asian countries: MNC home-country and host-country effects. *International Journal of Human Resource Management, 9*, 653–670.

Baliga, B. R., & Jaeger, A. M. (1984). Multinational corporations: control systems and delegation issues. *Journal of International Business Studies, 15*, 25–40.

Barkema, H. G., Bell, J. H. J., & Pennings, J. M. (1996). Foreign entry, cultural barriers, and learning. *Strategic Management Journal, 17*, 151–166.

Barkema, H. G., Shenkar, O., Vermeulen, F., & Bell, J. H. J. (1997). Working abroad, working with others. How firms learn to operate international joint ventures. *Academy of Management Journal, 40*(2), 426–442.

Barkema, H. G., & Vermeulen, F. (1998). International expansion through start-up or acquisition: a learning perspective. *Academy of Management Journal, 41*, 7–26.

Barney, J. B. (1989). Asset stocks and sustained competitive advantage: A comment. *Management Science, 35*(12), 1511–1513.

Barney, J. B. (1991). Firm resources and sustained competitive advantage. *Journal of Management, 17*, 99–120.

Barry, D., & Elmes, M. (1997). Strategy retold: Toward a narrative view of strategic discourse. *Academy of Management Review, 22*(2), 429–452.

Bartlett, C. A., & Ghoshal, S. (1986). Tap your subsidiaries for global reach. *Harvard Business Review, 64*(6), 87–94.

Bartlett, C. A., & Ghoshal, S. (1989). *Managing across borders: The transnational solution*. Boston: Harvard Business School Press.

Bartlett, C. A., & Ghoshal, S. (1990). Matrix management: Not a structure, a frame of mind. *Harvard Business Review, 68*(4), 138–145.

Bartlett, C. A., & Ghoshal, S. (1997). *International management: Text, cases and readings in cross-border management* (2nd ed.). Boston: Irwin.

Beer, M., Spector, B., Lawrence, P. R., Mills, D. Q., & Walton, R. E. (1985). *Human resource management*. New York: Free Press.

Begin, J. (1997). National HR systems: concepts and contexts. (pp. 1–30) In J. Begin (Ed.), *Dynamic human resource systems: Cross-national comparisons*. Berlin: de Gruyter.

Berger, P. L., & Luckman, T. (1967). *The social construction of reality*. Garden City, NY: Doubleday.

Best, M. H. (1990). *The new competition: Institutions of industrial restructuring*. Oxford: Polity Press.

Birkinshaw, J. M., & Morrison, A. J. (1995). Configurations of strategy and structure in subsidiaries of multinational corporations. *Journal of International Business Studies, 26*(4), 729753.

Birnbaum, P. H., & Wong, G. Y. (1985). Organizational structure of multinational banks in Hong Kong from a culture-free perspective. *Administrative Science Quarterly, 30*(2), 262–277.

Björkman, I. (2006). International human resource management research and institutional theory. pp. 463–479. In I. Bjorkman & G. Stahl (Eds.), *Handbook of research into international HRM*. London: Edward Elgar.

Björkman, I., & Lu, Y. (2001). Institutionalization and bargaining power explanations of HRM practices in international joint ventures: The case of Chinese-Western joint ventures. *Organization Studies, 22*(3), 491–512.

Bonache, J., & Brewster, C. (2001). Knowledge transfer and the management of expatriation. *Thunderbird International Business Review, 43*(1), 145–168.

Bourdieu, P., & Wacquant, L. J. D. (1992). *An invitation to reflexive sociology*. Chicago: University of Chicago Press.

Braun, W., & Warner, M. (2002). The "culture-free" versus the "culture-specific" management debate. In M. Warner & P. Joynt (Eds.), *Managing across cultures* (2nd ed., pp. 13–25). London: Thomson Learning.

Brewster, C., Mayrhofer, W., & Morley, M. (2004). *Human resource management in Europe: Evidence of convergence?* London: Elsevier.

Brewster, C., Sparrow, P. R., & Harris, H. (2005) Towards a new model of globalizing human resource management. *International Journal of Human Resource Management, 16*, 953–974.

Brewster, C., Tregaskis, O., Hegewisch, A., & Mayne, L. (1996). Comparative survey research in human resource management: A review and an example. *International Journal of Human Resource Management, 7*(3), 585–604.

Buckley, P. J., & Ghauri, P. N. (2004). Globalisation, economic geography and the strategy of multinational enterprises. *Journal of International Business Studies, 35*(2), 81–98.

Burt, R. S. (1992). *Structural holes*. Cambridge, MA: Harvard University Press.

Burt, R. S. (2000). The network structure of social capital. pp. 345–423. In B. M. Staw & R. I. Sutton (Eds.), *Research in organizational behavior: An annual series of analytical essays and critical reviews* (Vol. 22). New York: JAI Press.

Caves, R. E. (1996). *Multinational enterprise and economic analysis.* Cambridge: Cambridge University Press.

Chandler, A.D. (1962). *Strategy and structure: Chapters in the history of the industrial enterprise.* Cambridge, MA: MIT Press.

Chen, T.-J., Chen, H., & Ku, Y.-H. (2004). Foreign direct investment and local linkages. *Journal of International Business Studies, 35*(4), 320–333.

Child, J. (1981). Culture, contingency and capitalism in the cross-national study of organizations. pp. 265–339. In L. L. Cummings & B. M. Staw (Eds.), *Research in organizational behavior* (Vol. 3). Greenwich: JAI Press.

Child, J. (1984). Organization: A guide to problems and practice. London: Harper and Row.

Child, J., & Kieser, A. (1979). Organization and managerial roles in British and West German companies: An examination of the culture-free thesis. (pp. 251–271) In C. J. Lammers & D. J. Hickson (Eds.), *Organizations alike and unlike.* London: Routledge.

Cohen, W. M., & Levinthal, D. A. (1989). Innovation and learning: The two faces of R&D. *Economic Journal, 99*, 569–596.

Cohen, W. M., & Levinthal, D. A. (1990). Absorptive capacity: A new perspective on learning and innovations. *Administrative Science Quarterly, 35*, 128–152.

Collis, D. J. (1991). A resource-based analysis of global competition: The case of the bearings industry. *Strategic Management Journal, 12*, 49–68.

Daniels, J. D. (1986). Approaches to European regional management by large U.S. multinational firms. *Management International Review, 26*(2), 27–42.

Daniels, J. D. (1987). Bridging national and global marketing strategies through regional operations, *International Marketing Review*, Autumn, 29–44.

DeCieri, H., Cox, J. W., & Fenwick, M. (2001). Think global, act local: From naïve comparison to critical participation in the teaching of strategic international human resource management. *TAMARA Journal of Critical Postmodern Organization Science, 1*(1), 68–78.

DeCieri, H., & Dowling, P. J. (1997). Strategic international human resource management: An Asia-Pacific perspective [Special issue]. *Management International Review, 37*(1), 21–42.

DeCieri, H., & Dowling, P. J. (1998). *The tortuous evolution of strategic human resource management in multinational enterprises* (Working Paper in Human Resource Management and Industrial Relations, No. 5). Melbourne, Australia: University of Melbourne, Department of Management.

De Saá-Pérez, P., & García-Falcón, J. M. (2002). A resource-based view of human resource management and organisational capabilities development. *International Journal of Human Resource Management, 13*(1), 123–140.

Dierickx, I., & Cool, K. (1989). Asset stock accumulation and sustainability of competitive advantage. *Management Science, 25*(12), 1504–1511.

DiMaggio, P. J., & Powell, W. W. (1983). The iron cage revisited: Institutional isomorphism and collective rationality in organizational fields. *American Sociological Review, 48*, 147–160.

Dowling, P. J.; Schuler, R. S., & Welch, D. E. (1994). *International dimensions of human resource management* (2nd ed.). Belmont, CA: Wadsworth Publishing Company.

Dowling, P. J.; Welch, D. E., & Schuler, R. S. (1998). *International human resource management. Managing people in a multinational context.* Cincinnati: South-Western College Publishing.

Doz, Y. L., & Prahalad, C. K. (1981). Headquarters influence and strategic control in MNCs. *Sloan Management Review, 23*(1), 15–29.

Dunning, J. H. (1993). *Multinational enterprises and the global economy.* Reading, MA: Addison-Wesley.

Dunning, J. H. (2002). Relational assets, networks and international business activity. In F. J. Contractor & P. Lorange (Eds.), *Co-operative strategies and alliances* (pp. 569–594). Pergamon: New York.

Dyer, J., & Chu, W. (2000). The determinants of trust in supplier-automaker relationships in the U.S., Japan and Korea. *Journal of International Business Studies, 31*(2), 259–285.

Edström, A., & Galbraith, J. (1977a). Transfer of managers as a coordination and control strategy in multinational organizations. *Administrative Science Quarterly, 22*, 248–263.

Edström, A., & Galbraith, J. (1977b). Alternative policies for international transfers of managers. *Management International Review, 17*, 11–22.

Edström, A., & Galbraith. J. R. (1978). The impact of managerial transfers on headquarters-subsidiary relationships in a multinational company. In M. Ghertman & J. Leontiades (Eds.), *European research in international business* (pp. 331–349). Amsterdam: North-Holland.

Egelhoff, W. G. (1991). Information-processing theory and the multinational enterprise. *Journal of International Business Studies, 22*(3), 341–369.

Egelhoff, W. G. (1999). Organizational equilibrium and organizational change: Two different perspectives of the multinational enterprise. *Journal of International Management, 5*, 15–33.

Evans, P., Pucik, V., & Barsoux, J.-L. (2002). *The global challenge. Frameworks for international human resource management.* Boston: McGraw-Hill.

Faulkner, D., Pikethy, R., & Child, J. (2002). International mergers and acquisitions in the UK 1985–94: A comparison of national HRM practices. *International Journal of Human Resource Management, 13,* 106–122.

Fenton-O'Creevy, M. (2003). The diffusion of HR practices within the multinational firm: Towards a research agenda, *Beta: Scandinavian Journal of Business Research, 17*(1), 36–47.

Fenton-O'Creevy, M., Gooderham, and P., Nordhaug, O. (2005). Diffusion of HRM to Europe and the role of U.S. MNCs [Special Issue 1]. *Management Revue, 16,* 5–15.

Ferner, A. (1994). MNCs and human resource management: An overview of research issues. *Human Resource Management Journal, 4,* 79–102.

Ferner, A., & Quintanilla, J. (1998). Multinational, national business systems and HRM: The enduring influence of national identity or a process of "Anglo Saxonization"? *International Journal of Human Resource Management, 9*(4), 710–731.

Fladmoe-Lindquist, K., & Tallman, S. (1994). Resource-based strategy and competitive advantage among multinationals. pp. 45–72. In P. Shrivastava, A. Huff, and J. Dutton (Eds.), *Advances in strategic management* (Vol. 10). Greenwich, CT: JAI Press.

Flood, P. C., Ramamoorthy, N., & Liu, W. (2003). Knowledge and innovation: Diffusion of HRM systems. *Beta: Scandinavian Journal of Business Research, 17*(1), 59–68.

Ford, J. D., & Ford, L.W. (1995). The role of conversations in producing intentional organizational change. *Academy of Management Review, 20*(3), 541–570.

Foss, N. J., & Pedersen, T. (2004). Organizing knowledge processes in the multinational corporation: An introduction, *Journal of International Business Studies, 35*(5), 340–349.

Galbraith, J. R. (1973). *Designing complex organizations.* Reading, MA: Addison-Wesley.

Galbraith, J. R. (1977). *Organization design.* Reading, MA: Addison-Wesley.

Ghemawat, P. (1986). Sustainable advantage. *Harvard Business Review,* September–October, 53–58.

Ghoshal, S., & Bartlett, C. A. (1988). Creation, adoption, and diffusion of innovations by subsidiaries of multinational corporations, *Journal of International Business Studies, 29,* 365–388.

Glaister, K. W., & Buckley, P. J. (1996). Strategic motives for international alliance formation. *Journal of Management Studies, 33* 301–332.

Gooderham, P. N., Nordhaug, O., & Ringdal, K. (1999). Institutional and rational determinants of organizational practices: Human resource management in European firms. *Administrative Science Quarterly, 44,* 507–531.

Grant, R. M. (1996). Toward a knowledge-based theory of the firm. *Strategic Management Journal, 17*(S2), 109–122.

Grant, R. M., Almeida, P., & Song, J. (2000). Knowledge and the multi-national enterprise. In C. J. M. Millar, R. M. Grant, and C. J. J. Choi (Eds.), *International business: Emerging Issues and emerging markets* (pp. 102–114). Basingstoke: Macmillan.

Guest, D. E. (1991). Personnel management: The end of orthodoxy? *British Journal of Industrial Relations, 29,* 149–175.

Guest, D. E. (1997). Human resource management and performance: A review and research agenda. *The International Journal of Human Resource Management, 8,* 263–276.

Guest, D., & Hoque, K. (1996). The influence of national ownership in human resource management practices in UK greenfield sites. *Human Resource Management Journal, 6*(4), 50–74.

Gupta, A., & Govindarajan, V. (1991). Knowledge flows and the structure of control within multinational corporations. *Academy of Management Review, 16,* 768–792.

Hamel, G., & Prahalad, C. K. (1985). Do you really have a global strategy? *Harvard Business Review,* July–August, 139–148.

Hamilton, R. D., & Kashlak, R. J. (1999). National influences on multinational corporation control system selection. *Management International Review, 39*(2), 167–189.

Hannon, J. M., Huang, I.-C., & Jaw, B.-S. (1995). International human resource strategy and its determinants: The case of subsidiaries in Taiwan. *Journal of International Business Studies, 26*, 531–554.

Hansen, M. T. (2002). Knowledge networks: Explaining effective knowledge sharing in multiunit companies. *Organization Science, 13*, 290–302.

Hansen, M. T., Nohria, N., & Tierney, T. (1999). What is your strategy for managing knowledge? *Harvard Business Review 77*(2), 106–116.

Harbison, F., & Myers, C. A. (1959). *Management in the industrial world.* New York: McGraw-Hill.

Harzing, A.-W. K. (1999). *Managing the multinationals. An international study of control mechanisms.* Cheltenham, U.K.: Edward Elgar.

Haspeslagh, G., & Jemison, D. B. (1991). *Managing acquisitions: Creating value through corporate renewal.* New York: Free Press.

Hedberg, B. (1981). How organizations learn and unlearn. pp. 3–27. In P. C. Nystrom & W. H. Starbuck (Eds.), *Handbook of organizational design.* London: University Press.

Hedlund, G. (1986). The hypermodern MNC: A heterarchy? *Human Resource Management, 25*(1), 9–35.

Hedlund, G. (1993). Assumptions of hierarchy and heterarchy: An application to the multinational corporation. In S. Ghoshal & E. Westney (Eds.), *Organization theory and the multinational corporation* (pp. 211–236). London: Macmillan.

Hedlund, G., & Ridderstråle, J. (1997). Toward a theory of self-renewing MNCs. In B. Toyne & D. Nigh (Eds.), *International business: An emerging vision.* Columbia: University of South Carolina Press.

Hennart, J.-F. (1991). Control in multinational firms: The role of Price and hierarchy [Special issue]. *Management International Review, 31*, 71–96.

Hickson, D. J., Hinings, C. R., McMillan, C. J., & Schwitter, J. P. (1974). The culture-free context of organization structure: A tri-national comparison. *Sociology, 8*, 59–80.

Huselid, M. (1995). The impact of human resource management practices on turnover, productivity and corporate financial performance. *Academy of Management Journal, 38*(3), 635–672.

Iles, P., & Yolles, M. (2002). International joint ventures, HRM and viable knowledge migration. *International Journal of Human Resource Management, 13*(4), 624–641.

Inkpen, A. (1996). Creating knowledge through collaboration. *California Management Review, 39*, 123–140.

Jackson, S. E., Hitt, M. A., & DeNisi, A. S. (2003). Managing human resources for knowledge-based competition: New research directions. In S. E. Jackson, M. A. Hitt, & A. S. DeNisi (Eds.), *Managing knowledge for sustained competitive advantage: Designing strategies for effective human resource management* (pp. 399–428). San Francisco: Jossey-Bass.

Kale, P., Singh, H., & Perlmutter, H. (2000). Learning and protection of proprietary assets in strategic alliances: Building relational capital. *Strategic Management Journal, 21*, 217–237.

Kamoche, K. (1996). The integration-differentiation puzzle: A resource-capability perspective in international human resource management. *International Journal of Human Resource Management, 7*, 230–244.

Kanungo, R. N., & Jaeger, A. M. (1990). Introduction: The need for indigenous management in developing countries. pp. 1–23. In A. M. Jaeger & R. N. Kanungo (Eds.), *Management in developing countries.* London: Routledge.

Kenter, M. E. (1985). *Die steuerung ausländischer tochtergesellschaften. Instrumente und effizienz.* Frankfurt: P. Lang.

Kerr, C., Dunlop, J. T., Harbison, F. H., & Myers, C. A. (1960). *Industrialism and industrial man.* Cambridge, MA: Harvard University Press.

Kim, K., Park, J.-H., & Prescott, J. E. (2003). The global integration of business functions: A study of multinational businesses in integrated global industries. *Journal of International Business Studies, 34*, 327–344.

Kogut, B. (1997). The evolutionary theory of the multinational corporation: Within and across country options. pp. 329–354. In B. Toyne & D. Nigh (Eds.), *International business: An emerging vision.* Columbia: University of South Carolina Press.

Kostova, T. (1999). Transnational transfer of strategic organizational practices: A contextual perspective. *Academy of Management Review, 24*(2), 308–324.

Kostova, T., & Roth, K. (2002). Adoption of an organizational practice by subsidiaries of multinational corporations: Institutional and relational effects, *Academy of Management Journal, 45*(1), 215–233.

Kostova, T., & Roth, K. (2003). Social capital in multinational corporations and a micro-macro model of its formation. *Academy of Management Review, 28*(2), 297–317.

Krishnan, H. A., Miller, A., & Judge, W. Q. (1997). Diversification and top management team complementarity: Is performance improved by merging similar or dissimilar teams? *Strategic Management Journal, 18*, 361–374.

Lado, A., & Wilson, M. (1994). Human resource systems and sustained competitive advantage: A competency based perspective, *Academy of Management Review, 19*, 699–727.

Lane, P., & Lubatkin, M. (1998). Relative absorptive capacity and interorganizational learning. *Strategic Management Journal, 19*, 461–478.

Laurent, A. (1986). The cross-cultural puzzle of international HRM. *Human Resource Management, 25*, 91–102.

Lawler, E. E. (1997). *From the ground up.* San Francisco: Jossey-Bass.

Lawrence, J. W., & Lorsch, P. R. (1967). *Organization and environment.* Boston: Harvard University Press.

Lengnick-Hall, M. L., & Lengnick-Hall, C. (2006). International human resource management research and social network/social capital theory. pp. 475–487. In I. Bjorkman & G. Stahl (Eds.), *Handbook of research into international HRM.* London: Edward Elgar.

Levinthal, D. A., & March, J. G. (1993). Exploration and exploitation in organizational learning. *Strategic Management Journal, 14*(Winter), 95–112.

Levitt, B., & March, J. G. (1988). Organizational learning. *Annual Review of Sociology, 14*, 319–340.

Lu, Y., & Björkman, I. (1997). HRM practices in China-Western joint ventures: MNC standardization versus localization. *International Journal of Human Resource Management, 8*, 614–627.

Lubatkin, M., Florin, J., & Lane, P. (2001). Learning together and apart: A model of reciprocal interfirm learning. *Human Relations, 54*(10), 1353–1382.

Malbright, T. (1995). Globalization of an ethnographic firm. *Strategic Management Journal, 16*, 119–141.

March, J. G., & Olsen, J. P. (1988). The uncertainty of the past: Organizational learning under ambiguity. In J. G. March (Ed.), *Decisions and organizations* (pp. 335–358). Oxford: Basil Blackwell.

March, J. G., & Simon, H. A. (1958). *Organizations.* New York: John Wiley.

Martin, G., & Beaumont, P. (2001). Transforming multinational enterprises: Towards a process model of strategic human resource management change. *International Journal of Human Resource Management, 12*(8), 1234–1250.

Martin, X., & Salomon, R. (2003). Knowledge transfer capacity and its implications for the theory of the multinational corporation. *Journal of International Business Studies, 34*, 356–373.

Martinez, J. I., & Jarillo, J. C. (1989). The evolution of research on coordination mechanisms in multinational corporations. *Journal of International Business Studies, 20*(3), 489–514.

Maurice, M., Sorge, A., & Warner, M. (1980). Societal differences in organizing manufacturing units: A comparison of France, West Germany, and Great Britain. *Organization Studies, 1*, 58–86.

Meyer, J. W., & Rowan, B. (1977). Institutionalized organizations: Formal structure as myth and ceremony. *American Journal of Sociology, 83*(2), 340–863.

Meyer, J. W., Scott, W. R., & Strang, D. (1987). Centralization, fragmentation, and school district complexity. *Administrative Science Quarterly, 32*, 186–201.

Miller, D. (1993). The architecture of simplicity. *Academy of Management Review, 18*, 116–138.

Miller, D., & Chen, M.-J. (1996). The simplicity of competitive repertoires: An empirical analysis. *Strategic Management Journal, 17*, 419–439.

Miller, D., Droge, C., & Vickery, S. (1997). Celebrating the "essential": The impact of performance on the functional favoritism of CEOs in two contexts. *Journal of Management, 23*, 147–168.

Miller, D., & Friesen, P. H. (1980). Momentum and revolution in organizational adaptation. *Academy of Management Journal, 23*, 591–614.

Miller, D., & Friesen, P. H. (1984). A longitudinal study of the corporate life cycle. *Management Science, 30*, 1161–1183.

Miller, D., Lant, T. K., Milliken, F. J., & Korn, H. J. (1996). The evolution of strategic simplicity: Exploring two models of organizational adaptation. *Journal of Management, 22*, 863–887.

Milliman, J., Von Glinow, M. A., & Nathan, M. (1991). Organizational life cycles and strategic international human resource management in multinational companies: Implications for congruence theory. *Academy of Management Review, 16*, 318–339.

Minbaeva, D., Pedersen, T., Björkman, I., Fey, C. F., & Park, H. J. (2003). MNC knowledge transfer, subsidiary absorptive capacity, and HRM. *Journal of International Business Studies, 34,* 586–599.

Mintzberg, H. (1979). *The structuring of organizations.* Englewood Cliffs, NJ: Prentice Hall.

Mintzberg, H. (1983). *Structure in fives. Designing effective organizations.* Englewood Cliffs, NJ: Prentice Hall.

Montealegre, R. (2002). A process model of capability development: Lessons from the electronic commerce strategy at Bolsa de Valores de Guayaquil. *Organization Science, 13*(5), 514–531.

Morris, S. S., Snell, S. A., & Wright, P. M. (2006). A resource-based view of international human resources: Towards a framework of integrative and creative capabilities. pp. 433–448. In I. Bjorkman & G. Stahl (Eds.), *Handbook of research into international HRM.* London: Edward Elgar.

Muller, M. (1998). Human resource and industrial relations practices of U.K. and U.S. multinationals in Germany. *International Journal of Human Resource Management, 9,* 732–749.

Nahapiet, J., & Ghoshal, S. (1998). Social capital, intellectual capital, and the organizational advantage. *Academy of Management Review, 23,* 242–266.

Napier, N., Tibau, J., Jenssens, M., & Pilenzo, R. (1995). Juggling on a high-wire: The role of the international human resources manager. In G. Ferris, S. Rosen, & D. Barnum (Eds.), *Handbook of human resource management* (pp. 217–242). Oxford: Blackwell.

Neghandi, A. R. (1974). Cross-cultural management studies: Too many conclusions, not enough conceptualizations. *Management International Review, 14,* 59–72.

Nohria, N., & Ghoshal, S. (1997). *The differentiated network: Organizing multinational corporations for value creation.* San Francisco: Jossey-Bass.

Novicevic, M. M., & Harvey, M. (2001). The changing role of the corporate HR function in global organizations of the twenty-first century. *International Journal of Human Resource Management, 12*(8), 1251–1268.

Oliver, C. (1991). Strategic responses to institutional processes. *Academy of Management Review, 16*(1), 145–179.

Ouchi, W. G. (1977). The relationship between organizational structure and organizational control. *Administrative Science Quarterly, 22,* 95–112.

Ouchi, W. G. (1979). A conceptual framework for the design of organizational control mechanisms. *Management Science, 25*(9), 833–848.

Ouchi, W. G. (1980). Markets, bureaucracies and clans. *Administrative Science Quarterly, 25,* 129–141.

Parker, B. (1998). *Globalization and business practice: Managing across boundaries.* London: Sage.

Penrose, E. T. (1959). *The theory of growth of the firm.* New York: Wiley.

Perlmutter, H. V. (1969). The tortuous evolution of the multinational corporation. *Columbia Journal of World Business, 4,* 9–18.

Perlmutter, H. V., & Heenan, D. A. (1974). How multinational should your top managers be? *Harvard Business Review, 52*(6), 121–132.

Perlmutter, H. V., & Trist, E. (1986). Paradigms for societal transition. *Human Relations, 39*(1), 1–27.

Peteraf, M. A. (1993). The cornerstones of competitive advantage: A resource-based view. *Strategic Management Journal, 14*(3), 179–191.

Pettigrew, A. M. (1995). Longitudinal field research on change: Theory and practice. pp. 91–125. In G. P. Huber & A. Van de Ven (Eds.), *Longitudinal field research methods: Studying the processes of organizational change.* London: Sage.

Pfeffer, J., & Cohen, Y. (1984). Determinants of internal labor markets in organization. *Administrative Science Quarterly, 29,* 550–572.

Pfeffer, J., & Davis-Blake, A. (1987). Understanding organizational wage structure: A resource-dependence approach. *Academy of Management Journal, 30,* 437–455.

Pfeffer, J., & Moore, W. (1980). Power in university budgeting: A replication and extension. *Administrative Science Quarterly, 25,* 637–653.

Pfeffer, J., & Salancik, G. (1978). *The external control of organizations: A resource dependence perspective.* New York: Harper and Row.

Pieper, R. (1990). *Human resource management: An international comparison.* Berlin: de Gruyter.

Pilkington, A. (1996). Learning from joint ventures: The Rover-Honda relationship. *Business History, 38,* 90–116.

Poole, M. (1990). Editorial: Human resource management in an international perspective. *International Journal of Human Resource Management, 1*, 1–15.

Porter, M. E. (1986). Changing patterns of international competition. *California Management Review, 28*, 9–40.

Prahalad, C. K. (1975). *The strategic process in multinational corporation* (unpublished doctoral dissertation). Boston: Harvard Graduate School of Business Administration.

Prahalad, C. K., & Doz, Y. L. (1987). *The multinational mission.* New York: The Free Press.

Prahalad, C. K., & Hamal, G. (1990). The core competence of the corporation. *Harvard Business Review, 68*(3), 79–91.

Prange, C. (1999). Desperately seeking theory? pp. 23–43. In M. Easterby-Smith, J. Burgoyne, & L. Araujo (Eds.), *Organizational learning and the learning organization.* London: Sage.

Pucik, V., & Katz, J. H. (1986). Information, control, and human resource management in multinational firms. *Human Resource Management, 25*, 121–132.

Redding, S. G. (1994). Comparative management theory: Jungle, zoo or fossil bed? *Organization Studies, 15*, 323–359.

Rosenzweig, P. M. (2006). The dual logics behind international human resource management: Pressures for global integration and local responsiveness. In G. Stahl & I. Björkman (Eds.), *Handbook of research in international human resource management.* Cheltenham, U.K.: Edward Elgar.

Rosenzweig, P. M., & Nohria, N. (1994). Influences on human resource management practices in multinational corporations. *Journal of International Business Studies, 25*, 229–251.

Roth, K., Schweiger, D. W., & Morrison, A. J. (1991). Global strategy implementation at the business unit level: Operational capabilities and administrative mechanisms. *Journal of International Business Studies, 22*(3), 369–402.

Rugman, A. M., Cruz, J. R., & Verbecke, A. (1995). Internationalisation and de-internationalisation: Will business networks replace multinationals? In G. Boyd (Ed.), *Competitive and co-operative macro-management* (pp. 107–129). Aldershot: Edward Elgar.

Rumelt, R. P. (1987). Theory, strategy, and entrepreneurship. In D. Teece (Ed.), *The competitive challenge* (pp. 137–158). Cambridge, MA: Ballinger.

Sanders, W. and Carpenter, M. (1998). Internationalization and firm governance: the roles of CEO compensation, top team composition, and board structure. *Academy of Management Journal, 41*, 158–78.

Saparito, P. A., Chen, C. C., & Sapienza, H. J. (2004). The role of relational trust in bank-small firm relationships. *Academy of Management Journal, 47*(3), 400–410.

Schuler, R. S. (2000a). Human resource issues and activities in international joint ventures. *International Journal of Human Resource Management, 12*(1), 1–52.

Schuler, R. S. (2000b). The internationalization of human resource management. *Journal of International Management, 6*, 239–260.

Schuler, R. S. (2001). Human resource issues and activities in international joint ventures. *International Journal of Human Resource Management, 12*(1), 1–52.

Schuler, R. S., Budhwar, P. S., & Florkowski, G. W. (2002). International human resource management: Review and critique. *International Journal of Management Reviews, 4*(1), 41–70.

Schuler, R. S., Dowling, P. J., & DeCieri, H. (1993). An integrative framework of strategic international human resource management. *International Journal of Human Resource Management, 4*, 717–764.

Schuler, R. S., & Jackson, S. E. (1987). Linking competitive strategy and human resource management practices. *Academy of Management Executive, 1*, 207–219.

Schuler, R. S., & Jackson, S. E. (1995). Understanding human resource management in the context of organizations and their environments. *Annual Review of Psychology, 46*, 237–264.

Schuler, R. S., & Jackson, S. E. (2001). HR issues and activities in mergers and acquisitions. *European Management Journal*, June, 253–287.

Schuler, R. S., & Jackson, S. E. (2005). A quarter-century review of human resource management in the U.S.: The growth in importance of the international perspective. *Management Revue, 16*(1), 11–35.

Schuler, R. S., Jackson, S. E., & Luo, Y. (2003). *Managing human resources in cross-border alliances.* London: Routledge.

Schuler, R. S., Jackson, S. E., & Storey, J. (2001). HRM and its link with strategic management. In J. Storey (Ed.), *Human resource management: A critical text* (pp. 114–130). London: Thomson Learning.

Schuler, R., & MacMillan, I. C. (1984). Gaining competitive advantage through human resource management practices. *Human Resource Management, 23*(3), 241–255.

Schuler, R. S., & Rogovsky, N. (1998). Understanding compensation practice variations across firms: The impact of national culture. *Journal of International Business Studies, 29*(1), 159–177.

Schuler, R. S., & Tarique, I. (2006). International joint venture system complexity and human resource management. pp. 385–404. In I. Bjorkman & G. Stahl (Eds.), *Handbook of research into international HRM*. London: Edward Elgar.

Schütte, H. (1996). *Regional headquarters of multinational corporations* (unpublished doctoral thesis). St. Gallen: Universität St. Gallen, Hochschule für Wirtschafts-, Rechts- und Sozialwissenschaften (HSG).

Schütte, H. (1998). Between headquarters and subsidiaries: The RHQ solution. In J. Birkenshaw & N. Hood (Ed.), *Multinational corporate evolution and subsidiary development* (pp. 102–136). New York: St. Martin's Press.

Scott, W. R. (1983). Health care organizations in the 1980s: The convergence of public and professional control systems. In J. W. Meyer & W. R. Scott (Eds.), *Organizational environments: Ritual and rationality* (pp. 99–113). Beverly Hills, CA: Sage Publications.

Scott, W. R. (1987). The adolescence of institutional theory. *Administrative Science Quarterly, 32,* 493–511.

Scott, W. R., & Meyer, J. W. (1989). *The rise of training programs in firms and agencies: An institutional perspective* (Stanford University working paper). Stanford, CA: Stanford University.

Scott, W. R. (1995). *Institutions and organizations.* London: Sage Publications.

Sparrow, P. R. (2006). Knowledge management in global organizations. (pp. 113–140) In I. Bjorkman & G. Stahl (Eds.), *Handbook of research into international HRM*. London: Edward Elgar.

Sparrow, P. R., Brewster, C., & Harris, H. (2004). *Globalizing human resource management*. London: Routledge.

Sparrow, P. R., & Hiltrop, J. M. (1997). Redefining the field of European human resource management: A battle between national mindsets and forces of business transition. *Human Resource Management, 36*(2), 1–19.

Staehle, W. (1994). *Management* (7th ed.). München: Verlag Franz Vahlen.

Stonehouse, G., Hamill, J., Campbell, D., & Purdie, T. (2000). *Global and transnational business: Strategy and management*. Chichester: Wiley.

Stopford, J. M., & Wells, L. T. (1972). *Managing the multinational enterprise. Organization of the firm and ownership of subsidiaries*. New York: Basic Books.

Storey, J. (1995). Human resource management: Still marching on, or marching out? In J. Storey (Ed.), *Human resource management* (pp. 3–32). London: Routledge.

Szulanski, G. (1996). Exploring internal stickiness: Impediments to the transfer of best practice within the firm. *Strategic Management Journal, 17,* 27–44.

Tallman, S., & Fladmoe-Lindquist, K. (2002). Internationalization, globalization and capability-based strategy. *California Management Review, 45*(1), 116–135.

Taylor, S., Beechler, S., & Napier, N. (1996). Toward an integrative model of strategic international human resource management. *Academy of Management Review, 21*(4), 959–985.

Teece, D. J., Pisano, G., & Shuen, A. (1997). Dynamic capabilities and strategic management. *Strategic Management Journal, 18*,(7), 509–533.

Thompson, J. D. (1967). *Organizations in action. Social science base of administrative theory*. New York: McGraw-Hill.

Tichy, N. M., Fombrun, C. J., & Devanna, M. A. (1982). Strategic human resource management. *Sloan Management Review, 23,* 47–61.

Tsai, W. (2000). Social capital, strategic relatedness and the formation of intra-organizational linkages. *Strategic Management Journal, 21,* 925–939.

Tsai, W. (2002). Social structure of cooperation within a multiunit organization: Coordination, competition, and intraorganizational knowledge sharing. *Organization Science, 13,* 179–192.

Tsai, W., & Ghoshal, S. (1998). Social capital and value creation: The role of inter-firm networks. *Academy of Management Journal, 41*(4), 464–476.

Tushman, M. L., & Nadler, D. A. (1978). Information processing as an integrating concept in organizational design. *Academy of Management Review, 3,* 613–624.

Ulrich, D. 1987. Organizational capability as competitive advantage: Human resource professionals as strategic partners. *Human Resource Planning, 10*, 169–184.

Ulrich, D., & Lake, D. (1990). *Organization capability: Competing from the inside out.* New York: Wiley.

Van Dijk, J. J. (1990). Transnational management in an evolving European context. *European Management Journal, 8*, 474–479.

Vermuelen, F., & Barkema, H. (2001). Learning through acquisitions. *Academy of Management Journal, 44*(3), 457–476.

Wächter, H. (1987). Professionalisierung im Personalbereich. *Die Betriebswirtschaft, 47*, 141–150.

Weber, W., Festing, M., Dowling, P. J., & Schuler, R. S. (1998). *Internationales personalmanagement.* Wiesbaden: Gabler.

Weick, K. E., & Van Orden, P. (1990). Organizing on a global scale. *Human Resource Management, 29*, 49–62.

Wernerfelt, B. (1984). A resource-based view of the firm. *Strategic Management Journal, 5*(2), 171–180.

Westney, D. E. (1993). Institutional theory and the multinational corporation. In S. Ghoshal & D. E. Westney (Eds.), *Organization theory and the multinational corporation* (pp. 53–76). New York: St. Martin's Press.

White, R., & Poynter, T. (1990). Organizing for world-wide advantage. In C. A. Bartlett, Y. Doz, & G. Hedlund (Eds.), *Managing the global firm* (pp. 95–113). London: Routledge.

Whitley, R. D. (Ed.). (1992). *European business systems: Firms and markets in their national contexts.* London: Sage.

Whitley, R. D. (1999). *Divergent capitalisms: The social structuring and change of business systems.* Oxford: Oxford University Press.

Wolf, J. (1997). From "starworks" to networks and heterarchies? Theoretical rationale and empirical evidence of HRM organization in large multinational corporations [Special issue]. *Management International Review, 37*, 145–169.

Wright, P. M., Dunford, B. B., & Snell, S. A. (2001). Human resources and the resource based view of the firm. *Journal of Management, 27*, 701–721.

Wright, P. M., & McMahan, G. C. (1992). Theoretical perspectives for strategic human resource management. *Journal of Management, 18*(2), 295–320.

Wright, P. M., McMahan, G. C., & McWilliams, A. (1994). Human resources and sustained competitive advantage: A resource-based perspective. *International Journal of Human Resource Management, 5*(2), 301–326.

Yip, G. S. (1992). *Total global strategy.* Englewood Cliffs, NJ: Prentice-Hall.

Yli-Renko, H., Autio, E., & Sapienza, H. (2001). Social capital, knowledge acquisition, and knowledge exploitation in young technology-based firms. *Strategic Management Journal, 22*, 587–613.

Youndt, M. A., Subramaniam, M., & Snell, S. A. (2004). Intellectual capital profiles: An examination of investments and returns. *Journal of Management Studies, 41*, 335–361.

Yuen, E., & Hui, T. K. (1993). Headquarters, host-culture and organization influences on HRM policies and practices. *Management International Review, 33*, 361–383.

6 Research on Selection in an International Context: Current Status and Future Directions

Filip Lievens

CONTENTS

Due to the globalization of the economy, organizations continue to move beyond national borders. This is reflected in international collaborations, joint ventures, strategic alliances, mergers, and acquisitions. As a consequence, it is necessary for organizations to view the labor market in an international scope. In addition, there is a need for human resource (HR) systems that can be used across multiple countries while at the same time recognizing local particularities (Schuler, Dowling, & DeCieri, 1993). One of these HR challenges is selecting people in an international labor market.

The aim of this chapter is to review prior research dealing with personnel selection in a global context. Generally, prior studies about selection in an international context can be grouped in three research streams. First of all, there is a large body of research that has examined whether there are differences in the use of common selection procedures from one country to another. Relatedly, some studies have also tried to explain why some selection procedures are more used across various countries. A second more narrow line of research studies has focused on the perceptions of selection procedures in different countries. Again, the main thrust of these studies was to ascertain whether commonly used procedures in personnel selection are differentially perceived across countries. Third, a limited number of prior studies has examined whether the criterion-related validity of selection procedures differed across countries. These three streams of research are reviewed and possible avenues for future research are proposed. We pay special attention to the fundamental issue as to whether selection techniques that are valid in one culture will necessarily be valid in another culture. Table 6.1 summarizes the main international findings related to each of these three research streams. Note that

TABLE 6.1

Overview of Main Findings of International Selection Research in Different Continents

	Use of Selection Procedures	Perceptions of Selection Procedures across Countries	Criterion-Related Validity of Selection Procedures across Countries
North America	Canada and the U.S. were surveyed. Detailed results per country and selection procedure are reported in Ryan et al. (1999).	In the U.S., interviews, resumes, biodata, and work samples received favorable reactions, whereas cognitive ability tests, personal references, and personality inventories were rated in the middle of the scale. Honesty tests, graphology, and personal contacts were poorly perceived (Steiner & Gilliland, 2001).	Schmidt and Hunter's meta-analysis (1998) reviewed 85 years of research on the validity of common selection procedures.
Europe (including U.K.)	Germany, France, Belgium, Spain, Sweden, the U.K., Greece, Ireland, Portugal, Italy, and the Netherlands were surveyed. Detailed results per country and selection procedure are reported in Ryan et al. (1999).	In France, Belgium, Spain, and Portugal interviews, resumes, and work samples received favorable reactions. The other tests (ability tests, references, and personality tests) were rated in the middle of the scale. Biodata received mixed ratings across countries. Graphology, and personal contacts were poorly perceived in all European countries surveyed (Steiner & Gilliland, 2001).	The meta-analysis of Salgado et al. (2003) reviewed research on the validity of general mental ability in Europe. Another meta-analysis of Salgado (1997) reviewed research on the validity of personality in Europe. Generally, the results of these meta-analyses mirrored results found in North American meta-analyses.
Asia (including Australia)	Singapore, Hong Kong, Australia, and New Zealand were surveyed. Detailed results per country and selection procedure are reported in Ryan et al. (1999).	Work samples, resumes, and interviews were rated most favorably in the U.S. and Singapore. Personality tests were rated more favorably in Singapore (Phillips & Gully, 2002).	No information available.
Africa (including the Middle East)	South Africa was surveyed. Detailed results per selection procedure are reported in Ryan et al. (1999).	In South Africa, interviews, resumes, work samples, biodata, and ability tests were favorably perceived. Personality tests, references, and honesty tests were rated in the middle of the scale. Graphology and personal contacts were poorly perceived (Steiner & Gilliland, 2001).	No information available.
South/Central America	No information on these countries was presented in Ryan et al. (1999).	No information available.	No information available.

Note: "No information available" means that we did not find *published* studies about this issue that were written in English.

this chapter does *not* deal with the selection of expatriate employees. This issue is discussed at length in another chapter of this handbook.

USE OF SELECTION PROCEDURES ACROSS COUNTRIES

In the past, many studies have examined the usage of selection procedures in different countries. Early studies were conducted on a national level in one specific country and were descriptive in nature because surveys simply asked respondents to report how frequently they used various selection procedures. For example, in 1991, the European Review of Applied Psychology published a special issue with several separate studies about selection procedure use in France, Germany, the United Kingdom, the Netherlands, Norway, and Spain. Another example is the special issue of the International Journal of Selection and Assessment (1994) that contained information about usage of selection procedures in the United States, Canada, Australia, and various European countries. Given that these studies were conducted at the national level, broader conclusions could be drawn only by pooling the results across many individual studies (e.g., Bruchon-Schweitzer, 1996; Levy-Leboyer, 1994). However, meaningful across-country comparisons were hampered because the surveys (e.g., data gathering method, selection procedures surveyed, question type, response scale) were not the same across countries. In addition, direct comparisons across countries were often difficult to make because the type of companies and industries surveyed differed considerably across countries.

To overcome these methodological problems of earlier studies, other studies used the same survey and sampling plan across different countries (Shackleton & Newell, 1997; M. Smith & Abrahamsen, 1992). For example, in their large-scale survey, Shackleton and Newell asked respondents in Germany, Italy, Belgium, France, and the United Kingdom to indicate the frequency of use of selection procedures. Their results revealed significant across-country variability in terms of use of selection procedures. Examples included the more frequent use of assessment centers in British and German companies as compared to other countries. German and Italian organizations were relatively infrequent users of psychological tests. An interesting conclusion was that the size of the organizations surveyed had a much less significant impact on the use of different selection procedures than the country of the organization. A recent study (Ryan, McFarland, Baron, & Page, 1999) surveyed 959 organizations in 20 countries and confirmed that national differences accounted for considerable variance in selection practices.

EXPLANATIONS FOR VARIABILITY IN USE OF SELECTION PROCEDURES ACROSS COUNTRIES

Various scholars (Herriot & Anderson, 1997; Newell & Tansley, 2001; Ryan, Wiechmann, & Hemingway, 2003; Schuler et al., 1993; Wiechmann, Ryan, & Hemingway, 2003) have proposed a host of contextual factors as explanations for the potential variability in terms of selection procedure use. Generally, the contextual factors proposed refer to cultural value differences, economic differences, employment legislation differences, educational differences, institutional network differences, and technological differences. Although the potentially influencing contextual factors are abounding, empirical research to test the impact of these factors has been limited. To our knowledge, only one study (Ryan et al., 1999) linked cultural differences to the variability in selection procedure use. Ryan et al. (1999) examined the influence of two dimensions of Hofstede's (1991) model on differential usage of selection techniques across countries. For example, Ryan et al. hypothesized that organizations in cultures high in power distance would be the ones where selection decision making is more hierarchical and where peers are less likely to be interviewers. Other hypotheses were that organizations in cultures high in uncertainty avoidance would use a more extensive selection process, would be more likely to use a fixed set of interview questions, and would be more likely to audit selection processes in some manner. Results showed that cultural dimensions explained some of the variability in staffing practices. Yet, there was only mixed support for the hypotheses regarding

TABLE 6.2

Summary of Directions for Future International Selection Research

Use of Selection Procedures

Which cultural factors affect the differential use of selection procedures across countries?

What is the impact of legal factors on the differential use of selection procedures across countries?

How do users' familiarity with selection procedures impact on the differential use of selection procedures across countries?

How do applicants' perceptions impact on the differential use of selection procedures across countries?

Which factors might bolster the introduction and acceptance of selection procedures in different countries?

Which factors discourage the use of selection procedures in different countries?

Perceptions of Selection Procedures across Countries

Do cultural dimensions predict the differential perception of selection procedures across countries?

What's the role of privacy perceptions in the differential perception of selection procedures across countries?

Criterion-Related Validity of Selection Procedures across Countries

Does the criterion-related validity of common selection procedures generalize in across-country applications?

Is there a difference in the international generalizability of the criterion-related validity of sign-based tests (e.g., ability and personality tests) versus sample-based tests (e.g., assessment centers, situational judgment tests, behavior description interviews)?

What is the impact of careful predictor-criterion matching on the criterion-related validity of common selection procedures in across-country applications?

Are common selection procedures in across-country applications related to organizational success?

Are objective measures of work output more generalizable across cultures as criterion measures than subjective performance ratings?

Does the job moderate the importance of matching predictor and criterion domains in establishing the criterion-related validity of common selection procedures in across-country applications?

What is the international generalizability of the constructs underlying selection procedures versus the international generalizability of the methods used to measure these constructs?

Is the same information about predictor constructs (selection procedures) differently combined into an overall selection decision across countries?

Do potential cultural differences in predictor weighting schemes affect the criterion-related validity of a selection battery in an international context?

Hofstede's culture dimensions. Whereas the hypotheses for power distance were not confirmed, some of the hypotheses for uncertainty avoidance were supported. Organizations in cultures high in uncertainty avoidance used more selection methods, used them more extensively, and conducted more interviews.

In short, these two recent studies illustrate that there is some empirical support that country-specific differences in the use of selection procedures are rooted in deeper cultural beliefs. Yet, as noted in Table 6.2, it is clear that we need more research about the determinants of the differential use of selection procedures across countries. Granted, the examination of cultural, national, legal, economic, or technological influences on selection procedure use is challenging because these influences are often intertwined. We believe that research on organizational determinants of selection procedure use in a national context might serve as inspiration here. A good example is the recent study of Wilk and Cappelli (2003). They investigated how organizational characteristics (specific work characteristics such as skill requirements of a position, training, and pay) lead a representative sample of U.S. companies to use other selection procedures.

Table 6.2 also mentions other avenues that deserve attention in future research. First, the impact of legal factors on selection procedure use should be scrutinized. It is generally known that the legal framework and codes of practice differ from country to country. For instance, in North America (the United States and Canada), there is a heavy emphasis on job-relatedness and equal opportunity, as evidenced by the Uniform Guidelines on Employee Selection Procedures (1978) or the Principles for the Validation and Use of Personnel Selection Procedures (2003). This legal framework in the United States has increased the popularity of specific selection procedures such as structured interviews (Williamson, Campion, Malos, Roehling, & Campion, 1997). In other countries, the threat of legal action on the basis of adverse impact is perceived by employers to be far less likely. For example, Arvey, Bhagat, and Salas (1991) noted that in Japan there is apparently little enforcement of formal laws prohibiting discrimination and bias. A similar situation seems to be present in many European countries. Even though standards of testing exist (e.g., the European Federation of Professional Psychologists' Association, Bartram & Coyne, 1998), these standards are often not compulsory.

Second, users' familiarity with selection procedures are worthy of investigation. It is possible that HR practitioners in other countries are simply unfamiliar with specific selection procedures and therefore do not use them (Rowe, Williams, & Day, 1994). For example, people might be unaware of different types of interviewing methods (see also Terpstra & Rozell, 1997). Professional associations play a role in divulging information about selection procedures. Levy-Leboyer (1994) noted that professional associations such as the American Psychological Association or the Society for Industrial and Organizational Psychology have a strong role in the United States. They actively encourage professional practices by publishing guidelines for professional practice, funding research projects, organizing conferences, and disseminating professional publications among their members. In other countries, professional associations might have a much weaker influence on practice.

Research that furthers our understanding of the determinants of the use of selection procedures across countries is important because it can help multinational organizations to reduce resistance when introducing a specific selection procedure in a specific country. This brings us to a last avenue for future research. We need studies that identify factors that might bolster the introduction and acceptance of selection procedures in different countries. Similarly, case studies about successful and unsuccessful implementations of selection procedures in other countries would be welcome. Even on a national level, we know very little about the organizational factors that enable or hinder implementation of selection procedures. Along these lines, Johns (1993) posited that we have typically placed too much emphasis on selection practices as rational technical interventions (e.g., attempts to "sell" utility information or structured interviews). Conversely, practitioners in organizations perceive the introduction of new selection procedures as an organizational intervention that is subject to the same pressures (power games, etc.) as other organizational innovations. In an international context, these introduction and implementation issues become even more complex. So far, primarily exportive tactics have been used when introducing a selection procedure in another country. On the basis of the diffusion of innovation literature (DiMaggio & Powell, 1983; O'Neill, Pouder, & Buchholtz, 1998) other tactics might be explored and studied.

PERCEPTIONS OF SELECTION PROCEDURES ACROSS COUNTRIES

Although many studies have examined applicant perceptions on a national level (Ryan & Ployhart, 2000), only a few studies have explored how applicants in different countries perceive selection procedures. Steiner and Gilliland (1996) conducted the first study that examined applicant reactions to selection procedures in an international context. Specifically, they compared how people in the United States and France perceived various selection procedures. They used Gilliland's (1993) justice model as a theoretical framework for representing applicant perceptions. Inspired by Steiner and Gilliland (1996), similar studies were conducted in South Africa (De Jong & Visser, 1999), the Flemish part of Belgium (Lievens, De Corte, & Brysse, 2003), the French part of Belgium

(Stinglhamber, Vandenberghe, & Brancart, 1999), Spain, Portugal (Salgado & Moscoso, 2004), and Singapore (Phillips & Gully, 2002). Steiner and Gilliland (2001) reviewed most of these studies. Although Steiner and Gilliland anticipated considerable variations in the perceptions across countries, results were fairly consistent. Interviews, resumes, and work samples consistently received favorable reactions, whereas cognitive ability tests, personal references, and personality inventories were typically rated in the middle of the scale. In all countries, job-relatedness (face validity) emerged as the key determinant of favorable perceptions. Phillips and Gully (2002) reached similar conclusions for their U.S.–Singapore comparison. Again, interviews, resumes, and work samples were rated most favorably and job-relatedness was the crucial driver of these perceptions. A difference was that personality tests were rated more favorably in Singapore.

Steiner and Gilliland (2001) suggested sampling reasons as a possible explanation for these consistent findings. In particular, all of the aforementioned countries shared a European heritage. Hence, Steiner and Gilliland expected more diverging results in applicant reactions when a more diverse set of countries was surveyed. Along these lines, they posited that cultural dimensions might serve as powerful influences of applicant reactions. For instance, Steiner and Gilliland (2001) expected that the equality and special needs rule of distributive justice would be more prevalent in collectivistic cultures because these cultures are more concerned with group harmony or individuals in need. Conversely, they asserted that the equity rule would be most salient in individualistic cultures. So far, these assertions have not been fully tested. Thus, as noted in Table 6.2, they constitute an important avenue for future research on applicant perceptions in an international context.

Apart from exploring the generalizability of selection procedure perceptions, future research about applicant perceptions in an international context should broaden the type of perceptions investigated. In particular, candidates' perceptions of invasion of privacy have remained unexplored, even though there exists a large literature on organizational privacy that might be integrated into the organizational justice literature (Eddy, Stone, & Stone-Romero, 1999; Stone & Stone, 1990). There are a couple of reasons invasion of privacy perceptions might be useful dimensions in an international context. First, there is evidence that there are cultural differences in terms of privacy perceptions. In fact, in many European countries legislation is much stricter in terms of invasion of privacy than in the United States (see also H. J. Smith, 2001) so that European industrial and organizational psychologists seem to be more concerned with protecting the privacy of the candidate. That might be the reason drug testing, honesty testing, or polygraph testing is virtually never used in Europe. Second, the emergence of Web-based testing systems that might be used across countries is another reason for focusing on candidate's privacy perceptions. Along these lines, Harris, Van Hoye, and Lievens (2003) found that the discrepancies between privacy legislation in the United States and Europe were related to different privacy perceptions of Web-based testing applications among candidates in the United States versus Europe.

THE CRITERION-RELATED VALIDITY OF SELECTION PROCEDURES ACROSS COUNTRIES

VALIDITY GENERALIZATION VERSUS SITUATIONAL SPECIFICITY

When organizations use selection procedures in other cultures and across cultures, it is of key importance for them to know whether a specific selection procedure is transportable to another culture and whether the criterion-related validity of the selection procedure is generalizable. Essentially, two hypotheses have been proposed, namely the validity generalization hypothesis and the situational specificity hypothesis (Salgado & Anderson, 2002). The *validity generalization* hypothesis states that observed criterion-related validity coefficients vary only because of statistical artifacts (such as sampling error, range restriction, and criterion unreliability). When these statistical artifacts are accounted for, criterion-related validity coefficients will generalize across different situations (jobs, occupational groups, and organizations) (Schmidt & Hunter, 1984).

In an international context, this means that criterion-related validity coefficients associated with a specific selection procedure obtained in one country will generalize to another country.

Exactly the opposite is posited by the *situational specificity* hypothesis. According to this hypothesis, there will be high variability in the observed criterion-related validity coefficients obtained in different situations (jobs, occupational groups, organizations, etc.). Whenever the situation changes, the observed criterion-related validity coefficient might also change (Schmidt & Hunter, 1984). Applied to an international context, this means that selection procedures might be valid in one country but not in another country. The following quote from Herriot and Anderson (1997) further illustrates the basic arguments behind the situational specificity hypothesis:

> The findings from [the American] meta-analyses have been unreservedly cited by personnel psychologists in other countries and appear to have been unquestioningly accepted as being generalizable to different national contexts. Social, cultural, legislative and recruitment and appraisal differences have been overlooked, and certainly in many European countries the results of meta-analyses conducted in the United States have been cited without caveat. These findings may indeed be transferable to other countries, but then again they may not be, given the pervasive cultural differences. (p. 28)

DOES THE CRITERION-RELATED VALIDITY OF SELECTION PROCEDURES GENERALIZE?

To date, few empirical studies have tested the two aforementioned hypotheses, examining whether the criterion-related validity of selection procedures differed across countries. To our knowledge, only the criterion-related validity of cognitive ability tests and personality inventories has been put to the test in an international context. Generally, results have provided support for the validity generalization hypothesis. For example, Salgado and colleagues (Salgado, Anderson, Moscoso, Bertua, & De Fruyt, 2003a; Salgado, Anderson, Moscoso, Bertua, De Fruyt, & Rolland, 2003b) examined the criterion-related validity of cognitive ability tests in several countries of the European Community (Belgium, France, Germany, Ireland, the Netherlands, Portugal, Sweden, Norway, Spain, and the United Kingdom). They found evidence for validity generalization for cognitive ability tests as the magnitude of the criterion-related validity coefficients was very similar across European countries as different as Spain and the United Kingdom. As compared to previous meta-analyses in the United States (Hartigan & Wigdor, 1989; Hunter & Hunter, 1984; Schmidt & Hunter, 1998; Schmidt, 2002), this European Community meta-analysis showed a somewhat larger operational validity for cognitive ability for predicting job performance. For training success, the European and U.S. results were very similar. In addition, similar to earlier North American findings, the European results revealed that job complexity moderated the magnitude of the operational validities of cognitive ability tests, with higher coefficients for more complex jobs. All of this underscored that the criterion-related validity of cognitive ability tests generalized across jobs, occupations, and national borders.

Evidence for validity generalization has also been obtained with regard to personality tests. Specifically, Salgado (1997) conducted a meta-analysis of the criterion-related validity of the Big Five personality traits in Europe. He found that Conscientiousness and Emotional Stability were valid predictors across job criteria and occupational groups. Extraversion emerged as a predictor for two occupations, and Openness and Agreeableness were valid predictors of training proficiency. These results are fairly consistent with results found in North American meta-analyses (Barrick & Mount, 1991; Hough, Eaten, Dunnette, Kamp, & McCloy, 1990; Hurtz & Donovan, 2000; Tett, Jackson, & Rothstein, 1991). It is also important to note that the Big Five personality characteristics have been replicated in an impressive series of studies, across raters and rating scales, but also in different countries and cultures (Collins & Gleaves, 1998; Ghorpade, Hattrup, & Lackritz, 1999; Saucier, Hampson, & Goldberg, 2000).

Whereas the previous studies were meta-analyses, we also retrieved some primary studies that explored the criterion-related validity of common selection procedures across different countries. Ployhart, Sacco, Nishii, and Rogg (2004) examined whether the criterion-related validity of various predictors (measures of team skills, work ethic, commitment, customer focus, and cognitive ability) differed across 10 countries. They found that criterion-related validity was largely constant across countries and unaffected by culture. Such and Hemingway (2003) concluded that a biodata measure was valid in seven countries. Finally, Such and Schmidt (2004) validated a situational judgment test in four countries. Results in a cross-validation sample showed that the situational judgment test was valid in two countries, namely the United Kingdom and Australia. It was not predictive in Mexico.

Taken together, research dealing with the criterion-related validity of different selection procedures in an international context is scarce. On the one hand the limited number of prior studies in this domain has already produced quite some interesting findings. A key conclusion for cognitive ability and personality seems to be that the criterion-related validity of these two predictors generalizes across countries. This runs counter to the situational specificity hypothesis. On the other hand we also believe that prior research about the criterion-related validity of different selection procedures in an international context has only scratched the surface. Hence, the following section is uniquely devoted to avenues for future research on the criterion-related validity of selection procedures in an international context.

DIRECTIONS FOR FUTURE INTERNATIONAL VALIDITY RESEARCH

In this section, we discuss four directions for future international validity research. As will be detailed below, we first suggest that researchers make a clear distinction between within-country and across-country applications of selection techniques. Second, studies need to address the importance of matching the predictor and the criterion in an international context. Third, the constructs measured should be clearly distinguished from the methods used to measure these constructs. Finally, future international studies should not only focus on the criterion-related validity of individual selection procedures but also on the validity of selection batteries, thereby acknowledging the impact of predictor weighting schemes. Similar to the previous research streams, we summarized the main research questions that need to be addressed in future research about the criterion-related validity of selection procedures in an international context in Table 6.2.

WITHIN-COUNTRY APPLICATIONS VERSUS ACROSS-COUNTRY APPLICATIONS

It is important that future studies about personnel selection practices in an international context distinguish between within-country and across-country contexts. If the criterion data are gathered in the same country as the country wherein the selection procedure was developed and used, this can be termed a *within-country application* (e.g., the selection procedures are used in South Korea and the job performance data are also gathered in South Korea). Most prior studies of selection procedures in an international context investigated these so-called within-country applications. When the selection procedures and criteria are carefully developed and matched within a given country, we believe that the selection procedure will be valid (regardless of the country under examination). When framed in this way, it is less surprising that Salgado et al. (2003a, 2003b) found that cognitive ability tests in various European countries were good predictors of criterion data gathered in *those* respective countries. Examples of within-country applications of selection procedures that turned out to be valid are widespread (e.g., assessment centers developed, used, and validated in the Netherlands [Jansen & Stoop, 2001] or situational judgment tests developed, used, and validated in Singapore [Chan & Schmitt, 2002]).

The story is different in *across-country applications*. In these applications, a selection procedure might be developed and used in a specific country, whereas the criterion data might be gathered in another country. For example, a selection procedure might be developed and used in the United States, whereas the criterion data might be gathered in France. Similarly, a selection procedure might be developed and used in Europe, whereas the criterion data might be gathered in Japan. The selection of expatriates might constitute an example of such an across-country application of selection procedures. In these instances, it is crucial that one ensures a matching between the predictor and criterion domains across cultures, as will be discussed below.

Although we presented the within-country and across-country contexts as a dichotomy, this does not necessarily have to be so. In both within-country and across-country applications, it is assumed that the predictor is developed in one specific country (culture). However, this should not always be the case. For example, Schmit, Kihm, and Robie (2000) used judgments of various personality experts around the globe for constructing a personality inventory. In such a combined emic and etic approach the predictor is developed with cross-cultural input.

IMPORTANCE OF MATCHING THE PREDICTOR TO THE CRITERION

Conceptually, using a selection procedure across cultures (i.e., in a different culture than originally intended) is not different from using a selection procedure for another job or occupation than originally intended. All of this is based on the well-known notion that validity is about matching predictor and criterion domains (Binning & Barrett, 1989). A drawback of prior research was that it did not factor in this relation between predictor and criterion. Prior studies concentrated either solely on the generalizability of selection predictors across countries (e.g., Salgado et al., 2003a, 2003b) or solely on the generalizability of job performance ratings (e.g., Ployhart, Wiechmann, Schmitt, Sacco, & Rogg, 2003).

We believe it is a crucial issue that the selection procedures used in a given culture are matched with the definition of performance adopted by that culture (see also Hough and Oswald, 2000). Let us illustrate this assertion with a couple of examples. Consider the employment interview. Eder and Harris (1999) discussed that the employment interview and especially the structured employment interview represents something of a "contest" wherein the candidate has to prove that he or she has the knowledge, skills, and abilities necessary for the job. Hence, the employment interview as we know it seems to represent achievement-oriented and individualistic cultural styles. Eder and Harris (1999) warned that this may not be the case in collectivistic cultures. In these cultures, lengthy unstructured interviews about one's family, childhood, education, and interests may not be uncommon. In these cultures, unstructured interviews may also reflect much more a collaborative and modest style where the candidate is reluctant to boost up his or her own individual performance and accomplishments. We also heard from HR personnel working in China that behavior description interviews do not yield useful information in China because it is socially more acceptable to construct fictitious stories about one's achievements than not to answer the question (from my part, I also experienced this when I got lost in China and asked for directions). These cultural differences might undermine the usefulness of behavior description interviews in these cultures. Yet, this does not mean that lengthy unstructured interviews reflecting a more collaborative and collectivistic cultural style that seem to be prevalent in collectivistic cultures will be necessarily invalid. The key point is whether the constructs measured in these interviews match the criterion. If supervisors, peers, and managers also value a collaborative and modest style, such interviews might still produce useful information about people's performance according to the predictor-criterion matching logic. Conversely, this will not be the case if North American or European managers who typically value a more achievement-oriented and individualistic style are required to rate work performance in these cultures.

The importance of matching predictor and criteria can also be illustrated with assessment centers. The dimensions and exercises that are typically used in assessment centers in North America and Europe may be less relevant in other countries. Perhaps, in a high-power-distance culture, candidates may be extremely uncomfortable engaging in role-plays. Again, this does not mean that assessment centers will be invalid in these cultures. The question is: Are these role-plays indeed relevant for the criterion domain that one tries to predict in these cultures? Empirical research attests to this. Lievens, Harris, Van Keer, and Bisqueret (2003) examined whether two assessment center exercises were valid predictors of European executives who were selected to work in Japan. They found that one of the exercises, the group discussion exercise, was a very powerful predictor of future performance as rated by Japanese supervisors later on. The presentation exercise, however, was not a valid predictor. According to Lievens, Harris, et al. (2003), the group discussion exercise reflected the team-based decision culture inherent in Japanese culture. This result underscores the importance of using assessment center exercises that match the culture in terms of key features and then assessing requisite skills in that context.

A final example deals with a Japanese division of a U.S. firm that selects people in Japan. The divisional HR department uses a selection technique (e.g., a situational judgment test to measure teamwork) imposed by the corporate HR headquarters in the United States. However, when the individuals enter the job, Japanese supervisors rate them. Clearly, these supervisors' view on teamwork is different than teamwork as seen by the corporate HR department in the United States. Hence, the Japanese supervisors might rate the performance of their personnel differently than the test predicted, resulting in low criterion-related validity.

All these examples demonstrate that it makes little sense to posit that a specific selection procedure will be or will not be useful in a culture without carefully examining the criterion domain. Although this logic is fundamental to the notion of validity (Binning & Barrett, 1989), it is often ignored in international selection. Yet, three caveats are in order with respect to this predictor-criterion matching logic. First and most important, the criterion measures used in foreign countries should be related to organizational success of the multinational corporation. Although there may be a match between predictor and criterion domains in a specific country, this does not guarantee that the theory of performance adopted in a specific country is aligned with the general theory of performance of the multinational corporation. Actually, it is possible that the performance measures gathered in the foreign country do not contribute to organizational success. Rereading the above examples from this perspective illustrates this. This underscores the importance of relating selection predictors to the success of the organization instead of using subjective performance measures as the final criterion.

Along these lines, one might expect that criterion-related validity in an international context will be different for subjective criterion measures (supervisory performance ratings) than for objective criterion measures (e.g., measures of quantity of work or work quality on an assembly line). This is because subjective criterion measures may reflect the theory of performance adopted in a specific country, whereas objective criterion measures represent aspects of work output that may generalize from one country to another. In other words, subjective criterion measures gathered in a specific country may deviate from performance indicators set by the multinational. Conversely, it is more likely that objective measures of work output are aligned with organizational success. Future research is needed to test these ideas.

Second, careful attention to matching predictor and criterion domains in international use of selection procedures may be less important for cognitive predictor constructs. This is because the cognitive ability test has emerged as the best stand-alone predictor whose validity generalizes across jobs, occupations, and countries (Salgado et al., 2003a, 2003b). Relatedly, we expect that attention to matching predictor and criterion domains in international use of selection procedures may be especially crucial for externally constructed predictor measures, such as work samples, situational judgment tests, assessment center exercises, or situational interviews because these predictors typically sample behaviors directly from the criterion. In that case, it should be guaranteed that the behaviors sampled and the scoring key used represent criterion behavior and performance (in a different culture). This is illustrated by the aforementioned results of Such and Schmidt (2004) as their situational judgment test was valid in the United Kingdom and Australia but not in Mexico.

Third, the job at hand might moderate the importance of matching predictor and criterion domains. In fact, when the job domain is not drastically different from culture to culture, a mismatch between the predictor and the criterion will have fewer deleterious effects on criterion-related validity. Conversely, if the job is culture-dependent and the selection procedure development was done in a different culture from the culture in which the selection procedure is used, it will matter in terms of criterion-related validity. As argued by Furrer, Liu, and Sudharshan (2000), customer service quality might be an example of a job dimension that is especially susceptible to cultural differences (see also Ployhart et al., 2003).

METHOD VERSUS CONSTRUCT DISTINCTION

In prior research about the criterion-related validity of selection procedures in an international context the distinction between "constructs" and "methods" was typically ignored. In personnel selection, constructs refer to the content that is being measured (Arthur, Day, McNelly, & Edens, 2003; Chan & Schmitt, 1997; Schmitt & Chan, 1998; Schmitt & Mills, 2001). Examples are cognitive ability, extraversion, manual dexterity (see Peterson et al., 1990, for a detailed overview of the predictor construct space). Conversely, methods refer to the myriad of specific techniques that measure these constructs. A specific construct such as extraversion can be measured via various methods, such as specific interview questions, specific inventory items, or specific situational judgment test items.

Our general proposition is that the broader constructs will generalize across countries and cultures. As shown in our review above, the available research is consistent with this premise as both the validity of general mental ability and personality constructs was about the same in the United States as in Europe. Equally important, we propose that even though the underlying constructs might be the same, the measurements (e.g., specific items used) of these constructs will be different across countries.

These general propositions can be illustrated in various ways. First, the large body of research on the cross-cultural equivalence of cognitive ability and personality tests shows that item and/or wording changes are typically necessary when cognitive ability and personality tests are transported and translated to another language and culture. The underlying structure of the tests, however, remains typically the same. For example, the basic underlying construct of conscientiousness may not be different across cultures, although the behavioral expressions of this construct are likely to differ (Church & Katigbak, 1988).

The development of the global personality inventory of Schmit, Kihm, and Robie (2000) is a second illustration that the behavioral indicators of personality constructs may vary, although the broader underlying constructs are similar across countries. Schmit et al. developed a global personality inventory with input from a panel of experts around the world. Despite the fact that 70 psychologists around the world wrote items in their own language for the constructs as defined in their own language, construct validity studies provided support for the same underlying structure of the global personality inventory across countries.

Third, the cultural sensitivity of methods (in the sense of the items used and the behaviors elicited) as compared to the cultural robustness of constructs is also illustrated by the use of situational judgment tests (Lievens, 2006) or assessment center exercises across cultures (Briscoe, 1997). The scores generated in this kind of selection procedures may be especially prone to cultural sensitivity because there is ample evidence that the behavioral expressions and interpretations for common constructs measured in assessment centers or situational judgment tests may differ from one culture to another. The extensive work of P. B. Smith and colleagues (e.g., Smith et al., 2002; Smith, Dugan, Peterson, & Leung, 1998) is probably the best example of how managerial behavior (e.g., handling disagreement, seeking guidance) is valued differently across countries. As another example, Adler, Doktor, and Redding (1986) showed that there were differences in decision making and information processing across cultures and countries. Given these well-established cross-cultural differences, the same situation or the same response to the same situation may be differently scored/rated across cultures.

A final example is given by Lawler, Walumbwa, and Bai in this handbook (Chapter 2). They argue that in China the method of face reading is often used to discover essential aspects of a candidate's personality because the face is believed to hold clues to one's "fate." Again, the measures used differ across cultures (face reading versus rigorously developed inventories) but the constructs measured may be the same.

In short, no studies have made this explicit distinction between constructs and methods in the context of research on selection procedures in an international context. Yet, it should be fairly easy for future research to test our propositions through tests of structural and measurement equivalence. A good example on a national level is the study of Hattrup, Schmitt, and Landis (1992), which revealed that two different types of cognitive ability tests (a cognitive ability test with traditional items versus a cognitive ability test with business-related items) measured the same underlying constructs.

IMPACT OF PREDICTOR WEIGHTING

Our review of prior selection research in a cross-cultural context illustrated that only the criterion-related validity of individual selection procedures was examined. An additional set of issues arises if we move from an individual selection procedure (a univariate prediction model) to a selection battery (a multivariate prediction model). A multivariate prediction model implies that decisions have to be taken about how to combine or weight the several predictors into a composite predictor score[1] (Murphy & Shiarella, 1997).

Many studies have already demonstrated the impact of predictor weighting schemes on criterion-related validity (e.g., De Corte, 1999; Hattrup, Rock, & Scalia, 1997; Sackett & Roth, 1996; Schmitt, Rogers, Chan, Sheppard, & Jennings, 1997). In particular, Murphy and Shiarella (1997) found that the criterion-related validity of a selection battery depended substantially on how predictors were combined. Roughly 23% of the variance in the criterion-related validity of the selection battery could be explained in terms of the weights assigned to the predictors of the battery. On a national level, there is also evidence that practitioners assign implicit weights to the predictors in making overall hirability ratings. Dunn, Mount, Barrick, & Ones (1995) presented American managers with applicant profiles who were described on general mental ability (GMA) and the Big Five. Policy-capturing analysis showed that GMA and conscientiousness were viewed as the most important attributes. Dunn et al. also found that the relative importance attached to the personal attributes was consistent across six occupations, although some minor differences were found (see also Ones & Viswesvaran, 1999). A similar study of Lievens, Highhouse, and De Corte (2005) demonstrated that the method of selection used (paper-and-pencil test versus unstructured interview) affected the relative importance attached to the constructs among Belgian supervisors. Specifically, the importance attached to extraversion and GMA was significantly moderated by the selection method, with extraversion and GMA decreasing in importance when store supervisors knew that scores on extraversion and GMA were derived from a paper-and-pencil test as opposed to from an unstructured interview.

In an international context, there is similar evidence that predictor constructs are differentially weighted. A good example is the large-scale survey of Huo, Huang, and Napier (2002) (see also Von Glinow, Drost, & Teagarden, 2002). They surveyed selection preferences in ten countries all over the world and concluded that companies in these countries differed in how they valued specific characteristics to be used in selection. Countries such as Australia, Canada, Germany, and the United States assigned great importance to proven work experience in a similar job and technical skills for deciding whether someone should have the job (see also Arvey et al., 1991). Conversely, companies in Japan, South Korea, and Taiwan placed a relatively low weight on job-related skills. In these countries, people's potential and teamwork skills seemed much more important (see also Morishima, 1995). Other evidence comes from Triandis and Vassiliou (1972) who asked both Americans and Greeks to make decisions about job candidates. The Greek sample emphasized much more information from interpersonal sources than the American sample. In countries such as Mexico (Kras, 1988) or South Korea (Koch, Nam, & Steers, 1995) it has also been found that recruiters attach much more importance to information provided by interpersonal sources of information, such as friends or relatives of the candidate.

---

[1]	Note that Murphy and Shiarella (1997) also discuss the impact of combining or weighting the criterion dimensions into an overall criterion (job performance) on the validity of selection procedures.

Although these studies revealed that predictors may be differentially weighed from one culture to another culture, no studies have taken this further. Specifically, we do not know whether the same information about predictor constructs on the basis of a specific selection battery may be differently combined into an overall selection decision across cultures. Given the aforementioned differences in the importance of predictors across cultures, we expect that this will be the case. Even more important, future studies are needed to investigate whether these potential cultural differences in predictor weighting schemes affect the criterion-related validity of a selection battery. In light of the well-documented evidence of the impact of predictor weighting schemes on criterion-related validity on a national level, we also expect that the criterion-related validity of the selection battery will differ from one culture to another.

CONCLUSIONS

This chapter gave an overview of prior research about personnel selection in an international context. Although we tried to use a truly "international" perspective, Table 6.1 exemplified that the large majority of studies were conducted in North America and Western Europe. Therefore, future studies should be conducted in other parts of the world (South America, Africa, and Asia). Only then can we obtain a full understanding of the cultural influences on personnel selection.

We believe that prior international selection research has only scratched the surface. Prior research was descriptive and primarily explored differential usage of selection techniques. The more fundamental issue of whether the criterion-related validity of selection procedures generalized across countries has been largely ignored so far. Therefore, a large part of this chapter focused on criterion-related validity issues in an international context. We posited that in most cases the criterion-related validity of most selection procedures will generalize and that researchers should put forward explicit hypotheses as to why criterion-related validities should *not* generalize. To this end, we proposed various testable hypotheses. First, researchers should carefully distinguish between within-country and across-country applications of selection procedures. If the predictor is used for within-culture applications (predictor and criterion are developed and gathered in the same culture, e.g., an organization in Germany hires German individuals for a given job in Germany), criterion-related validity should be ensured when the predictor is carefully developed (based on job analysis, etc.). Conversely, cultural differences might threaten the criterion-related validity of selection procedures in across-country applications (predictor and criterion data are gathered in different cultures, e.g., a multinational hires an individual for a given job in the host culture). This might be especially the case if the performance theory used in a specific culture is different from the performance theory adopted by the multinational organization. A second general conclusion was that the predictor constructs will often be very similar across countries. Third, we posited that even though the predictor constructs are similar, the behavioral content and measurement of the predictors might be different across countries and cultures. Therefore, it is crucial that the predictor specifications are matched with the criterion specifications in another culture so that the culture-specific theory of performance is taken into account. We also argued that both subjective and objective criterion measures should be used as the latter seem to be more generalizable across cultures. As a fourth conclusion, we posited that even though the criterion-related validity coefficient associated with an individual selection procedure (univariate model) might be the same across cultures, this does not necessarily mean that the criterion-related validity coefficient associated with a selection battery (multivariate model) will be the same across countries because the relative importance attached to predictor components is likely to differ across countries.

REFERENCES

Adler, N. J., Doktor, R., & Redding, S. G. (1986). From the Atlantic to the Pacific century: Cross-cultural management reviewed. *Journal of Management, 12*, 295–318.

Arthur, W., Jr., Day, E. A., McNelly, T. L., & Edens, P. S. (2003). A meta-analysis of the criterion-related validity of assessment center dimensions. *Personnel Psychology, 56*, 125–154.

Arvey, R. D., Bhagat, R. S., & Salas, E. (1991). Cross-cultural and cross-national issues in personnel and human resources management: Where do we go from here? In G. R. Ferrris & K. M. Rowland (Eds.), *Research in personnel and human resource management* (Vol. 9. pp. 367–407). Greenwich: JAI Press.

Barrick, M. R., & Mount, M. K. (1991). The big five personality dimensions and job performance: A meta-analysis. *Personnel Psychology, 44*, 1–26.

Bartram, D., & Coyne, I. (1998). The ITC/EFPPA survey of testing and test use within Europe. *Proceedings of the British Psychological Society's Occupational Psychology Conference*, 12–18.

Bartram, D., & Coyne, I. (1998). Variations in National Patterns of Testing and Test Use: The ITC/EFPPA International Survey. *European Journal of Psychological Assessment, 14*, 249–260.

Binning, J. F., & Barrett, G. V. (1989). Validity of personnel decisions: A conceptual analysis of the inferential and evidential bases. *Journal of Applied Psychology, 74,* 478–494.

Briscoe, D. R. (1997). Assessment centers: Cross-cultural and cross-national issues. *Journal of Social Behavior and Personality, 12*, 261–270.

Bruchon-Schweitzer, M. (1996). Some French studies in selection and assessment. In M. Smith and V. Sutherland (Eds.), *International review of professional issues in selection and assessment* (Vol. 2, pp. 165–168). New York: Wiley.

Chan, D., & Schmitt, N. (1997). Video-based versus paper-and-pencil method of assessment in situational judgment tests: Subgroup differences in test performance and face validity perceptions. *Journal of Applied Psychology, 82*, 143–159.

Church, A. T., & Katigbak, M. S. (1988). The emic strategy in the identification and assessment of personality dimensions in a nonwestern culture: Rationale, steps, and a Philippine illustration. *Journal of Cross-Cultural Psychology, 19*, 140–163.

Collins, J. M., & Gleaves, D. H. (1998). Race, job applicants, and the five-factor model of personality: Implications for black psychology, I/O psychology, and the five-factor model. *Journal of Applied Psychology, 83*, 531–544.

De Corte, W. (1999). Weighing job performance predictors to both maximize the quality of the selected workforce and control the level of adverse impact. *Journal of Applied Psychology, 84*, 695–702.

De Jong, A., & Visser, D. (1999). *Black and white employees' fairness perceptions of personnel selection techniques* (Unpublished manuscript).

DiMaggio, P., & Powell, W. (1983). The iron cage revisited: Institutional isomorphism and collective rationality in organizational fields. *American Sociological Review, 4*, 147–160.

Dunn, W. S., Mount, M. K., Barrick, M. R., & Ones, D. S. (1995). Relative importance of personality and general mental ability in managers' judgments of applicant qualifications. *Journal of Applied Psychology, 4*, 500–509.

Eddy, E. R., Stone, D. L., & Stone-Romero, E. F. (1999). The effects of information management policies on reactions to human resource information systems: An integration of privacy and procedural justice perspectives. *Personnel Psychology, 52*, 335–358.

Eder, R. W., & Harris, M. M. (1999). Employment interview research: Historical update and introduction. In R. W. Eder and M. M. Harris (Eds.), *The employment interview handbook* (pp. 1–28). Thousand Oaks, CA: Sage Publications.

Furrer, O., Liu, B. S., & Sudharshan, D. (2000). The relationship between culture and service quality perceptions: Basis for international market segmentation and resource allocation. *Journal of Service Research, 2*, 355–371.

Ghorpade, J., Hattrup, K., & Lackritz, J. R. (1999). The use of personality measures in cross-cultural research: A test of three personality scales across two countries. *Journal of Applied Psychology, 84*, 670–679.

Gilliland, S. W. (1993). The perceived fairness of selection systems: An organizational justice perspective. *Academy of Management Review, 18*, 694–734.

Harris, M. M., Van Hoye, G., & Lievens, F. (2003). Privacy and attitudes towards Internet-based selection systems: A cross-cultural comparison. *International Journal of Selection and Assessment, 11*, 230–236.

Hartigan, J. A., & Wigdor, A. K. (1989). *Fairness in employment testing.* Washington, DC: National Academy Press.

Hattrup, K., Rock, J., & Scalia, C. (1997). The effects of varying conceptualizations of job performance on adverse impact, minority hiring, and predictor performance. *Journal of Applied Psychology, 82*, 656–664.

Hattrup, K., Schmitt, N., & Landis, R. S. (1992). Equivalence of constructs measured by job-specific and commercially available aptitude tests. *Journal of Applied Psychology, 77*, 298–308.

Herriot, P., & Anderson, N. (1997). Selecting for change: How will personnel and selection psychology survive? In N. R. Anderson and P. Herriot (Eds.), *International handbook of selection and assessment*. London: Wiley.

Hofstede, G. (1991). *Cultures and organizations: Software of the mind*. London: McGraw-Hill.

Hough, L. M., Eaton, N. K., Dunnette, M. D., Kamp, J. D., & McCloy, R. A. (1990). Criterion-related validities of personality constructs and the effect of response distortion on those validities. *Journal of Applied Psychology, 75*, 581–595.

Hough, L. M., & Oswald, F. L. (2000). Personnel selection: Looking toward the future—remembering the past. *Annual Review of Psychology, 51*, 631–664.

Hunter, J. E., & Hunter, R. F. (1984). Validity and utility of alternative predictors of job performance. *Psychological Bulletin, 96*, 72–98.

Huo, Y. P., Huang, H. J., & Napier, N. K. (2002). Divergence or convergence: A cross-national comparison of personnel selection practices. *Human Resource Management, 41*, 31–44.

Hurtz, G. M., & Donovan, J. J. (2000). Personality and job performance: The big five revisited. *Journal of Applied Psychology, 85*, 869–879.

Jansen, P. G. W., & Stoop, B. A. M. (2001). The dynamics of assessment center validity: Results of a 7-year study. *Journal of Applied Psychology, 86*, 741–753.

Johns, G. (1993). Constraints on the adoption of psychology-based personnel practices: Lessons from organizational innovation. *Personnel Psychology, 46*, 569–592.

Koch, M., Nam, S. H., & Steers, R. M. (1995). Human resource management in South Korea. In L. F. Moore and P. D. Jennings (Eds.), *Human resource management on the Pacific Rim* (pp. 217–242). Berlin: Walter de Gruyter.

Kras, E. S. (1988). *Management in two cultures: Bridging the gap between U.S. and Mexican managers*. Yarmouth, ME: Intercultural Press.

Levy-Leboyer, C. (1994). Selection and assessment in Europe. In H. C. Triandis, M. D. Dunnette, & L. M. Hough (Eds.), *Handbook of industrial and organizational psychology* (Vol. 4, pp. 173–190). Palo Alto, CA: Consulting Psychologists Press.

Lievens, F. (2006). International situational judgment tests. pp. 279–300. In J. A. Weekley and R. E. Ployhart (Eds.), *Situational judgment tests* (SIOP Frontier Series). Mahwah, NJ: LEA

Lievens, F., De Corte, W., & Brysse, K. (2003). Applicant perceptions of selection procedures: The role of selection information, belief in tests, and comparative anxiety. *International Journal of Selection and Assessment, 11*, 67–77.

Lievens, F., Highhouse, S., & De Corte, W. (2005). The importance of traits and abilities in supervisors' hirability decisions as a function of method of assessment. *Journal of Occupational and Organizational Psychology, 78*, 453–470.

Lytle, A. L., Brett, J. M., Barsness, Z. I., Tinsley, C. H., & Janssens, M. (1995). A paradigm for confirmatory cross-cultural research in organizational behavior. *Research in Organizational Behavior, 17*, 167–214.

Morishima, M. (1995). The Japanese human resource management system: A learning bureaucracy. In L. F. Moore and P. D. Jennings (Eds.), *Human resource management on the Pacific Rim* (pp. 119–150). Berlin: Walter de Gruyter.

Murphy, K. R., & Shiarella, A. H. (1997). Implications of the multidimensional nature of job performance for the validity of selection tests: multivariate framework for studying test validity. *Personnel Psychology, 50*, 823–854.

Newell, S. & Tansley, C. (2001) International uses of selection methods. In C. L. Cooper and I. T. Robertson (Eds.), *International review of industrial and organizational psychology* (Vol. 21, pp. 195–213). Chichester: Wiley.

O'Neill, H. M., Pouder, R. W., & Buchholtz, A. K (1998). Patterns in the diffusion of strategies across organizations: Insights from the innovation diffusion literature. *Academy of Management Review, 23*, 98–114.

Ones, D. S., & Viswesvaran, C. (1999). Relative importance of personality dimensions for expatriate selection: A policy capturing study. *Human Performance, 12*, 275–294.

Peterson, N., Hough, L., Dunnette, M., Rosse, R., Houston, J., Toquam, J. L. & Wing, H. (1990). Project A: Specification of the predictor domain and development of new selection/classification tests. *Personnel Psychology, 43*, 247–276.

Phillips, J. M., & Gully, S. M. (2002). Fairness reactions to personnel selection techniques in Singapore and the United States. *International Journal of Human Resource Management, 13*, 1186–1205.

Ployhart, R. E., Sacco, J. M., Nishii, L. H., & Rogg, K. L. (2004, April). *The influence of culture on criterion-related validity and job performance*. Poster presented at the Annual Conference of the Society for Industrial and Organizational Psychology, Chicago, IL.

Ployhart, R. E., Wiechmann, D., Schmitt, N., Sacco, J. M., & Rogg, K. L. (2003). The cross-cultural equivalence of job performance ratings. *Human Performance, 16*, 49–79.

Principles for the validation and use of personnel selection procedures (3rd ed.). (2003). College Park, MD: Society for Industrial and Organizational Psychology, Inc.

Rowe, P., Williams, M., & Day, A. (1994). Selection procedures in North America. *International Journal of Assessment and Selection, 2*(2), 74–79.

Ryan, A. M., McFarland, L., Baron, H., & Page, R. (1999). An international look at selection practices: Nation and culture as explanations for variability in practice. *Personnel Psychology, 52*, 359–391.

Ryan, A. M., & Ployhart, R. E. (2000). Applicants' perception of selection procedures and decisions: A critical review and agenda for the future. *Journal of Management, 26*, 565–606.

Ryan, A. M., Wiechmann, D. & Hemingway, M. (2003). Designing and Implementing global staffing systems. Part II: Best practices. *Human Resource Management, 42*, 85–94.

Sackett, P. R., & Roth, L. (1996). Multistage selection strategies: A Monte Carlo investigation of effects on performance and minority hiring. *Personnel Psychology, 49*, 549–572.

Salgado, J. F. (1997). The five-factor model of personality and job performance in the European Community. *Journal of Applied Psychology, 82*, 30–43.

Salgado, J. F., & Anderson, N. R. (2002). Cognitive and GMA testing in the European Community: Issues and evidence. *Human Performance, 15*, 75–96.

Salgado, J. F., Anderson, N., Moscoso, S., Bertua, C., & De Fruyt, F. (2003a). International validity generalization of GMA and cognitive abilities: A European community meta-analysis. *Personnel Psychology, 56*, 573–605.

Salgado, J. F., Anderson, N., Moscoso, S., Bertua, C., De Fruyt, F., & Rolland, J. P. (2003b). A meta-analytic study of general mental ability validity for different occupations in the European Community. *Journal of Applied Psychology, 88*, 1068–1081.

Salgado, J. F., & Moscoso, S. (2004). Fairness reactions to personnel selection techniques in Spain and Portugal. *International Journal of Selection and Assessment, 12*, 187–196.

Saucier, G., Hampson, S. E., & Goldberg, L. R. (2000). Cross-language studies of lexical personality factors. In S. E. Hampson (Ed.), *Advances in personality psychology* (Vol. 1, pp. 1–36). Philadelphia: Psychology Press.

Schmidt, F. L. (2002). The role of general cognitive ability and job performance: Why there cannot be a debate. *Human-Performance, 15*, 187–211.

Schmidt, F. L., & Hunter, J. E. (1984). A within setting test of the situational specificity hypothesis in personnel selection. *Personnel Psychology, 37*, 317–326.

Schmidt, F. L., & Hunter, J. E. (1998). The validity and utility of selection methods in personnel psychology: Practical and theoretical implications of 85 years of research findings. *Psychological Bulletin, 124*, 262–274.

Schmitt, M. J., Kihm, J. A., & Robie, C. (2000). Development of a global measure of personality. *Personnel Psychology, 53*, 153–193.

Schmitt, N., & Chan, D. (1998). *Personnel selection: A theoretical approach*. Thousands Oaks, CA: Sage.

Schmitt, N., & Mills, A. E. (2001). Traditional tests and job simulations: Minority and majority performance and test validities. *Journal of Applied Psychology, 86*, 451–458.

Schmitt, N., Rogers, W., Chan, D., Sheppard, L., & Jennings, D. (1997). Adverse impact and predictive efficiency of various predictor combinations. *Journal of Applied Psychology, 82*, 719–730.

Schuler, R., Dowling, P., & DeCieri, H. (1993). An integrative framework of strategic international human resource management. *Journal of Management, 19*, 419–459.

Shackleton, V., & Newell, S. (1997). International assessment and selection. In N. Anderson & P. Herriot (Eds.), *International handbook of selection and assessment*. New York: Wiley.

Smith, H. J. (2001). Information privacy and marketing: What the U.S. should (and shouldn't) learn from Europe. *California Management Review, 43,* 8–33.

Smith, M., & Abrahamsen, M. (1992). Patterns of selection in six countries. *The Psychologist, 5,* 205–207.

Smith, P. B., Dugan, S., Peterson, M. F., & Leung, K. (1998). Individualism/collectivism and the handling of disagreement: A 23-country study. *International Journal of Intercultural Relations, 22,* 351–368.

Smith, P. B., Peterson, M. F., Schwartz, S. H., Ahmad, A. H., Akande, D., Andersen, J. A., Ayestaran, S., Bochner, S., Callan, V., Davila, C., Ekelund, B., Francis, P.-H., Graversen, G., Harb, C., Jesuino, J., Kantas, A., Karamushka, L., Koopman, P., Leung, K., Kruzela, P., Malvezzi, S., Mogaji, A., Mortazavi, S., Munene, J., Parry, K., Punnet, B. J., Radford, M., Ropo, A., Saiz, J., Savage, G., Setiadi, B., Sorenson, R., Szabo, E., Teparakul, P., Tirmizi, A., Tsvetanova, S., Viedge, C., Wall, C., & Yanchuk, V. (2002). Cultural values, sources of guidance, and their relevance to managerial behavior: A 47-nation study. *Journal of Cross-Cultural Psychology, 33,* 188–208.

Steiner, D. D., & Gilliland, S. W. (1996). Fairness reactions to personnel selection techniques in France and the United States. *Journal of Applied Psychology, 81,* 134–141.

Steiner, D. D., & Gilliland, S. W. (2001). Procedural justice in personnel selection: International and cross-cultural perspectives. *International Journal of Selection and Assessment, 9,* 124–137.

Stinglhamber, F., Vandenberghe, C., & Brancart, S. (1999). Les réactions des candidats envers les techniques de sélection du personnel: Une étude dans un contexte francophone (Reactions of job applicants to personnel selection techniques: An investigation in a French-speaking context). *Le Travail Humain, 62,* 347–361.

Stone, E. F., & Stone, D. L. (1990). Privacy in organizations: Theoretical issues, research findings, and protection mechanisms. *Research in Personnel and Human Resources Management, 8,* 349–411.

Such, M. J., & Hemingway, M. A. (2003, April). *Examining the usefulness of empirical keying in the cross-cultural implementation of a biodata inventory.* Paper presented at the Annual Conference of the Society of Industrial and Organizational Psychology, Orlando, FL.

Such, M. J., & Schmidt, D. B. (2004, April). *Examining the effectiveness of empirical keying: A cross-cultural perspective.* Paper presented at the Annual Conference of the Society of Industrial and Organizational Psychology, Chicago, IL.

Terpstra, D. E., & Rozell, E. J. (1997). Why some potentially effective staffing practices are seldom used. *Public Personnel Management, 26 (4),* 483–495.

Tett, R. P., Jackson, D. N., & Rothstein, M. (1991). Personality measures as predictors of job performance: A meta-analytic review. *Personnel Psychology, 44,* 703–742.

Triandis, H. C., & Vassiliou, V. (1972). Interpersonal influence and employee selection in two cultures. *Journal of Applied Psychology, 36,* 140–145.

Uniform Guidelines on Employee Selection Procedures (1978). *Federal Register,* 1978, 43, No. 166, 38290-38309.

Von Glinow, M. A., Drost, E. A., & Teagarden, M. B. (2002). Converging on IHRM best practices: Lessons learned from a globally distributed consortium on theory and practice. *Human Resource Management, 41,* 123–140.

Wiechmann, D., Ryan, A. M., & Hemingway, M. (2003). Designing and implementing global staffing systems. Part I: Leaders in global staffing. *Human Resource Management, 42,* 71–83.

Wilk, S. L., & Cappelli, P. (2003). Understanding the determinants of employer use of selection methods. *Personnel Psychology, 56,* 103–124.

Williamson, L. G., Campion, J. E., Malos, S. B., Roehling, M. A., & Campion, M. A. (1997). Employment interview on trial: Linking interview structure with litigation outcomes. *Journal of Applied Psychology, 82,* 900–912.

7 International Performance Management and Appraisal: Research Perspectives

Caroline Bailey and Clive Fletcher

CONTENTS

Interest in employee performance and foundations of contemporary research into performance appraisal (PA) processes can be traced as far back as early organizational theories such as scientific management (Taylor, 1911). Not surprisingly, over the course of the twentieth century, as well as post-2000, a large amount of research literature continues to be produced—from numerous disciplines—concerned with various aspects of PA (Fletcher, 2001). In part, this growing body of work can be seen as a response to the continual evolution of PA. Until recently—and in many organizations, still—appraisal took the form of an annual process whereby a manager reviewed a subordinate's performance, perhaps producing a written report on it containing an assessment, then held an interview with the subordinate concerned to discuss the evaluation, set objectives, and look at how performance can be improved. Now, however, it has evolved into a series of linked processes that take varying forms, though still centering on the evaluation, reward, and development of employees (Fletcher, 2004). In addition, the concept of performance management (PM), with its more strategic and holistic approach to organizational and individual performance, gives performance appraisal a central role in a more integrated and dynamic set of human resource (HR) systems. Although there is no universally accepted definition of PM, the most prevalent notion describes it as a set of mechanisms creating a shared vision of the purpose and aims of the organization, helping each individual employee to understand and recognize his or her part in contributing to them, and thereby managing and enhancing the performance of both individuals and the organization (Williams, 2002).

This chapter deals mainly with PA, as most of the available literature relates to that, but PM will be referred to where there are relevant studies or papers. The focus of what follows is a review and critique of research pertaining to PA practices across the world (though, as will be seen in the following paragraph, there are some limitations on this), and the identification of some key challenges for future research activity in this area. In relation to the latter, the second half of this chapter advances some hypotheses as to how various cross-cultural dimensions may impact upon different elements of the PA process. The role of technology and advances in assessment methods are also considered as viable directions for future research.

In providing an international perspective, relevant literature has been sought from Europe (including Britain), Asia (including Australia), Africa (including the Middle East), South/Central America, and North America. However, as with many areas of industrial and organizational psychology, the vast majority of research into performance management and appraisal has been published by U.S. researchers (and to a lesser extent Western European), utilizing samples of Western employees. From the limited amount of PA research published for the rest of the world, it seems not only are organizations in certain countries less likely to have a formal PA system (Kim, Park, & Suzuki, 1990), but where a system is in place, the very nature of the assessments (what purpose they are put to, who has an input to them, whether they are framed in terms of competencies or personal qualities, and so forth) may differ from Western practices. Accordingly, there are no global trends as such in research into PA systems. Instead specific avenues of research have developed for discrete geographical areas, which mirror countries' cultural, political, and economic conditions. Moreover, research (and in fact PA practice) in many "developing" countries, such as those in Africa, is largely inchoate. As a result, for these countries we summarize recent reviews of emerging human resource management (HRM) practices, and consider possible directions for PA, as based upon an analysis of cultural and economic factors.

The diversity of PA research is not surprising given the work of Hofstede (1980, 1991), Trompenaars (1993), and multiauthor collaborations, such as the Global Leadership and Organizational Behavior Effectiveness (GLOBE) research program (led by Robert House), which have provided empirical evidence of stable cultural differences in individual behavior, all of which impact on the concept of employee performance and suitable approaches to its assessment. In the theoretical and empirical literature, Hofstede's (1980) model of cultural values is used by the vast majority of theoretical and empirical investigations. National cultures are described in terms of their position along four dimensions: power distance, uncertainty avoidance, masculinity/femininity, and individualism/collectivism. These are described by Hofstede (1994, p. 5) and might be summarized as follows:

Power distance (PD): In high PD cultures there is acceptance of unequal distribution of power within a culture, whereas in low PD cultures it is not. In low PD cultures relationships between individuals across hierarchical levels are closer and less formal in nature than high PD cultures.

Uncertainty avoidance (UA): The degree to which people in a country prefer structured over unstructured situations. Low UA cultures are more risk taking and tolerant of organizational ambiguity and change than high UA cultures.

Masculinity/femininity (M/F): Masculine cultures are associated with values such as assertiveness, performance, success, and competition (associated with the male role in almost
all societies). Female cultures are associated with values such as quality of life, maintaining warm personal relationships, service, and care for the weak.

Individualism/collectivism (I/C): Individualistic cultures value personal identity and choice,
whereas collectivist cultures emphasize group values over individual goals, and the welfare of the group over individual needs.

Given the steady increase in globalization and increasing diversity of citizens' ethnic or
national origin in many Western countries, we regard cross-cultural issues to be a key challenge
for future research—not just for those countries currently underrepresented in PA literature, but
also for many organizations in the West. As background to these research directions, the next
section presents a critical overview of research into PA practices throughout different geographical areas.

NORTH AMERICA/WESTERN EUROPE

PA research in North America and Western Europe can be seen to have gone through a series
of phases, reflecting the changes in PA practices. Historically, in these countries the PA process
was regarded as separate from other HRM practices, such as selection, training, and organizational development. Appraisal systems in the 1950s were typically personality-based assessments
of employees' work behavior, with individuals' line managers providing "top-down" ratings, taking
a retrospective view of their behavior (McGregor, 1957). The ratings were generally not shared
with the employees themselves, and provided little or no guidance as to the activities the individual
should engage in order to improve. Given the lack of feedback in the PA process at this time,
research was largely concerned with the assessment aspects of the PA system.

Various critiques (e.g. McGregor, 1957; Maier, 1958) drew negative conclusions on this form of
appraisal, urging organizations to adopt a more participative and forward-looking approach instead.
This, and theoretical influences such as goal-setting theory (Locke & Latham, 1990) and the development of methods such as management by objectives (MBO) (Drucker, 1955), led to organizations
adapting their performance criteria to assess employees' behaviors in relation to task objectives.
Although the responsibility for assessment still lay largely with the employees' line manager, there
was more participation from employees, in that objective setting encouraged their involvement in
their performance goals and discussion of processes by which these objectives were best achieved.
This very individualized approach to managing employees' performance was subsequently found
by research to be one of its main limitations; providing specific targets for individual employees
meant comparisons across employees was difficult. It was recognized that some form of systematic
assessment was needed (at least for individuals of similar function), leading to more widespread use
of appraisal rating forms.

This next evolution in PA practice (in the late 1960s and throughout the 1970s) also coin-
cided with the activity of the Civil Rights movement in America and equal opportunities legislation
introduced across much of Europe. Organizations now had a greater concern for the accuracy and
fairness of employee assessments. As a result, research attention turned toward issues such as the
psychometric properties of ratings (e.g. Schwab, Heneman, & DeCotiis, 1975) and ways in which
ratings could be made more accurate. For example, a considerable amount of research into rater
cognition and bias (DeNisi and colleagues), rater training (e.g. Smith, 1986), and the use of rating
scales (e.g. Smith & Kendall, 1963) was produced.

Many of the investigations comparing different ratings formats had disappointing effect sizes;
Landy and Farr (1980) concluded that less than 4% of the variance in the psychometric properties of
ratings could be attributed to rating format. Although research into rating scales has mainly abated,
investigations into rater cognition and bias (DeNisi, 1996) and rater training (e.g. Smith, 1986)

continue to be popular themes, reflecting an increasing awareness that rater motivation arguably has more to do with the accuracy of PA ratings than assessment form design.

With the economic downturn in Western economies in the late 1980s and early 1990s, PA practice moved on again, with the latest step being the integration of PA systems with wider HRM processes. Many organizations were faced with increased global competition, and a need to become leaner and less hierarchical. As a result, organizations began to take a more holistic view and have an ongoing concern for employees' performance; as indicated earlier, this is usually referred to as performance management (PM). A key element of this is to tie in the individual's objectives with the broader business objectives, and to target individual development strategy in line with the needs of the business as a whole.

In PM, typically, two forms of assessments are conducted; those for evaluative purposes (which can then be used to inform decisions around employee remuneration and career progression) and those for developmental purposes, which may guide personal development plans and training activities. Although the evaluative element of the PM process is similar to the "traditional" PA approach (e.g. conducted "top-down," requiring retrospective evaluation of employees' individual achievements), the developmental aspects of PM are often far more participative, with employees establishing and agreeing to commit to future individual goals with their line manager that align with ongoing organizational objectives (Ainsworth & Smith, 1993). As part of this goal-setting exercise, employees and their manager will also identify individual development goals and formulate personal development plans for training or other developmental activities, as needed for goal attainment.

The increased focus on performance development within the PM cycle compared to earlier PA systems is arguably one factor contributing to the proliferation from the late 1990s onwards of techniques such as 360-degree feedback (or other forms of multisource feedback system) as well as ongoing developmental support from schemes such as mentoring and coaching. The rate at which organizations adopted multisource assessments initially outpaced empirical research (Fletcher & Baldry, 1999). However, over recent years the amount of research available for multisource feedback systems has grown considerably. Since its introduction, 360-degree feedback research has focused on three main issues. First, as with traditional PA research, there was much concern for the psychometric properties of ratings from different rater sources, as well as situational and systemic factors influencing the characteristics of ratings made (Fletcher & Baldry, 1999). U.S.-based research suggested that self-assessments tended to be more favorable than ratings from other sources, and generally levels of agreement between raters at different hierarchical levels was seen to be fairly low. The reliability and validity of ratings from "alternative" sources such as subordinates and peers were just as good, if not better, than traditional sources (i.e. the line manager). Finally, a number of situational factors were identified as correlates of development following feedback (e.g., amount of organizational support, Walker & Smither, 1999), which led to the identification of various best practice principles.

A second trend in multisource research has been the investigation of the predictive validity of ratings. In particular, the issue of rater congruence has been explored, the general conclusion being that those employees whose self-assessments are highly congruent with ratings made of them by others (sometimes characterized as showing "self-awareness") are found to be assessed significantly more positively on independent measures of performance (Fletcher, 2001). This avenue of research promoted much discussion about the appropriate statistical representation and operationalization of congruence (with early research utilizing a range of measures, from profile similarity indices based on correlation coefficients and difference scores to those based on multivariate statistical tests). It is now generally accepted that the extent to which the interaction between self and others' ratings predict criterion measures is best represented by multivariate approaches such as polynomial regression.

Most recently research has explored how feedback predicts other organizational indicators of performance, such as PA ratings (e.g. Bailey & Fletcher, 2002a), selection of developmental goals (Brutus, London, & Martineau, 1999), types of developmental activities (Hazucha, Hezlett, & Schneider, 1993), and focal individuals' subsequent involvement in both on-the-job and off-the-job development activities (Maurer, Mitchell, & Barbeite, 2002). All have generally had positive findings regarding the value of receiving feedback from one's coworkers. Finally, research has also begun to consider factors influencing focal individuals' responsiveness to feedback, such as rater source credibility (e.g. Bailey & Fletcher, 2002b), facilitation of feedback by an executive coach (Smither, London, Flautt, Vargas, & Kucine, 2003), and discussion of feedback with certain rating constituencies (e.g. Walker & Smither, 1999). Overall, then, research to date has generally been favorable about the practice of providing feedback; it seems the majority of focal individuals do improve following participation, according to changes in the self-assessment and ratings provided by others (e.g. Smither et al., 2003). Less is known about the long-term effects of multisource feedback; however, given that the technique has become an established diagnostic tool for employee development in many organizations, it is likely that further research into such systems will continue. A number of directions are provided in the second section of this chapter.

In summary, PA practices (and the majority of PA research) in North America and Western Europe can be seen to be reflective of certain cultural values, as well as economic and political conditions of the time. According to Hofstede (1980), individuals from Western cultures are high in individualism, medium in levels of power distance and uncertainty avoidance, and are masculine more than feminine cultures. Within the context of PA, this manifests itself as a need for individual achievement and recognition, with individuals being encouraged to express assertive, challenging, and ambitious behaviors over group-oriented actions and nurturing behaviors. Subsequently, appraisal systems are generally focused upon the individual (not the group) and, whether task-focused or person-focused, have emphasized stereotypically masculine values over feminine ones. As a result, the appraisal system can be seen as an arena for negotiation between the individual and the organization. Perhaps for this reason, whether conducted for evaluative or developmental purposes, PA continues to be regarded by both organizations and employees as a "necessary evil" in the majority of North American and West European organizations. Will countries in other parts of the world follow the same pattern of development as has been outlined here? In its entirety, probably not, because they have access to the literature of the research that has already been done, which hopefully will help them avoid some of the earlier pitfalls, and because their social, economic, and legal contexts all tend to differ in varying ways, which as we have seen are important influences in terms of the PA and PM approaches that evolve.

ASIA (INCLUDING AUSTRALIA)

Schneider and Barsoux (1997) observe that contrary to most Western organizations where the focus of the appraisal is on what the employee does, Asian organizations focus on what the employee *is*, with greater concern for the employee's personality and other characteristics. The vast geographical distance of this continent has led to a diverse range of cultural values within different nations and regions. Moreover, as certain countries have been subjected to colonialism by one European country or another (e.g. India, colonized by Britain and to a lesser extent Portugal) or primarily inhabited by European descendants (e.g. Australia), an analysis of PA practices is presented, as available, for all countries that constitute a major economic power within this continent.

Australia

Despite its geographic location in the Far East, economically, politically and culturally, Australia is currently closely allied with the West. This is largely a result of early colonization by the British, and previous immigration policy favoring European migrants, resulting in a population where European descendants far outnumbered indigenous Australians, Asians, and other ethnic groups. However, since the political reforms of the 1970s, stronger links have been made with Asia and particularly Japanese organizations. Not surprisingly, empirical research suggests Australia's cultural values are very similar to those of Western rather than Asian countries (Ashkanasay, 1997). As a result, historically many of the HRM and PA practices of North America and Western Europe are found in Australian organizations, including development-oriented PA schemes (Clayton & Ayres, 1996), which may utilize competency-based assessments and interventions such as 360-degree feedback (Nagel, 2002). Consequently, the research issues raised in the preceding section are also applicable to Australian organizations.

CHINA

Research has found that there are a number of distinct differences between Chinese and Western PA practices, which may be explained in terms of differences in national culture. Snape, Thompson, Ka-Ching Ya, and Redman (1998) comment that societies such as China are characterized by Confucian cultural values, and have a strong collectivist orientation, a sense of hierarchy, and acceptance of authority. Furthermore, they suggest that in more collectivist societies (such as Hong Kong), the focus of "Western" PA practices on individual performance, accountability, and open confrontation are unlikely to be seen as appropriate. Their propositions are supported by Huo and von Glinow (1995), who found that Chinese managers were reluctant to engage in two-way communication or provide counselling in the PA appraisal process, because of the high PD values of Chinese culture. As such, employees' participation in appraisal was low in comparison to Western practices. They also note that peer evaluation was virtually nonexistent in China; again, because of power distance only the immediate manager is regarded as sufficiently qualified to evaluate employees' performance.

The function of PA systems in China has also been found to be different from those of Western organizations. In a survey of organizations' appraisal practices, Tang, Lai, and Kirkbride (1995) concluded that the general purpose of the appraisal in Hong Kong organizations is to review past performance only. This contrasts with many British and American systems, where appraisal not only looks backwards in this way, but also forwards, to assess training and development needs, set objectives, and assess promotion potential (Mackay & Torrington, 1986).

In a study comparing appraisal practices (and employee reactions to appraisal) between Hong Kong Chinese and British managers and professional staff, Snape et al. (1998) concluded that although Hong Kong employees perceived a high level of "negative" appraiser behavior from their supervisors, they were more positive about the utility of the appraisal process than the British employees. Differences were noted in the confidence placed in the performance ratings of line managers, with Hong Kong employees having significantly greater acceptance of ratings from senior sources than British employees. Finally, although there was no difference between the British and Hong Kong employees in their preference for group-based appraisal criteria, they did find more support for the use of personality constructs in appraisal criteria by Hong Kong employees than their British counterparts. This raises the interesting question as to whether in Hong Kong, China, and some other countries the way appraisal evolves may follow a different track from that seen in the United States and Europe, where personality-oriented ratings have been largely rejected. Among other things, it is possible that the rather disappointing impact of different rating formats in Western countries might not be found elsewhere, because with greater acceptance of ratings, the benefits of more structured rating approaches may have a better chance to show themselves.

In summary, the findings of this research suggest Chinese PA processes are radically different from Western systems. As a result, it seems questionable how much the vast majority of PA research (with its Western orientation) can be generalized and applied successfully to Chinese organizations.

INDIA

In a survey of organizations' HRM practices in India, Sparrow and Budhwar (1997) concluded that employee performance appraisal is a relatively "under emphasised factor in managerial practices" (p. 225). As a result, very little research literature could be identified for this vast country. However, one cannot assume Western practices prevail, given the cultural differences between India and the

West. Specifically, Hofstede (1980) found empirical evidence to suggest that as a nation, Indian culture is low UA, high PD, and medium in both collectivist orientation and masculinity.

Amba-Rao, Petrick, Gupta, and Von der Embse (2000) appear to provide the only current detailed analysis of PA practices and management values among both foreign and domestic firms in India. As with most of the world's economies, they note that the Indian government has implemented policies on privatization and globalization, resulting in a number of reforms to HRM practices and management values. They suggest three broad socioeconomic factors have shaped Indian organizations: (a) the caste system, (b) British colonization, and (c) postindependence socialism. In turn, they propose that these factors have led to a stratified, hierarchical socioeconomic class system, administrative bureaucratization, polarization of manager-nonmanager groups, and finally a socialist ideology, with increasing concern for the welfare of workers (Amba-Rao et al., 2000).

Amba-Rao et al. (2000) conducted an empirical survey of HRM and PA practices in 116 public- and private-sector organizations. They concluded that there were significant differences in PA processes across types of organization. Although all firms utilized some form of PA system and did provide some amount of feedback to employees, the multinational corporations/joint venture firms were significantly more likely to discuss PA feedback with employees than private investor firms. They also found that the former had a much greater drive toward using PA as a tool to enhance globally competitive quality performance than other types of organization. Finally, along with private investor firms and private family firms, multinational/joint venture firms were much more likely to use PA in an evaluative rather than developmental manner than public-sector firms.

In explanation, Amba-Rao et al. (2000) suggest that until recently, the majority of Indian firms were mainly under domestic competition, and so did not give much importance to providing employees with performance feedback. Virmani and Guptan (1991) found empirical evidence to support the hypothesis that Indian employees' dislike of PA was because it was perceived as a means for managers to control and maintain the loyalty of their subordinates, without providing any direct links to actual performance.

In summary, Amba-Rao et al. (2000) conclude that there appears to be a variety of PA systems in operation in Indian organizations, which are reflective of the particular organization's business objectives. However, they predict that increasingly a PM approach will be adopted throughout various industries, with emphasis on employee development and productivity. That said, they suggest that the collectivist Indian concept of "dharma" (moral duty toward others) will be retained in any PM approach. As a result, we suspect that Indian PM may focus organizational objectives at the group level, rather than for individual workers, and techniques like coaching rather than upward feedback seem likely developmental tools.

JAPAN

Japanese culture is characterized in terms of Hofstede's dimensions as one that is strongly collectivist, very hierarchical (i.e., high PD), high UA, and more masculine than feminine in orientation. As a result, workers in organizations are regarded as part of a "family" with an expectation that they will show loyalty to both their team and the organization, as well as respond to a clearly defined management hierarchy, members of which have a right to exert power in an autocratic rather than participative, democratic manner.

Again, very little research appears to have been produced describing the subjective aspects of PA processes in Japan. Historically, the wages of Japanese workers are heavily influenced by their age and seniority rather than their performance per se, so although PA systems were applied to blue-collar and white-collar workers in Japanese firms, Shibata (2002) suggests that prior to the 1990s, the appraisal methods did not thoroughly evaluate white-collar employees' performance. Similarly, Endo (1996) claims that PA systems in Japanese firms at that time were subjective, disorganized, and closed. Following the crash of the Japanese economy in the 1990s, radical reforms were observed in a number of large Japanese firms (Shibata, 2002). Examples of changes included an increased use of Western practices such as MBO appraisal methods as well as applying annual wage systems to managers (Fuji Sogo Kenkyujo, 1998). Generally PA at managerial levels appears to have become more systematic, with top management utilizing performance appraisal questionnaires to evaluate managers' performance. Also, whereas previously wages were linked primarily to age and tenure rather than performance, age-linked wages for managers has declined. However, these changes in PA were largely seen at the managerial level only, with employees' appraisal still relying upon the more subjective, closed appraisal methods traditionally used.

Ariga, Brunello, and Ohkusa (2000) speculate there are three possible directions for Japanese wage and PA systems: (a) adoption of the more Western market-driven systems; (b) maintenance of current practices (as described above); or (c) development of more flexible systems, which maintain the benefits of current practices. Shibata (2002) regards the third option as most likely, with Japanese organizations increasing their focus on differentiating performance at the individual level, and across all types of employees (not just managerial staff). He also suggests that the differentiation between blue-collar and white-collar workers will remain relatively small (compared to Western practices) and that various performance incentive systems could be introduced to technical roles (e.g., sales and engineering). Thus, in comparison to many other countries, it may be seen that Japanese organizations could lead the way in their adoption of systems that represent an East–West hybridization of PA practices.

EASTERN EUROPE AND RUSSIA

In a survey of national culture and leadership profiles across 21 European countries (which included Russia), the GLOBE project (Koopman, Den Hartog, & Konrad, 1999) found significant cultural differences between north-western countries (e.g., England, Ireland, Denmark, Germany, Switzerland, Sweden, the Netherlands, Finland, and Austria) and south-eastern countries (e.g., France, Italy, Spain, Portugal, Greece, Turkey, Hungary, the Czech Republic, Slovenia, Russia, Albania, and Georgia). In particular, Eastern European countries such as Russia, Georgia, and Turkey were found to have significantly higher scores on the dimension of "family collectivism" (the extent to which individuals are integrated with their family, exemplified by whether individuals live at home with their parents until they themselves get married). As such, Koopman et al. (1999) suggest these countries are culturally more similar to Asia than Western Europeans.

In terms of differences in leadership style, Koopman et al. (1999) found that managers from central and eastern Europe had significantly less negative attitudes toward autocratic behavior and valued diplomacy as a managerial behavior significantly more than Western managers. They propose that this may be a legacy of previous command economies, which endorsed formal and obedient behavior in both employees and managers through bureaucratized business practices (Den Hartog, House, Hanges, Ruiz-Quintanilla, Dorfman, 1999). Similarly, Maczynski, Lindell, Motowidlo, Sigrids, and Jarmutz (1997) note the directive influence of the communist party on organizational practices in the majority of Eastern European organizations until the end of the 1980s, which in turn reinforced managerial behaviors of compliance and diplomacy.

In a review of PA literature, no reference at all was found to empirical research for any Eastern European countries. One study was identified for Russia, that by Elenkov (1998), which compares Russian and American perceptions of performance feedback. He concluded that Russian managerial culture is characterized by higher power distance than in American managerial culture, and that as such, American concepts of subordinate participation in managerial decisions (i.e., performance appraisal) may be incompatible with Russian culture. He also found that direct feedback is perceived as undesirable between managers and employees. He concluded that this was a result of the collectivist value orientation, which regards direct feedback as harmful to group harmony, the employee's self-image, and loyalty to the organization. As a result, he suggests that appraisals that focused on group rather than individual achievements were likely to be more acceptable.

Given that so little appears to have been written about PA practices in this area, at best one can speculate (on the basis of cultural values observed) that any PA systems in operation are likely to be top-down and nonparticipative, with assessors having concern for maintaining group harmony rather than isolating individual contributions. However, as with other non-Western countries, considerably more research attention needs to be given to all areas of PA practice for organizations in this region.

AFRICA (INCLUDING THE MIDDLE EAST)

Seemingly no direct PA research has been produced for this continent; however, some reviews of broader HRM practices are available. For example, in a comprehensive analysis of HRM practices throughout Africa, Jackson (2002) suggests that the majority of management literature for African countries regards management's approach to employees as "fatalistic, resistant to change, reactive, short-termist, authoritarian, risk reducing, context dependent and basing decisions on relationship criteria rather than universalistic criteria" (p. 998). However, he argues that this may not be an accurate (nor particularly useful) representation of HRM practices in this continent, but instead an inappropriate stereotype that is a legacy of colonialism. Indeed, many African countries are now facing the economic conditions felt throughout the rest of the world, including organizational downsizing, increased accountability in public-sector organizations, and a drive for private-sector organizations to be increasingly competitive at a global level (Ibru, 1997).

In terms of the cultural values of this geographic area, Jackson suggests previous empirical analysis of culture has also been fairly limited. He notes that Hofstede's (1980) data on African culture is based on two small sample sizes from West and East African countries that he combined into two regional samples, and a Whites-only sample from South Africa. A number of researchers have concluded that African cultures can be regarded as collectivist (e.g., Blunt & Jones, 1992; Noorderhaven & Tidjani, 2001). Kanungo and Jaeger (1990) suggest developing countries (including those in Africa) are high UA, low in individualism, low in masculinity, and high PD. However, it is apparent that much more empirical research needs to be conducted with African populations to verify these profiles.

Jackson (2002) suggests that as a result of previous political and economic factors, three differing management paradigms currently prevail in African management practices: (a) a post-colonial approach, (b) a post-instrumental approach, and (c) an African Renaissance, all of which have differing perceptions on the nature of the managerial role, how to best manage and coordinate the work of personnel, and facilitate employee development. He describes the post-colonial approach as the stereotypical system of management most commonly labeled as "African" in most management literature. Typically this management style is akin to McGregor's (1957) theory X, where the manager generally mistrusts workers, believing them to be motivated primarily by financial reward and having a strong concern for the control (rather than empowerment) of workers. Organizations are characterized as having a lack of strategic results orientation, clear mission statement, or sense of direction. Leadership is highly centralized, authoritarian, and hierarchical (Blunt & Jones, 1997). As a result, there is often an emphasis on "control mechanisms, rules and procedures rather than performance, and a high reluctance to judge performance" (Jackson, 2002, p. 1001). Finally, many internal policies are seen as discriminatory, being based upon in-group or family membership rather than meritocratic principles.

In strong contrast to this, the post-instrumental paradigm advocates a more Westernized theory Y perspective to management; managers regard their function as consulting and empowering employees, and providing clear objectives and rules of action. Flatter organizational hierarchies are preferred, and HRM practices are nondiscriminatory and provide employees with access to equal opportunities. Finally promotion is based on achievement and management practices are said to value self-enhancement, autonomy, and open communication between employees and management.

The African Renaissance represents a management style that is reflective of African values and knowledge systems. Largely driven by political reforms in South Africa (Jackson, 2002), this has led to the introduction of terms such as *ubuntu* into management theory, which reflects the value for community. Dia (1996) suggests that within the African Renaissance there will be deference to rank.

However, Jackson (2002) suggests it is not in the manner described by Hofstede's power distance dimension. Although there is an awareness of one's place in the social hierarchy, individuals at all levels are free to express opinions and dissent. Furthermore, just as lower levels are expected to show respect for those at higher levels, the more senior person is expected to show humility and respect for those at more junior levels. Thus, management principles are based on both status and achievement orientation. Finally, openness and good social and personal relations are valued, resulting in flatter, accessible hierarchies and a humanistic rather than individualistic orientation.

Jackson (2002) concludes that for many African organizations each paradigm is unlikely to exist in its purest form, but instead some form of hybrid of the three will be in operation. Unfortunately, no empirical survey evidence of current people management (and specifically PA) practices in different African countries could be found by the authors of this chapter. Surprisingly, despite the radical reforms in employment law in post-apartheid South Africa, no research to date appears to have been conducted that presents an analysis or evaluation of PA practices in this particular African country. In a review of literature, one report was identified that presented an analysis of various case studies of employee litigation around discrimination in remuneration and promotion decisions (Horwitz, Browning, Jain, & Steenkamp, 2002). Throughout this, it was noted that legal judgements of discrimination were based upon retrospective evaluations of employee performance, conducted purely as evidence for the trial (rather than as an ongoing HRM practice). Given the considerable political pressure upon organizations to have transparent, nondiscriminatory employment and promotion procedures, development of PA practice (and research) is sorely needed in this country, as well as the rest of the continent.

CENTRAL AND SOUTH AMERICA

Again, this is an area of the world that seems to have been largely missed in terms of research on this topic, and only brief observations have been made. For example, Triandis (1989) reports that in Latin America power distance is high and participation as a management technique has not been successful. One might expect a mixed set of findings from any research that is done, partly because of the size and disparity of the countries included, but also because of their varying historical links with different European countries (such as Portugal and Spain). For the most part, we are left to look for indirect indications, such as those provided by Bastos and Fletcher (1995) in their study of feedback. They conducted an investigation of cross-cultural differences (the United Kingdom versus Brazil) in employees' perceptions of the credibility of different sources of performance feedback. They found that there were similarities between the two countries in terms of sources of performance feedback; in both, task feedback and self-mediated feedback accounted for more variance than other feedback sources (e.g., coworkers, feedback from supervisor, promotion, or financial feedback). There were also similarities in the perceived credibility of sources, with the organization and the supervisor accounting for most variance in feedback credibility ratings in both samples. The main difference between the two countries lay in the perceived credibility of coworkers' feedback, with this accounting for much less variance in the Brazilian sample, in comparison to those ratings made by British employees. However, Bastos and Fletcher (1995) concluded that this may be a function of the sample characteristics rather than cross-cultural differences. In the British sample, appraisal was not linked to reward decisions; for the Brazilian sample, the individual's performance was more closely allied to pay increases and promotion. Such as they are, these findings imply that responses to PA might show some similarities between the two countries, though the use of 360-degree feedback might be more problematic in Brazil.

SUMMARY

Given the significant differences that can be observed between countries on issues such as the conceptualization of performance, deference to organizational hierarchies, and individual choice and decision making, it seems unlikely that contemporary, participative Western PA practices can (or should) be directly transplanted into other geographical areas. This, and the increased cultural diversity of citizens in many Western countries, leads to the conclusion that future PA research would do well to consider how cultural factors impact upon aspects of the PA process. The next section focuses upon a number of directions for PA research, including consideration of cross-cultural differences in the PA process.

FUTURE DIRECTIONS: EMERGING TRENDS IN PERFORMANCE MANAGEMENT RESEARCH

ADVANCES IN ASSESSMENT METHODS

By far the biggest development seen in assessment methods since the introduction of the competency approach in the early 1980s has been the adoption of multirater developmental appraisal systems such as 360-degree feedback. The notion of providing performance feedback from sources other than the line manager has been around for a long time. For example in a meta-analysis of subordinate, peer, and supervisor ratings, Conway and Huffcutt (1997) found research dating from 1950 onwards. However, the practice did not reach mainstream popularity (at least in North America and Britain) until the early 1990s. There are reports that it has also become a popular practice within Australia (Nagel, 2002) and a number of northern European countries. However, it seems not yet to have spread to Asia, Central and South America, or Africa, except in those organizations with North American or Western European headquarters.

As discussed in the previous section, the impact of participation upon employees' performance has been a major theme for multisource research, and one that is likely to continue. London and Smither (1995) provide a very comprehensive model of feedback impact, describing how a number of individual differences and situational variables combine with feedback characteristics (favorability and agreement between raters, including the self-assessment) to produce feedback impact (operationalized by changes in self-image, goal setting and goal attainment, and ultimately behavior change). This model can be seen to have influenced much empirical research to date, and support for its propositions continues to be produced from various sources (e.g., Bailey & Fletcher, 2002a; Walker & Smither, 1999).

However, despite the growing body of research into feedback impact, there is still much to be understood about the factors and processes at play within multisource systems. In particular, future research should expand the scope of the predictors of impact to include individual difference variables, such as emotional intelligence and personality traits, and self-image variables, such as self-esteem, as well as more "performance-oriented" factors, such as self-efficacy. In addition, situational factors, such as organizational climate and culture, as well as systemic factors (such as geographic proximity of raters) could also be fruitful. Similarly, future research should expand the scope of impact criteria beyond changes in successive feedback ratings and other PA ratings, to short-term issues (such as immediate impact on organizational commitment, motivation, and relations with coworkers), midterm issues (such as commitment to developmental goals), and long-term developmental outcomes. Finally, there is a significant gap in the current literature in terms of longitudinal descriptive research that adequately explains the actual process of development, from immediate reactions to behavior change and performance improvement.

A small number of authors have acknowledged how these multisource appraisals may have much stronger implications for the social relations and motivation of employees, over traditional appraisal. For example, London, Smither, and Adsit (1997) proposed that many aspects of a 360-degree feedback methodology are fundamentally flawed in the extent to which different constituencies can be held accountable (e.g. focal individuals' subsequent use of feedback ratings to decide developmental goals, anonymous raters' responsibility for the accuracy of their ratings, and the organization's responsibility for support and facilitation of development following feedback). In a similar vein, Flint (1999) presents a detailed theoretical model outlining the fairness (distributive and procedural justice) issues associated with multisource feedback ratings. In particular he discusses a number of factors (including the ratee's perceptions of voice and opportunity to challenge the evaluation, choice of raters, support from appraisers for their development, and so on) that he argues will determine the extent to which an individual may perceive both the assessment process, and the resultant feedback received, to be fair. Empirical evidence remains to be published that explores how multisource feedback influences employees' motivation, despite the obvious implications this has for both individual and organizational performance.

Neither of the models put forward by London and Smither (1995) and Flint (1999) explicitly address cultural issues, however. Although they might be considered under more general headings such as self-image, feedback seeking, and self-monitoring (one group of factors included in the London and Smither model), much of the language and assumptions of these approaches are rooted in the Western concepts of PA and PM. The very notion of providing feedback to anyone other than a subordinate is less acceptable in high-power-distance cultures, as we have seen. Concepts of procedural justice are likely to be rather different in say, China, than in the United States. Indeed, in some countries what is accepted as justice in general is fundamentally different, and the issue of equal opportunities and associated legislation may hardly feature. It might be a useful step as a precursor to further research in this area if the existing models were reviewed and revised to accommodate cultural differences, though this may prove to be quite a substantial undertaking as it is quite likely that the only viable approach will be to have different models for specific cultural groupings.

TECHNOLOGICAL DEVELOPMENTS

The technological boom post-2000 has had a number of effects upon organizations' appraisal processes. First, there have been advances in administration methods. Most Western organizations now have some form of intranet or Web access, enabling appraisal forms to be administered and completed online. Not only can this be seen to significantly reduce PA administration time, but as a paper-free system also significantly reduces the costs of the process.

A limited number of studies to date have compared the psychometric properties of computer-administered versus paper-and-pencil ratings. Penny (2003) compared the differential item functioning of 360-degree feedback ratings (self-assessments, line managers' ratings, peers' and subordinates' assessments). He concluded that despite sufficient statistical power, there was no evidence that the method of survey delivery influenced the characteristics of ratings ascribed. More recently Smither, Walker, and Yap (2004) investigated the equivalence of Web-based versus paper-and-pencil upward feedback (subordinate) ratings. Overall they surmised that response mode accounted for 1% or less of the variance in favorability of feedback ratings. Thus, at least from these two studies, it appears that computer administration may provide a number of benefits to the administrative process, without significantly influencing the psychometric properties of ratings made. Further research is needed to replicate these findings; however, it would be useful for future comparative research to extend this research design and also examine employees' and appraisers' reactions to electronic versus paper-based systems.

Another way in which technology may impact upon PA processes is by virtue of enabling rapid (even real-time) communication across vast geographic distances. Having the capacity to e-mail PA questionnaires or provide Web-based online assessment systems arguably increases the ease with which organizations may utilize the same PA system across different geographic locations, and timeliness of appraisal feedback to individual employees. As noted by Chen and DiTomaso (1996) typically, most HRM processes are chosen by the international headquarters of the organization and then rolled out to subsidiaries in other geographic locations. Thus, the use of the Internet in PA can be seen to have both positive and negative consequences. Although it may engender an awareness of head office organizational values and development of organizational culture, it may also lead to conflict. The nature of the assessments and very philosophies underpinning their use may strongly conflict with the cultural values of local employees (Groeschl, 2003). The extent to which such positive and negative consequences may result from global rollout of PA practices is underpinned by much of what has been said in this chapter, and arguably is a key issue for future empirical research.

Quite apart from the danger that the Internet may encourage a more unthinking application of corporate policies across cultural boundaries, there is also the possibility that the technology itself may elicit different reactions in different countries. For example, in another but not far removed area, namely selection, Harris, Van Hoye, and Lievens (2003) found differences between Belgian and U.S. samples in privacy concerns and willingness to supply employment-related information over the Internet. On another theme, one might speculate that in countries such as China where there is more acceptance of autocratic leadership styles and direct feedback, communicating the latter via computer rather than seeking to handle it more sensitively face to face might be perfectly acceptable and appropriate. In addition to such differences in attitudes that may exist, it is also possible that variations in computer literacy and familiarity, not to mention availability, may temporarily reduce or slow the impact of technological development on PA and PM in some countries.

Finally, computer software has also contributed to recent advances in PA rating techniques. Schneider, Goff, Anderson, and Borman (2003) conducted a trial of a performance appraisal questionnaire designed to assess both task and contextual aspects of managerial performance that utilized computer adaptive rating scales (CARS), with very positive results. The main benefits of a CARS approach over common PA rating formats (e.g., Likert-type rating scales) is felt to be that they produce interval rather than ordinal-level ratings (Schneider et al, 2003). They concluded that administration times may be dramatically reduced, because assessments can be made using fewer items, without compromising the precision of the performance assessment. However, they also note that further work is needed, to ascertain the concurrent and predictive validity of such assessments.

In summary, much research on this topic tends to focus on administrative convenience and psychometric qualities offered by IT-based delivery, rather less on psychological responses and acceptance. Given that Cleveland and Murphy (1992) and others have concluded that arriving at an objective and accurate assessment of an individual is not always the top priority for managers doing appraisal—other, more interpersonal, motivations come into the picture—and that appraisees have a wide variety of motivations (Fletcher, 2002), perhaps the focus should shift more to user acceptability and impact. Anecdotally, the second author of this chapter has just encountered a beautifully designed IT-based appraisal system that was introduced into a large multinational organization and that offered a detailed and sophisticated performance assessment methodology—within a year, top management wanted to strip it of many of its features because they wanted something quick and simple! However, as with much else in relation to PA, it is unwise to generalize across different countries until we have more hard facts to go on.

Hypothesized Linkages between Performance Appraisal and Culture

As previously noted, research into PA processes has continued at a relentless pace in North America and parts of Europe. However, despite the cultural diversity within these geographic areas, as we have seen in the earlier sections of this chapter, little has been written (and even less empirical evidence produced) that considers how national culture can affect different types of appraisal processes. In a review of management, organizational psychology, cross-cultural psychology, and human resource management literature only a handful of reviews were identified (e.g., Fletcher & Perry, 2001; Groeschl, 2003; Milliman, Nason, Gallagher, Huo, von Glinow, & Lowe, 1998). Given this deficit, it may be helpful to present a number of hypotheses regarding the impact of cross-cultural dimensions on various aspects of the PA process that could stimulate and guide future research in this area; this section seeks to do that, organizing the suggestions under specific headings. To be consistent with the analysis presented throughout, the hypotheses offered are couched in terms of Hofstede's dimensions. However, as noted at the outset, there are other writers and theorists who have described alternative (though sometimes overlapping) analyses of cultural differences (e.g., Trompenaars, 1993), and a broader research objective might be to see if these too can be used to generate additional ideas and directions for PA research. However, this is beyond the scope of the present chapter.

Appraisal Objectives

Schneider and Barsoux (1997) note that there are strong differences between Western and Asian organizations in the nature of the employee-employer relationship, which may impact upon the purpose of the appraisal. Employees in the West are expected to have a more transactional and individualistic relationship than their collectivist Asian counterparts. The former are seen to contribute their individual skills and abilities to the performance of the organization, in return for individual fair reward and career progression. In contrast, Asian employees' personality and other personal characteristics are regarded as more important than actual performance, as their presence in the organization contributes to the collective, facilitating the status of the organization.

Hypothesis 1
Formal PA systems that focus on individual achievements and future personal goals are more acceptable to organizations and employees in individualistic than collectivist cultures.

Hypothesis 2
Masculine countries are more likely to emphasize evaluative rather than developmental aspects of the PA process (the rationale being that they are more comfortable with competition and achievement compared to feminine cultures, which should value "nurturing" employees, i.e., skill development).

Hypothesis 3
Appraisers and appraisees in high-uncertainty-avoidance cultures will show more adherence to PA policies and guidance than their counterparts in low UA cultures.

Performance Criteria

The employee behaviors valued by an organization are likely to vary as a function of the organization's national culture (Groeschl, 2003). In turn, these values are likely to be reflected in organizations' competency frameworks, leadership models, and performance assessment criteria, as well as individual appraisers' own implicit theories of behavior. In a study of implicit leadership theory (ILT), Epitropaki and Martin (2004) conclude that individuals' ILT consistently affect their perceptions and ratings of others' behaviors. Individuals who are perceived to behave in a manner concordant with the assessors' schema of appropriate behavior were rated more favorably. Thus, from a cross-cultural perspective:

Hypothesis 4
Ratings of managerial performance in a masculine culture (for example) will be biased towards stereotypically masculine behaviors, whereas in feminine cultures the opposite behaviors will be regarded as appropriate.

Type of Appraisers

Given the rapid uptake of multisource feedback in the West, it is tempting to suggest it may become a global practice over time. However, cross-cultural studies of employees' value systems, communication styles, and behaviors in countries such as China, southern Europe, and Central and South America (as outlined in the previous section) suggest there are a number of factors that may limit its usefulness in these geographical areas. In 360-degree feedback, individuals are appraised by their line manager, their peers, and personnel who report to them. Fletcher and Perry (2001) note that this may be acceptable for those individuals in a low-power-distance culture (e.g., the United States), where flatter, less hierarchical organizations are favored, and communication across organizational levels is acceptable. However, in high-power-distance cultures (e.g., China), employees have strong regard for the organizational hierarchy. Thus, the ratings required from subordinate personnel, and response required by the focal individual to his or her appraisal, is likely to be a difficult process for both parties. As a result, employees may refuse to participate or confound their participation by providing uniformly favorable ratings.

There is some empirical evidence to support this. North American investigations comparing self-assessments to external raters (peers, subordinates, and line managers) have generally found self-assessments to be more lenient than rating others' ratings. However, this is not replicated in other countries, with studies of British managers (e.g., Bailey & Fletcher, 2002a) and Chinese managers (e.g., Furnham & Stringfield, 1994) finding support for modesty, rather than leniency in self-assessments (relative to others' ratings).

Hypothesis 5
Credibility (and thus acceptability) of ratings from different sources is predicted by PD values; low PD cultures will accept assessments from all hierarchical levels (peers, subordinates, and line managers), whereas high PD cultures find assessments credible and acceptable from senior levels only.

Hypothesis 6
High PD cultures have greater confidence in the ability of their seniors (line managers) to provide appraisal ratings than low PD cultures.

Appraisal Process

One of the common principles of PA processes in Western literature is the practice of ensuring employee "buy-in" to the appraisal process to engender its success. For example, as noted by Snape et al. (1998), in Britain appraisals have to be "sold" to employees in terms of how it can be of benefit to their individual needs (development, fair remuneration, and career progression) and playing down of the judgmental aspects of the process. Conversely, in Hong-Kong, they suggest the traditional, top-down judgment appears to be more acceptable, to the point that it is expected by most employees (Snape et al., 1998). Therefore, it is proposed that power-distance values are a key factor in determining the importance of employee buy-in to the appraisal process to the overall success of the performance appraisal system. Whereas employees in Western countries may require detailed briefing and opportunities to comment upon the nature of the PA process, autocratic decisions by management about the PA process are more likely to be accepted by employees in Eastern countries.

A second aspect of the PA process that may be affected is the extent to which the assessment process itself is formal and standardized, utilizing appraisal questionnaires. Cultures that have high UA, such as France and Spain, are those that like to have "structure" (Hofstede, 1980). Individuals are typically uncomfortable with high levels of ambiguity and uncertainty, and prefer to follow set rules. Conversely, low UA cultures (e.g., Sweden) value flexibility and the freedom of ambiguous situations. This cultural dimension may even impact upon the extent to which organizations actually implement a formal appraisal process (or employees rely on informal feedback from their colleagues) as well as how formal the appraisal process is (e.g., format and standardization of assessments).

Hypothesis 7
High levels of consultation with appraisees and their representatives in the development of an appraisal scheme will lead to greater acceptance of the scheme and more positive appraisee attitudes in low-power-distance cultures, but not in high-power-distance cultures.

Hypothesis 8
Formal appraisal systems are likely to be implemented with more detailed guidance, rest on more comprehensive and structured appraisal forms, and be consistent in the way they are applied across an organization in cultures high on UA compared to those low on UA.

CONCLUSION

The previous section and the eight general hypotheses it puts forward simply crystallizes what went before in this chapter, and the hypotheses are by no means comprehensive. The main point is that more cross-cultural and comparative research is needed in this field, and without it what is left is speculation. In compiling material for this chapter we have attempted to identify relevant research across a broad perspective. This has spanned a variety of fields, including organizational psychology, management, human resource management, cross-cultural and even anthropological research. However, what is most striking is the overall paucity. One theme has been alluded to only briefly, and that is the interaction of national and organizational cultures, and the impact of one on the other. It has been pointed out before (Fletcher & Perry, 2001) that the influence of the—often very strong—cultures of multinational organizations can overlay and offset the behavioral mores of national cultures; understanding the extent to which this is true, and how it comes about, is especially relevant to the study of performance management, and indeed of leadership (Trompenaars & Wooliams, 2002). Ultimately, the picture is not a static one, as cultures change rapidly and what is not acceptable as an HRM practice in a particular country can become commonplace there in but a few years (Fletcher, 2001). Research, if it is to be current in value, may have to take a more longitudinal approach to developments in performance management than has hitherto been the case.

REFERENCES

Ainsworth, M., & Smith, M. (1993). *Making it happen: Managing performance at work.* Sydney, Australia: Prentice Hall.

Amba-Rao, S., Petrick, J., Gupta, J., & Von der Embse, T. (2000). Comparative performance appraisal practices and management values among foreign and domestic firms in India. *International Journal of Human Resource Management, 11,* 1, 60–89.

Ariga, K., Brunello, G., & Ohkusa, Y. (2000). *International labor markets in Japan.* Cambridge, U.K.: Cambridge University Press.

Ashkanasy, N. (1997). A cross-national comparison of Australian and Canadian supervisors' attributional and evaluative responses to subordinate performance. *Australian Psychologist, 32,* 1, 29–36.

Bailey, C., & Fletcher, C. (2002a).The impact of multi-source feedback on management development: Findings from a longitudinal study. *Journal of Organizational Behavior, 23,* 853–867.

Bailey, C., & Fletcher, C. (2002b, January). *When do other people's opinions matter? The credibility of feedback from co-workers.* Paper presented at the British Psychological Society Occupational Psychology Conference, Blackpool.

Bastos, M., & Fletcher, C. (1995). Exploring the individual's perceptions of sources and credibility of feedback in the work environment. *International Journal of Selection and Assessment, 3,* 1, 29–40.

Blunt, P., & Jones, M. (1992). *Managing organisations in Africa.* Berlin: Walter de Gruyter.

Blunt, P., & Jones, M. (1997). Exploring the limits of Western leadership theory in East Asia and Africa. *Personnel Reveiw, 26,* 1-2, 6–23.

Brutus, S., London, M., & Martineau, J. (1999). The impact of 360-degree feedback on planning for career development. *Journal of Management Development, 18,* 8, 676–693.

Chen, C., & DiTomaso, N. (1996). Performance appraisal and demographic diversity: Issues regarding appraisals, appraisers and appraising. pp. 137–163. In E. Kossek and S. Lobel (Eds.), *Managing diversity.* Cambridge, MA: Blackwell Publishers.

Clayton, P., & Ayres, H. (1996). Performance appraisal or performance development? A tale of two schemes. *Australian Journal of Public Administration, 55*, 1, 63–71.

Cleveland, J. N., & Murphy, K. R. (1992). Analyzing performance appraisal as goal-directed behavior. *Research in Personnel and Human Resources Management, 10,* 121–185.

Conway, J., & Huffcutt, A. (1997). Psychometric properties of multisource performance ratings: A meta-analysis of subordinate, supervisor, peer and self-ratings. *Human Performance, 10*(4), 331–360.

Den Hartog, D., House, R., Hanges, R., Ruiz-Quintanilla, S., Dorfman, P., et al. (1999). Culture specific and cross-culturally generalizable implicit leadership theories: Are attributes of charismatic/transformational leadership universally endorsed? *Leadership Quarterly, 10,* 219–256.

DeNisi, A. (1996). *Cognitive approach to performance appraisal: A programme of research.* London: Routledge.

Dia, M. (1996). *Africa's management in the 1990's and beyond.* Washington, DC: World Bank.

Drucker, P. F. (1955). *The practice of management.* London: Heinemann.

Elenkov, S. (1998). Can American management concepts work in Russia? A cross-cultural comparative study. *California Management Review, 40,* 133–156.

Endo, K. (1996). Jinjisatei-seido no Nichibei Hikaku (A comparison of Japanese and American performance appraisals). *Ohara Shakaimondai Kekyujo Zasshi, 449,* 1–29.

Epitropaki, O., & Martin, R. (2004). Implicit leadership theories in applied settings: Factor structure, generalizability and stability over time. *Journal of Applied Psychology, 89*(2), 293–310.

Fletcher, C. (2001). Performance appraisal and management: The developing research agenda. *Journal of Occupational and Organizational Psychology, 74*(4), 473–488.

Fletcher, C. (2002). Appraisal—An individual psychological analysis. In Sonnentag S. (Ed.), *Psychological management of individual performance: A handbook in the psychology of management in organisations.* New York: John Wiley & Sons.

Fletcher, C. (2004). Appraisal and feedback: Making performance review work. London: Chartered Institute of Personnel & Development.

Fletcher, C., & Baldry, C. (1999). Multi-source feedback systems: A research perspective. In C. Cooper & I. Robertson (Eds.), *International review of organizational and industrial psychlogy* (Vol. 14, pp. 149–193). New York: John Wiley & Sons.

Fletcher, C., & Perry, C. (2001). Performance appraisal and feedback: A consideration of national culture and a review of contemporary research and future trends. In N. Anderson, D. Ones, H. Sinangil, & C. Viswesvaran (Eds.), *Handbook of industrial and organizational psychology* (Vol. 1, pp. 127–144). Beverly Hills, CA: Sage.

Flint, D. (1999). The role of organizational justice in multi-source performance appraisal: Theory-based applications and directions for research. *Human Resource Management Review, 9*(1), 1–20.

Fuji Sogo Kenkyujo (1998). *Jitsuryoku-shugi, Seika-shugi teki Shogu ni kansuru Jittai Hokokusho (Report on performance-oriented personnel management).* Tokyo: Fuji Research Institute.

Furnham, A., & Stringfield, P. (1994). Congruence in job performance ratings: A study of 360 degrees feedback examining self, manager, peers and consultants' ratings. *Human Relations, 51*(4), 517–530.

Groeschl, S. (2003). Cultural implications for the appraisal process. *Cross Cultural Management, 10*(1), 67–80.

Harris, M. M., Van Hoye, G., & Lievens, F. (2003). Privacy attitudes towards Internet-based selection systems: A cross-cultural comparison. *International Journal of Selection and Assessment, 11,* 230–236.

Hazucha, J., Hezlett, S., & Schneider, R. (1993). The impact of 360-degree feedback on management skills development. *Human Resource Management, 32* (2–3), 325–351.

Hofstede, G. (1980). *Cultures' consequences: International differences in work-related values.* Beverly Hills, CA: Sage.

Hofstede, G. (1991). *Cultures and organizations: Software of the mind.* London: McGraw-Hill.

Hofstede, G. (1994). Management scientists are human. *Management Science, 40,* 4–13.

Horwitz, F., Browning, V., Jain, H., & Steenkamp, A. (2002). Human resources practices in South Africa: Overcoming the apartheid legacy. *International Journal of Human Resource Management, 13*(7), 1105–1118.

Huo, Y., & von Glinow, M. (1995). On transplanting human resource practices to China: A culture driven approach. *International Journal of Manpower, 16,* 3–15.

Ibru, O. (1997). The development of international business in Africa (1947–1997). *International Executive, 39*(2), 117–133.

Jackson, T. (2002). Reframing human resource management in Africa: A cross-cultural perspective. *International Journal of Human Resource Management, 13*(7), 998–1018.

Kanungo, R., & Jaeger, A. (1990). Introduction: The need for indigenous management in countries. In A. Jaeger & C. Myers (Eds.), *Management in developing countries* (pp. 1–23). London: Routledge.

Kim, I., Park, H., & Suzuki, N. (1990). Reward allocations in the United States, Japan and Korea: A comparison of individualistic and collectivist cultures. *Academy of Management Journal, 33,* 188–198.

Koopman, P., Den Hartog, D., Konrad, E. (1999). National culture and leadership profiles in Europe: Some results from the GLOBE study. *European Journal of Work and Organizational Psychology, 8*(4), 503–520.

Landy, F., & Farr, J. (1980). Performance rating. *Psychological Bulletin, 87,* 72–107.

Locke, E. A., & Latham, G. P. (1990). *A theory of goal setting and task performance.* Englewood Cliffs, NJ: Prentice Hall.

London, M., & Smither, J. (1995). Can multi-source feedback change perceptions of goal accomplishment, self-evaluations and performance related outcomes? Theory based applications and directions for research. *Personnel Psychology, 48,* 803–839.

London, M., Smither, J., & Adsit, D. (1997). Accountability: The Achilles heel of multisource feedback. *Group and Organization Management, 22*(2), 162–184.

Mackay, L., & Torrington, D. (1986). *The changing nature of personnel management.* London: Institute of Personnel Management.

Maczynski, J., Lindell, M., Motowidlo, S., Sigfrids, C., & Jarmuz, S. (1997). A comparison of organisational and societal culture in Poland and Finland. *Polish Psychological Bulletin, 28,* 269–278.

Maier, N. (1958). Three types of appraisal interview. *Personnel*, March/April, 27–40.

Maurer, T. J., Mitchell, R. D., & Barbeite, F. G. (2002). Predictors of attitudes toward a 360 feedback system and involvement in post-feedback management development activity. *Journal of Occupational and Organizational Psychology, 75*(1), 87–107.

McGregor, D. (1957). An uneasy look at performance appraisal. *Harvard Business Review, 35,* 89–94.

Milliman, J., Nason, S., Gallagher, E., Huo, P., von Glinow, M., & Lowe, K. (1998). The impact of national culture on human resource management practices: The case of performance appraisal. *Advances in International Comparative Management, 12,* 157–183.

Nagel, R. (2002). *360 degree feedback.* Article presented on the International Public Management Association for Human Resources Web site: http://www.ipma-hr.org.

Noorderhaven, N., & Tidjani, B. (2001). Culture, governance and economic performance: An exploratory study with a special focus on Africa. *International Journal of Cross Cultural Management, 1*(1), 31–52.

Penny, J. (2003). Exploring differential item functioning in a 360-degree assessment: Rater source and method of delivery. *Organizational Research Methods, 6*(1), 61–79.

Schneider, R., Goff, M., Anderson, S., & Borman, W. (2003). Computerized adaptive rating scales for measuring managerial performance. *International Journal of Selection and Assessment, 11* (2/3), 237–246.

Schneider, S., & Barsoux, J. (1997). *Managing across cultures.* Hemel Hempstead: Prentice Hall Europe.

Schwab, D., Heneman, H., & DeCotiis, T. (1975). Behaviourally anchored rating scales: A review of the literature. *Personnel Psychology, 28,* 549–562.

Shibata, H. (2002). Wage and performance appraisal systems in flux: A Japan-United States comparison. *Industrial Relations, 41*(4), 629–652.

Smith, D. (1986). Training programs for performance appraisal: A review. *Academy of Management Review, 11*(1), 22–40.

Smith, D., & Kendall, L. (1963). Retranslation of expectations: An approach to the construction of unambiguous anchors for rating scales. *Journal of Applied Psychology, 47,* 149–155.

Smither, J. W., London, M., Flautt, R., Vargas, Y., & Kucine, I. (2003). Can working with an executive coach improve multisource feedback ratings over time? A quasi-experimental field study. *Personnel Psychology, 56*(1), 23–44.

Smither, J., Walker, A.. & Yap, M. (2004). An examination of the equivalence of Web-based versus paper-and-pencil upward feedback ratings: Rater and ratee-level analyses. *Educational and Psychological Measurement, 64*(1), 40–61.

Snape, E., Thompson, D., Ka-Ching Ya, F., & Redman, T. (1998). Performance appraisal and culture: Practice and attitudes in Hong Kong and Great Britain. *International Journal of Human Resource Management, 9*(5), 841–861.

Sparrow, P., & Budhwar, P. (1997). Competition and change: Mapping the India HRM recipe against world-wide patterns. *Journal of World Business, 32*(3), 224–243.

Tang, S., Lai, E., & Kirkbride, P. (1995). *Human resource management practices in Hong Kong: Survey report.* Hong Kong: Hong Kong Institute of Human Resource Management.

Taylor, F. (1911). *Principles of scientific management.* New York: Harper and Row.

Triandis, H. (1989). *Handbook of cross-cultural psychology* (6 vols.). Boston, MA: Allyn & Bacon.

Trompenaars, F. (1993). *Riding the waves of culture: Understanding cultural diversity in business.* London: Economist Books.

Trompenaars, F., & Wooliams, P. (2002). Model behaviour. *People Management, 5*(12), 30–35.

Virmani, B., & Guptan, S. (1991). *Indian management.* New Delhi: Vision Books.

Walker, A., & Smither, J. (1999). A five year study of upward feedback: What managers do with their results matters. *Personnel Psychology, 52,* 393–423.

Williams, R. (2002). *Managing employee performance: Design and implementation in organizations.* London: Thomson.

8 International Compensation

Michael M. Harris and Seungrib Park

CONTENTS

Like domestic compensation research, international compensation has, for the most part, been the focus of limited attention by researchers. Rynes and Gerhart's (2000) volume, for example, did not address international compensation issues. A recent book chapter by Heneman, Fay, and Wang (2001), however, provided some coverage to international compensation. Nonetheless, their chapter focused primarily on North American approaches to compensation, emphasizing the strategic compensation process, pay-for-performance systems, and the setting of pay policies (using job evaluation methods and market surveys), as well as on alternatives to the traditional pay structure (e.g., skill-based pay). They also commented on employee benefits, such as cash balance pension plans, with primarily a North American orientation.

    The purpose of this chapter is to review and extend what is known with regard to cross-cultural compensation practices. Specifically, our focus is on surveying international research on compensation, and offering suggestions where there is a lack of such research. We found that the vast majority of compensation research has been conducted in North American settings and relatively little is known regarding the generalizability of this research to other countries and cultures.

    Our major organizing structure for this chapter focuses on the two possible effects of culture on compensation. First, culture may have a *direct effect* on pay practices. That is, culture may directly affect the factors that managers consider in making pay raises or how pay is set for different jobs. Second, culture may have an *indirect effect* on compensation practices. For example, the relationship between a pay-for-performance plan and job performance may be moderated by the employees' culture. As we will show, there is a sufficient amount of research to draw some conclusions regarding the direct effect of culture on compensation. As we will also explain, however, there has been too little research on the indirect effect of culture to draw even very tentative conclusions regarding those relationships.

In the section that follows, we review the literature discussing culture as having a direct effect on compensation. This section is further subdivided into: (a) micro-level studies, which look at how culture affects individual decisions, (b) macro-level studies, which address decisions at the organizational level, and (c) research on basic compensation practices, such as job evaluation. We begin first, however, with a discussion as to why culture should affect pay practices. Although this may seem like an obvious question, surprisingly little literature has considered this point.

WHY SHOULD CULTURE AFFECT COMPENSATION?

There are two potential explanations as to why culture should affect pay practices. First, we consider compensation as symbolic of cultural values. Second, there may be cultural differences in terms of how individuals perceive money. These are not meant to be exclusive explanations; both may be correct.

PAY PRACTICES AS SYMBOLIC OF CULTURAL VALUES

Pay practices may reflect cultural values in terms of collectivism, power distance, and so forth. In a highly collectivistic culture, for example, a pay-for-performance plan that emphasizes team performance reinforces culturally appropriate norms and values. In the same culture, a pay-for-performance plan based on individual performance might be perceived quite negatively. In this view, cultural values govern the nature of compensation practices and policies. This is similar to a perspective offered by Tosi and Greckhamer (2004), who found that differences in chief executive officer compensation across countries was related to power distance and individualism. Thus, this explanation assumes that compensation policies and practices are an expression of cultural values.

CULTURAL DIFFERENCES IN PERCEPTIONS OF MONEY

A second possible explanation for the relationship between culture and compensation is that culture affects individual perceptions of money, which in turn affect compensation practices and policies. Money has important symbolic properties, including achievement and recognition, status and respect, freedom and control, and power (Mitchell & Mickel, 1999). Although only limited cross-cultural work has been done in this area, several measures have been developed to measure perceptions of the meaning of money. The most researched measure is the Money Ethic scale (MES), developed by Tang and his colleagues. Their short version of the MES assumes three factors, including a "money is evil" factor (e.g., "money is the root of all evil"), a "money should be budgeted" factor (e.g., "I use my money very carefully"), and a "money is a measure of success" factor (e.g., "money represents one's achievement"). Tang, Furnham, and Davis (2002) examined the MES using samples from the United States, Taiwan, and the United Kingdom. They found that for the U.S. data, a confirmatory factor analysis fit the data quite well. For the U.K. and Chinese data, the model fit was poor. The difference appeared to be due to the correlations between the factors; whereas U.S. data reflected a very low correlation between the three factors, the Taiwan data and the U.K. data reflected more highly correlated factors. Tang et al. also found that there were mean differences between the countries on three of the items. Based on their results, Tang et al. concluded that "the meaning of money is in the eye of the beholder and is different across cultures." (p. 558). The meaning of money scales may be helpful in understanding how employees across different cultures respond to pay-for-performance plans. We recommend that further investigations be performed in terms of how perceptions of money vary across cultures, and how this construct affects various other aspects of compensation and reactions to compensation.

Forgas, Furnham, and Frey (1989) examined perceptions of money from a somewhat different perspective. Specifically, they examined attributions for wealth and economic success using respondents from Australia, the United Kingdom, and Germany. In the first part of their questionnaire, subjects were asked to list the six most important explanations for why some people are more financially successful than others. Two judges ultimately reduced these open-ended responses to seven distinct categories, including individual effort, individual ability, family background (e.g., inheritance), exploitation of others, social rewards, having an occupation with special powers (e.g., membership in a union), and luck (e.g., gambling). Based on frequency of mention and order of importance, each of these seven categories was weighted by country. Large differences were found between countries. Family, for example, was perceived as the most important factor in both the United Kingdom and Germany, whereas effort was the most important factor in Australia. Luck was the least important factor in Germany and Australia; social rewards was the least important in the United Kingdom. Using multiple regression analyses, Forgas et al. (1989) also examined the unique effects of national and demographic (e.g., educational level) variables, and found that each of them contributed significantly to attributions of financial success.

This study suggests that there may be cultural differences in understanding how wealth is attained, which in turn may affect pay-for-performance perceptions and perhaps other pay practices. Pay-for-performance plans, for example, may work best in cultures where effort is seen as the most important factor in achieving financial success. Pay-for-performance plans may be least effective in cultures where family is seen as the most important factor in financial success.

Next, we discuss the literature looking at the direct effect of culture on compensation practices.

THE DIRECT EFFECT OF CULTURE ON COMPENSATION

The largest amount of international compensation research has considered the direct effect of culture on pay practices. This is probably due, at least in part, to the fact that data are relatively easy to gather, as compared to culture as a moderator, where data may be more difficult to obtain. Some of the studies here have used micro-level designs (e.g., studying pay decisions by individual managers), while other studies have used macro-level designs, looking at company-level data (e.g., pay rates set by different companies in different countries).

Micro-Level Studies

Based on an expectation that reward allocation decisions in general, and pay decisions specifically, will differ as a function of culture, several researchers have conducted policy-capturing studies focusing on individual managers' pay decisions. Beatty, McCune, and Beatty (1988) performed a policy-capturing study comparing U.S. ($N = 63$) and Japanese ($N = 41$) managers. The stimulus materials consisted of 40 hypothetical employees, who varied in terms of their performance level, worth of their job to the organization, seniority, and several other variables (e.g., need for achievement). For U.S. managers, performance was by far the most important predictor of pay increase, with the other variables having little effect. The reverse was true for Japanese managers. U.S. managers were also more likely to give either relatively large or relatively small raises; Japanese managers had much less variance in their raise decisions.

Zhou and Martocchio (2001) performed a policy-capturing study, comparing Chinese and American managers' bonus decisions (as well as nonmonetary rewards) for hypothetical employees. Subjects (71 Chinese and 281 U.S. participants) made ratings on 16 vignettes, which varied with regard to performance level, coworker relationship (i.e., excellent or poor), manager relationship (excellent or poor), and family's financial need. For the most part, Zhou and Martocchio's hypotheses were supported. In making bonus allocations, Chinese managers placed less emphasis on performance as compared with the U.S. managers. Likewise, as they predicted, Chinese managers placed greater importance on interpersonal relationships and on family financial needs than did U.S. managers. The one finding that was in the opposite direction than predicted was that Chinese managers placed greater weight on performance than U.S. managers when making nonmonetary recognition decisions.

Finally, Hundley and Kim (1997) argued that there are at least three sets of factors that determine pay fairness. Based on organizational justice theory, they hypothesized that distributive justice (i.e., the ratio of one's inputs to outcomes, as compared to the referent other's ratio of inputs to outcomes) would affect perceptions of pay fairness. A second factor, referred to as the "status-value" approach, assumed that salary is affected by various statuses or positions that are considered prestigious, including seniority and education. The third factor included by Hundley and Kim (1997) was employee need, which was operationalized as the stimulus employee's family size (i.e., number of dependents). Based on their understanding of cultural differences, Hundley and Kim (1997) proposed that U.S. and Korean subjects would place different weights on these factors. For example, they hypothesized that size of one's family would have a bigger effect on fairness ratings of Korean respondents than U.S. respondents. To test their hypotheses, Hundley and Kim created hypothetical vignettes that manipulated these factors and obtained independent samples of U.S. and Korean junior and senior college students, who rated the fairness of the employee's situation in each vignette. Their findings supported the hypotheses; work performance was weighted more heavily by U.S. respondents, whereas seniority, education, and family size were weighted less heavily, as compared to Korean subjects.

Although the findings seem reasonable, these studies do not prove that culture accounts for the results. First, there was no direct measure of culture in any of these studies. Thus, differences between the subjects from the United States and the subjects from the Asian countries may be due to other factors, such as the threat of litigation in the United States as compared to China, differences in business conditions, and so forth. Second, even if the differences are due to culture, it is not entirely clear which aspects of culture may account for these differences. Using Hofstede's (2001) framework, for example, we don't know whether the findings are due to differences in collectivism, time orientation, or power distance. Of course, because the judgments were based on hypothetical employees, it is not known whether the same decisions would be made in an actual organization. Studies with subjects representing several different countries, which vary in terms of key cultural values, would enable researchers to better assess the relationship between culture and the weights assigned to the various factors.

MACRO-LEVEL STUDIES

Several studies have looked at the relationship between culture and a wide variety of pay practices on a macro-level. These studies range in sophistication as well. Lowe, DeCieri, and Dowling (2002) reported a descriptive study of companies' compensation and benefit practices in nine different countries (i.e., Australia, Canada, China, Indonesia, Japan, Korea, Mexico, Taiwan, and the United States) and one region (i.e., Latin America), as reported by respondents (managerial and nonmanagerial employees) from these countries. Specifically, respondents rated incentive pay issues (e.g., "pay incentives are important to compensation strategy"), the role of seniority (e.g., "seniority influences pay decisions"), long-term pay orientation (e.g., "pay system has a future orientation") and benefits (e.g., "benefits are generous"). For each question, respondents rated both the degree to which the item reflected current practice and the degree to which they felt it "should be" this way, using a five-point scale (1 = not at all; 5 = to a very great extent).

Some selected findings are particularly interesting. Beginning first with the ratings on current practices, only three countries, China, Japan, and Taiwan, had mean ratings of 3.0 ("to a moderate extent") or higher on the item "pay incentives are important to compensation strategy."

By comparison, the mean rating for the United States was 2.77. Somewhat similar findings were reported for the link between pay and group/organizational performance; specifically, only Taiwan and China had average ratings above 3.0 on this item. Regarding seniority entering into pay decisions, only three of the countries (Taiwan, Japan, and Indonesia) had means that were above 3.0. Although Australia (M = 2.52) and Canada (M = 2.61) had relatively low ratings on this item, the average U.S. ratings were slightly higher (M = 2.96).

Finally, in terms of the long-term emphasis on pay, the most individualistic countries had the lowest means (e.g., the U.S. mean was 2.01), whereas the more collectivist countries tended to have higher means (e.g., Taiwan had a mean rating of 3.47, while China had a mean of 3.04). There were exceptions even here, however, as Korea had a mean rating of only 2.39. A possible explanation is that these collectivist countries also have a long-term time orientation.

Turning next to the findings for the "should be" ratings, respondents from all countries expressed greater desire for pay incentives to be linked to compensation strategy. Respondents from three countries (the United States, Taiwan, and Mexico) and Latin America had means above 4.0 on the "should be" ratings. The lowest "should be" rating was for Australia (M = 3.52). Finally, in terms of whether seniority *should* enter into pay decisions, ratings were more consistent with culture in that all three individualistic countries had relatively low mean ratings (under 2.5) on this question. Conversely, the highest mean ratings on this item were from collectivist countries, including Mexico (M = 3.61), Taiwan (M = 3.51), and China (M = 3.38).

Although Lowe et al. (2002) did not make specific hypotheses, they offered post hoc explanations for some of their findings. For example, they concluded that there was *some* support for their predictions regarding country culture (e.g., individualism versus collectivism) and various perceptions of pay practices, but the results were not always consistent. Furthermore, they observed that "though the pay systems between these various countries do have a number of important differences, they seem to share more similarities than we had anticipated." (p. 61). Lowe et al.'s study also may have suffered from several methodological issues. First, they did not measure the cultural values of the respondents, so it is not clear if they shared their country's culture. Second, some of the items may have had different meanings in different countries. Although the questionnaire was subjected to rigorous development, the term "pay incentives" may have had different meanings in different cultures (Geringer, Frayne, & Milliman, 2002). In some cultures "pay incentives" may refer to pay level (i.e., lower or higher pay levels); in other cultures, "pay incentives" may refer to pay-for-performance programs (e.g., individual incentive systems).

Schuler and Rogovsky (1998) also examined the relationship between culture and compensation practices. Based on Hofstede's dimensions of culture, they developed a series of hypotheses regarding the relationship between culture and status-based pay, individual performance-based pay, benefits, and employee ownership plans. For example, they predicted that countries that are high on uncertainty avoidance will tend to use compensation practices that are based on seniority, because that type of system is highly predictable. Similarly, they hypothesized that countries that are more individualistically oriented will be more likely to have a focus on individual performance-based pay. Finally, regarding benefits, they theorized that countries with higher levels of masculinity would be less likely to have workplace child-care practices. Their hypotheses were generally supported. For example, four of the eight hypotheses regarding benefits were completely supported, but the four other hypotheses were supported only for certain employee groups. There was quite strong support, however, for their hypotheses regarding employee ownership and culture.

Finally, Townsend, Scott, and Markham (1990) conducted a macro-level study of compensation-related costs. Their dependent variables included average hourly earnings, benefit costs, and the ratio between hourly earnings and benefit costs for 41 manufacturing industries in 28 countries. Based on a cultural cluster model derived by Ronen and Shenkar (1985) in which countries are grouped into five distinct clusters (i.e., Anglo, Asian, Latin European, Nordic, and Germanic), Townsend et al. found that the cultural clusters explained a substantial amount of variance in all three dependent variables. Conversely, industry type had no effect on compensation practices, except within Anglo industries. They concluded that "culture is a predominant factor that influences certain compensation patterns" (p. 674).

Taken together, Lowe et al. (2002), Schuler and Rogovsky (1998), and Townsend et al. (1990) indicate support for relationships between culture and pay practices. It is important to emphasize, however, that their research does not examine whether those compensation practices that are *congruent* with the country's culture are more effective in achieving their goals. Rather, this research indicates that certain cultures tend to have certain kinds of compensation practices. It seems safe to conclude, however, that culture does have a direct effect on organizational pay practices.

Next, we turn to an examination of basic compensation tools and practices, such as job evaluation, salary surveys, and pay structures. We briefly review these processes, then offer comments regarding culture and its effects on these practices.

BASIC COMPENSATION PRACTICES: JOB EVALUATION, SALARY SURVEYS, AND PAY STRUCTURES

Although job evaluations, salary surveys, and pay structures form the "bread-and-butter" of compensation practice, a review of research and practice indicates that these are primarily North American activities. As we will discuss, however, some interesting cross-cultural questions do arise.

JOB EVALUATION

Job evaluation is a systematic procedure for determining the worth of each job to the organization (Madigan & Hoover, 1986) and it appears to be primarily practiced in a North American and U.K. (Childs, 2004) context. There are a variety of different job evaluation procedures (Collins & Muchinsky, 1993), but the point method system is one of the most common approaches. A point method system involves the selection of the compensable factors, or dimensions, that determine the value of jobs. Typical compensable factors include education, accountability, mental demands, and physical demands. Once the compensable factors are determined and carefully defined, the levels on each compensable factor are determined. Education, for example, may have four levels, ranging from high school diploma to graduate degree. Points are then assigned to each level (e.g., 10 points for high school diploma, 20 points for two-year college degree, and so forth). Compensable factors are usually weighted, indicating that some are more highly valued to the organization than others. Weights may be determined subjectively, or objectively, using pay information from other companies. Research shows that different job evaluation methods may arrive at different conclusions about job worth (Madigan & Hoover, 1986). Even decisions regarding how to set the weights may produce different job worth results.

In terms of international implications, it is unclear whether organizations in other cultures use a system like job evaluation or some similar process to determine job worth. Perhaps a much more informal process is used instead, and job worth is determined more casually than in North America and the United Kingdom. If job evaluation methods were to be used in other cultures, several interesting questions emerge. Would different compensable factors, for example, be used? Would compensable factors be weighted the same way? It seems reasonable to expect that culture would affect the development of a job evaluation tool in a number of ways. As an example, it seems likely that cultures high in masculinity would weight compensable factors such as instructing lower than cultures high in femininity. Cultures high in power distance would be likely to weight supervisory responsibilities higher than cultures low in power distance.

COLLECTING SALARY SURVEY INFORMATION

Salary survey information gathered from other companies plays an important role in determining pay for different jobs. Judgments must be made at each stage in conducting a salary survey (Rynes

& Milkovich, 1986). For example, decisions must be made as to which organizations to include in a salary survey, how to weight information, and which jobs in the organization sufficiently match jobs in the salary survey.

With a few exceptions, little empirical research has been conducted on how salary survey information is chosen. What research does exist has primarily been conducted in North American settings. Viswesvaran and Barrick (1992) examined how compensation specialists chose organizations for inclusion in a pay survey. Viswesvaran and Barrick conducted a two-part study, first examining how organizations were chosen in an initial screening, and then whether a particular organization would be retained in the actual data analysis. For the first decision step, Viswesvaran and Barrick varied five features of each organization: union status, industry similarity, geographic proximity, organization size, and frequency of hiring (e.g., "seldom hires" to "frequently hires"). Using a policy-capturing methodology, they reported that union status was the most important feature based on subjects' self-reports, but geographic location was the most important factor based on the regression analyses.

For the second decision step, Viswesvaran and Barrick varied five different factors, including method used to collect information (e.g., phone interview, mailed survey), title of person providing the information (e.g., clerk, compensation specialist), degree of job match, completeness of the data provided (e.g., base pay only, base pay plus incentives and overtime), and completeness of information about the organization. For this decision, the most important self-reported factor was the method used to collect information; but the most important factor based on a regression analysis was degree of job match. As noted by Gerhart and Rynes (2003), the discrepancies between the self-reported weights and the regression derived weights reported by Viswesvaran and Barrick (1992) indicate that pay structure decisions "might occur through unintentional decision processes than through differences in strategic intent." (p. 35).

Whereas Viswesvaran and Barrick (1992) examined salary survey decisions for a relatively low-level position (i.e., secretary), Trevor and Graham (2000) compared the use of different pay surveys for different jobs. Specifically, they examined the relative importance of product market surveys (where the concern is for cost containment) versus labor market surveys (where the concern is for attracting and retaining employees) in determining job pay. Trevor and Graham varied factors such as the job salary (i.e., above or below $40,000), ratio of labor costs to total costs, attraction/retention difficulty, and job types (i.e., core job, noncore job, managerial job). They found that core jobs and more highly paid jobs were associated with greater reported use of product market surveys; the ratio of labor costs to total costs was *not* associated with use of product market surveys.

As with job evaluation, it would be useful to obtain basic information as to how salary surveys are conducted in other cultures. We suspect that the processes associated with salary surveys are much more informal than in North American settings, but there is insufficient information to draw any firm conclusions in this regard. Furthermore, the methods used to choose companies to survey, as well as other aspects of the salary survey process, are in need of investigation across different cultures.

ESTABLISHING A PAY STRUCTURE

The purpose of a pay structure is to provide a pay range for each position in the organization, thereby enabling managers to make pay decisions such that they are not paying too much or too little in attracting and retaining employees. The establishment of a pay structure requires several decisions. In this section, we briefly summarize how a pay structure is devised, review relevant research (which is not targeted towards international issues), and briefly comment on the implications for international pay practices.

Several decisions must be made in order to create a pay structure. First, the organization must decide whether to lead, match, or lag in terms of pay relative to other organizations. That is, the organization must determine whether to pay more, match, or pay less than other relevant organizations. Another decision that must be made is whether to treat each job separately, or to collapse the jobs into a smaller number of grades. Most commonly, jobs are collapsed into a smaller number of grades. A major question then becomes how many grades to have. Another decision concerns the amount of range within each grade. Specifically, a decision must be made as to whether there will be some degree of variation allowed in pay within the grade, or whether all job incumbents will be paid the same within a grade. In the United States, there typically is some degree of variation allowed within grades to allow higher performers to earn more than people who are lower performers. Variation within grades also allows managers to reward employees with more seniority or job experience. Yet another important decision is how much overlap to have between grades. The less overlap between grades, the greater the difference in pay between job grades. Conversely, the more overlap between grades, the less the difference in pay between job grades.

Research on developing a pay structure is sparse even in a North American context. In one of few such studies, Weber and Rynes (1991) examined the relative importance of salary surveys and job evaluation in determining pay rates. Subjects were compensation specialists, who recommended pay rate changes in nine situations. Each situation involved the manipulation of a salary survey (showing that pay was either 6% above, equal to, or 6% below the target organization) and job evaluation points (indicating that the jobs were either 6% above, equal to, or 6% below, the number of points equating to current job pay). Job pay was also manipulated so that different jobs were examined, with different pay rates associated with them. Weber and Rynes found that although both salary surveys and job evaluation factors affected pay decisions, salary survey information was far more important to subjects.

Because most of this research was conducted in North American settings, we know virtually nothing about how pay structures are established in other cultures, to the extent that they even exist. We suspect that pay rates are determined using far more informal, unsystematic approaches, particularly in non-Western countries, but there is far too little information on this matter. A consideration of the purposes of a pay structure suggests certain cross-cultural hypotheses. For example, we predict that cultures with high uncertainty avoidance would have less within-grade range, as more range in a particular grade would create ambiguity in the eyes of employees and managers. Similarly, in highly collectivistic cultures, we expect that the within-grade range in pay would be much lower than in highly individualistic cultures. The reason for this prediction is that employees in collectivist cultures are likely to be paid more similarly to one another, as compared to individualistic cultures. We also predict that in high-power-distance cultures, there will be more grades within the pay structures, as having more pay grades reinforces status differences. Alternatively, in high-power-distance cultures, there may be more pay structures, reflecting sharp differences between positions at different hierarchical levels.

In sum, research on the main effect of culture on pay practices is modest in scope. What research does exist, however, suggests that culture does affect certain pay practices. This is true for both micro-level research (e.g., individuals making pay decisions) and macro-level research (e.g., use of seniority in determining pay). By contrast, there is a dearth of research examining the effect of culture on basic pay practices, such as job evaluation, salary surveys, and pay structures. We offered some predictions as to how culture is likely to affect some of these processes. Next, we address culture as a moderator of the relationship between pay practices and various outcomes of interest.

THE INDIRECT EFFECT OF CULTURE ON COMPENSATION PRACTICES

In this section, we address the indirect effect of culture on pay practices. We primarily address indirect effects in terms of a moderator relationship (i.e., moderating the relationship between pay practices and job outcomes (e.g., job performance). In terms of pay practices, we focus on pay level and pay-for-performance programs. With regard to job outcomes, we refer to the full range of criteria that may be affected by pay practices, including pay satisfaction and job performance. In considering the indirect effect of culture, we first examine what general theories of motivation have to say about compensation. Next, we summarize research on pay level and various outcomes. We conclude with a discussion of pay-for-performance research. Unfortunately, as we will discuss, there is little research regarding the moderating effect of culture on the pay practices–outcomes relationship, and therefore much of our thinking here must be speculative.

WHAT DO MOTIVATION THEORIES SAY ABOUT PAY?

Because there are many different motivation theories, it is useful to divide them into two somewhat arbitrary categories: classical theories and contemporary theories. Although much research has been conducted with the classical theories of motivation, there is far less research regarding contemporary theories.

Classical Theories of Motivation

Researchers have developed numerous general theories of motivation. Although one might think that compensation would be a central variable in many of these theories, Rynes, Gerhart, and Park (2005) noted that three major theories of motivation had downplayed the role of pecuniary rewards in employee behavior. These three theories include Maslow's need hierarchy, Herzberg's two-factor theory, and Deci and Ryan's cognitive evaluation theory. However, Rynes et al. (2005) summarized a wide variety of studies suggesting that pay serves as a greater motivator than these three theories had suggested. Despite some research suggesting that pay is not important to most people, Rynes, Gerhart, and Minette (2004) observed that research conducted during the 1980s attributed a greater importance to pay. Along these lines, Rynes et al. (2004) argued that there are various situational contingencies that affect the importance of pay. As an example, Rynes et al. (2004) asserted that pay will be more important to applicants when pay varies widely across companies compared to when pay is relatively uniform. Recent research has also suggested that individual differences affect the importance of pay; risk seekers, for example, place greater importance on pay (e.g., Cable & Judge, 1994). Furthermore, Rynes et al. (2004) asserted that people may be reluctant to admit that pay is an important factor to them, which may lead researchers to mistakenly conclude that compensation is not motivating. Much of this research has been conducted in North American settings, however, and we know very little about the importance of pay in other cultures.

Although there is little research using even the classical motivation models as they relate to compensation in other cultures, Arnolds and Boshoff (2002) used Alderfer's (1969) ERG (existence, relatedness, and growth needs) theory in examining the relationship between need satisfaction, self-esteem, and performance intentions in a South African sample. They hypothesized that self-esteem would completely mediate the relationship between need satisfaction and performance intentions. Their study is particularly relevant here because they divided existence needs into two scales: a scale measuring pay need satisfaction (e.g., "I get enough money from my job to live comfortably") and a scale measuring fringe benefit need satisfaction (e.g., "Compared to other places, our fringe benefits are excellent"). They found that pay need satisfaction and fringe benefit need satisfaction did not affect self-esteem. Clearly, research is needed to explore the role of compensation on various underlying psychological attitudes and perceptions, as well as on behavior.

In short, classical theories either disparage the importance of money as a motivator, or have little specific to say about the topic. Rynes and colleagues (e.g., Rynes et al., 2004; Rynes et al., 2005) offer a more optimistic conclusion about the importance of compensation, which in turn suggests a reconsideration of pay as a motivator. Whether the importance of pay varies across cultures also needs to be studied. We turn now to contemporary theories of motivation.

Contemporary Theories of Motivation

Kehr (2004) presented a relatively new approach to understanding motivation. At the core of his model is the notion that there are two sets of motives that drive behavior: implicit motives and explicit motives. Explicit motives, or values, are "the reasons people self-attribute for their actions" (p. 481). Explicit motives are consciously accessible and are most closely related to goals and intentions. Explicit motives influence cognitive choices and goal setting. The notion of implicit motives, although it has a long history in psychology, has rarely been discussed in the context of HRM theory. Implicit motives influence *long-term* behavior trends. According to Kehr, implicit motives "lead to affective preferences and implicit behavioral impulses" (p. 480). Implicit motives cannot be directly measured, which makes them difficult, though not impossible, to assess.

Kehr (2004) hypothesized that although implicit and explicit motives are independent of one another, they often interact together. Specifically, explicit motives may "channel" or influence the way in which implicit motives are expressed. Thus, although an implicit motive for achievement may exist, the explicit motive may determine how that implicit motive is enacted. An individual who has an implicit motive for achievement and an explicit motive for solitude, for example, may prefer to write books. An individual with the same implicit motive for achievement may have an explicit motive for interaction with others. Thus, he prefers a sales position where he can have a great deal of customer contact.

In addition to implicit and explicit motives, Kehr assumed that perceived abilities are another factor in determining motivation. The bulk of his model, then, focuses on what happens when there are discrepancies between implicit motives, explicit motives, and perceived abilities. Toward that end, Kehr hypothesized the existence of volitional regulation, which may be defined as "an array of self-regulatory strategies to support explicit action tendencies against competing behavioral impulses" (p. 485), and includes such tactics as will-power, self-control, and so forth. According to Kehr, discrepancies between implicit and explicit motives create conflict, which in turn necessitates the use of volitional regulation mechanisms. Problem-solving strategies, on the other hand, are associated with perceived inadequacies in one's abilities. Kehr assumed that volitional regulation is an exhaustible resource, which may eventually become depleted.

In terms of compensation, Kehr discussed the link between his model and organizational rewards, such as pay. Although Kehr seems to consider pay to be an external motive, pay may be an internal motive (Rynes et al., 2005). Regardless, Kehr suggests that organizational rewards will "not necessarily arouse implicit motives," and may even produce discrepancies between explicit and implicit motives, which will in turn require volitional regulation. Worse yet, because volitional regulation is a finite resource, it may be depleted over time, producing alternative negative reactions (e.g., absenteeism or turnover). Increasing organizational rewards for certain desired behavior, however, may increase overall motivation. Indeed, Kehr argued that the inconsistent literature regarding the effects of extrinsic rewards on intrinsic motivation might be better understood using his model. Specifically, he noted that extrinsic rewards only negatively impact intrinsic motivation if they activate new goals and deactivate the initial implicit motives. Kehr observed that intrinsic motivation might be strengthened by extrinsic rewards if they enhance the implicit motives. In the present context, if someone enjoys producing publishable research, receiving a financial inducement for each article published would serve to increase intrinsic motivation. In terms of international compensation issues, it would be interesting to investigate whether extrinsic and intrinsic motives are similar across cultures and whether money functions similarly.

Another contemporary development has been the generation of motivational theories that explicitly take into account culture as a variable. Steers and Sanchez-Runde, 2000 (cited in Latham & Pinder, 2005), described a theory that assumes culture affects three key distal sources of motivation, including individuals' self-concept (e.g., beliefs, needs, and values), norms about work ethic and other psychological variables (e.g., tolerance for ambiguity), and environmental factors, such as economic prosperity. In turn, these distal factors were said to affect self-efficacy, work motivation, and incentives. This theory would seem to provide the basis for more empirical research in terms of the motivational properties of pay as it is indirectly affected by culture, through various other factors. We suggest that international HRM researchers consider this theory more closely in trying to understand the effects of compensation.

In sum, although classical theories may be somewhat uninspiring (Steers, Mowday, & Shapiro, 2004), contemporary theories offer some interesting possibilities and frameworks for testing the indirect effect of culture on compensation. We should not lose sight of the fact, however, that there may be considerable *agreement* in terms of the effect of compensation on motivation in different cultures. Chiu, Luk, & Tang (2002), for example, examined perceptions regarding the most important compensation practices by workers from Hong Kong and mainland China. Along with a detailed description of the cultural views towards compensation, Chiu et al. reported that base pay, merit increases, annual bonuses, mortgage loans, and profit sharing were regarded as the most important compensation practices to retain and motivate employees in Hong Kong. These top three practices were also perceived as being the most important by Chinese employees. With the exception of mortgage loans, these views could just as well have been provided by North American workers.

Next, we turn to research specifically addressing the pay practices–individual outcomes relationship. Like the research described above, however, there is a dearth of such research in international settings. Much of our discussion about the indirect effects of culture on pay practices must therefore be speculative.

Pay Practices–Outcomes Relationship

In this section, we selectively summarize research regarding the effects of pay level on satisfaction and attraction/retention, as well as studies examining pay level from a cost-benefit approach. We then briefly review the pay-for-performance literature.

Pay Level and Satisfaction

In an extensive meta-analysis, Williams et al. (2006) reported a corrected correlation of .29 between pay and pay satisfaction. Although this correlation is higher than has previously been reported (e.g., Heneman & Judge, 2000), there are clearly more factors involved in pay satisfaction than simply one's actual pay level. In this vein, Gerhart and Rynes (2003) observed that pay satisfaction is generally viewed as the difference between one's pay and what one believes he or she should earn. As an example, an executive earning $250,000 might feel somewhat dissatisfied because she feels that $350,000 is the appropriate pay. Distributive justice models assume a variety of factors (e.g., the comparison of other's inputs and outputs) that affect one's sense of equity with regard to pay. It is important, then, to measure what the relevant social comparisons earn in order to understand reactions to one's own pay (Rice, Philips, & McFarlin, 1990). Borrowing from the social psychological literature on social comparisons, Harris, Anseel, and Lievens (unpublished paper) examined downward, lateral, and upward comparisons as predictors of pay satisfaction. They found that an upward comparison (i.e., what higher-paid workers were assumed to be earning) was significantly related to pay satisfaction, but downward and lateral comparisons were not. They offered several explanations for this finding, including that individuals generally consider their performance above average and therefore compare themselves to others who are presumably at the top end of the pay spectrum.

In a conceptual paper, Toh and DeNisi (2003) applied social comparison concepts to host country nationals' (HCNs) reactions to their pay. Specifically, they developed a model of the factors that determine whether HCNs choose expatriates as pay referents. Factors included salience of the expatriates, availability of information about expatriates, and relevance of the expatriates for pay comparisons. Toh and DeNisi's hypotheses regarding culture were particularly interesting. In high-power-distance cultures, for example, they predicted that younger or lower-status workers would be less likely to use older and higher-status workers as a comparison group. They also predicted that in low-masculinity cultures, compensation fairness would be of less importance than quality of life and social interactions. Although these hypotheses were made in the context of HCNs' reactions to pay, it would seem that they would apply more generally as well. Similarly, in a study of pay comparisons in different countries, Sweeney and McFarlin (2004) speculated that the masculinity-femininity cultural dimension may affect the importance of pay comparisons. Despite a paucity of empirical data to support these hypotheses, there is good reason to expect that there will be a relationship between cultural values and one's choice of social comparisons, as well as the importance of pay. Clearly, the question of how social comparisons affect pay satisfaction deserves more research across different cultures.

In a book chapter reviewing a number of different empirical studies, Diener and Oishi (2000) described data collected from a variety of different countries to test relationships between income, financial satisfaction, and life satisfaction. They also outlined several different theories explaining the relationship between income and satisfaction, including livability theory, relativistic judgment or social comparison, cultural explanations, and the material desires concept.

Very briefly, livability theory proposes that income increases subjective well-being insofar as it enables one to afford basic (e.g., food, housing, and clothing) needs. Beyond those basic needs, however, higher income will not increase one's satisfaction. Thus, livability theory would predict that differences in satisfaction will be found between many income groups in poorer countries. Conversely, livability theory predicts that satisfaction levels will not differ between the most affluent individuals in poor countries, nor will satisfaction levels differ between most income groups in wealthier countries.

Relativistic theory assumes that people rely on relevant social comparisons to determine their satisfaction. This theory hypothesizes that individuals more readily compare themselves to nearby neighbors and residents in assessing satisfaction with income, while placing less importance on comparisons to people in other nations, who live far away. Relativistic theory would therefore lead one to predict that within-nation correlations between income and satisfaction will be quite high. In other words, within a particular country, such as the United States, individuals' income should correlate relatively highly with their satisfaction. However, according to Diener and Oishi (2000), relativistic theory would also predict that satisfaction levels will not be affected by a nation's overall income. Hence, the correlation between the average income level across countries and the average satisfaction level across these countries should be zero.

Cultural theory, as explained by Diener and Oishi (2000) assumes that satisfaction and income will be highly correlated in cultures where money is valued and less highly correlated in cultures where money is not highly valued. This theory is, unfortunately, somewhat general and no explanation is given as to how to independently determine what value a particular country places on wealth. Thus, it is somewhat difficult to test this theory.

According to Diener and Oishi (2000), the fourth theory, the material desires theory, can encompass all of the above theories (see also Crawford-Solberg, Diener, Wirtz, Lucas, & Oishi, 2002). The material desires theory assumes that people will report high levels of satisfaction to the extent that they can obtain, or at least progress in their ability to have, the items they desire (e.g., clothing, recreational goods, or whatever objects are sought after). If the desired items are not obtained, dissatisfaction will result. Of course, desires can change; when faced with the realization that one may not be able to obtain the desired items, one may pursue different objects. Conversely, a person who attains a desired object may be satisfied for only a short time until he or she seeks a new item.

To test the theories described above, Diener and Oishi (2000) analyzed data from several different sources. We will discuss some of the more pertinent findings; interested readers wishing more details are encouraged to read their work. First, Diener and Oishi (2000) reported a modest correlation between *financial* satisfaction and income within countries. The highest correlation reported was for Slovenia ($r = .52$); the lowest correlation was for Austria ($r = .05$). Across 19 countries, the average correlation was .25 (note that this is very close to the *uncorrected* correlation between pay level and pay satisfaction reported by Williams et al., 2006). Diener and Oishi (2000) also provided correlations between *life* satisfaction and income for the same countries. These correlations were lower, with the highest correlation being reported for South Africa ($r = .38$) and the lowest correlation for Brazil and Finland ($r = -.02$). The average correlation between life satisfaction and income was .13. As Diener and Oishi (2000) pointed out, there are clearly other factors that affect one's financial and life satisfaction beyond income.

In a second set of analyses, Diener and Oishi (2000) compared the two top groups of income earners in terms of life satisfaction and financial satisfaction. Recall that livability theory predicted that income only makes a difference in satisfaction for individuals earning relatively little income. Contrary to livability theory, they reported that the differences between top income earners were statistically significant.

Third, Diener and Oishi (2000) examined between-country differences, by correlating the average income of the country with average life satisfaction levels. Based on data from over 40 countries, they found a correlation of .69 between average income and life satisfaction. Although researchers need to be careful in comparing correlations based on individual-level versus aggregated data (Ostroff, 1993), this result contradicts the prediction made by relativistic theory that there will be no correlation across countries between satisfaction and income.

Diener and Oishi (2000) also summarized some results from other studies, including a finding that income was related to satisfaction across different nations, even when various other factors, such as health indices, amount of sanitary drinking water available, and amounts of food were included. On that basis, they concluded that income is not merely related to satisfaction to the extent that it enables people to purchase the basic needs that they have, but that income appears to have other effects on satisfaction. This finding fits with the notion that income serves many purposes (e.g., recognition; status), beyond simply enabling one to purchase more goods and services, and supports Rynes et al.'s (2005) argument that compensation may serve both intrinsic and extrinsic needs.

By way of summary, some of the relationships examined in Diener and Oishi (2000) suggest there may be cultural differences; other relationships suggest that there are not cultural differences. In terms of the correlation between income and financial satisfaction, for example, across 19 countries, the results seem to differ somewhat (e.g., for Austria, the correlation was .05; for Slovenia, it was .52). It is possible, however, that these apparent differences are due to statistical artifacts (e.g., sampling error) or other unimportant differences (e.g., differences in the characteristics of the sample). Of particular interest to us is the richness of the theories tested by Diener and Oishi and the cleverness with which they used different samples to test them. A major weakness, however, was that no measure of culture was included, thus limiting the ability to examine the indirect or moderating effect of culture on these relationships.

Diener and Oishi's (2000) research leads to the following thoughts. First, it remains to be seen whether or not there is a universal model that relates income to satisfaction. Second, most of the research we reviewed above focused on *work-related* explanations for pay satisfaction. The material desires theory discussed by Diener and colleagues, however, focused on nonwork-related variables that affect pay satisfaction. To date, management scholars have tended to ignore nonwork-related variables that may affect pay satisfaction. We suspect that there may be cultural differences in the degree to which work-related (e.g., pay system features), as compared to nonwork-related variables (e.g., to what degree one is able to obtain sought-after objects) affect pay satisfaction. Third, we suggest that individuals studying cultural issues in compensation should gather data from a larger sample of countries. By looking at pay across a relatively large number of countries, one is likely to be able to draw much stronger conclusions about culture. Finally, there is growing evidence that pay satisfaction is related to a variety of organizational outcomes. Currall, Towler, Judge, and Kohn (2005), for example, reported that teachers' pay satisfaction was related to organizational-level outcomes such as intentions to quit and students' academic performance. We urge researchers to obtain both organizational-level outcomes and behavioral measures wherever possible.

Pay Level and Attraction/Retention

Most researchers reviewing the literature have concluded that pay level can help increase the number of applicants, the likelihood that applicants accept job offers, and the quality of job applicants who apply. Gerhart and Rynes (2003), however, concluded that although higher pay levels are associated with improved attraction and retention, "further work is needed to determine the precise size of these relationships and the degree to which they are affected by moderators" (p. 67). Similarly, it would be interesting to examine the pay level–attraction/retention relationship across cultures.

It seems plausible that in cultures where pay is more valued, pay level will be more strongly linked to employee attraction and retention.

Pay Level and Cost-Benefit Analyses

Although there is some research to indicate that higher pay levels are associated with several organizational outcomes, some researchers have investigated whether the benefits associated with higher pay (e.g., greater retention) outweigh the costs of higher pay. Klaas and McClendon (1996) varied several factors in their simulation to assess the effect of pay level. Specifically, they varied pay level (20% above market, at market, and 20% below market), and assumed an average turnover rate of 32%. Based on studies of the relationship between pay level and turnover rates, they estimated that turnover would drop to 29% when pay was 20% above market and increase to 35% when pay was below market. Similarly, various estimates were made for the effect of pay level on retention. They also estimated the standard deviation of job performance for their analyses. Given these estimates, it is noteworthy that above-market pay actually produced the *lowest* utility. In other words, relatively speaking, the advantages (e.g., lower turnover and higher retention) of paying above market failed to overcome the costs of paying higher salaries. Nevertheless, Gerhart and Rynes (2003) cautioned that certain assumptions made by Klaas and McClendon may have been incorrect (e.g., that top performers are less likely to leave the organization than low performers), and that Klaas and McClendon may have underestimated the gains of paying above-market wages. Obviously, in another culture, some of these parameter values may change, which in turn may affect the conclusions.

PAY-FOR-PERFORMANCE PLANS

Although pay-for-performance plans have a long history in the United States, in some ways the research has lagged far behind practice. It is important to note that there are different kinds of pay-for-performance plans, ranging from merit pay increases, which are based on subjective evaluations of individual performance, to gain-sharing plans, which focus on cost cutting at the plant or facility level. In the last ten or so years, some experts have critiqued the use of pay-for-performance plans, arguing that use of such plans can diminish motivation and produce negative reactions (Kohn, 1993). Rynes et al. (2005), however, conducted an extensive review of empirical studies regarding pay-for-performance plans and drew much more positive conclusions. With regard to merit pay plans, for example, Gerhart and Rynes (2003) concluded that the evidence for such plans is primarily positive and they were cautiously optimistic about the value of this approach. Likewise, they concluded that research was quite positive about the effects of individual incentive and gain-sharing programs on performance. Even profit-sharing plans received positive accolades, although they found that this approach demonstrated much larger effects in certain organizations (i.e., employee-managed) compared to other organizations (i.e., traditional organizations). In terms of international research, however, there has been relatively little research on pay-for-performance plans. Although it seems logical that a highly individualized pay-for-performance plan will not fare well in a highly collectivistic culture, for example, there is no empirical data to support this notion. Furthermore, it will be interesting to study compensation in countries, such as China, where major cultural changes are occurring rapidly.

Furthermore, even in domestic settings, there is relatively little writing as to *why* pay-for-performance plans may be effective. Gilbreath and Harris (2002) provided a list of positive and negative effects of pay-for-performance plans. Among the positive effects of pay-for-performance plans they included were increased motivation, improved role clarity, and an increased sense of fairness on the part of employees. Gilbreath and Harris also pointed out some possible negative effects of a pay-for-performance plan, including decreased positive motivation for certain activities (e.g., cooperation with other employees), an increase in negative motivation (e.g., unethical behavior to achieve one's goals), and more resentment, stemming from a perception of being manipulated. These, as well as related factors, should be measured in order to better understand the causal linkages between pay-for-performance and job performance. Research across several different cultures would be useful in examining whether the causal linkages differ by culture.

Sturman, Trevor, Boudreau, and Gerhart (2003) examined the utility of varying the pay levels in a merit pay system, by comparing an organization's current system (i.e., where there was a moderate relationship between performance and pay raise), a more aggressive merit pay plan (i.e., top performers received a higher raise than the present system), and an extremely aggressive merit pay plan (i.e., top performers received a higher raise and low performers received a lower raise than in the current system). They also varied the magnitude of the variance in performance of employees (i.e., SDy). Sturman et al. found that, in general, a more aggressive merit pay plan had greater utility than the current merit pay plan.

It would well be worth reexamining this study in the international context to determine whether the relevant parameters change. In cultures that have a high collectivist orientation, for example, would the potential negative effect of an individually oriented pay-for-performance system on group cohesion impact the overall cost-benefit? Will resentment based on a feeling of being controlled be more prevalent in a very low-power-distance culture? Given that we located no research on the effects of pay-for-performance plans on various criteria (e.g., performance, job satisfaction) outside of North America, there is much opportunity here for future investigators.

Finally, in an interesting study, DeVoe and Iyengar (2003) investigated whether culture affected managers' perceptions of employee motivation. Toward that end, DeVoe and Iyengar had both managers and employees make ratings on the degree to which worker motivation was intrinsic (i.e., finding the job enjoyable and interesting) and the degree to which worker motivation was extrinsic (i.e., motivated by pay). In a North American sample, managers rated employee extrinsic motivation to be higher than employee intrinsic motivation. The opposite effect was found for self-ratings; employees rated themselves as being more motivated by intrinsic factors than extrinsic factors. Conversely, Asian managers did not perceive a difference between their employees' intrinsic and extrinsic motivation. Asian employee ratings indicated that they perceived themselves as being slightly more motivated by intrinsic, as compared to extrinsic, factors. Finally, Latin American employees and their managers were more congruent in their ratings; both the managers and the self-ratings showed that intrinsic motivation was slightly more important than extrinsic motivation.

DeVoe and Iyengar (2003) also reported cross-cultural differences in the degree to which managerial ratings of extrinsic and intrinsic motivation correlated with the employee's performance rating. Specifically, North American and Latin American managers weighted intrinsic motivation more heavily than extrinsic motivation in making performance ratings, whereas Asian managers weighted them equally.

DeVoe and Iyengar (2003) pointed out what they referred to as a paradox in the ratings by North Americans managers in the sense that although they reward their subordinates more heavily when their performance is due to intrinsic factors, they believe that extrinsic factors have a greater effect on their subordinates' performance. DeVoe and Iyengar attributed this finding to a preference for valuing uniquenesses (i.e., deviation from the norm) in highly individualistic cultures. Alternatively, in more collectivist cultures, such as Asia, a high value is placed on conformity and therefore there is consistency between managerial perceptions of what motivates employees and what is emphasized in rewards. More studies using creative designs like the one employed by DeVoe and Iyengar would be helpful in understanding cross-cultural differences in perceptions of pay-for-performance processes. Social desirability measures should also be included, as this factor may affect self-reported measures of pay importance, which may also differ across cultures.

CONCLUSIONS

By way of conclusion, cross-cultural issues in compensation represent a fertile area for further investigation. Of the topics we reviewed here, there are only two that seem to be relatively well researched, both of which concerned the main effect of culture on compensation. There appears to be sufficient evidence that U.S. managers, compared to Asian managers, use different factors in making reward allocation decisions. We also found relatively strong support for the thesis that on a macro-level, culture is related to the presence of various pay practices, such as seniority-based pay, chief executive officer pay, and the provision of various benefits. At the same time, we know very little about cross-cultural differences regarding basic compensation practices such as job evaluation, salary surveys, and pay structures.

We know even less about culture as a *moderator* of the relationship between compensation and various outcomes, such as employee performance. Nevertheless, our literature review revealed some interesting potential developments regarding this question, including some interesting research by Diener and Oishi (2000) that deserves further investigation, as well as a new motivation theory that explicitly incorporates culture.

With these points in mind, we believe that there are two critical areas for investigation. First, we believe that a more complete model of pay satisfaction across different cultures should be developed. This model should include both actual pay and relevant pay comparisons as predictors of pay satisfaction, as well as other possible factors. Pay satisfaction may also affect life satisfaction, though this linkage has not been examined much (e.g., see Williams et al., 2006). Culture may have a moderating effect on several of these relationships, including the actual pay–pay satisfaction link and the pay comparisons–pay satisfaction link. A measure of the meaning of money should also be included, as it may moderate some of the same factors as culture. We also recommend that where possible, relevant organizational measures (e.g., productivity) be gathered and examined relative to pay satisfaction, as described by Currall et al. (2005).

A second critical area for future investigators is to examine cross-cultural differences in terms of pay as a motivator. This research might be performed in an applied context (e.g., the effects of a pay-for-performance program) in different cultures, but it is important to ground such investigations in a theoretical framework.

In sum, there is a great deal of opportunity for researchers in the area of international compensation. We encourage others to conduct this research using innovative designs and with a variety of measures, including cultural values, perceptions of money, various measures of satisfaction, and to the extent possible, behavioral measures such as turnover and performance.

REFERENCES

Alderfer, C. P. (1969). An empirical test of a new theory of human needs. *Organizational Behavior & Human Performance, 4*, 142–175.

Arnolds, C., & Boshoff, C. (2002). Compensation, esteem valence and job performance: An empirical assessment of Alderfer's ERG theory. *The International Journal of Human Resource Management, 13*, 697–719.

Beatty, J., McCune, J., & Beatty, R. (1988). A policy-capturing approach to the study of United States and Japanese managers' compensation decisions. *Journal of Management, 14*, 465–474.

Cable, D. M., & Judge, T. A. (1994). Pay preferences and job search decisions: A person-organization fit perspective. *Personnel Psychology, 47*, 317–348.

Childs, M. (2004, October 19). Putting a value on evaluation. *Personnel Today, 33*.

Chiu, R., Luk, V. W., & Tang, T. L. (2002). Retaining and motivating employees: Compensation practices in Hong Kong and China. *Personnel Review, 31*, 402–431.

Collins, J., & Muchinsky, P. (1993). An assessment of the construct validity of three job evaluation methods: A field experiment. *Academy of Management Journal, 36*, 895–904.

Crawford-Solberg, E., Diener, E., Wirtz, D., Lucas, R., & Oishi, S. (2002). Wanting, having, and satisfaction: Examining the role of desire discrepancies in satisfaction with income. *Journal of Personality and Social Psychology, 83*, 725–734.

Currall, S. C., Towler, A. J., Judge, T. A., & Kohn, A. (2005). Pay satisfaction and organizational outcomes. *Personnel Psychology, 58*, 613–640.

DeVoe, S. E., & Iyengar, S. S. (2003). Managers' theories of subordinates: A cross-cultural examination of manager perceptions of motivation and appraisal of performance. *Organizational Behavior and Human Decision Processes, 93*, 47–61.

Diener, E., & Oishi, S. (2000). Money and happiness: Income and subjective well-being across nations. In E. Diener & E. Suh (Eds.), *Culture and subjective well-being.* (pp. 185–218) Cambridge, MA: MIT Press.

Forgas, J., Furnham, A., & Frey, D. (1989). Cross-national differences in attributions of wealth and economic success. *Journal of Social Psychology, 129*, 643–657.

Gerhart, B., & Rynes, S. (2003). Compensation: Theory, evidence, and strategic implications. Thousand Oaks, CA: Sage.

Geringer, J. M., Frayne, C. A., & Milliman, J. F. (2002). In search of "best practices" in international human resource management: Research design and methodology. *Human Resource Management, 41*, 5–30.

Gilbreath, B., & Harris, M. (2002). Performance-based pay in the workplace: Magic potion or malevolent poison? *Behavioral Analyst Today, 3*, 311–322.

Heneman, H., & Judge, T. A. (2000). Compensation attitudes. In S. L. Rynes, & B. Gerhart (Eds.), *Compensation in organizations: Current research and practice.* pp. 61–103. San Francisco, CA: Jossey-Bass.

Heneman, R., Fay, C., & Wang, Z. (2001). Compensation systems in the global context. In N. Anderson, D. Ones, H. K. Sinangil, & C. Viswesvaran (Eds.), *Handbook of industrial, work and organizational psychology* (Vol. 2 pp. 77–92). Thousand Oaks, CA: Sage.

Hofstede, G. (2001). Culture's consequences: Comparing values, behaviors, institutions, and organizations across nations, Thousand Oaks, CA: Sage.

Hundley, G., & Kim, J. (1997). National culture and the factors affecting perceptions of pay fairness in Korea and the United States. *International Journal of Organizational Analysis, 5*, 325–341.

Kehr, H. (2004). Integrating implicit motives, explicit motives, and perceived abilities: The compensatory model of work motivation and volition. *Academy of Management Review, 29*, 479–499.

Klaas, B., & McClendon, J. (1996). To lead, lag, or match: Estimating the financial impact of pay level policies. *Personnel Psychology, 49*, 121–141.

Kohn, A. (1993). *Punished by rewards.* New York: Houghton Mifflin.

Latham, G., & Pinder, C. (2005). Work motivation theory and research at the dawn of the twenty-first century. *Annual Review of Psychology, 56*, 485–516.

Lowe, J., DeCieri, H., & Dowling, P. (2002). International compensation practices: A ten-country analysis. *Human Resource Management, 41*, 45–66.

Madigan, R., & Hoover, D. (1986). Effects of alternative job evaluation methods on decisions involving pay equity. *Academy of Management Journal, 29*, 84–100.

Mitchell, T., & Mickel, A. (1999). The meaning of money: An individual-difference perspective. *Academy of Management Review, 24*, 568–578.

Ostroff, C. (1993). Comparing correlations based on individual-level and aggregated data. *Journal of Applied Psychology, 78*, 569–574.

Rice, R., Phillips, S., & McFarlin, D. (1990). Multiple discrepancies and pay satisfaction. *Journal of Applied Psychology, 75*, 386–393.

Ronen, S., & Shenkar, O. (1985). Clustering countries on attitudinal dimensions: A review and synthesis. *Academy of Management Review, 10*, 435–454.

Rynes, S., & Gerhart, B. (2000). *Compensation in organizations: Current research and practice.* San Francisco, CA: Jossey-Bass.

Rynes, S., Gerhart, B., & Minette, K. (2004). The importance of pay in employee motivation: Discrepancies between what people say and what they do. *Human Resource Management, 43*, 381–395.

Rynes, S., Gerhart, B., & Park, L. (2005). Performance evaluation and pay for performance. *Annual Review of Psychology, 56*, 571–600.

Rynes, S., & Milkovich, G. (1986). Wage surveys: Dispelling some myths about the "market wage." *Personnel Psychology, 39*, 71–90.

Schuler, R., & Rogovsky, N. (1998). Understanding compensation practice variations across firms: The impact of national culture. *Journal of International Business Studies, 29*, 159–177.

Steers, R., Mowday, R., & Shapiro, D. (2004). The future of work motivation theory. *Academy of Management Review, 29*, 379–387.

Sturman, M., Trevor, C., Boudreau, J., & Gerhart, B. (2003). Is it worth it to win the talent war? Evaluating the utility of performance-based pay. *Personnel Psychology, 56*, 997–1035.

Sweeney, P., & McFarlin, D. (2004). Social comparisons and income satisfaction: A cross-national examination. *Journal of Occupational and Organizational Psychology, 77*, 149–154.

Tang, T. L., Furnham, A., & Davis, G. M. W. (2002). The meaning of money: The money ethic endorsement and work-related attitudes in Taiwan, the U.S.A. and the U.K. *Journal of Managerial Psychology, 17*, 542–563.

Toh, S. M., & DeNisi, A. (2003). Host country national reactions to expatriate pay policies: A model and implications. *Academy of Management Review, 28*, 606–621.

Tosi, H., & Greckhamer, T. (2004). Culture and CEO compensation. *Organization Science, 15*, 657–670.

Townsend, A., Scott, K. D., & Markham, S. E. (1990). An examination of country and culture-based differences in compensation practices. *Journal of International Business Studies, 21*, 667–678.

Trevor, C., & Graham, M. (August, 2000). *Discretionary decisions in market wage derivation: What do compensation professionals rely upon and does it really matter?* Paper presented at the Academy of Management Meetings, Toronto, Canada.

Viswesvaran, C., & Barrick, M. (1992). Decision-making effects on compensation surveys: Implications for market wages. *Journal of Applied Psychology, 77*, 588–597.

Weber, C., & Rynes, S. (1991). Effects of compensation strategy on job pay decision. *Academy of Management Journal, 34*, 86–109.

Williams, M. L., McDaniel, M. A., & Nguyen, N. T. (2006). A meta-analysis of the antecedents and consequences of pay level satisfaction. *Journal of Applied Psychology, 91*, 392–413.

Zhou, J., & Martocchio, J. (2001). Chinese and American managers' compensation award decisions: A comparative policy-capturing study. *Personnel Psychology, 54*, 115–145.

9 International Labor Relations

Greg Hundley and Pamela Marett

CONTENTS

Arguably, in no area of human resources do organizations face greater pressures for adaptation to local (national) conditions than they do in the field of labor–management relations. The extent of union organization and the influence of unionism and labor relations institutions on employment relationship and other aspects of economic and political life vary widely across nations. Differences in macro-institutional frameworks likely contribute significantly to these variations through the ways that public policies and national institutions encourage or discourage labor unions, regulate the subject matter of labor–management negotiations, and define roles for other important labor relations actors, including management, governments, and third party representatives. In some countries, particularly those of northern Europe, labor unions are accepted as an integral element of national life, and their influences affect organizations in ways that go beyond outcomes traditionally encompassed by the terms and conditions of collectively bargained agreements in the United States. In other countries, unions are actively discouraged as part of strategies for economic development or political strategies. Recently, the situation has become even more complicated, as the forces of globalization relentlessly expose more areas of national economies to worldwide competition and affect national industrial relations systems in ways that are not easily predicted. Some of the world's most populous nations and potentially largest economies, such as Brazil, Russia, India, and China, are transitioning from state dominated or controlled economies and are in the throes of developing industrial relations frameworks suited to full-fledged market economies.

Given the diversity of industrial relations institutions, it is not surprising that much of the scholarship in international labor relations contributes to a descriptive tradition, seeking to identify the characteristics of national industrial relations systems, and to explain how and why these systems take the shape they do. Other analytical developments focus on particular aspects of industrial and employment relations, such as workplace governance, the extent of unionization and collective bargaining, and the effects of unionism and other attributes of industrial relations systems on outcomes such as macroeconomic performance, productivity, industrial innovation, and employee compensation.

This chapter addresses the broad area of international labor relations. It reviews the foundational literatures that have sought to develop frameworks for explaining international diversity in labor relations systems and the analysis of outcomes of labor relations systems and practices. The structure and functions of industrial relations systems in industrial market economies are described. The systems of the long-established market economies are compared along several dimensions, including union density, coverage, and bargaining structure. Attempts to analyze the effects of labor relations policies and institutions on important outcomes, such as firm performance, productivity, and industrial innovation are assessed. The challenges of understanding industrial relations phenomena in economies that are either newly industrializing or transitioning from centrally planned systems to market economies are discussed. This chapter concludes with an agenda for future research, including a call for fresh approaches that go beyond the usual focus on institutions of collective bargaining and labor unions to embrace the contributions of major social science disciplines and explore the diversity of contemporary employment relationships, including nonunion relationships.

NATIONAL INDUSTRIAL RELATIONS SYSTEMS

Early analyses of international labor relations relied upon descriptive studies of labor relations in specific countries. Many of these can be viewed as attempts to understand the rise during the early part of the twentieth century of labor unions and collective bargaining as major forces in national economic and political life of frequently studied market economies such as the United States and the United Kingdom (Sturmthal, 1973).

Analytical frameworks seeking to provide insight into the forces shaping industrial relations systems were not slow to develop. Dunlop's (1958) system is an influential attempt to provide a framework for the study of a nation's industrial relations. The dependent variable is "web of rules"—the set of formal (legal) and informal guidelines governing the relationships of major system "actors"—employers, workers, and the state—shaped by an environment of technology, market forces, and the relative power and status of the actors. Although the industrial relations system may be defined as a sector (for example the construction industry), Dunlop's model was frequently applied to explain the web of rules governing the behavior of parties in a particular country. Dunlop's model contributes in that it provides a focus (the web of rules) and embeds the systems in a wider socioeconomic and political framework. From the viewpoint of scholars seeking to inform contemporary human resource practitioners, Dunlop's system has several limitations. It does not consider the decisions that the parties in the system make about aspects of the employment relationship at the more disaggregate levels (such as the firm), it excludes the types of "behavioral variables" that have provided insight in other areas of organizational behavior and human resources management, and it provides little guidance scope for prediction of key outcomes of the operation of an industrial system, including the course of industrial conflict, distribution of organizational rewards, and the adoption of particular work practices.

An ambitious, large-scale investigation by Kerr, Dunlop, Harbison, and Myers (1960) sought to identify the major forces shaping national industrial relations systems by studying the experiences of national economies at various stages of industrialization. They saw national industrial relations systems as a product of the forces of industrialization, including pervasive and changing industrial technologies and science requiring a wide range of skills and capabilities, rapid change, an open society, industrial mobility, an educational system conditioned to meet the demands of industrial economy, a labor force stratified by occupational specialization and hierarchical position in industrial organizations, large-scale organizations, and an expanding governmental role in the provision of infrastructure and services, coordinating trade and mediating the complex relationships in industrial society. The dynamics forces of industrialization required systems of workplace governance involving managers, workers, and government. According to Kerr et al. (p. 42):

> In the fully industrialized society, regardless of the relative balance and roles of enterprise managers, workers, and government in the transition, all three have a significant part in the establishment, adaptation, and administration of the work place and the work community. The industrial relations system of the industrial society is genuinely tripartite.

Two hypotheses advanced by Kerr et al. continue to have an important role in discussions about national industrial relations systems. The first proposes that key characteristics of the industrial relations system at a point in time are determined by the societal elite governing the industrializing process. Five elites are identified: dynastic, middle-class, revolutionary intellectuals, colonial administrators, and nationalistic leaders. The identity of the dominant industrializing elite has a distinct set of implications for systems when they are in control, determining the power and position of managers, the development of the industrial workforce, and rules and mechanisms for governing rule making. The second hypothesis is one of system convergence, with industrial societies converging to a plural market economy in which parties share a consensus about industrialism, the efficacy of the market economy, and the role of an industrial relations system that provides mechanisms for representing diverse interests, and reconciling differences.

The question as to whether or not employment relations systems converge remains unanswered, as at present not all nations have similar industrial relations systems. It might be argued that convergence should be viewed as a tendency and different national industrial relations systems will continue to coexist for a long while. One reason for the failure to converge, however, may be that national economies—or significant parts of them—have in different ways been protected from the full force of international competition. But now, there is the prospect that globalization (including elimination of barriers to capital flows and the deregulation of major sectors within each country) place ever-greater pressures to converge toward those practices confirmed to be most efficient.

Subsequent developments in comparative industrial relations recognize the strategic element wherein main actors have choices in determining how they achieve desired outcomes, including the design of the system. Poole (1986) distinguishes between four classes of strategy, each stemming from an alternative orientation toward social action: utilitarian (where agents behave in pursuit of their own rationally determined ends), idealistic (based on a commitment to ethical, religious, or political values), affectual (based on emotion), and traditional (ingrained habituation). The key actors include the usual players: managers and employers' associations, unions, governments, and political parties, but the decision-making environment expands to include socially constructed meaning attached to cultural values and ideologies. More so than historically deterministic or functionalist approaches, Poole's framework lends itself to predictions of key employment relations outcomes, including the degree of industrial conflict (say the incidence and length of strikes and industrial action), the distribution of economic rewards (for example, patterns of pay differentials), and industrial democracy (for example, the choices made between methods of workplace representation, including self-management, producer cooperatives, co-determination, works councils, trade union action, or shop floor action).

A strategic approach guides the recent work of a set of scholars based at the Masachusetts Institute of Technology (MIT), and their international collaborators (Locke, Kochan, & Piore, 1995), who initially examined employment relationship trends in 11 established industrialized economies and then followed up with analysis of emerging economies. They make two empirical observations. First, the anticipated convergence in industrial relations systems has not yet transpired, with major industrial economies exhibiting substantial and seemingly persistent differences. Second, there is considerable heterogeneity in the nature of employment systems and practices within national boundaries. Although the pressures of global competition (for example, pressures for cost competitiveness and rapid responses to market conditions) may be omnipresent, the responses made by firms and unions may vary considerably, resulting from the strategic choices of managers, unions, and governments. Four areas of emerging employment practices were discerned:

1. Changes in work organization emanating from the introduction of new technologies and the alternative competitive strategies, such as the degree of team-based production, decentralized decision making, changes in work rules, and employee participation.
2. New compensation systems, involving group incentives, employee ownership, and policies affecting the level and structure of relative pay for all employee groups.
3. Changing patterns of skill acquisition and training to meet changing firm needs, taking account of the balance of public and private provision of education, training, and the range of social welfare benefits and services.
4. Staffing issues, such as employment security and job mobility, including how employers react to changes in workforce demands stemming from cyclical and long-term or structural adjustments in demand.

The authors focused on these employment practices at the firm level, seeking to identify the major actors responsible for shaping employment practices and the level at which the shaping occurs (national, industry, region, or firm). Thus, their approach contrasts with the more "centralized" approach identified with European scholars, and with the deterministic views of earlier American scholars.

Several patterns emerge from the empirical work. First, throughout the industrial world, managements are the key actors driving change in employment relations. Second, there is a trend toward decentralization of workplace practices as employers seek more focused yet more adaptable structures to meet the challenges of market forces. Third, the development of human capital through training and educational investments continues as a major concern. Fourth, formal union organizations have been subject to continuing pressures due to the rapid pace of organizational change, and changes in work methods that may be less suited to union representation.

The strategic choices give rise to several areas of tension. First, there are the firm-level choices between cost-cutting and high value-added strategies. Second, the drive toward new forms of organization with a core of committed, well-trained employees and a periphery of less well-attached employees can cause a divide between those with access to jobs and those without. Third, with the decline of union structures, there is a need for alternative methods of employee voice and representation.

The empirical work of the MIT-centered group suggests that there is no one best approach that can be used to adapt to market forces. Existing institutions and practices affect what is achievable and the path taken to adjust to market exigencies and opportunities. Thus, for example, corporatist systems are likely to follow a consultative approach that considers the interests of system participants. In decentralized market economies (typically those associated with the Anglo-Saxon model of corporate governance), individualistic approaches where one group may have to bear all the costs of transitions are relatively more likely to be favored.

INDUSTRIAL RELATIONS SYSTEMS IN ESTABLISHED MARKET ECONOMIES

International industrial relations scholars are interested in two main areas. First, there is the identification and explanation of key differences in industrial relations systems of the industrialized market economies. Second, there is a recent concern with the way that system characteristics (institutions and policy frameworks) affect important firm-level outcomes and management practices.

Given the apparently persistent cross-national differences in industrial relations systems, it is important to explore major characteristics of these systems. These include the extent of union membership, extent of bargaining coverage, and various elements of the structure of labor–management bargaining. In addition to providing information on the labor relations environment for practitioners and researchers seeking to understand environmental impact at the firm level, these attributes provide a basis for analyzing the effects of industrial relations systems on key outcomes.

The decisions of policymakers and analysts about the efficacy of industrial relations institutions and the outcomes associated with specific institutional configurations are informed by alternative views of the roles that unions play in work organizations and in society. Such differences are reflected in the two "faces of unionism" popularized by Freeman and Medoff (1984). The first face, which dominates the work of many economists concerned with the economic impact of unionism, is that of the monopoly union, where the union seeks gains for its members through threats of withholding their labor and the exercise of bargaining power vis-à-vis employers. Although union monopoly effects advance the economic interests of current union members and others covered by union agreements, the consequences for other groups are mostly negative. Unionized employers have fewer profits to share with stockholders and will find it more difficult to attract capital for future growth. Nonunion workers have lower wages than they might have had in the absence of union monopoly wage effects because the reduced job opportunities in the unionized sector caused by higher wages increase the competition among workers for nonunion jobs. Although some nonunion workers may benefit from "threat effects" and enjoy higher wages (Hundley, 1987), nonunion workers will be worse off on average, as the presence of monopoly unions generally detracts from firm economic performance by distorting of relative wages and prices and the effects of other contractual restrictions that curtail the ability of management to allocate resources to their best available ends. Future generations will suffer as union wage gains contribute to the decline of unionized industries and union restrictions dampen innovation and technological progress.

The second face of unionism, where the union serves as the "voice" of workers in noneconomic matters is seen to have more generally positive effects. American scholars, Katz and Kochan (2003), for example, emphasize voice benefits at the level of the individual workplace or firm where the union distills the preferences of employees and negotiates terms of employment that more efficiently accommodate heterogeneous needs of a workforce obliged to share common working conditions. By providing dissatisfied workers with an outlet to redress their grievances the union reduces turnover and facilitates the accumulation of firm-specific human capital, thus enhancing productivity. According to European policy analysts, voice can also occur at broader levels, up to and including society as a whole. Where a union is encouraged or required to represent for the interests of larger groups, they may work to restrain the demands of militant, strategically placed subgroups in order to benefit the larger collectivities up to and including society as a whole (Hall & Soskice, 2001).

The characteristics of national industrial relations systems vary widely on a number of dimensions, including the extent of union organization and coverage and arrangements for labor representation and negotiations. In several ways these variations derive from differences in the roles that unions and formal labor relations processes are assigned by major policy decision makers in the various countries.

UNION DENSITY AND COVERAGE

Union density refers to the proportion of workers who are union members. Union coverage refers to the percentage of the workers covered by union-negotiated employment agreements. Although density and coverage are often treated as conveying the same information about the power or influence of labor unions within the relevant group, Table 9.1 shows that in many established market economies, the measure of union coverage and union density diverge substantially.

In some countries, including the United States, Canada, and Korea, where collective bargaining takes place at the firm level, where agreements apply only to those employee groups whose members have demonstrated a strong preference for union representation, and where there are strong incentives for covered employees to join or contribute to a union either because of union security provisions or informal pressures, there is strong correspondence between density and coverage measures. Unions in these settings generally do not provide voice for those workers outside the organized workplace, there is little incentive for workers not covered by a union-negotiated agreement to become union members, and any difference between coverage and membership is due to covered workers who are not union members (free riders). In these countries, the preeminent concern of policymakers is the mitigation of the monopoly effects of unions. Individuals are given the right to organize for collective bargaining if a majority of workers desire formal union representation. However, negotiated

TABLE 9.1

Percentage Union Membership Density and Collective Bargaining Coverage

	Membership	Density	Bargaining	Coverage
	1980	2000	1980	2000
Australia	48	25	>80	>80
Austria	57	37	>95	>95
Belgium	54	56	>90	>90
Canada	35	28	37	32
Czech Republic		27		>25
Denmark	79	74	>70	>80
Finland	69	76	>90	>90
France	18	10	>80	>90
Germany	35	25	>80	68
Greece	39	27	>80	68
Hungary		20		>30
Iceland	57	38		
Italy	50	35	>80	>80
Japan	31	22	>25	>15
Korea	15	11	>15	>10
Luxembourg	52	34		>60
Mexico		18		
Netherlands	35	23	>70	>80
New Zealand	69	23	>60	>25
Norway	58	54	>70	>70
Poland		15		>40
Portugal	61	24	>70	>80
Slovak Republic		36		>50
Spain	7	15	>60	>80
Sweden	80	79	>80	>90
Switzerland	31	18	>50	>40
Turkey		33		
United Kingdom	51	31	>70	>30
United States	22	13	26	14

Source: Organisation for Economic Co-operation and Development (OECD). (2004). *Employment outlook*. Paris: OECD.

benefits do not extend outside the certified scope of the union, thus leaving unionized workforces open to nonunion competition, serving to curtail excesses of bargaining power.

There are a number of countries where coverage rates are markedly higher than union membership rates. Here, wage rates and other terms and conditions of employment that are arrived at by negotiations between union officials at a centralized level, for example at the industry or the national level, with the results applying to all employees in the sector regardless of their desire to be union members. Examples of such countries include France, Germany, and Greece. In common with most other industrial economies, the industrial relations systems of these nations do not allow for strong union security provisions.

Finally, there are several nations, mostly northern European, where there are high rates of union membership and union coverage. In these areas, greatest weight is attached to the union as a macro voice and participant in society. The industrial relations systems of these countries are characterized as "corporatist" where unions are part of a social compact, in which unions are accorded a wider institutional role in representing members' interests to both employers and government, and union membership is not discouraged by employers or other third parties. In exchange for a wider societal role, unions generally refrain from pursuing narrow sectional gains, especially in areas where they might have great bargaining power. In several of these countries, unions are given an official role in distributing welfare and social security benefits. For example, Belgium, Denmark, Iceland, Finland, and Sweden are in the Ghent system where unemployment benefits are administered by the union organizations. The relatively high union membership rate in Taiwan in the 1980s is also associated with public policies providing health insurance through occupational or craft unions (see Table 9.2). The higher membership rates in Argentina also coincide with union management of employee health plans funded by an employer contribution, providing them with a source of income and patronage power conducive to high membership levels.

For all the cross-sectional differences, Table 9.1 shows that over the last two decades, there has been a distinctive downward trend in the level of union organization in nearly all the established market economies. The exceptions to the pattern include the northern European strongholds such as Belgium, Sweden, Denmark, Norway, and Finland, where unions play a broader role in economic and social life. Membership declines are particularly marked for several nations where, it has been generally recognized, there are long-established, often powerful union movements in labor relations systems characterized by adversarial union–management relations: Australia, France, New Zealand, Italy, the United Kingdom, and the United States. The decline of the extent of unionism is consistent with a number of explanations. Economic deregulation, trade liberalization, increased globalization of competition in basic industries that have been the traditional

TABLE 9.2
Union Densities and Bargaining Coverage: Selected Non-OECD Countries

	Membership	Density	Coverage
	Mid 80s	Late 90s	Late 90s
China	59	42	
Singapore	21	17	19
Philippines	24	30	4
Taiwan	33	50	3
Malaysia	14	12	3
India	7	3	
South Africa	18	41	49
Kenya	42	33	35
Zambia	40	58	30
Argentina	67	51	73
Brazil		44	
El Salvador	10	11	13
Chile	23	27	13
Poland	47	18	
Russia	91	58	

Source: Visser, J. (2003). Unions and unionism around the world. In J. T. Addison & C. Schnabel (Eds.), *International handbook of trade unions* (pp. 415–460). Cheltenham: Edward Elgar.

foundation of unionism all are likely to have played a role. In some cases, such as the United Kingdom, there have been significant declines in the legal protections afforded unions. Empirical research to explain the differences in unionization rates of different countries and the general decline of union densities across nations (Rose & Chaison, 2001) shows that only a small part of these effects are due to structural factors, such as relative size of public sectors and traditionally unionized occupations, supporting arguments that decline is due to broader economic forces and policy measures that decrease both the institutional legitimacy or power of labor unions.

Bargaining Structure

A nation's bargaining structure is determined by the institutional rules or practices that affect the level of bargaining, the degree of coordination of bargaining, and the extension of agreements to jurisdictions not involved in the original agreement. Across countries, collective bargaining takes place at different levels. At the most decentralized level, characteristic of several major industrialized nations, such as Canada, Japan, the United Kingdom, and the United States (Table 9.3), bargaining takes place at the level of the workplace or the firm. Such practices are, however, not the norm in many other countries. In many of the countries of continental Europe, for example, negotiation on compensation levels is much more centralized, occurring typically at the industry level. In some, such as Iceland and Finland, bargaining is even more centralized, with agreements covering all industries, or periodic agreements between employers, governments, and union federations at the national level setting important parameters for sector agreements.

Bargaining coordination occurs when bargaining at a lower level is affected coordination by peak (central) unions, employer's associations, and tripartite arrangements. Thus, although agreement may be at a local level, it will in many ways be affected by patterns that are spread throughout firms or workplaces in a major sector or even at the level of the national economy. Not surprisingly, the degree of coordination increases agreements with centralization, although there are exceptions, such as Japan, where there is the spring offensive that ensures wage uniformity across employers in a covered sector while leaving all other matters to the local level. One reason for the much greater reach (that is, coverage) of collective bargaining in Western industrialized countries outside North America is the existence of extension provisions whereby settlements between unions and management representatives are automatically extended to other areas not covered by other employers. In some countries, extensions are generally made voluntarily wherein employers extend agreements to nonmembers. The motivations may include the preservation of labor harmony, including nondiscrimination between union members and nonmembers and the tamping down of any incentives to engage in union activism or join a union (Bamber, Lansbury & Wailes, 2004a, 2004b). Other countries are characterized by legal or administrative extension mechanisms. Extension in these countries may be made by labor ministries, which can make unilateral extensions, often consistent with past practice, or make extension as a result of petition by union or management representatives. Often, the petitioners for the extension of negotiated terms are required to show so-called "representativeness" where the agreement is extended to employee populations that are by some logic similar to those covered by the agreement. In Germany, Greece, or Switzerland, for example, extension will be granted to all employees in an industry if the initial signatories already cover 50% or more of the industry workforce. Extension provisions may explain the lack of interest in union security provisions in collective bargaining agreements outside the Anglo-Saxon countries. Union officials are able to extend the terms of their agreements to nonunion workforces without needing to garner the resources (such as financial resources from membership dues) to increase bargaining power. Extension practices are, however, encountering increased hostility from academic economists and market-oriented reformers, who argue that these procedures dampen competitive forces, and increase rigidities in the economy (OECD, 2004).

TABLE 9.3

Collective Bargaining Structure in Selected OECD Nations: Degrees of Centralization, Coordination, and Existence of Bargaining Extension

	Centralization[a]	Coordination[b]	Extension
Australia	2	2	Yes
Austria	3	4	Yes
Belgium	3	4.5	Yes
Canada	1	1	No
Czech Republic	1	1	
Denmark	2	4	No
Finland	5	5	
France	2	2	Yes
Germany	3	4	Yes
Hungary	1	1	Yes
Iceland	5		
Ireland	4	4	No
Italy	2	4	No
Japan	1	4	No
Korea	1	1	
Netherlands	3	4	
New Zealand	1	1	No
Norway	4.5	4.5	No
Poland	1	1	Yes
Portugal	4	4	Yes
Slovak Republic	2	2	Yes
Spain	3	3	Yes
Sweden	3	3	No
Switzerland	2	4	
United Kingdom	1	1	No
United States	1	1	No

Note:

[a]*Centralization*

1 = Company or plant level

2 = Combined industry and plant with many plant-level agreements

3 = Industry level predominant

4 = Mainly industry-level with some recurrent central-level agreements

5 = Central-level agreements of overriding importance

[b]*Coordination*

1 = Fragmented company/plant, little upper coordination

2 = Fragmented company/plant level, little or no pattern setting

3 = Industry bargaining with irregular pattern setting

4 = Regular pattern setting or coordination by multiple peak federations or government arbitration mechanisms

5 = Pattern or coordination by single peak federation or government

Source: Organisation for Economic Co-operation and Development (OECD). (2004). *Employment outlook.* Paris: OECD.

OUTCOMES OF INDUSTRIAL RELATIONS SYSTEMS
IN ESTABLISHED MARKET ECONOMIES

Recently, debates over the effects of attributes of industrial relations systems on outcomes at national and organizational levels, together with persistent, measurable differences in the characteristics of the national systems, has led to a large body of empirical work on the effects of industrial relations systems (Metcalf, 1993; Flanagan, 1999).

INDUSTRIAL RELATIONS AND NATIONAL ECONOMIC PERFORMANCE

According to the standard economic theory, the effects of unionism on the national economy are relatively straightforward. The real wages of the employed workers increase (because output is distributed away from profits and consumer prices are increased), unemployment is increased (because labor is too expensive for employers), and national output is reduced (because human resources are priced out of the market). Aspects of the bargaining framework may well affect the trade-offs between real wage levels, inflation, and unemployment. Under more centralized systems, where negotiations occur at the national level, union negotiators may be more aware of the broader negative effects of higher wage demands on price levels and output, thereby moderating their demands in the interests of the workforce as a whole. Under decentralized arrangements, union bargaining power is diminished by the prospect that unionized firms will lose business (and jobs) to nonunion competitor firms. It follows then, that the effects of bargaining structure on real wages, employment, and economic growth conform to the "hump" hypothesis, with nations where bargaining occurs at an intermediate (industry) level experiencing high real wages, high unemployment, high inflation, and economic stagnation—a relationships that describes the data from the continental European economies (Calmfors & Drifill, 1988).

The effects of labor relations institutions on long-term unemployment rates are of considerable interest. Although unemployment may increase in response to many exogenous economic shocks that have nothing to do with labor–management relations (for example, sudden increases in oil prices, shifts in product demand or exchange rates), labor relations systems may affect how quickly the labor market adjusts to such shocks and restore full employment. It has been argued that European labor market rigidities served to translate the supply side shocks of increased oil prices in the 1970s into persistently high unemployment rates, and there is some evidence that high union density or coverage has tended to magnify the effects of macroeconomic shock on unemployment (Blanchard & Wolfers, 2000). These issues are far from resolved for, as Flanagan (1999) notes, the effect of labor relations institutions on economic performance has weakened in recent periods.

FIRM PERFORMANCE, PRODUCTIVITY, AND INNOVATION

A large body of evidence confirms that workers covered by union agreements have higher wage and salary levels than those who do not (Addison & Hirsch, 1989; Lewis, 1986; Blanchflower & Bryson, 2003). The effects of unionism on other important outcomes, such as firm financial performance, productivity, innovation, and human capital accumulation remain very much at issue, however.

The effects of unions on organizational efficiency depend on the extent to which the positive voice effects offset or outweigh the negative monopoly effects. Studies of the firm-level effect of unionized employment relations in several countries confirm that the relative sizes of these effects are likely to vary considerably with differences in industrial relations systems. In addition, there is evidence of significant within-country variation of the effects of unionism attributable to differences in the types of relationship that management chooses to have with their union.

Unionism is associated with higher productivity in the United States, particularly when associated with a high performance work system characterized by commitments to training, employee involvement, and teamwork (Black & Lynch, 2001; Capelli & Neumark, 2001), and in Japan where unions tended to be associated with lower turnover costs and longer tenure (Benson, 1994). The United Kingdom and Australia, two nations that used to be characterized by multi-unionism (where a single firm confronts several unions representing different segments of their employee populations), unionized firms tended to be less productive. Since the 1980s, however, where regulatory changes sharply curtailed multiunionism and generally increased exposure to competitive pressures, the negative effects of unions on productivity have disappeared (Metcalf, 2003). Thus, in competitive environments where unions and managements are more strongly obliged to cooperate to ensure their mutual survival, unions do not necessarily have a negative effect on productivity and may even be one of those tools that enhance the application of productivity-enhancing techniques.

The possibility that union voice functions might have a positive effect on organizational outcomes makes more salient the empirical findings about works councils in Germany. Although such councils are designed to expedite pure worker voice effects at the plant level after economic bargains have been concluded at the industry level, the reality is somewhat different as often work councils are dominated by union officials who informally seek further bargaining gains at the local level. It appears that works councils increase productivity and reduce profitability (Addison, Schnabel and Wagner, 2001)—a mixed record that contrasts with the greater success of the less formally structured employee involvement programs in German firms (Hassel, 1999).

The overall effect of unionism on firm financial performance (such as profitability or return on investments) depends on the extent to which productivity enhancements, if any, offset the greater costs per unit of labor. Most international evidence shows that unionism is associated with lower levels of financial performance in the United States (Addison & Hirsch, 1989; Kleiner, 2001), Japan (Tachibanaki & Noda, 2000), the United Kingdom (Metcalf, 1993, 2003). Again, however, the effects of unionized labor relations may depend on the broader economic and institutional forces prevailing at a point in time. Metcalf (2003) observes that the negative effects of unionism on firm performance in the United States are much less pronounced for smaller, newer firms in more competitive environments. Similarly, the firm performance effects found in recent data from the United Kingdom are negligible compared to earlier years when the institutional framework posed fewer disincentives for uncooperative labor–management relations).

The impact of unionism on innovation is also subject to competing effects. To the extent that union firms have lower profits, the economic residual available for investments in process improvements, new equipment, and R&D expenditures is depleted. Additionally, the presence of the union may discourage profit-enhancing investments in R&D, to the extent that management might expect some of the gains for increased wage claims to be bargained away in the future. On the other hand, the union may have a positive effect on innovation if it can encourage its members to withhold wage gains in the short term in exchange for R&D investments that in the long term make both the employer and union employees better off (Ulph & Ulph, 2001). Empirical work shows that unions reduce R&D expenditures and numbers of innovation in the United States (Menezes-Filho & van Reneen, 2003), a result that is broadly consistent with the widely held notion that American unions have tended to trade off long-term employment gains in exchange for short-run gains to be enjoyed by their current membership. In contrast, European studies do not show that unionism has any substantial effect on innovation. Why the U.S. and European results differ is not clear, but it could be due to the generally more centralized bargaining structures in Europe where wage increases are more broadly spread across competing firms in the same industry.

LABOR RELATIONS IN TRANSITIONING MARKET ECONOMIES

A major set of challenges for students of international industrial relations is presented by the potentially very large economies that are moving from various forms of state control towards free markets. These nations include those of the former Soviet bloc, the emerging Asian powers of India and China, and major South American economies, such as Brazil.* Large labor organizations existed in each of these nations before the transition to open markets that commenced over the last 15 years, but in many ways, they were the product of institutional environments and historical precursors that were markedly different from those distinguishing the longer-established market economies of Europe, North America, and Japan.

POST-SOVIET ERA TRANSITION ECONOMIES: POLAND AND RUSSIA

In the case of former communist countries, such as Russia and the Eastern European countries, industrial relations systems were designed to play roles prescribed by Kerr et al.'s (1960) revolutionary elite, serving a wide range of the interests of the state in production, distribution, and employee welfare. The Soviet era unions were organized in a hierarchy from the official federation, the All Union Central Council of Trade Unions, down to the enterprise level union committees. Firm-level union officials were accountable to the national hierarchy, local party officials, and the company management. Union enterprise committees managed the social insurance funds, pensions, and determined eligibility for health care, education, housing, and recreation facilities.

With the end of communism, the All Union Central Council reconstituted itself as the Federation of Independent Trade Unions of Russia (FNPR). Although the FNPR has retained its dominant position, several independent unions have been formed in some strategically placed industries.

Movement toward an institutional framework for Russian labor relations has proceeded fitfully. A Tripartite Commission for the Regulation of Social and Labor Relations was formed in 1992 to set parameters for national, regional, and sector agreements that were to guide enterprise-level agreements (Sil, 2001). Against the backdrop of weak and divided unions, worker distrust, lack of peak employer associations, strong government control, diverse regional interests, the Commission worked poorly. Under President Putin, a new Labor Code replaced the patchwork of old and new regulations that prevailed during the 1990s. The Russian Labor Code obliges management to accept collective bargaining and specifies detailed dispute resolution procedures and provides protections for employee attempts to form independent unions. Nonetheless, independent collective bargaining has been slow to develop, due to a predilection of union leaders to negotiate with the state, and economic weakness in many sectors.

Unlike Russia, Poland had independent trade unions before World War II. Under communism, Polish unions were committed to building socialism on the Soviet model (Chobot, 1992). The weakening of the Soviet system in the late 1970s saw the rise of the popular independent union movement, Solidarity, and the eventual election of its pioneering leader Lech Walesa as the first popularly elected president in 1990. The Solidarity-led governments of the 1990s refrained from establishing formal, centralized bargaining structures for fear of undermining the drastic economic reform that they believed were necessary to permanently end communism (Orenstein & Hale, 2001). Workers acquiesced in a strike moratorium and at the plant level Solidarity branches pressured management to carry out corporate restructuring and downsizing. The dual and contradictory role played by Solidarity crucially influenced Polish industrial relations (Thirkwell, Scase, & Vickerstaff, 1994), but the movement's popularity waned and lost power in the 2001 election. Poland has created numerous paths to privatization, and the number of small and medium-sized enterprises has grown. In this process unions and workers councils have been marginalized and most new enterprises are nonunion. As shown in Table 9.2, union membership declined from 47.1% in 1989 to 18.5% in 1999 and is now almost totally concentrated in the old state-owned sector.

---

* Hence the concern among international trade and business specialists with the 'BRIC's - Brazil, Russia, India, and China.

New Asian Giants: China and India

According to official figures, China in the late 1990s had the largest number of union members, 91 million. The All-Chinese Federation of Trade Unions (ACFTU), which oversees more than half a million local unions operating at the plant level, is a relic of the tightly controlled Marxist-Leninist economy, serving mainly to promote industrial harmony and promote workplace discipline. Since the opening up of the Chinese economy, the union role has weakened considerably (Hong & Warner, 1998). After a period of attempts to promote labor management cooperation, management authority has become preeminent. Unionization rates remain high in the state-owned sector, which accounts for nearly all Chinese members, but there is relatively little unionization in the new non-state and multinational sectors where management policies ignore and discourage unions (Kuruvilla, Das, Kwon, & Kwon, 2002).

Before 1990, Indian labor unions benefited from policies of import substitution and trade protection and the support of major political parties. For example, the Indian National Trades Union Congress (INTUC) has operated as an adjunct of the Congress Party, which has governed India for most of the time since independence from Britain in 1948 and which again assumed power in 2004. The INTUC has tended to be influenced more by its political counterparts than by a desire to represent industrial membership (Bhattacherjee, 2002). Indian unions have not prospered with economic liberalization, and are now concentrated almost exclusively in the public sector, covering a much smaller portion of the Indian workforce in the 1990s (3%) than the United States (Visser, 2003).

Brazil

Brazil began redemocratizing in 1985 after 21 years of military rule, and successive governments, including the administration of the socialist Luis Inacio Lula da Silva (Lula), moved toward a liberalized market economy (Branford & Kucinski, 2003). Like India, for most of the post-World War II era, successive governments focused on industrialization through subsidization and protection of import-competing industries. A significant feature of this model was the construction of corporatist institutions for workers (Drake, 1996). The government implemented a social service system that provided workers with a minimum wage and unemployment insurance. Retirement benefits, medical benefits, sickness benefits, workers compensation, and pension were brought together under the National Institute for Social Provision (INPS) and financed by worker and employer contributions.

The Consolidation of Labor Laws (CLT), collective bargaining, and labor court rulings set employment conditions. The CLT is a corporatist law that provides a range of protections and employment guarantees, including 30 days of annual leave, minimum wage, maternity leave, severance pay, unemployment insurance, and a 44-hour week. It encourages a hierarchical union structure. Local unions may affiliate with state federations and national confederations in their professional category. Only one union may represent workers in a given profession and geographical area. All formal sector workers must contribute a day's wages each year in support of unions, which in turn must negotiate on behalf of all covered workers.

A three-tier labor justice system has broad powers to set the terms of collective bargaining agreements and adjudicate millions of disputes concerning wages, benefits, working conditions, and dismissals. Collective bargaining in Brazil takes place between local unions and an employer association. The employer groups represent companies with employees in the specific geographic area and occupational category. Only one union may represent workers from each geographic/occupational group, thus limiting scope for competition between unions and for enterprise-level agreements, and restricting pluralism (O'Connell, 1999).

Collective bargaining in the formal sector is widespread, with more than 18,000 agreements registered in 2000. The importance of collective bargaining increased in the 1980s as parties broadened the content of negotiated agreements. Brazilian industrial relations suffer from a fragmented labor movement, limited firm-level representation, and a culture of negotiations through the labor courts (U.S. Department of Labor, 2002). Brazilian employers are an active force for liberalization of Brazil's labor relations institutions as the only way to increase competitiveness.

INDUSTRIAL RELATIONS AND GLOBALIZATION

The forces of globalization pose special challenges for major industrial relations actors, particularly organized labor. These challenges arise from trade liberalization and economic integration, and the rise of the transnational corporation.

Unions in the established market economies have worked toward the inclusion of core labor standards in bilateral trade agreements, such as the North American Free Trade Agreement (NAFTA) and the US–Australia Free Trade Agreement. The experience of labor unions with what they consider to be the failure of the labor-side agreement in NAFTA has led North American unions to reject future trade liberalization and underscored the importance of international unionism (MacDonald, 2003). However, whereas labor sees its efforts as focused on improved working standards, employers and policymakers see it as a form of disguised protectionism (Mazur, 2000). The impact of organized labor's national and international strategies appear limited, with unions retarding the pace of change and defending the interests of some occupational groups such as airline pilots (Blyton, Martinez Lucio, McGurk, & Turnbull, 2001).

Research indicates that the activities of transnational corporations seek to actively manage the tensions of executing low-cost strategies and high-value localization strategies are affected by the varying labor relations environments in the countries in which they potentially operate. Bognanno, Keane, and Yang (2005) examined the operations of U.S. multinationals in seven manufacturing industries and 22 countries over ten years to determine the effects of tariffs, wages, and industrial relations environments on location decisions, finding that tariffs had negligible significance but industrial relations environment was very important, with the companies preferring locations with decentralized bargaining structure and few lay-off restrictions. There is some evidence that the experience that U.S. companies have in operating in both union and nonunion facilities serve them well in coordinating operations across diverse institutional environments. Ferner, Almond, Colling, and Edwards (2005) examined policies toward unions and collective representation of U.S. multinationals in the United Kingdom and found that the dominant ideological norms of anti-unionism in U.S. business shaped but did not determine the policies of their British subsidiaries who adapted to their institutional environment to construct industrial relations models that differed from their parent's. The diversity of approaches is also reflected in non-American companies operating in the United States. For example, some, not all, Japanese multinational electronics corporations starting in the United States were characterized by antiunionism and labor law violations (Marett, 1984), with the diverse behaviors depending greatly upon the information sources and advice received prior to start-up. Kujawa (1983) showed that industrial relations practices of manufacturing subsidiaries were influenced by technology strategies, with those that competed on innovations in organizational or management practices tending to be more aggressively nonunion than those that competed on transfer of process or product technologies.

Although globalization surely contributes to convergence in international practices, cross-national diversity remains a reality. Black's (2005) extensive analysis of cross-national patterns of industrial relations institutions shows that national culture is the primary determinant of cross-national variation in institutions, leading him to forecast ongoing diversity in labor market systems. Not surprisingly then, Frege's (2005) recent review of industrial relations research reveals that industrial relations research remained strongly embedded in nationally specific research cultures and traditions.

CONCLUSIONS

Industrial relations institutions are complex and vary significantly across national borders. Even though terminology is similar, understandings developed by scholars and practitioners within and about a specific national system do not necessarily transfer directly to other systems. For these reasons alone, international labor relations will continue to be informed by careful institutional and descriptive studies characteristic of industrial research. In addition, however, future research must be directed toward understanding how social and economic forces shape the essential characteristics of the national labor relations systems, and how these elements in turn combine to affect important outcomes of the employment relationships, such as firm performance, employee productivity, and other work-related outcomes.

Such analytical work is made more important by worldwide shifts in the industrial and economic contexts of the employment relationship. It is apparent that in most major industrial economies—especially those where unions are not accorded any special role in the broader social compact—the influence of organized labor has lessened considerably over the last two decades. Moreover, there is little indication that organized labor and labor relations institutions will be as integrally involved in the development of the newly emerging economies as they were in the industrialization of the older market economies. Not surprisingly, there is considerable contention as to the long-term future of organized labor. Scholars and practitioners with a stake in established institutions tend to see fluctuations in unionism as episodic, with unions rising and falling in response to periodic shifts in public policy, the attitudes of public and private policymakers and employee sentiments. An alternative view is that the emergence of labor unions is a product of a distinctive set of structural forces that are unlikely to be replicated. Unions have typically been concentrated in large-scale manufacturers, regulated telecommunications and transportation, and the public sector, areas in which there is some mitigation of the negative employment effects of higher union wages, and union workplace voice mechanisms might be expected to have some positive contribution to organizational efficiency. But the extent to which structural conditions are amenable to traditional labor relations practices and institutions can be expected to continue to diminish as industries are deregulated, governmental workforces contract, and established industries in the old industrial democracies become exposed to more and more competition on the global scale.

There is considerable unresolved conjecture as to whether existing labor organizations will have a new role as counterweights to the forces of global competition. According to Polanyi (2001), movements towards self-regulated markets have inevitably been accompanied by counter-movements to circumvent the more adverse consequences of the treatment of labor as a market commodity. Although established industrial relations institutions can be cast as a response to the rise of industrial market economies, there is yet no strong argument or evidence to suggest that they will be a major counterbalance to the effects of globalization (Castells, 2002; Munck, 2004).

Studies of international labor relations need to be informed by other disciplines or fields of study. The persistent cross-national differences in extent of unionism and the roles that unions play in society invite explicit consideration of the effects of national culture. However, by the standards of the widely used cultural typologies of Hofstede (1983) and Triandis and colleagues (Triandis, 1996; Singelis, Triandis, Bhawuk, & Gelfand, 1995), many of the oft-studied market economies of Western Europe and North America would be regarded as culturally similar in that they are generally classified as individualistic. A more fine-grained approach to national differences in values, beliefs, and attitudes as they bear directly on the employment relationship, and industrial and political organization may be more fruitful. For example, English-speaking market economies are characterized by beliefs about the role of the individual in the market. Employee rights to organize into unions are seen to be based on the individual freedom of association, and there is no presumption that collective organization of workers is inherently necessary or beneficial for the society as a whole. In addition, some parts of influential business and academic elites question whether or not union organizations have a useful role. Not coincidentally, these nations are also characterized by adherence to a model of corporate governance where the firm's stockholders are the preeminent stakeholder in the organizations. Competing European and Japanese visions view other groups, including employees, to be important stakeholders and these differing conceptions of the role of the corporation and firm governance could parallel differences in models of industrial relations (Dore, 1973, 2003). Historical approaches are clearly important, especially where scholars attempt to come to grips with the experiences and future directions of the newly industrializing and transition economies whose historical contexts differ markedly from those of the long-established market economies of North America, Western Europe, and the former British Commonwealth.

Topical research focus needs to expand to cover related areas of employment relations outside the areas of formal collective bargaining relationship. These include alternative forms of employee representation, and the role of protective labor legislation. Legislation establishing or encouraging work councils in the European Union and Korea has been designed to provide for employee voice without the inefficiencies associated with the monopoly face of unionism, and have encountered mixed reaction from union representatives (Bamber, Lansbury, & Wailes, 2004b). We need to determine how employees embrace these institutions, and how they affect organizational outcomes. Arguably, both works councils and protective employment laws that ensure minimal acceptable employment conditions and nondiscrimination might supplant employee interest in union representation, substituting for formal union voice and protective mechanisms, and contributing to the decline of union membership.

The widespread uncertainties about the future course of labor relations worldwide poses challenges that may well require, as Kaufman (2004) has argued, that industrial relations scholars abandon frameworks that over the last 30 years have become myopically focused on institutions of collective bargaining in the unionized sector. A new model for labor relations research should afford an explicit role for management decision makers, recognize new forms of employment relationships, including those where labor unions prospectively have little if any role to play, and embrace the contributions of broader social science disciplines.

REFERENCES

Addison, J. T., Schnabel, C., & Wagner, J. (2001). Works councils in Germany: Their effects on establishment performance. *Oxford Economic Papers, 53*(4), 659–694.

Addison, J. Y., & Hirsch, B. T. (1989). Union effects on productivity, profits, and gowth: Has the long run arrived? *Journal of Labor Economics, 7*(1), 72–105.

Bamber, G. J., Lansbury, R. D., & Wailes, N. (2004a). Conclusions. In G. J. Bamber & R. D. Lansbury (Eds.), *International and comparative employment relations: Globalisation and the developed market economies* (4th ed., pp. 329–346). London: Sage Publications.

Bamber, G. J., Lansbury, R. D., & Wailes, N. (2004b). Introduction. In G. J. Bamber & R. D. Lansbury (Eds.), *International and Comparative Employment Relations: Globalisation and the Developed Market Economies* (4th ed., pp. 1–35). London: Sage Publications.

Benson, J. (1994). The economic effects of unionism on Japanese manufacturing enterprises. *British Journal of Industrial Relations, 32*(1), 1–21.

Bhattacherjee, D. (2002). Organized labor and economic liberalization in India: Past, present, and future. In A. V. Jose (Ed.), *Organized Labor in the 21st Century* (pp. 307–345). Geneva: International Institute for Labor Studies.

Black, B. (2005). Comparative industrial relations theory: The role of national culture. *International Journal of Human Resource Management, 16*(7), 1137–1158.

Black, S. E., & Lynch, L. M. (2001). How to compete: The impact of workplace practices and information technology on productivity. *Review of Economics and Statistics, 83*(3), 434–445.

Blanchard, O., & Wolfers, J. (2000). The role of shocks and institutions in the rise of European unemployment: The aggregate evidence. *Economic Journal, 110*(462), C1–C33.

Blanchflower, D. G., & Bryson, A. (2003). Changes over time in union relative wage effects in the U.K. and the U.S. revisited. In J. T. Addison & C. Schnabel (Eds.), *International handbook of trade unions* (pp. 197–245). Cheltenham: Edward Elgar.

Blyton, P., Martinez Lucio, M., McGurk, J., & Turnbull, P. (2001). Globalization and trade union strategy: Industrial restructuring and human resource management in the international civil aviation industry. *International Journal of Human Resource Management, 12*(3), 445–463.

Bognanno, M. F., Keane, M. P., & Yang, D. (2005). The influence of wages and industrial relations environments on the production location decisions of U.S. multinational corporations. *Industrial and Labor Relations Review, 58*(2), 171–200.

Branford, S., & Kucinski, B. (2003). *Lula and the Workers Party in Brazil.* New York: The New Press.

Calmfors, L., & Drifill, J. (1988). Bargaining structures, corporatism, and macroeconomic performance. *Economic Policy, 3*(6), 13–61.

Capelli, P., & Neumark, D. (2001). Do "high performance" work practices improve establishment level outcomes? *Industrial and Labor Relations Review, 54*(4), 737–775.

Castells, M. (2002). *The Information Age. Vol. 2. The power of identity.* Oxford: Blackwell Publishing.

Chobot, A. (1992). Poland. In J. Campbell (Ed.), *European Labor Unions* (pp. 341–356). Westport, CT: Greenwood Press.

Dore, R. (1973). *British factor, Japanese factor: The origins of national diversity in industrial relations.* Berkeley: University of California Press.

Dore, R. (2003). *New forms and meanings of work in an increasingly globalized world.* Tokyo: International Institute for Labour Studies.

Drake, P. W. (1996). *Labor movements and dictatorships: The southern cone in comparative perspective.* Baltimore: The John Hopkins University Press.

Dunlop, J. T. (1958). *Industrial relations systems.* New York: Holt, Rinehart & Winston.

Ferner, A., Almond, P., Colling, T., & Edwards, T. (2005). Policies on union representation in U.S. multinationals in the U.K.: Between micro-politics and macro-institutions. *British Journal of Industrial Relations, 43*(4), 703–728.

Flanagan, R. J. (1999). Macroeconomic performance and collective bargaining: An international perspective. *Journal of Economic Literature, 37*(3), 1150–1175.

Freeman, R. B., & Medoff, J. L. (1984). *What do unions do?* New York: Basic Books.

Frege, C. M. (2005). Varieties of industrial relations research: Take-over, convergence or divergence? *British Journal of Industrial Relations, 43*(2), 179–207.

Hall, P., & Soskice, D. (2001). An introduction to varieties of capitalism. In P. Hall & D. Soskice (Eds.), *Varieties of capitalism: The institutional advantages of comparative advantage* (pp. 1–68). Oxford: Oxford University Press.

Hassel, A. (1999). The erosion of the German system of industrial relations. *British Journal of Industrial Relations, 37*(3), 483–505.

Hofstede, G. (1983). *Culture's consequences: International differences in work-related values.* Beverly Hills, CA: Sage Publications.

Hong, N. S., & Warner, M. (1998). *China's trade unions and management.* New York: St Martin's Press.

Hundley, G. (1987). The threat of unionism and wage coverage effects. *Journal of Labor Research, 8* (Summer): 236–251.

Katz, H., & Kochan, T. (2003). *An introduction to collective bargaining and industrial relations* (3rd ed.). New York: McGraw-Hill, Irwin.

Kaufman, B. E. (2004). *The global evolution of industrial relations events, ideas, and the IIRA.* Geneva: International Labor Organization.

Kerr, C., Dunlop, J. T., Harbison, F. H., & Myers, C. A. (1960). *Industrialism and industrial man.* Cambridge, MA: Harvard University Press.

Kim, D.-O., & Kim, H.-K. (2004). A comparison of the effectiveness of unions and non-union works councils in Korea: Can non-union employee representation substitute for trade unionism? *International Journal of Human Resource Management, 15*(3), 1069–1093.

Kleiner, M. (2001). Intensity of management resistance: Understanding the decline of unionization in the private sector. *Journal of Labor Research, 22*(3), 519–540.

Kujawa, D. (1983). Technology strategy and industrial relations: Case studies of Japanese multinationals in the United States. *Journal of International Business Studies, 14*(3), 9–22.

Kuruvilla, S., Das, S., Kwon, H., and Kwon, S. (2002). Trade unions growth and decline in Asia. *British Journal of Industrial Relations, 40*(3), 431–461

Lewis, H. G. (1986). *Union relative wage effects: A survey.* Chicago: University of Chicago Press.

Locke, R. M., Kochan, T., & Piore M. J. (1995). *Employment relations in a changing world economy.* Cambridge, MA: MIT Press.

MacDonald, I. T. (2003). NAFTA and the emergence of continental labor cooperation. *American Review of Canadian Studies, 33*(2), 173–197.

Marett, P. (1984). Japanese firms in the United States: Do they resist unionization? *Labor Law Journal, 35*(4), 240–250.

Mazur, J. (2000). Labor's new internationalism. *Foreign Affairs, 79*(1), 79–93.

Menezes-Filho, N., & Van Reenen. (2003). Unions and innovation: A survey of the theory and empirical evidence. In J. T. Addison & C. Schnabel (Eds.), *International handbook of trade unions* (pp. 415–460). Cheltenham: Edward Elgar.

Metcalf, D. (1993). Industrial relations and economic performance. *British Journal of Industrial Relations, 31*(2), 249–266.

Metcalf, D. (2003). Unions and productivity, financial performance and investment: International evidence. In J. T. Addison & C. Schnabel (Eds.), *International handbook of trade unions* (pp. 118–171). Cheltenham: Edward Elgar.

Munck, R. (2004). Globalization, labor and the "Polanyi problem." *Labor History, 45*(3), 251–269.

O'Connell, L. D. (1999). *Collective bargaining systems in six Latin American countries: Degrees of autonomy and decentralization* (Working paper No. 399). Washington, DC: Inter-American Development Bank, Office of the Chief Economist.

OECD (Organisation for Economic Co-operation and Development). (2004). *Employment outlook 2004.* Paris: OECD.

Orenstein, M. A., & Hale, L. E. (2001). Corporatist renaissance in post-communist Central Europe. In C. Candland & R. Sil (Eds.), *The politics of labor in a global age: Continuity and change in late-industrializing and post-socialist economies* (pp. 258–284). New York: Oxford University Press.

Osterman, P., Kochan, T. A., Locke, R. M., & Piore, M. J. (2001). *Working in America: A blueprint for the new labor market.* Cambridge, MA: MIT Press.

Pencavel, J. (2005). Unionism viewed internationally. *Journal of Labor Research, 36*(1), 65–97.

Polanyi, K. (2001). *The great transformation: The political and economic origins of our time.* Boston: Beacon Press.

Poole, M. (1986). *Industrial relations: Origins and Ppatterns of national diversity.* London: Routledge and Kegan Paul.

Riethof, M. (2002). Responses and strategies of the Brazilian labor movement towards Economic Restructuring Paper presented at the Annual Convention of International Studies Association, New Orleans, March 25–27.

Rose, J. B., & Chaison, G. N. (2001). Unionism in Canada and the United States: The prospects for revival. *Relations Industrielles, 56*(1), 34–65.

Schnabel, C., & Wagner, J. (1994). Industrial relations and trade union effects on innovation in Germany. *Labour, 8*(3), 489–503.

Sil, R. (2001). Privatization, labor politics, and the firm in post-Soviet Russia: Non-market norms, market institutions, and the Soviet legacy. pp 205–232. In C. Candland & R. Sil (Eds.), *The politics of labor in a global age: Continuity and change in late-industrializing and post-socialist economies.* New York: Oxford University Press.

Singelis, T. M., Triandis, H. C., Bhawuk, D. P. S., & Gelfland, M. J. (1995). Horizontal and vertical dimensions of individualism and collectivism: A theoretical and measurement refinement. *Cross-Cultural Research, 29*, 240–275.

Sturmthal, A. (1973). Industrial relations strategies. pp. 34–57. In A. Sturmthal & J. G. Scoville (Eds.), *The international labor movement in transition: Essays on Africa, Asia, Europe, and South America.* Urbana: University of Illinois Press.

Tachibanaki, T., & Noda, T. (2000). *The economic effects of trade unions in Japan.* Basingstoke: Macmillan.

Thirkwell, J., Scase, R., & Vickerstaffs (1994). Labour relations in transition in Eastern Europe. *Industrial Relations Journal, 25*(2), 84–95.

Triandis, H. C. (1996). The psychological measurement of cultural syndromes. *American Psychologist, 51*, 407–415.

Triandis, H. C., & Gelfland, M. J. (1998). Converging measurement of horizontal and vertical individualism and collectivism. *Journal of Personality and Social Psychology, 74*, 118–128.

Ulph, A., & Ulph, D. (2001). Strategic innovation with complete and incomplete labor market contracts. *Scandanavian Journal of Economics, 103*(2), 265–272.

U.S. Department of Labor. (2002). Brazil. In *Foreign labor trends* (FLT 02-04, pp. 1–33). Sao Paulo: U.S. Embassy.

Verma, A., Kochan, T. A., & Lansbury, R. D. (1995). *Employment relations in Asian economies*. London: Routledge.

Visser, J. (2003). Unions and unionism around the world. In J. T. Addison & C. Schnabel (Eds.), *International handbook of trade unions* (pp. 415–460). Cheltenham: Edward Elgar.

10 Expatriate Management: A Review and Directions for Research in Expatriate Selection, Training, and Repatriation

Jessica R. Mesmer-Magnus and Chockalingam Viswesvaran

CONTENTS

In today's ever-expanding marketplace, few organizations are able to operate solely within the confines of a specific country or distinct geographic locale. Rather, the workplace is becoming increasingly global (Oddou & Mendenhall, 1991), and such globalization presents a number of challenges for the ways in which organizations select, develop, and manage their human resources (Tannenbaum, 2002). To effectively compete, organizations have found it necessary to employ expatriates in a variety of international assignments. An *expatriate* is an employee of a business or government organization who is sent to another (nonnative) country to accomplish a job or organizational goal for a specific, temporary time-frame. Expatriate assignments typically range in length from 6 months to 5 years (Aycan, 1997).

As the globalization of the marketplace has progressed, international work experience has become a crucial component of the repertoire of aspiring managers of multinational corporations (MNCs; Carpenter, Sanders, & Gregersen, 2001). In many MNCs, international experience is considered a pre-requisite to advancement within managerial positions (Carpenter et al., 2001; Takeuchi, Tesluk, Yun, & Lepak, 2005). Current estimates suggest corporations worldwide are employing over 1.3 million expatri-ates from American nations alone (Van Vianen, De Pater, Kristof-Brown, 2004). Expatriate managers are frequently responsible for the management, administration, and implementation of new technologies, product lines, or services to a new region (Dunbar, 1992). These expatriates are operating in a number of positions (CEO, functional department heads, troubleshooters, line managers, etc.; Hays, 1974) and in a variety of functions (transfer of technologies, joint ventures, transmission of organizational culture, developing new markets, developing skills of international employees; Graf & Harland, 2005). Such variability in function and position warrants an examination into the most effective strategies for staff-ing, training, and managing expatriate positions. Indeed, international assignments are one of the most expensive per-person investments made by MNCs, as the yearly cost of an expatriate assignment fre-quently exceeds U.S.$1 million (Stroh, Black, Mendenhall, & Gregersen, 2005).

Expatriate failure remains a salient problem for those responsible for managing expatriate assignments (Feldman & Thomas, 1991). Failure may include termination or recall of an expatriate due to his or her inability to perform successfully in the overseas function or requesting to return prematurely because the expatriate or spouse is unable to adjust (Caligiuri, Hyland, Joshi, & Bross, 1998; Tung, 1987). Costs associated with the failure of an expatriate may range from U.S.$250,000 to over U.S.$1.25 million in expenses associated with moving, downtime, and a myriad of other direct and indirect costs (Black & Gregersen, 1999; Mervosh & McClenahen, 1997). Moreover, failed international assignments are potentially destructive to the career potential of the returning expatriate. These individuals often suffer decrements in self-esteem, self-confidence, reputation, and motivation following an unsuccessful international assignment (Takeuchi et al., 2005). Fur-ther, expatriate failure often reduces the potential for future expatriate assignments. Even when the expatriate completes the assignment, inadequate adjustment to the host country may yield dis-satisfaction, suboptimal work performance, and decreased organizational commitment (Bhuian & Menguc, 2002; Shaffer & Harrison, 1998; VanVianen et al., 2004). And, even though international assignments are valued by the MNC, many potential expatriates feel that such an assignment is a risky career move (Gregersen & Black, 1992; Oddou & Mendenhall, 1991). Such issues present the MNC and its human resources constituents with a unique set of problems associated with preparing and managing expatriates. Given the costs associated with expatriate failure, ensuring expatriate success is the key issue of concern to human resources practitioners responsible for the management of expatriate positions (Black & Gregersen, 1991; Black, Mendenhall, & Oddou, 1991). As such, much research about expatriate assignments has focused on improving the potential for success.

Research suggests five factors are of key importance to expatriate success in international assignments: (a) family situation, (b) adaptability and flexibility, (c) job knowledge and motivation, (d) relational skills, and (e) extra-cultural openness (Arthur & Bennett, 1995; Caligiuri et al., 1998; Kraimer, Wayne, & Jaworski, 2001). In fact, expatriate failure occurs for a number of reasons, namely: (a) inability of the expatriate's spouse to adjust, (b) expatriate inability to adjust, (c) other family problems, (d) expatriate personality or emotional immaturity, (e) expatriate inability to meet responsibilities of overseas work, (f) expatriate lack of technical competence, and (g) expatriate lack of motivation (Tung, 1987). Interestingly, little attention is paid to these factors when selecting and preparing the expatriate for an overseas assignment. Rather, expatriates are typically selected solely for their technical skills relevant to the overseas assignment. Following the selection process, these employees are often left to tackle the new country, culture, and work assignment with little assistance from their parent organization.

The vast majority of research in the area of expatriation, though anecdotal and prescriptive in nature, has focused on selection, preparation and training, and repatriation (Brewster & Pickard, 1994; Mendenhall, Dunbar, & Oddou, 1987). We review this research and offer insights into avenues fruitful for future research. Further, to enhance the reader's access to salient conclusions drawn by expatriation researchers, we provide tables summarizing (a) current research findings; (b) research conclusions unique to five regions of the world—Asia and Australia, Europe and the United Kingdom, Africa and the Middle East, and North and South America; and (c) fruitful avenues for future research in expatriate selection, training, and repatriation.

EXPATRIATE SELECTION

POTENTIAL PREDICTORS OF EXPATRIATE SUCCESS

The majority of U.S. firms staff global assignments solely on the basis of technical capabilities of the candidates (Stroh et al., 2005; Tung, 1987). Importantly, this aspect of the candidate's repertoire is only one piece of the puzzle. Other factors may be of greater importance in predicting success on an international assignment, and thus should be incorporated within the selection process. Below we review such predictors.

Person-Related Predictors

The earliest attempts at expatriate selection can be traced to the efforts of the Peace Corps to predict the suitability of volunteers for overseas assignments. These assessments were typically made by clinical psychologists and field officers (Adler, 1991). Little attempt was made to perform comprehensive psychological assessments, and not surprisingly, the predictive value of these assessments was poor. This failed attempt resulted in some pessimistic conclusions about the role of using personality factors to predict expatriate success (cf. Dicken & Black, 1965; Harris, 1973).

Despite the not-so-optimistic predictive utility of personality assessments, researchers have hypothesized various aspects of personality as potential predictors of expatriate success. For example, Copeland and Griggs (1988) suggest individuals selected for expatriate assignments should be resourceful, curious, and have positive regard for others. Brislin (1981) suggests predictors of intercultural adjustment and expatriate success include intelligence, conscientiousness, nondogmatism, nonauthoritarianism, tolerance, self-esteem, tolerance for ambiguity, etc. Gudykunst, Hammer & Wiseman (1977) also suggest empathy, nonjudgmentalness, and tolerance for ambiguity, etc., as potential predictors of expatriate success. Unfortunately, many of these studies have failed to collect the empirical data necessary to establish a link between such personality facets and expatriate success. Although the theoretical reasoning presented in these accounts (cf. Ones & Viswesvaran, 1997) serves as a good guide to expatriate selection, their empirical validation is also required. In part due to the lack of standardized measures of personality, earlier attempts to empirically validate these hypotheses were not promising. Sinangil and Ones (2001) provide a good summary of some of the statistical problems encountered in the earlier validation attempts.

Recently, researchers have sought to overcome these shortcomings and establish the criterion-related validity of person-related factors for predicting expatriate success. Although several personality variables have been postulated in the literature, personality psychologists (e.g., Costa & McCrae, 1992; Goldberg, 1993; Hogan, Hogan, & Roberts, 1996) have accepted five factors as giving an overview of individual personality. The five factors are: agreeableness, conscientiousness, emotional stability, extraversion, and openness to experience. Agreeableness refers to how likable the person is and may be an important factor in expatriate success as expatriates are expected to work in team settings with local host country nationals to get the job done. Conscientiousness refers to how dependable, diligent, and persistent an individual is and is a likely predictor of success in any venture. In fact, conscientiousness has been related to job performance in domestic contexts in both North American (Barrick & Mount, 1991) and European samples (Salgado, 1997). Emotional stability is also referred to by its polar opposite, neuroticism, and has been linked to performance in high-stress situations as well as in ambiguous situations. Given the need for expatriates to deal effectively with uncertainty, emotional stability is a likely predictor. Extraversion assesses how sociable and ambitious an individual is whereas openness to experience, also referred to as intellect, assesses how flexible the individual is to novel situations. As can be seen from these descriptions, each of these factors may play a role in expatriate success (see also Ones & Viswesvaran, 1997, for an elaboration of these mechanisms).

Caligiuri (1997) investigated the relationships between the Big Five factors of personality and important outcomes like expatriate willingness to continue with an international assignment and expatriate performance. Data were collected from 143 expatriates assessing personality and job performance. Job performance assessments were made by their supervisors reflecting the expatriates' technical knowledge, technical application, organizational commitment, communication competence, motivation, and teamwork. Expatriates also reported their intentions to prematurely terminate the overseas assignment. Caligiuri (1997) found that extraversion, agreeableness, and emotional stability were negatively related to intentions of quitting and conscientiousness was positively related to supervisor ratings of job performance. Contrary to past predictions, openness to experience was not predictive of job performance. In a follow-up investigation, Caligiuri (2000) found that openness to experience moderated the relationship between contact with host country nationals and cross-cultural adjustment. That is, individuals who were high on openness to experience benefited more from contact with host country nationals than those who scored low on this personality dimension. These findings underscore the fact that personality variables have predictive value in expatriate selection.

Other researchers have also linked personality variables to expatriate success. Sinangil and Ones (1998) found that conscientiousness did not predict overseas job performance but was highly predictive of overseas counterproductive behaviors. Deller (1998) reported that ambition (an aspect of extraversion) and openness to experience were predictive of expatriate job performance. Similar findings emerge when personality is correlated with expatriate performance ratings by host-country coworkers (Caligiuri, 1997; Sinangil & Ones, 1998). The importance of considering both the views of supervisors and host-country coworkers has been increasingly emphasized over the past two decades (e.g., Kealey, 1989) and this is more appropriate in an era when teamwork and team-level performance is emphasized. It is important to note that managers and coworkers place a great deal of importance on the role of personality in expatriate success (Ones & Viswesvaran, 1999). Using a policy-capturing approach, Ones and Viswesvaran (1999) found managers of expatriates placed substantial weight on personality factors during the expatriate selection process. Zeira and Banai (1985) found factors that host-country nationals viewed as important predictors were also considered important by parent-country managers, providing further credence to the idea that the host-country workforce should be engaged in the expatriate selection process.

Other person-related factors are also potentially useful predictors of expatriate success. General mental ability, for example, has been related to job performance in many studies; multiple meta-analyses attest to the predictive validity of general mental ability for predicting job performance (Ones, Viswesvaran, & Dilchert, 2005; Schmidt, 2002). In fact, if we can assess only one predictor about our potential applicants for a job, the best predictor will be general mental ability. This is especially true as the complexity of the job increases (Schmidt & Hunter, 1998) as is inevitably the case in expatriate assignments (e.g., Brislin, 1981).

Technical knowledge, or job-specific knowledge, is also an important predictor of expatriate success. In fact, task performance is what the organization is employing the individual for. Although an important predictor of job performance, it may not be a critical component for expatriate selection because individuals will have already been preselected in technical competence. That is, there will be a range-restricted sample (with only technically qualified applicants) being considered for expatriate assignments. To the extent the overseas assignment requires unique technical knowledge, possession of such information will be critical for expatriate success.

It is axiomatic in personnel selection that past behavior is the best predictor of future behavior. Biodata instruments, training and experience measures, application blanks, situational interviews, and even personality inventories rely on this principle. As such, prior (successful) expatriate experience is a valid predictor of expatriate success. In a meta-analysis of available empirical studies, Hechanova, Beehr, and Christiansen (2003) found that across eight studies involving 1635 respondents, previous overseas experience correlated .08 with cross-cultural adjustment, .09 with interactional adjustment (3 studies, 524 respondents) and .07 with work adjustment (7 studies, 1240 respondents). Although the magnitude of the correlations was not high, there were consistent positive correlations across samples. Furthermore, because performance is a multiplicative product of ability and motivation, to the extent previous overseas experience reflects both ability and motivation, it is a valuable predictor (compared to either measures of only ability—general mental ability, job knowledge, etc.—or only measures of motivation—personality variables).

Job-Related Predictors

Person-related factors are important determinants of success; nevertheless, success also depends upon situational factors or constraints. This is especially true in expatriate assignments where the tasks are complex, interdependent, and impacted by many contextual factors. Hechanova et al. (2003) found that job level is negatively related to overall adjustment but is positively related to interactional adjustment. These findings probably reflect the higher levels of stressors found in high-level jobs, as well as the fact that interactions at higher levels of jobs are with more intelligent and culturally suave individuals. Frequency of interaction with host-country nationals required in the job was also found to be positively related to expatriate success. This is consistent with studies conducted in the United States on improving race relations during the 1960s (Allport, 1954; Zajanoc, 1968). The rationale here is that as an individual has more contact with a cultural group, interpersonal communication will improve. Interestingly, the more a job involves contact with the parent-country offices, the greater is the likelihood of success. Perhaps, continued interaction with parent-country employees provides the expatriates with social support and prevents feelings of isolation. One of the concerns of expatriates is that they will miss promotion opportunities when they are overseas (Miller & Cheng, 1978), and frequent consultation with the parent company likely mitigates this concern.

Role conflict and role ambiguity are likely to contribute to stress levels (Beehr, 1995), which in turn will affect job performance. These relationships have been confirmed in several different meta-analyses (e.g., Jackson & Schuler, 1985) wherein the correlations between role conflict and ambiguity and job performance have been robust. Conflict and ambiguity are more likely in expatriate assignments where the jobs are more complex and involve many different stakeholders than in the domestic context. Cross-cultural training has been found to be effective in enhancing job performance and cross-cultural adjustment. In a meta-analytic review of the effectiveness of training programs, Deshpande and Visweswaran (1992) found cross-cultural training to be substantially correlated with expatriate performance. Thus, organizations should strive to reduce role conflict, ambiguity, and provide adequate training. However, these good management practices do not form the basis for selection. Selection should be based on job-related personal factors (individual differences; see Schmitt & Chan, 1998).

Nonwork-Related Predictors

In addition to person- and job-related factors, several nonwork-related variables have been postulated as predictors of expatriate job performance. For example, gender and marital status have been related to expatriate success. Also predictive is the number of school-age children. The rationale is that expatriates find adjustment more difficult when they are faced with the additional stress of finding good educational opportunities for their children and helping their children adjust to the new culture and educational system. Selmer and Leung (2003) compared the characteristics of male and female expatriates and found that female expatriates were younger and less frequently married. Researchers have argued that women may find adjustment to be more difficult in some cultures (Adler, 1987). Although there may be some truth in these claims, use of these nonwork-related factors for personnel selection is professionally unethical (especially when there are other standard measures to assess job-related characteristics) and may be illegal in some countries (e.g., the United States).

POTENTIAL CRITERIA FOR ASSESSING EXPATRIATE SUCCESS

Job performance is a central construct in human resource management (Austin & Villanova, 1992; Campbell, 1990; Viswesvaran, Ones, & Schmidt, 1996); in fact all human resources systems and interventions (including selection) are in some way focused on improving job performance (both individual and unit-level). Given this, we would expect the assessment of job performance to be well developed and the mediating mechanisms well understood. Unfortunately, we are far from even delineating clearly the content domain of job performance. Different taxonomies of job performance dimensions have been postulated.

Campbell, McCloy, Oppler, and Sager (1992) postulate that eight dimensions make up the domain of performance; Viswesvaran et al. (1996) divide the content domain of job performance into ten dimensions. The eight dimensions hypothesized by Campbell et al. are job-specific task proficiency, nonjob-specific task proficiency, written communication, oral communication, demonstrating effort, personal discipline, facilitating peer and team performance, and management or administration. According to Viswesvaran et al. (1996) the content domain of job performance includes dimensions such as productivity, interpersonal competence, communication competence, effort, job knowledge, problem solving, etc. Several other taxonomies (e.g., Hunt, 1996) have also been proposed. Viswesvaran and Ones (2001) review the different models of job performance postulated in the extant literature and propose a two-dimensional grid to classify the different taxonomies.

In the expatriate performance assessment literature, researchers (e.g., Birdseye & Hill, 1995; Caligiuri, 2000) have assessed expatriate success with the following criteria: (a) completion of overseas stay, (b) job performance assessments, and (c) cross-cultural adjustment. Completion of stay is akin to turnover. In domestic contexts, turnover or tenure are not considered to be good proxies for (or indicative of) job performance. Rather, turnover and tenure are likely influenced by a myriad of other factors (e.g., economic conditions) and as such are not appropriate indicators of performance (Naumann, 1992). An argument can be made that in expatriate selection, completion of overseas stay is the most important criteria to consider as it takes a huge investment to send an expatriate overseas. However, in the rapidly changing workplace today, there are substantial costs with turnover in domestic assignments also. Thus, unless there are more relevant reasons, the use of turnover as a criterion for expatriate selection is not recommended. This is especially the case when researchers resort to "intent to complete" a global assignment as a criterion (Naumann, 1992).

Cross-cultural adjustment is another potential criterion that may be better conceptualized as a predictor than a criterion. In expatriate literature, employee adjustment has been considered as both a predictor and a criterion; different models have postulated the components of adjustment (workplace adjustment, general adjustment, interactional adjustment, etc.). Assessments of job performance in these studies have been idiosyncratic to each researcher, thus a clean relationship between adjustment and performance has not been established. It is likely that the comprehensive models of job performance developed in the within-country selection research (e.g., Austin & Villanova, 1992; Viswesvaran & Ones, 2001) are more appropriate for expatriate selection research. It is also likely that the actual indicators of the dimensions of adjustment will differ though they will generalize from a domestic to expatriate selection context.

MODELS OF EXPATRIATE SELECTION

In this chapter, we have covered the different predictors of expatriate success under three different categories: (a) person-related or individual differences variables, (b) job-related or situational factors, and (3) nonwork-related predictors. We have postulated that job-relevant person-related variables likely have the most viability as predictors. Although we have addressed each predictor individually, they are likely to interact when predicting expatriate success. In fact, in recognition of these interactions, researchers have proposed several integrated models of expatriate success. Below we review three such models but would like to reiterate that expatriate selection should be based on job-related individual differences variables only (for both ethical and perhaps legal concerns).

Tung (1981) identified four clusters of variables related to expatriate success. The four categories were technical skills, personality or relational skills, family situation, and environmental variables. Technical skills refer to procedural and declarative job knowledge and are potentially crucial to success as expatriates are sent internationally in large part because of the technical expertise they are able to share with the host-country workforce. Thus, it is crucial to assess expatriate assignees' competence in this factor. Given that overseas assignments are likely to involve novel cultural situations, personality variables, especially individual differences in interpersonal acumen, will play a crucial role in success. Family factors, such as the presence of children and family/spousal adjustment, will affect performance via spillover and support mechanisms.

Black and Gregersen (1999) also identify characteristics of successful expatriates; foremost among them is a "drive to communicate." This includes proficiency in different languages, being extraverted in personal dealings, enthusiastic, and sociable. According to Black and Gregersen (1999), successful expatriates also tend to have contact with host-country nationals in nonwork contexts, cultural flexibility, a cosmopolitan orientation, and a collaborative negotiation style. The frequency of interaction with host-country nationals likely facilitates greater insight into local markets, develops important contacts with key stakeholders, and fosters successful completion of overseas assignment.

Arthur and Bennett (1995), in an extensive literature review, identified 54 characteristics with the potential to impact expatriate success. These characteristics were grouped into the following five categories: family situation, flexibility/adaptability, job knowledge and motivation, relational skills, and extracultural openness. Across the three models outlined here, several individual differences variables have been postulated and are likely to be valid predictors. Unfortunately, there is scant empirical testing of such comprehensive models. We revisit this issue when discussing avenues for fruitful future research.

A summary of research findings regarding expatriate selection is provided in Table 10.1. Further, given broad differences in research and practice regarding expatriate selection across major world regions, we provide a summary of such differences in Table 10.2. For example, whereas U.S. MNCs typically select expatriates based upon technical expertise, Asian and European MNCs tend to use predictors of both technical competence and cross-cultural adaptability. In addition, European MNCs have made effective use of realistic job previews when staffing expatriate functions. Importantly, Asian and European MNCs have reported a higher expatriate success rate than U.S. MNCs, presumably because greater attention has been paid to ensuring expatriate success prior to the commencement of the overseas assignment.

TRAINING EXPATRIATES

Research suggests greater than 70% of North American expatriates receive little or no preparation prior to embarking on a global assignment (Stroh et al., 2005). Worse, less than 10% of managerial-level expatriates are offered any cross-cultural training in host-country customs or practices, and the majority report being ill-prepared for interactions with host-country nationals (these numbers are somewhat more promising for expatriates originating from Asian countries; Brewster & Pickard, 1994). Although there is a great deal of literature on the preparation of expatriates for foreign assignments, much of this research is anecdotal and prescriptive in nature (Brewster & Pickard, 1994). Researchers agree, however, that most organizations provide little formal preparation for expatriation; training that is provided is rarely well planned (i.e., does not result from a thoughtful/competent needs assessment), and most expatriate training involves a "canned" approach (e.g., viewing videos about the host country, reading books on the host country's culture and traditions,

TABLE 10.1
Expatriate Selection: Current Research Findings

Predictors of expatriate success might be organized into four crucial factors: (1) technical competence, (2) personality traits, (3) environmental variables, and (4) family situation.

Expatriates are typically selected based solely upon their technical skills.

Other important predictors of expatriate success may include

> *Proficiency in host-country language*
> *Expertise in specific assignment*
> *Expertise in host-country business world*
> *Expertise in business world of the parent company*
> *Age*
> *Gender*
> *Seniority in the organization*
> *Adaptability of the expatriate's spouse*
> *Hierarchical position within the organization*
> *Previous success in foreign assignments, previous experience in foreign assignments*
> *Academic education*
> *Similarity of host country with the expatriate's country of origin*
> *Marital status*
> *Family situation*
> *Motivational state of the expatriate's spouse*

> *Personality factors, like drive to communicate, cultural flexibility, cosmopolitan orientation, openness to experience, etc.*

Criteria of expatriate success typically include (1) cross-cultural adjustment, (2) completion of the global assignment, and (3) performance on the global assignment.

The motivational state of the expatriate (and the expatriate's spouse) is potentially important to success (e.g., belief in mission, career path congruence, interest in overseas experience, professional intentions).

Most organizations have a relatively narrow view of the role of expatriate assignments in organizational success; the best expatriate management strategies incorporate a clear focus/understanding of how the expatriate's international experience will contribute to his or her future success within the organization. In other words, international assignments should be incorporated within managerial succession plans.

or conversing with people who have lived previously in a similar country; Oddou & Mendenhall, 1991; Tung, 1981). Moreover, organizations often approach expatriate training as though it is simply an expense (even a waste) of valuable resources rather than an investment in the career development of the expatriate (Feldman & Thomas, 1991). Researchers agree that the outcome of a well-designed and implemented expatriate training initiative likely outweighs its associated costs. Interestingly, many expatriates are unaware of their need for training prior to commencing their overseas assignment (Stroh et al., 2005). Thus, they are unprepared to actively solicit the training that would be beneficial (crucial) to their successful performance and adjustment in the new context.

TRAINING METHODS

More often than not, expatriates are selected for international assignments requiring substantially similar knowledge, skills, and abilities as were required for successful performance within their current domestic assignments. Expatriate training, then, is mainly focused on developing the cross-cultural knowledge and skills necessary for successful interaction with host-country nationals and for effective operation within the host-country culture (e.g., Brewster & Pickard, 1994; Black & Mendenhall, 1989; Selmer, Torbiorn, & de Leon, 1998). Importantly, research suggests cross-cultural training is effective in developing appropriate cultural perceptions within trainees, facilitating adjustment to host-country culture, and enhancing performance in international assignments (Black & Mendenhall, 1990; Deshpande & Visweswaran, 1992; Tung, 1981).

TABLE 10.2
Expatriate Selection: World Region-Specific Findings

Asia & Australia

Expatriates with previous experience/success with training host-country local managers will likely be successful in training Chinese local managers. Expatriates lacking such experience should be sent elsewhere.

Chinese managers are typically very reliant upon rules, procedures, and orders from supervisors.

The Chinese government favors expatriate arrangements that foster the development of host-country nationals. Therefore, the MNC should only send an expatriate who is certain to operate in ways consistent with the goals of the MNC and in ways that promote the development of the host-country workforce (Pazy & Zeira, 1985; Selmer, 2004; Sergent & Frenkel, 1998).

Many locations in China are not characterized as "family-friendly." Pollution, insufficient international schools, inferior housing, lack of Western medical facilities, etc., may make it difficult to persuade expatriates with spouse/family to accept an assignment in China. Many foreign nations attempt to staff expatriate assignments with single employees with few family obligations.

Asian expatriates assign a very high priority to the international marketplace due to the smaller size of their domestic marketplace. International assignments provide the opportunity for greater career mobility than would ordinarily be available.

U.S. expatriates fail in overseas assignments in large part due to the inability of their spouses to adjust. Japanese wives are typically seen as more obedient and dependent than are American wives (Black & Stephens, 1989). Thus, Japanese wives may strive to ensure that they are not the reason for their husband's failure in an international assignment. Research suggests that Japanese wives are much less likely to complain about the difficulties of adjusting to the host-country culture (Fukuda & Chu, 1994).

Contrary to expectations, female expatriates to Asia have not reported that their gender served as a significant impediment to successful (managerial) performance. However, they did perceive the presence of glass ceilings, sexist attitudes, and, at times, straightforward discrimination. Female expatriates should be selected when they possess the technical and interpersonal skills necessary for success in the overseas assignments and when they are confident in these skills. MNCs should avoid selecting "token" female expatriates for assignments to Asia.

Japanese MNCs typically consider the following criteria when selecting expatriates: technical competence, desire to work abroad, tenure with home office, family support for an international assignment, and familiarity with host country (see Beamish & Inkpen, 1998).

Many Asian MNCs will not select an expatriate who has not been identified as having potential for advancement to senior management positions. This selection factor has been adopted to reduce the probability that the returning expatriate will be without career opportunities or will be unable to utilize his or her international experience upon repatriation.

Europe & the United Kingdom

Realistic job previews are used with some frequency in European countries.

American expatriates positioned in Europe reported more satisfaction with the assignment and social conditions and expressed a greater intent to remain with the organization upon repatriation.

European expatriates assign a very high priority to the international marketplace due to the smaller size of their domestic marketplace. International assignments provide the opportunity for greater career mobility than would ordinarily be available.

European countries have a longer history of expatriation than other nations, a greater language capability than is seen in other world regions, and possess an international orientation.

European MNCs consider a number of factors when selecting expatriates, including proficiency in the host-country language, expertise relevant to the specific international assignment, expertise in the business environment of the host country, expatriate age, seniority, appearance (dress and attractiveness), and adaptability of the spouse, hierarchical position at headquarters, previous success in overseas assignments, academic education, and country of origin (Scullion, 1994).

Many European MNCs will not select an expatriate who has not been identified as having potential for advancement to senior management positions. This selection factor has been adopted to reduce the probability that the returning expatriate will be without career opportunities or will be unable to utilize his or her international experience upon repatriation.

(Continued)

TABLE 10.2 (Continued)

Expatriate Selection: World Region-Specific Findings Africa & the Middle East

Expatriates to Africa and the Middle East are frequently required to take assignments in these countries prior to being granted international assignment to more "desirable" countries. These assignments are typically viewed as a prerequisite to gaining other international experience.

North America

One of the most frequently cited criteria for success of North American expatriates is the mastery of cross-cultural communication.

North American expatriate tenure with the MNC is predictive of successful performance on international assignments.

U.S. MNCs typically select expatriates based solely upon technical expertise. Insufficient attention is placed on cross-cultural skills or cultural adaptability. Spouses are not typically taken into consideration during the selection or training process.

Recent surveys suggest that American expatriates consider international experience essential to their upward career mobility. The most significant fear reported by these expatriates, however, is that once they are "out of sight," they will be "out of mind" (e.g., lose out on promotions and career advancement opportunities).

Taxonomies of Expatriate Training

Brislin (1981) identified three key forms of cross-cultural training approaches utilized in the preparation of expatriates: (a) cognitive or information-giving approaches, (b) affective approaches, and (3) behavioral/experimental or immersion approaches. Cognitive or information-giving approaches typically utilize a lecture-based approach to present basic culture-related knowledge and facilitate the development of basic culture-related skills. These approaches may include area briefings, cultural briefings, films/books, use of interpreters, and basic language training. Affective approaches to expatriate training foster the learning of culture-related information/skills by using techniques that raise awareness of cultural differences and foster cultural insights. Such approaches include culture assimilator training, language training, role-playing, critical incidents techniques, case studies, and stress reduction training (Mendenhall et al., 1987).

Clearly affective approaches are more rigorous than information-giving approaches and likely require more time to implement (Brislin, 1981). Lengthy predeparture training programs are rarely provided by MNCs. However, these more in-depth approaches to expatriate preparation are thought to yield a greater degree of integration and adjustment with the host-country workforce (Mendenhall et al., 1987). The most rigorous methods of expatriate preparation, behavioral/experimental or immersion approaches, likely result in the greatest potential for adaptation and adjustment to the host country and the expatriate assignment. These approaches may include assessment centers, field experiences, shadowing opportunities, simulations, sensitivity training, and extensive language training. Although immersion approaches result in the greatest preparation for expatriate assignments, they also require the greatest investments in planning and of time and money. Cross-cultural researchers agree that a comprehensive expatriate training program would utilize methods of each type (Brislin, 1981; Mendenhall et al., 1987; Tung, 1981). Further, Mendenhall and colleagues (1987) proposed that greater emphasis should be placed on immersion approaches as the length of the expatriate's proposed international assignment increases. Other important considerations may include the degree of interaction the expatriate will have with host-country nationals and the novelty of the expatriate's job assignment (Mendenhall & Oddou, 1985).

Tung (1981) organized cross-cultural expatriate training programs into five complementary categories ascending in level of rigor: (a) area studies programs, (b) cultural assimilator, (c) language training, (d) sensitivity training, and (e) field experiences. According to Tung, area studies programs include environmental briefings and cultural orientation programs that provide the expatriate with information relevant to the host country's sociopolitical history, geography, economic development, and cultural institutions. The premise backing the use of this approach to expatriate preparation is that increased knowledge about another culture will increase empathy, ultimately improving the nature of intercultural relationships by attenuating the fear and uncertainty that typically arises in unusual contexts and unexpected situations (Tung, 1981). Tung argues, however, that the sole reliance on area studies programs for preparing expatriates will be inadequate, especially when the assignment requires extensive contact with host-country nationals.

The culture assimilator, another approach utilized in expatriate preparation, is considered to be more rigorous than area studies programs (Bhawuk, 1998). The culture assimilator typically consists of 75 to 100 episodes depicting intercultural encounters (Tung, 1981). This approach was traditionally utilized in situations where an expatriate assignment was made on short notice, and where insufficient time was available to utilize a more rigorous approach. Research suggests that this approach is effective in improving expatriate adjustment to and interaction with the host culture (Fiedler & Mitchell, 1971; Worchel & Mitchell, 1972). A third approach to expatriate preparation proposed by Tung involves training the expatriate to speak the language of the host country. As Brislin (1981) argued, language training may be offered in varying degrees of intensity, from basic "survival" language skills to very intensive "immersion" approaches. The intensity of language training offered to expatriates should be contingent upon the extent to which fluidity in the host-country language will be instrumental to successful performance in the international assignment and to adjustment to the host-country culture (Brislin, 1981; Mendenhall et al., 1987; Tung, 1981).

Sensitivity training, the fourth category of expatriate training proposed by Tung (1981), focuses learning at the affective level and is designed to result in flexibility with regard to the expatriate's attitudes toward and understanding of the values and actions of the host-country culture. Field experiences, Tung's fifth category, are the most rigorous form of expatriate training, and involve immersing the expatriate into the country of assignment or into a nearby "microculture" (e.g., Indian reservations, culturally homogeneous urban neighborhoods). Field experiences of this sort are thought to elicit the same types of emotional reactions that could be expected while on expatriate assignment. Tung (1981) argued that these expatriate training methods will be most effective when they are utilized in concert. Specifically, these training approaches focus on different types of learning (cognitive, skill, and affective) and vary in terms of the instructional media utilized, the informational content provided, and the time and monetary resources required.

Landis and Brislin (1983) proposed a six-part typology of cross-cultural training programs which, like Tung's, sought to enumerate different training options available to the trainers of expatriates. These programs include facts-oriented training, attributions training, cultural awareness training, cognitive-behavior modification training, experiential learning exercises, and interaction training (which involved interacting with host-country nationals or returning expatriates). Like Tung (1981), Landis and Brislin argued the importance of multiple training methods, especially when the expatriate's assignment would be lengthy or require extensive interaction with the host-country workforce.

EFFECTIVENESS OF VARIOUS TRAINING APPROACHES

Research in the area of expatriate training reveals that an important predictor of the utility of a cross-cultural training program is rigor (Black et al., 1991; Stroh et al., 2005). *Rigor* reflects not only the time requirements of the training program, but also the extent to which a particular training method requires the trainee to become mentally involved in learning training content (Stroh et al., 2005). Low rigor approaches, like videos/films, lectures, area briefings, and books, require less mental focus on the part of the trainee, and thus are likely to be less effective in facilitating learning (Black et al., 1991). Somewhat more rigorous approaches similarly require only passive learning, but offer the trainee the opportunity to practice learned skills in a "safe" environment. Such approaches include role modeling, language training, or discussion groups. High rigor approaches, like assessment centers, simulations, and interactive language and cultural skills training, require more involvement and interaction on the part of the trainee, and thus are more likely to result in learning and transfer to the host country.

Research suggests training programs of higher rigor result in retention rates that exceed those of less rigorous training by more than 70% (Stroh et al., 2005). In sum, programs provided in an effort to minimize time requirements or effort on the part of the trainee are likely to result in substantially less learning and return on investment than would be gained by training programs requiring more trainee effort and time (Black & Mendenhall, 1989).

According to Black et al. (1991), the level of rigor necessary for a successful expatriate training program depends upon the three dimensions of the host culture: cultural toughness, communication toughness, and job toughness. Cultural toughness refers to the degree to which the expatriate will find adjustment to the host country's culture difficult. This dimension is determined in part by the relative difference between the expatriate's home and host countries. Also relevant is the depth, quality, and similarity of previous overseas experience. Communication toughness is a function of the extent to which the expatriate is required to communicate extensively with host-country locals. When expatriates will be expected to communicate with host-country nationals in person and in an informal manner, more rigorous language training will be necessary than when the communication will be formal or unidirectional. Job toughness, the third relevant dimension, relates to the degree to which the expatriate's new job function will require more autonomy, responsibility, or advanced skills than his or her previous position. Frequently expatriates are promoted just prior to the overseas transition. In these cases, the expatriate must not only adapt to a new country, culture, and business customs, they must also adapt to a new or more challenging job. Rigorous training is necessary to more fully prepare the expatriate.

EVALUATING EXPATRIATE TRAINING

Research suggests that little formal evaluation of expatriate training programs is executed by organizations (Mendenhall et al., 1987). However, evaluation typically assesses the extent to which expatriates have adjusted to their new culture, the expatriate's performance on the international assignment, and whether the expatriate successfully completes the international assignment. Although the costs associated with expatriate failure to complete an assignment are salient (direct costs associated with selection, relocation, and replacement; downtime both prior to and after the move; and indirect costs, like damage to relationships with host-country nationals and constituents, decreased morale, loss of business opportunities, etc.), the costs associated with ineffective expatriate performance and insufficient expatriate adjustment to the host country are no less important to the bottom line performance of the MNC.

Expatriate Adjustment

Adjusting to a new culture is a gradual process. Cross-cultural training is thought to facilitate adjustment by introducing the trainee to cultural content that will be important to adaptation, and to help the trainee to more rapidly move through the phases of adjustment (Black & Mendenhall, 1990). Adjustment involves the development of familiarity, comfort, and proficiency with expected behaviors, cultural assumptions, and value systems. This process is made more challenging as the differences between the expatriate's home culture and the host culture become greater (Torbiorn, 1982). When evaluating the extent to which an expatriate has adjusted to the host country's culture, three factors are thought to be of importance: (a) maintenance of self, including psychological well-being, increased self-confidence, etc., (b) development of interpersonal relationships with host nationals, and (c) cognitive learning of host-country culture (e.g., understanding of host-culture social system and values, etc.; Black & Mendenhall, 1990; Deshpande & Viswesvaran, 1992; Mendenhall & Oddou, 1985). Importantly, research confirms that cross-cultural training is effective in promoting expatriate adjustment (Black & Mendenhall, 1990; Deshpande & Viswesvaran, 1992).

Performance on the Global Assignment

Upon immersion into a novel culture and work context, the expatriate is required not only to carry out the technical aspects of his or her job, but also to operate within a completely new context, with new individuals and new cultural requirements. Successful performance thus requires the ability to perform one's job while simultaneously adapting to these new requirements both in and out of the work context. Research suggests cultural adjustment (work and nonwork) to the host country is an important predictor of successful expatriate performance in overseas operations (Black & Mendenhall, 1990). Adjustment, although a gradual process, is fostered when the expatriate is offered predeparture and postarrival cross-cultural training (Selmer et al., 1998). In order to accurately evaluate expatriate performance, expatriate adjustment must also be taken into consideration.

Completion of the Global Assignment

Not surprisingly, the most salient indicator of expatriate success on a global assignment (and also a valuable criterion for expatriate training program evaluation) is whether or not the expatriate successfully completes the global assignment. Frequently, performance deficiencies or adjustment problems (on the part of the expatriate or his or her spouse or family) cause the expatriate or organization to prematurely terminate the assignment. Research suggests that when expatriates are provided with sufficient predeparture preparation and timely during-assignment training, the potential for successful completion of the global assignment is significantly enhanced (e.g., Black & Mendenhall, 1990; Caligiuri, 2000; Caudron, 1991; Garonzik, Brockner, & Siegel, 2000; Gregersen & Black, 1990; Selmer et al., 1998; Tung, 1981; 1988; 1998).

A summary of research findings regarding expatriate training is provided in Table 10.3. Further, Table 10.4 highlights broad world region differences in research findings and expatriation practice. For example, whereas U.S. MNCs typically have very short-term perspectives regarding expatriate preparation (typically implementing only "quick fix" or canned training programs, such as videos and information on the host country, short language preparation courses, etc.), Asian MNCs tend to plan farthest in advance of an expatriate assignment, facilitating an implementation of longer-term expatriate preparation initiatives (e.g., mentoring, language immersion programs, and graduate or professional training programs). European MNCs offer a unique focus on managing the expatriation process. These corporations often staff human resources representatives that are dedicated solely to expatriate preparation and management, improving the potential training initiatives will be tailored to the expatriate's needs.

REPATRIATION

One fifth of returning expatriates intend to leave their organization upon return; less than half receive a promotion upon return; two thirds feel the assignment had a negative impact on their career; half feel the reentry position is less satisfying than was the overseas assignment (Hammer, Hart, & Rogan, 1998). Still, repatriation remains the least carefully considered component of the management of international assignees. Ill-prepared repatriates are much more likely to leave their parent company upon return, an exceptionally costly form of turnover for the organization (Stroh et al., 2005; Stroh, Gregersen, & Black, 1998). Current estimates of repatriate turnover suggest that over one quarter of repatriates leave their companies within 2 years of repatriation (Oddou & Mendenhall, 1991; Stroh et al., 2005). Moreover, these repatriates often seek employment with competing organizations. When the international experience was provided as part of a managerial succession plan, a repatriate's turnover can be particularly devastating (i.e., the long-term goals of many MNCs involve the creation of globally experienced managers). High repatriate failure rates

TABLE 10.3

Expatriate Training: Current Research Findings

It is estimated that 90% of expatriates receive no predeparture cross-cultural training.

The most common forms of expatriate predeparture training include watching videos, reading books, and talking with current or past expatriates (Welch & Welch, 1997).

Research has identified five main areas of expatriate training: (1) area studies programs, (2) cultural assimilators, (3) language training, (4) cultural sensitivity training, and (5) field experience. Specific expatriate training methods include area briefings, lectures, books, films, classroom language training, case studies, interactive language training, role-plays, field trips, and simulations. The best method (or combination of methods) is contingent upon the cultural distance between the home and host country, the expatriate's experience with similar cultures, the readiness of the expatriate and the expatriate's family to commence with an international assignment. The utility of expatriate training methods appears to increase as the rigor of the method and the time invested in training increases.

Expatriate adjustment to international assignments includes two main components: (1) psychological adjustment and (2) sociocultural adjustment. Psychological adjustment involves the affective or perceived psychological well-being of the expatriate. This facet of adjustment is heavily influenced by the adjustment of the spouse. Sociocultural adjustment involves the expatriate's evaluation of how well he or she fits in with the host-country workforce. This may include perceived/actual adjustment to work, adjustment to interaction with the host-country nationals, and adjustment to the general nonwork environment.

Antecedents to adjustment may include (1) expatriate language skills, (2) past international work experience, (3) length of time on expatriate assignment, (4) host-country cultural distance/difference, (5) predeparture training content, rigor, and time investment, and (6) family adjustment.

Predictors or facilitators of adjustment may include (1) content and rigor of predeparture training, (2) previous overseas experience, (3) organization selection criteria, (4) individual characteristics of the expatriate, (5) cultural distance/difficulty of the host country, and (6) family adjustment. Research also suggests that expatriate training programs must take into account that adjustment occurs in two key phases: (1) anticipatory adjustment and (2) in-country adjustment. Anticipatory adjustment should be addressed in predeparture training; in-country adjustment develops through continued socialization and training during the expatriate assignment.

Personality characteristics, like openness to experience and sociability, may have implications for the effectiveness of expatriate training in promoting cross-cultural adjustment.

"One-size-fits-all" approaches to expatriate training are ill-advised (Vance & Paik, 2002).

---

are most likely a function of ill-conceived repatriation plans on the part of the organization. Insufficient attention to repatriation occurs because top management fails to realize that repatriation may represent a similar shock to the repatriate (and spouse) as was experienced during the initial expatriation (Tung, 1988). Neglecting this aspect of the expatriate management process only increases the potential for unreturned investment. A summary of key findings from the research and practice of expatriate repatriation is provided in Table 10.5.

MAJOR ISSUES IN REPATRIATION OF EXPATRIATES

Organizations select, train, and send expatriates for several reasons (Boyacigiller, 1990). Organizations may be attempting to fill positions overseas for which locals with required technical skills are not available. In the recent years of rapid development across the world, such shortages are less likely. It is more likely that organizations employ expatriates to develop managers with global mindsets (Black & Gregersen, 1999). This objective is unlikely to be met if expatriates quit the organization on return from the overseas assignment. Empirical data suggest a large percentage of returning expatriates quit their jobs within two years of their return (Hammer et al., 1998).

The high quit rate of repatriates reflects the oft-cited adjustment difficulties that they encounter upon return, which are typically unforeseen (Caligiuri, Joshi, & Lazarova, 1999). On the one hand, the expatriates have high expectations about career advancements due to their successful completion

TABLE 10.4
Expatriate Training: World Region-Specific Findings

Asia & Australia

Chinese employees tend to prefer more long-term relationships with their mentors than is common in Western countries; Expatriate managers may be expected to maintain both a work-focused and a long-term personal mentoring relationship well beyond the length of the international assignment.

Chinese are used to a more authoritative parental mode in teaching/training.

Japanese companies typically plan far in advance of an international assignment and use the time prior to expatriation to thoroughly prepare the expatriate for the assignment. In fact, 86% of Japanese MNCs have expatriate failure rates of below 10%.

Training of Japanese expatriates for international assignments typically takes place in both formal and informal, classroom and social situations. The trainer typically functions as a participant-observer and informal lecturer/interpreter. Trainers are expected to possess a competency in the target culture (Goldman, 1992).

Japanese MNCs provide both the expatriate and spouse with extensive language skills training, which typically includes a language-immersion element.

Japanese MNCs also make use of ongoing mentoring relationships between the expatriate and both home- and host-country managers. Company time is devoted to the preparation and ongoing training of the expatriate.

The Japanese have unique perspectives on the preparation of expatriates: (1) the expatriate manager must develop skills to facilitate effective performance in new subordinate relationships and in new political, regulatory, and market environments; (2) the expatriate and his or her family must develop coping skills for the new culture and must learn to accept, enjoy, and respect the potentially unfamiliar and inconvenient customs of the host culture.

Japanese MNCs offer employees the opportunity to attend graduate and professional training programs abroad. This fosters the development of cross-cultural skills well in advance of potential expatriate assignments.

Europe & the United Kingdom

European MNCs typically provide cross-cultural skills and language training to both the expatriate and his or her spouse.

European MNCs utilize repatriates in the expatriate training/preparation process, and establish longer-term mentoring relations.

The cultural assimilator method of expatriate training has been quite effective in preparing European expatriates for international assignments.

Many European MNCs have created specific organizational functions with the primary objective of selecting, training, monitoring, and managing expatriate positions.

Africa & the Middle East

Many expatriates to Africa and the Middle East report feeling isolated from the host-country culture. These expatriates and their families typically live in compounds isolated from the host-country nationals. The training requirements for these expatriates differ from those who will be living and operating exclusively within the host country.

North America

North American expatriates who endorse more culturally appropriate interpersonal skills and cognitions are most successful on international assignments; personnel with past international experience were more likely to use culturally appropriate behaviors and cognitions.

Research suggests that U.S. MNCs have some of the highest expatriate failure rates. U.S. MNCs typically have the short-sighted view of expatriate training programs as a waste of valuable resources due to the temporary nature of the expatriate assignment. Training should be modeled after more successful foreign MNCs, and include a focus on developing cross-cultural skills; the intensity of training should be contingent upon the expatriate's own experience with the specific culture and the degree of difference between the home and host cultures.

U.S. expatriates who reported feeling under little pressure to conform to the host-country culture were more satisfied with the international assignment.

North American MNCs do not make sufficient use of realistic job previews and do not provide sufficient cross-cultural training when preparing expatriates for international assignments.

TABLE 10.5
Repatriation: Current Research Findings

Common problems reported/experienced by repatriates: (1) loss of status, (2) loss of autonomy, (3) loss of career direction, (4) low value placed on the value of international experience by top management, (5) inability to use new skills gained in the international assignment.

Repatriation may be a more difficult experience than the initial expatriation because (1) the expatriate has a different/ inaccurate expectation regarding the difficulty of adjustment, (2) whereas the host-country workforce expected the expatriate to act differently than the host-country workforce, the home country does not have the same expectations, and (3) the expatriate expects change when leaving the home country but not when returning to it. The potential for these experiences increases with the length of time of the international assignment.

Potential predictors of successful repatriation include (1) individual factors, like age, previous intercultural experience, etc., (2) job factors, like length of assignment, the frequency and intimacy of social relations with host-country nationals, (3) organizational factors, like culture, perceived value placed on international experience, and (4) nonwork factors, like family and spouse adjustment.

of the overseas assignment. The experience of living and working abroad has most likely altered how the repatriates think and act (Brett, Stroh, & Reilly, 1993) and this, coupled with changes in the parent company during their absence, necessitates readjustment. Given that most organizations do not explicitly address this difference between expectations and reality, there is more likelihood of turnover. Organizations should attempt to provide mentors, career counseling, and other supportive services to actively prevent turnover and the subsequent loss of global expertise. More research in this area is needed, especially that which focuses on the best ways to foster successful repatriation, the design and evaluation of repatriation programs, and methods by which candidates for unsuccessful repatriation may be preemptively targeted.

Regional differences in repatriation programs are highlighted in Table 10.6. In general, repatriation efforts appear to be relatively uncommon within European and North American MNCs.

TABLE 10.6
Repatriation: World Region-Specific Research Findings

Europe & the United Kingdom

Few European MNCs implement formal repatriation programs, even though repatriates report a need/desire for such programs. Upon repatriation, U.K. repatriates report feeling a loss of status, loss of autonomy, loss of career direction, and a feeling that international experience is undervalued by the company.

North America

North American expatriate tenure with the MNC is predictive of successful repatriation.

U.S. expatriates guaranteed (desirable) positions/assignments upon return to the home country were most satisfied during the repatriation process.

Research suggests the most important factor relevant to reentry satisfaction of North American repatriates is spouse satisfaction with reentry and spouse ability to readjust to the home country. Other important factors include the degree to which the returning expatriate experiences "reverse culture shock," whether they are returning to the same location or whether relocation within the home country will be required, and whether the spouse is able to retain satisfactory employment in the home country.

Few North American MNCs implement formal repatriation programs, even though repatriates report a need for such programs. Upon repatriation, many U.S. repatriates report a feeling a loss of status, loss of autonomy, loss of career direction, and a feeling that international experience is undervalued by the company.

Few reports of repatriation practices from other world regions are available, indicating a need for future research.

FUTURE RESEARCH DIRECTIONS IN EXPATRIATE MANAGEMENT

STAFFING EXPATRIATES

Staffing is a central function in human resources management; hence the adage, "the people make the place" (Schneider, 1987). Therefore, a voluminous literature exists on personnel selection in domestic contexts. The literature on expatriate selection is more recent and an attempt was made here to review the findings reported in the extant literature. In this section, we hypothesize some promising new predictors, the need to develop comprehensive taxonomies of criteria, and the need to consider the applicant perspective in selection.

One predictor that appears to have potential value to expatriate selection is emotional intelligence (EI). Although the discussion of EI has increased in the 1990s (Goleman, 1995), the concept has been around for many decades under different labels, such as social intelligence (Thorndike, 1937), and interpersonal and intrapersonal intelligences (Gardner, 1983). The writings on EI can be grouped into two distinct camps (Van Rooy & Viswesvaran, 2004). In one camp, EI is conceptualized as an ability to recognize emotions, understand emotions (both one's own as well as others), and manage the emotions (Salovey, Brackett, & Mayer, 2004). Alternately, EI has also been conceptualized as a constellation of different personality traits (e.g., empathy; Bar-On & Parker, 2000). Both conceptualizations of EI are likely to be useful predictors of expatriate success. The comprehensive models reviewed here of the antecedents of expatriate success have components that reflect EI (Arthur & Bennett, 1995; Tung, 1981). Future research should assess the incremental validity of EI for predicting expatriate success beyond traditional individual differences variables, such as intelligence and personality. In fact, one need for future research is to assess the incremental validity of the plethora of predictors hypothesized in the extant literature as predictors of expatriate success.

On a related note, research is needed to develop theories of job performance. Several dimensions of performance have been postulated and future research should identify the links between the dimensions. For example, research should investigate whether adjustment results in performance or whether adjustment reduces turnover, which in turn improves unit performance. Another research question revolves around how individual performance is linked to organizational and team/unit performance. In extending our inferences to organizational performance the mediating and moderating effects of environmental variables need to be considered.

Research in expatriate selection has focused on the validity of different predictors or sets of predictors. However, the interaction of these predictors with organizational policies needs to be considered. For example, consider an organization that provides high pay for expatriate assignments. Many individuals (both high and low in openness to experience) will apply for the job. Alternately, an organization that does not provide high pay for expatriate assignments will attract only individuals seeking novelty to apply for these openings. This restriction of range in openness to experience will lower the estimated validity of this predictor in the second organization. Similarly, an organization that uses expatriate assignments for developing future leaders may have a restriction in the ambition scores of the applicants (with a subsequent lowering of validity for ambition). In short, the interaction between organizational motives for expatriate assignments, individual motives and predictors should be explicitly considered.

There is also a dearth of research on applicant reactions to selection procedures used in expatriate management. Researchers have identified several determinants and consequences of applicant reactions to personnel selection procedures (see the Special Issue of the *International Journal of Selection and Assessment*, 2005, for a review). Future research should address whether there are notable differences in expatriate selection. A summary of potentially profitable research questions is provided in Table 10.7.

TABLE 10.7
Expatriate Selection: Questions for Future Research

Is research on realistic job previews (RJPs) relevant to the expatriate selection process? Are RJPs useful in promoting expatriate success? How might past repatriates be employed in this process?

When is it better to fill an international position with a host-country national? What are the potential problems with this approach? What recommendations can be made to practitioners about addressing such issues?

Nonwork issues are understudied with regards to expatriate success. How do variables like dual careering, marital status/ family situation, and spousal support impact expatriate success? Should these factors be incorporated into the selection process?

The career orientation of expatriates is thought to be a crucial predictor of expatriate success. How might this variable be incorporated into expatriate selection models?

What are the antecedents of accepting international assignments? (Antecedents may include perceptions regarding career mobility or advancement, financial benefit, lack of other domestic opportunities, etc.). How do these reasons for accepting an international assignment impact the potential for expatriate success? What actions might be taken on the part of the organization to ensure that the expatriate accepts the position for the "right" reasons? (Selmer, 1998; Stahl, Miller, & Tung, 2002).

What role should the expatriate's spouse/family play in the selection process?

What role should the host-country workforce play in the selection process? How might surveys of the host-country workforce be utilized to select expatriates?

Can research findings relevant to the concept of person-environment fit be applied to expatriate research?

Can general selection research be applied to expatriates? Most expatriate research has focused on identifying the predictors/ criteria unique to expatriates. This focus, for the most part, has not yielded standard models for expatriate selection.

EXPATRIATE MANAGEMENT

Much research in the area of expatriate training has been prescriptive in nature, focusing on potential training methodologies and implementation strategies unique to the expatriate function (e.g., cross-cultural experiences, adjustment to host-country culture, etc.; Black & Mendenhall, 1989; Mendenhall et al., 1987; Stroh et al., 2005). Interestingly, there has been little effort to integrate research relevant to expatriate management with the more general literature on employee training and development. It is true that expatriates face unique challenges in the execution of their work assignments and thus comprehensive expatriate training programs require an added dimension that may not be required for many other job functions. It is unfortunate that expatriate researchers have not made use of the general learning and training principles explored within the extant training literature (e.g., Alliger & Janak, 1989; Goldstein & Ford, 2002; Kraiger, Ford, & Salas, 1993).

To advance our understanding of the design, implementation, and evaluation of expatriate training, it would be prudent for future research to assimilate the "tried and true" principles of training with the specificity of the expatriate function. Future researchers might consider how general training models (i.e., Goldstein & Ford, 2002) can be assimilated to expatriate research. On a similar note, the role of competent needs assessments prior to training has been neglected in the literature on expatriate training. Researchers might consider how this phase of the training process is unique for the expatriate function. Further, given the apparent importance of individual-level variables in expatriate success (i.e., expatriate adjustment), how should the "person analysis" component of the needs assessment process be approached?

Other related research questions or directions are summarized in Table 10.8. Space considerations do not allow an in-depth discussion of each direction here. However, a few avenues for future research in expatriate training may have particular potential for advancing our understanding in this area. For example, research in the area of expatriate training has focused in large part on ways in which expatriates may best be prepared to adapt to the culture of the host country. Research in organizational training has identified a number of individual difference variables (e.g., cognitive ability, learning styles, emotional

TABLE 10.8

Expatriate Training: Questions for Future Research

How might current research in the areas of training and development inform expatriate research? Can general training models (i.e., Goldstein & Ford, 2002) be incorporated into research on expatriates? Might these models serve as a basic framework for training expatriates? (See Vance, Boje, & Stage, 1991.)

How might past repatriates be employed in the preparation of future expatriates? Can research findings relevant to mentoring and organizational socialization be applied to the expatriate situation?

How might research relevant to the concept of person-environment fit be applied to expatriate research?

What are the implications of involving the host-country workforce in the training of expatriates? Should the host-country workforce receive training prior to the arrival of an expatriate? What form should such training take? (Toh & DeNisi, 2005; Vance & Paderon, 1993).

How does parent company culture impact perceptions of the host-country workforce?

What implications do the differences between more developed and less developed nations have for the training of expatriates?

Is it realistic for organizations to expect expatriates to engage in multiple international assignments? If no, then what are the implications for expatriate management? If yes, how might these individuals ("nomadic globetrotters") be selected and trained?

The role of competent needs assessments prior to training have been neglected in the literature on expatriate training. Is this phase of the training process unique for the expatriate function? Specifically, given the apparent importance of individual-level variables in expatriate success (e.g., expatriate and spouse adjustment), how should the person analysis component of the needs assessment process be approached?

How should expatriate training be evaluated? What are the most relevant/important criteria for success? How might training evaluation differ depending upon specific characteristics of the assignment and the host country?

How should the expatriate's spouse/family be involved in the preparation process? Do the training needs of the spouse/ family differ from those of the expatriate? How should spouse/family training be evaluated?

intelligence, personality, motivation to learn, etc.) with the potential of moderating the effectiveness of training programs and approaches (e.g., Ackerman, 1987; Anderson, 1996; Arthur, Bennett, Edens, & Bell, 2003; Baldwin & Ford, 1988; Colquitt, LePine, & Noe, 2000). The effects of such variables have not been examined with regard to the efficacy of expatriate training. Future research on the impact of individual difference variables in expatriate training will most certainly enhance our understanding of the expatriate preparation process.

TABLE 10.9

Repatriation: Questions for Future Research

What role does the organization have in the repatriation process? How might a "repatriation preparation program" be designed? What is the most appropriate content for such a program? What is the most appropriate delivery method?

Who should be targeted for repatriation preparation? How should successful repatriation be promoted? Evaluated?

How should "functional" and "dysfunctional" repatriate turnover be operationalized? What are the implications for repatriation management? Specifically, successful repatriation is typically evaluated using repatriate turnover as the key criterion. Functional and dysfunctional turnover are typically aggregated in these analyses.

Are there any individual difference variables predictive of repatriation success? If yes, should these be considered in expatriate selection? Training?

Most research in repatriation has been conducted using student samples. What implications does this artifact have for conclusions drawn about organizational repatriates?

How might past repatriates be incorporated into the repatriation process?

Can research on organizational socialization inform repatriation research?

Second, many researchers have called for the implementation of predeparture training for the expatriate's spouse and family, citing the high occurrence of expatriate failure resulting from the inability of the expatriate's spouse or family to adjust to the host-country culture (e.g., Tung, 1981). Many organizations have cited monetary and time-related constraints as justification for not providing such training. Future research focused on understanding and assessing the efficacy, utility, and cost-effectiveness of spouse and family predeparture training, as well as research exploring the design, implementation, and evaluation of such training, may well further our understanding in this area, as well as provide human resource practitioners with evidence necessary to justify such expense.

A final research area with great promise to benefit the practice of expatriate management is the utilization of repatriates in formal expatriate mentoring programs. Researchers might explore how research in the areas of mentoring, career development, and organizational socialization relate to the expatriate function. A summary of questions for future research in the repatriation of expatriates is provided in Table 10.9.

CONCLUSION

In closing, we are reminded that there are five components to effective people management; they are clearly applicable to the management of expatriates: (a) select the right people, (b) train people to be successful, (c) appraise their performance so that additional guidance and appropriate training can be offered, (d) reward desired performance, and (e) develop people so they may progress along their desired career path. For expatriate employees, this fifth step includes planning how an international assignment will help expatriates advance through their career, providing expatriates with the training and support important to success during and after the international assignment, competently repatriating returning expatriates into the home country and organizational culture, and placing them in positions where they will be able to make use of the experience they acquired while overseas (Stroh et al., 2005).

REFERENCES

Ackerman, P. L. (1987). Individual differences in skill learning: An integration of psychometric and information processing perspectives. *Psychological Bulletin, 102*(1), 3–27.

Adler, N. J. (1987). Pacific Basin managers: A Gaijin, not a woman. *Human Resource Management, 26,* 169–191.

Adler, N. J. (1991). *International dimensions of organizational behavior* (2nd ed). Boston: PWS-Kent.

Alliger, G. M., & Janak, E. A. (1989). Kirkpatrick's levels of training criteria: Thirty years later. *Personnel Psychology, 42,* 331–342.

Allport, G. W. (1954). *The nature of prejudice*. Cambridge, MA: Addison-Wesley.

Anderson, J. R. (1996). Skill acquisition: Compilation of weak-method problem solutions. *Psychological Review, 94,* 192–210.

Arthur, W., Jr., & Bennett, W., Jr. (1995). The international assignee: The relative importance of factors perceived to contribute to success. *Personnel Psychology, 48,* 99–114.

Arthur, W., Jr., Bennett, W., Jr., Edens, P. S., & Bell, S. T. (2003). Effectiveness of training in organizations: A meta-analysis of design and evaluation features. *Journal of Applied Psychology, 88*(2), 234–245.

Austin, J. T., & Villanova, P. (1992). The criterion problem: 1917–1992. *Journal of Applied Psychology, 77,* 836–874.

Aycan, Z. (1997). Expatriate adjustment as a multifaceted phenomenon: Individual and organizational level predictors. *International Journal of Human Resource Management, 8*(4), 434–456.

Baldwin, T. T., & Ford, J. K. (1988). Transfer of training: A review and directions for future research. *Personnel Psychology, 41,* 63–105.

Bar-On, R., & Parker, J. D. A. (Eds.). (2000). *The handbook of emotional intelligence*. San Francisco: Jossey-Bass.

Barrick, M. R., & Mount, M. K. (1991). The Big Five personality dimensions and job performance: A meta-analysis. *Personnel Psychology, 44,* 1–26.

Beamish, P. W., & Inkpen, A. C. (1998). Japanese firms and the decline of the Japanese expatriate. *Journal of World Business, 33*(1), 35–50.

Beehr, T. A. (1995). How job stress is teated. In L. R. Murphy, J. J. Hurrell, Jr., S. L. Sauter, & G. P. Keita (eds.), *Job Stress Interventions*. Washington, DC: American Psychological Association.

Bhawuk, D. P. S. (1998). The role of culture theory in cross-cultural training: A multimethod study of culture-specific, culture-general, and culture theory-based assimilators. *Journal of Cross-Cultural Psychology, 29*(5), 630–655.

Bhuian, S. N., & Menguc, B. (2002). An extension and evaluation of job characteristics, organizational commitment, and job satisfaction in an expatriate, guest worker, sales setting. *Journal of Personal Selling and Sales Management, 22*(1), 1–11.

Birdseye, M. G., & Hill, J. S. (1995). Individual, organizational/work and environmental influences on expatriate turnover tendencies: An empirical study. *Journal of International Business Studies, 26,* 787–813.

Black, J. S., & Gregersen, H. B. (1991). Antecedents to cross-cultural adjustment for expatriates in Pacific Rim assignments. *Human Relations, 44*(5), 497–515.

Black, J. S., & Gregersen, H. B. (1999). The right way to manage expats. *Harvard Business Review, 77*(2), 52–62.

Black, J. S., & Mendenhall, M. (1989). A practical but theory-based framework for selecting cross-cultural training methods. *Human Resource Management, 28*(4), 511–539.

Black, J. S., & Mendenhall, M. (1990). Cross-cultural training effectiveness: A review and a theoretical framework for future research. *Academy of Management Review, 15*(1), 113–136.

Black, J. S., Mendenhall, M., & Oddou, G. (1991). Toward a comprehensive model of international adjustment: An integration of multiple theoretical perspectives. *Academy of Management Review, 16*(2), 291–317.

Black, J. S., & Stephens, G. K. (1989). The influence of the spouse on American expatriate adjustment and the intent to stay in Pacific Rim overseas assignments. *Journal of Management, 15*(4), 529–544.

Boyacigiller, N. (1990). The role of expatriates in the management of interdependence, complexity, and risk in multinational corporations. *Journal of International Business Studies, 21,* 357–381.

Brett, J. M., Stroh, L. K., & Reilly, A. H. (1993). Pulling up roots in the 1990s: Who's willing to relocate? *Journal of Organizational Behavior, 14*(1), 49–60.

Brewster, C., & Pickard, J. (1994). Evaluating expatriate training. *International Studies of Management and Organization, 24*(3), 18–35.

Brislin, R. W. (1981). *Cross-cultural encounters: Face-to-face interaction*. New York: Pergamon Press.

Caligiuri, P. M. (1997). The Big Five personality characteristics as predictors of expatriate's desire to terminate the assignment and supervisor-rated performance. *Personnel Psychology, 53,* 67–88.

Caligiuri, P. M. (2000). Selecting expatriates for personality characteristics: A moderating effect of personality on the relationship between host national contact and cross-cultural adjustment. *Management International Review, 40,* 61–80.

Caligiuri, P. M., Hyland, M. M., Joshi, A., & Bross, A. S. (1998). Testing a theoretical model for examining the relationship between family adjustment and expatriates' work adjustment. *Journal of Applied Psychology, 83*(4), 598–614.

Caligiuri, P. M., Joshi, A., & Lazarova, M. (1999). Factors influencing the adjustment of women on global assignments. *International Journal of Human Resource Management, 10*(2), 163–179.

Campbell, J. P. (1990). Modeling the performance prediction problem in industrial and organizational psychology. In M. D. Dunnette & L. M. Hough (Eds.), *Handbook of industrial and organizational psychology* (2nd ed., Vol. 1, pp. 687–732). Palo Alto, CA: Consulting Psychologists Press.

Campbell, J. P., McCloy, R. A., Oppler, S. H., & Sager, C. E. (1992). A theory of performance. In N. Schmitt & W. C. Borman (Eds.), *Personnel selection in organizations* (pp. 35–70). San Francisco: Jossey Bass.

Carpenter, M. A., Sanders, W. G., & Gregersen, H. B. (2001). Building human capital with organizational context: The impact of international experience on multinational firm performance and CEO pay. *Academy of Management Journal, 44,* 493–511.

Caudron, S. (1991). Training ensures success overseas: Providing employees and their families with cross-cultural training before they're sent overseas can help prevent costly expatriate failures. *Personnel Journal, 70*(12), 27–30.

Colquitt, J. A., LePine, J. A., & Noe, R. A. (2002). Toward an integrative theory of training motivation: A meta-analytic path analysis of 20 years of research. *Journal of Applied Psychology, 85*(5), 678–707.

Copeland, L., & Griggs, L. (1988). The internationable employee. *Management Review, 77,* 52–53.

Costa, P. T., Jr., & McCrae, R. R. (1992). Four ways the five factors are basic. *Personality and Individual Differences, 13,* 653–665.

Deller, J. (August 9–14, 1998). *Personality scales can make a difference in expatriate selection: The case of Germans working in Korea.* A paper presented at the International Congress of Applied Psychology, San Francisco, CA.

Deshpande, S. P., & Viswesvaran, C. (1992). Is cross-cultural training of expatriate managers effective: A meta-analysis. *International Journal of Intercultural Relations, 16*(2), 295–310.

Dicken, C. F., & Black, J. D. (1965). Predictive validity of psychometric evaluations of supervisors. *Journal of Applied Psychology, 49,* 34–47.

Dunbar, E. (1992). Adjustment and satisfaction of expatriate U.S. personnel. *International Journal of Intercultural Relations, 16,* 1–16.

Feldman, D. C., & Thomas, D. C. (1991). Career management issues facing expatriates. *Journal of International Business Studies, 23,* 271–293.

Fiedler, F. E., & Mitchell, T. (1971). The culture assimilator: An approach to cross-cultural training. *Journal of Applied Psychology, 55*(2), 95–102.

Fukuda, K. J., & Chu, P. (1994). Wrestling with expatriate family problems: Japanese experience in East Asia. *International Studies of Management and Organization, 24*(3), 36–47.

Gardner, H. (1983). *Frames of mind: The theory of multiple intelligences.* New York: Basic Books.

Garonzik, R., Brockner, J., & Siegel, P. A. (2000). Identifying international assignees at risk for premature departure: The interactive effect of outcome favorability and procedural fairness. *Journal of Applied Psychology, 85*(1), 13–20.

Goldberg, L. R. (1993). The structure of phenotypic personality traits. *American Psychologist, 48,* 26–34.

Goldman, A. (1992). Intercultural training of Japanese for U.S.-Japanese interorganizational communication. *International Journal of Intercultural Relations, 16,* 195–215.

Goldstein, I. L., & Ford, J. K. (2002). *Training in organizations* (4th ed.). Belmont, CA: Wadsworth.

Goleman, D. (1995). *Emotional intelligence: Why it can matter more than IQ.* New York: Bantam.

Graf, A., & Harland, L. K. (2005). Expatriate selection: Evaluating the discriminant, convergent and predictive validity of five measures of interpersonal and intercultural competence. *Journal of Leadership and Organizational Studies, 11*(2), 46–62.

Gregersen, H. B., & Black, J. S. (1990). A multifaceted approach to expatriate retention in international assignments. *Group & Organization Studies, 15*(4), 461–485.

Gregersen, H. B., & Black, J. S. (1992). Antecedents to commitment to a parent company and a foreign operation. *Academy of Management Journal, 35*(1), 65–90.

Gudykunst, W., Hammer, M., & Wiseman, R. (1977). An analysis of an integrated approach to cross-cultural training. *International Journal of Intercultural Relations. 1*(2), 99–110.

Hammer, M. R., Hart, W., & Rogan, R. (1998). Can you go home again? An analysis of the repatriation of corporate managers and spouses. *Management International Review, 38,* 67–86.

Harris, J. G. Jr., (1973). A science of the South Pacific: Analysis of the character structure of the Peace Corps volunteer. *American Psychologist, 28,* 232–247.

Hays, R. D. (1974). Expatriate selection: Insuring success and avoiding failure. *Journal of International Business Studies, 5,* 25–37.

Hechanova, R., Beehr, T. A., & Christiansen, N. D. (2003). Antecedents and consequences of employees' adjustment to overseas assignment: A meta-analytic review. *Applied Psychology: An International Review, 52*(2), 213–236.

Hogan, R., Hogan, J., & Roberts, B. W. (1996). Personality measurement and employment decisions: Questions and answers. *American Psychologist, 51,* 469–477.

Hunt, S. T. (1996). Generic work behavior: An investigation into the dimensions of entry-level, hourly job performance. *Personnel Psychology, 49,* 51–83.

Jackson, S. E., & Schuler, R. S. (1985). A meta-analysis and a conceptual critique of research on role ambiguity and role conflict in work settings. *Organizational Decision and Human Decision Processes, 36,* 16–78.

Kealey, D. J. (1989). A study of cross-cultural effectiveness: Theoretical issues, practical applications. *International Journal of Intercultural Relations, 13,* 387–428.

Kraiger, K., Ford, J. K., & Salas, E. (1993). Application of cognitive, skill-based, and affective theories of learning outcomes to new methods of training evaluation. *Journal of Applied Psychology, 78*(2), 311–328.

Kraimer, M. L., Wayne, S. J., & Jaworski, R. A. (2001). Sources of support and expatriate performance: The mediating role of expatriate adjustment. *Personnel Psychology, 54,* 71–99.

Landis, D., & Brislin, R. (1983). *Handbook on intercultural training* (Vol. 1). Elmsford, NY: Pergamon Press.

Mendenhall, M. E., & Oddou, G. R. (1985). The dimensions of expatriate acculturation: A review. *Academy of Management Review, 10,* 39–47.

Mendenhall, M. E., Dunbar, E., & Oddou, G. R. (1987). Expatriate selection, training and career-pathing: A review and critique. *Human Resource Management, 26*(3), 331–345.

Mervosh, E. M., & McClenahen, J. S. (1997). The care and feeding of expats. *Industry Week, 246*(22), 68–72.

Miller, E. L., & Cheng, J. L. C. (1978). A closer look at the decision to accept an overseas position. *Management International Review, 18,* 25–34.

Naumann, E. (1992). A conceptual model of expatriate turnover. *Journal of International Business Studies, 23,* 499–531.

Oddou, G. R., & Mendenhall, M. E. (1991). Succession planning for the 21st century: How well are we grooming our future business leaders? *Business Horizons,* 26–34.

Ones, D. S., & Viswesvaran, C. (1997). Personality determinants in the prediction of aspects of expatriate job success. In D. M. Saunder (Series Ed.) & Z. Aycan (Vol. Ed.), *New approaches to employee management. Vol. 4. Expatriate management: Theory and research* (pp. 63–92). Greenwich, CT: JAI Press.

Ones, D. S., & Viswesvaran, C. (1999). Relative importance of personality dimensions for expatriate selection: A policy capturing study. *Human Performance, 12*(3/4), 275–294.

Ones, D. S., Viswesvaran, C., & Dilchert, S. (2005). Intelligence testing in applied settings: Issues and opportunities. In O. Wilhelm & R. W. Engle (Eds.), *Handbook of understanding and measuring intelligence* (pp. 431–468). London: Sage.

Pazy, A., & Zeira, Y. (1985). Compatibility of expectations in training parent-country managers and professionals in host-country organizations. *International Studies of Management and Organization, 15*(1), 75–93.

Salgado, J. F. (1997). The Five Factor model of personality and job performance in the European Community. *Journal of Applied Psychology, 82,* 30–43.

Salovey, P., Brackett, M. A., & Mayer, J. D. (Eds.). (2004). *Emotional intelligence: Key readings on the Mayer and Salovey model.* Port Chester, NY: National Professional Resources, Inc.

Schmidt, F. L. (2002). The role of general cognitive ability and job performance: Why there cannot be a debate. *Human Performance, 15,* 187–210.

Schmidt, F. L., & Hunter, J. E. (1998). The validity and utility of selection methods in personnel psychology: Practical and theoretical implications of 85 years of research findings. *Psychological Bulletin, 124,* 262–274.

Schmitt, N., & Chan, D. (1998). *Personnel selection.* Thousand Oaks, CA: Sage.

Schneider, B. (1987). The people make the place. *Personnel Psychology, 40,* 437–453.

Scullion, H. (1994). Staffing policies and strategic control in British multinationals. *International Studies of Management and Organization, 24*(4), 86–104.

Selmer, J. (1998). Expatriation: Corporate policy, personal intentions, and international adjustment. *International Journal of Human Resource Management, 9*(6), 996–1007.

Selmer, J. (2004a). Expatriates' hesitation and the localization of Western business operations in China. *International Journal of Human Resource Management, 15*(6), 1094–1107.

Selmer, J. (2004b). Psychological barriers to adjustment of Western business expatriates in China: Newcomers vs. long stayers. *International Journal of Human Resource Management, 15*(4), 794–813.

Selmer, J., & Leung, A. (2003). Personal characteristics of female vs. male business expatriates. *International Journal of Cross-Cultural Management, 3*(2), 195–212.

Selmer, J., Torbiorn, I., & deLeon, C. T. (1998). Sequential cross-cultural training for expatriate business managers: Pre-departure and post-arrival. *International Journal of Human Resource Management, 9*(5), 831–840.

Sergent, A., & Frenkel, S. (1998). Managing people in China: Perceptions of expatriate managers. *Journal of World Business, 33*(1), 17–34.

Shaffer, M. A., & Harrison, D. A. (1998). Expatriates' psychological withdrawal from international assignments: Work, nonwork, and family influences. *Personnel Psychology, 51,* 87–118.

Sinangil, H. K., & Ones, D. S. (1998, August). *Personality correlates of expatriate adjustment in Turkey.* Paper presented at the International Congress of Applied Psychology, San Francisco, CA.

Sinangil, H. K., & Ones, D. S. (2001). Expatriate management. In N. Anderson, D. S. Ones, H. K. Sinangil, & C. Viswesvaran (Eds.), *Handbook of industrial, work and organizational psychology: Organizational psychology* (pp. 424–443). Thousand Oaks, CA: Sage.

Stahl, G. K., Miller, E. L., & Tung, R. L. (2002). Toward a boundaryless career: A closer look at the expatriate career concept and the perceived implications of an international assignment. *Journal of World Business, 37,* 216–227.

Stroh, L. K., Black, J. S., Mendenhall, M. E., & Gregersen, H. B. (2005). *International assignments: An integration of strategy, research and practice.* Mahwah, NJ: Lawrence Erlbaum Associates.

Stroh, L. K., Gregersen, H. B., & Black, J. S. (1998). Closing the gap: Expectations versus reality among repatriates. *Journal of World Business, 33*(2), 111–124.

Takeuchi, R., Tesluk, P. E., Yun, S., & Lepak, D. P. (2005). An integrative view of the international experience. *Academy of Management Journal, 48*(1), 85–100.

Tannenbaum, S. (2002). A strategic view of organizational training and learning. In K. Kraiger (Ed.), *Creating, implementing, and managing effective training and development* (pp. 10–52). San Francisco, CA: Jossey-Bass.

Thorndike, R. L. (1937). An evaluation of the attempts to measure social intelligence. *Psychological Bulletin. 34*(5), 275–285.

Toh, S. M., & DeNisi, A. S. (2005). A local perspective to expatriate success. *Academy of Management Executive, 19*(1), 124–131.

Torbiorn, I. (1982). *Living abroad: Personal adjustment and personnel policy in the overseas setting.* New York: Wiley.

Tung, R. L. (1981). Selection and training of personnel for overseas assignments. *Columbia Journal of World Business, 16,* 68–78.

Tung, R. L. (1987). Expatriate assignments: Enhancing success and minimizing failure. *Academy of Management Executive, 1*(2), 117–126.

Tung, R. L. (1988). Career issues in international assignments. *Academy of Management Executive, 11*(3), 241–244.

Tung, R. L. (1998). American expatriates abroad: From neophytes to cosmopolitans. *Journal of World Business, 33*(2), 125–144.

Van Rooy, D. L., & Viswesvaran, C. (2004). Emotional intelligence: A meta-analytic investigation of predictive validity and nomological net. *Journal of Vocational Behavior, 65,* 71–95.

Vance, C. M., Boje, D. M., & Stage, H. D. (1991). An examination of the cross-cultural transferability of traditional training principles for optimizing individual learning. *Journal of Teaching in International Business, 2*(3/4), 107–120.

Vance, C. M., & Paderon, E. S. (1993). An ethical argument for host country workforce training and development in the expatriate management assignment. *Journal of Business Ethics, 12,* 635–641.

Vance, C. M., & Paik, Y. (2002). One size fits all in expatriate pre-departure training? Comparing the host country voices of Mexican, Indonesian, and US workers. *Journal of Management, 21*(7), 557–571.

Van Vianen, A., De Pater, I., & Kristof-Brown, A. (2004). Fitting in: Surface- and deep-level cultural differences and expatriates' adjustment. *Academy of Management Journal, 47*(5), 697–709.

Viswesvaran, C., & Ones, D. S. (2001). Perspectives on models of job performance. *International Journal of Selection and Assessment, 8,* 216–227.

Viswesvaran, C., Ones, D. S., & Schmidt, F. L. (1996). Comparative analysis of the reliability of job performance ratings. *Journal of Applied Psychology, 81,* 557–574.

Welch, D. E., & Welch, L. S. (1997). Pre-expatriation: The role of HR factors in the early stages of internationalization. *International Journal of Human Resource Management, 8*(4), 402–413.

Worchel, S., & Mitchell, T. R. (1972). An evaluation of the effectiveness of the culture assimilator in Thailand and Greece. *Journal of Applied Psychology, 56*(6), 472–479.

Zajanoc, R. B. (1968). Attitudinal effects of mere exposure. *Journal of Personality and Social Psychology, 9,* 1–27.

Zeira, Y., & Banai, M. (1985). Selection of expatriate managers in MNCs: The host-environment point of view. *International Studies of Management and Organization, 15*(1), 33–51.

11 Careers in a Global Context

Jean-Luc Cerdin and Allan Bird

CONTENTS

In this chapter we examine careers in a global context. The field of international human resource management (IHRM) may be divided into two main research streams: (a) the comparison of national cultural variation in HR practices and/or the comparison of national cultural variation in people's attitudes and behaviors; and (b) the study of international mobility and expatriation. The concept of career—from both an organizational and individual perspective—is a central issue in human resource management and in IHRM. This chapter on careers in a global context addresses both of these research streams.

The study of careers encompasses both the viewpoint of organizations and the viewpoint of individuals. Both individual and organizational perspectives vary across nationalities and ethnicity with regard to the way career practices are addressed and implemented. There are also differences in the way that researchers have studied the concept. Brewster (1999) termed the two paradigms stemming from these differences the universalist paradigm and the contextual paradigm. The universalist approach gives rise to the notion of a "best way" and encourages a search for best practices, whereas the contextual paradigm focuses on unique features of institutional environment, including the legal and cultural environments, which give rise to distinctive, environment-specific practices. Another debate that has invigorated career study in a global context centers on the opposition between traditional and boundaryless career conceptions.

We will examine careers in a global context with regard to these several paradigms. Nevertheless, we will adopt the paradigm of boundaryless career, particularly when we bring expatriates into focus. Expatriation amounts to crossing geographical boundaries and, quite often, crossing other types of boundaries, such as organizational or occupational ones as well.

We begin this chapter with a consideration of career in national comparative contexts. In a second section, we shift our focus to career experiences that take individuals out of their own cultural context and place them in another country. The expatriate experience historically was a one-time event in an individual career. It has been largely studied as such and there is an extensive body of research examining the expatriate experience. There have always been a small number of individuals who have pursued a large portion of their careers in an international arena. Until recently, the careers of these people had not been well studied, and often they have been lumped into the expatriate research. With the rise of globalization, however, there has been a significant increase in the number of individuals seeking international careers. The emergence of this cadre coincides with the development of the boundaryless career concept. In the third section of this chapter, we focus on international career and its relationship to the concept of boundarylessness. We conclude this chapter by summarizing implications for future research.

CAREERS IN NATIONAL COMPARATIVE CONTEXTS

Within the national comparison stream of research, the concept of career and other constructs related to career may be examined in terms of differences in cultural contexts. In this section we will consider two topics. First, we will explore the meaning of careers, including notions of career success and potential. Second, we will examine concepts related to career processes and events.

MEANING OF CAREER ACROSS CULTURES

Each cultural context may have an impact on how people define career, and particularly how they define career success and career potential. In this section, we will try to shed light on three related questions: (a) What does "career" mean across cultures? (b) What does "to succeed in one's career" mean across cultures? (c) How is career potential identified and developed across cultures?

Many disciplines, for example, sociology, psychology, anthropology, and so forth, have developed their own definitions of career (Arthur, Hall, & Lawrence, 1989). For example, in economics a career is defined as a "response to market forces," whereas in social psychology it is defined as an "individually mediated response to outside role messages" and in political science it is "the enactment of self interest" (Arthur et al., 1989, p. 10). Nevertheless, a common thread can be found running through the many definitions if we view a career as entailing "an evolving sequence of work experiences over time." That said, the very definition of a career might also vary across countries and cultures. Granrose (1997) provides a clear demonstration of the range of variability possible, even within a single geographic region, in her review of career conceptions across a number of Asian counties. She notes that many Hong Kong Chinese have quite vague notions of what constitutes a career and perceive themselves as having little chance of career development, whereas their Taiwanese counterparts see more opportunities, and view their own lack of ambition as the key barrier to advancement. In a similar vein, Taiwanese Chinese managers are more likely to see and pursue career opportunities beyond the boundary of a single firm than are Japanese managers.

At the same time, there may also be significant areas of overlap regarding career conceptions and behaviors from one region of the world to the next. Lin (1995), for example, finds a high degree of similarity in the career goals and tactics of Asian (Japanese, Hong Kong Chinese, Taiwan Chinese, and Singaporean) and U.S. managers.

In the 1990s a new school of researchers took aim at the traditional conception of careers, arguing that changes in the nature of the work environment and the nature of individuals' relations to their employers had opened the door to "boundaryless careers" (e.g., Arthur & Rousseau,

1996; Bird, 1994; DeFillippi & Arthur, 1994). Such careers are characterized by: awareness of individuals' personal career motivations and the way in which those motivations shape career choices; individuals' acceptance of personal responsibility for career development and direction; variation in individual capabilities, which allow for pursuit of opportunities outside the bounds of a single organization; and individuals viewing the individual-organizational relationship in more calculative, contractual terms (DeFillippi & Arthur, 1994). The concept of boundaryless careers may not apply in all national cultures. In some cultures, the traditional model may be prevalent, raising a potentially interesting line of research regarding why some cultures are more likely to favor boundaryless careers than others. Given its increasing influence in careers research, we will pursue a fuller discussion of the boundaryless career perspective later in the chapter.

CAREER SUCCESS ACROSS CULTURES

Beyond the definition of career, the meaning of a successful career may also vary across cultures. Wayne, Liden, Kraimer, and Graf (1999) point out that career success may be defined both objectively and subjectively. For these authors, objective success encompasses observable achievements such as salary increase or promotion rate, and subjective success is measured by the individual's satisfaction regarding his or her career, consisting of salary evolution, promotions, and professional development. Still, across disciplines and across cultures there is little, if any, agreement on what the essential substance of a career or career success should be. Still, in each of these contexts, differences in sequence, length, duration, and type of work experiences are commonly viewed as important dependent and independent variables in studying careers. These outward manifestations, or "external careers," stand in contrast to varying perceptions of "internal careers," that is, the inflows, outflows, and transformations of the individual that result from sequences of work experiences. Some cultural contexts may lead people to define their career success in objective terms whereas other cultures may lead them to place more emphasis on subjective terms.

MODELS OF CAREER POTENTIAL ACROSS CULTURES

While it may be possible to identify distinctive conceptions and models of careers and career processes across many countries and cultures, it is also the case, and more useful for purposes of research and conceptualization, that these varying perspectives can be grouped into several overarching categories. More specifically, four models have been proposed by which to categorize processes of identifying and developing career potentials (Evans, Lank, & Farquhar, 1989; Evans, Pucik, & Barsoux, 2002). These four career models—the Japanese model, the Latin model, the Germanic model, and the multinational corporation model—may serve as the basis for understanding how careers may be structured in different contexts. The very meaning of what is a career in terms of advancement in a given structure varies from context to context.

The *Japanese model*, or "elite cohort approach," depicts a career structure in which the identification of potential occurs at the time of initial recruitment followed by a long trial period of 7 to 8 years. Only the winners in this time-constrained tournament are given challenging responsibilities at each level of advancement within the organization.

The *Latin model*, or "elite political approach," of which France is a typical example, is an elitist and political process in which top leaders are selected, mainly from the "Grandes Ecoles." The elite move on a path of cross-functional challenges and engage in a political tournament in which visible achievement and coalitional maneuvering play a central role.

The *Germanic model* places a premium on functional expertise. Apprenticeships constitute trial periods, in order to identify individuals with potential who will climb up the functional ladder.

The *multinational corporation model* is not based on elite recruitment in identifying potential, but rather on decentralized recruitment at the local subsidiary level. Local subsidiaries recruit not just for jobs but also for potential. The subsequent development of potential within the organization is managed at the corporate level with no preference given to any one nationality. Those with greater potential for advancing in the ranks are identified, after 5 to 8 years of functional experience in the local subsidiary.

The first three models, though they have distinctive strengths, have come increasingly under pressure from progressive globalization (Evans et al., 2002). Their contextual approach may no longer fit an increasingly international labor market. For instance, given the emphasis on status and graduation from the "Grandes Ecoles," French organizations struggle with providing access to higher levels of management for non-French individuals, who have not passed through the French institutional education system. In a related vein, and viewed from an individual perspective, it can be difficult for French managers to market their elite educational qualifications on the worldwide labor market. By contrast, the fourth model fits a more global approach because it is more universalistic than the other three. Although these models are helpful in categorizing and depicting different career paths according to varying cultural and institutional contexts, we can speculate as to whether they are still relevant and how they may yet evolve.

It is important to note that these four models are structural, that is, careers are viewed as a "structural aspect of an organization" (Rosenbaum, 1993). In such a view, individuals' careers are strongly determined by the structure of the organization they work for. In turn, organizational structures may be influenced by the national culture in which they are located. The structural model defines the rules of the game that operate in a given context (Cerdin, 2004). When the context changes, such as when an individual relocates to another country, the rules of the game, such as valuing diplomas or professional experiences, also change. What may send a positive signal in one particular context (e.g. age, specific degree, etc.) may not send any signals, or may send a negative signal, in another context.

As organizations are becoming increasingly international in their operations, the complexity of the interaction of the different meanings of career, career success, and career potential becomes more ambiguous. One line of future research is to explore how multinational organizations resolve the multiple meanings in their career planning and processes.

CAREER-RELATED CONCEPTS ACROSS CULTURES

Just as with the meaning of career, other concepts related to careers may also be questioned taking into account the culture in which they are examined. For instance, what mentoring means in the context of a particular culture may differ from what it means in another cultural context (Granrose, 1997). Career stages may also follow different patterns depending on the cultural context. Another concept related to careers that requires more investigations in the global context of careers is that of career anchors and motivations. Future careers research should strive to understand the differences of meaning across cultures and also should address these differences when measuring such concepts.

CAREER SUPPORT

When their careers are at stake, individuals in different cultures may not resort to the same type of support. Individuals have around them multiple supports upon which they can rely for purposes of establishing, maintaining, or rescuing their careers. Cerdin (2000) has developed the concept of "360-degree support" (see Figure 11.1) by drawing an analogy to the 360-degree feedback approach used in performance appraisal settings. Individuals may not only rely on themselves in building their careers, but may also look to the support of others, including their supervisor, peers, mentor, network, and family members. The 360-degree support concept delineates the range of supports individuals may rely on during their career in order to advance and be successful, whatever their definition of success is. Nevertheless, the type and extent of support may vary from one culture to another.

Claiming that an employee is his or her own career support finds its place in the individualistic model of career (Rosenbaum, 1993). This model recognizes the individual as the main agent of his or

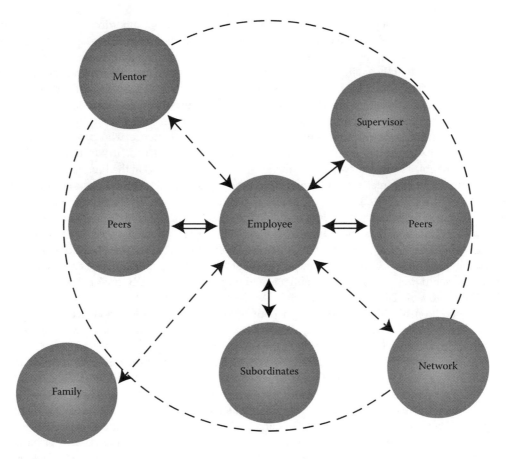

FIGURE 11.1

her career. In a culture high in individualism, people may be more prone to rely on their own resources, whereas in a culture characterized by collectivism, others' support may be of paramount importance.

The supervisor, because of hierarchical status, is both an evaluator and a developer of careers (Hill & Kamprath, 1995), but conflict can arise between these roles. Does the subordinate see the supervisor as an accelerator or as a threat to career advancement? Power distance is defined as "the degree to which members of an organization or society expect and agree that power should be stratified and concentrated at higher levels of an organization or government" (House & Javidan, 2004, p. 12). In a culture high in power distance, subordinates are likely to see their supervisor more as an evaluator than a developer of careers. As a result, individuals are less likely to seek career support from their supervisor in a high-power-distance culture than in a culture in which hierarchical status is less important. Leader-member exchange theory (Liden & Graen, 1980) can be used to characterize the sponsor relationship between an immediate supervisor and subordinates. The theory distinguishes "in-group" employees from those of the "out-group." For a subordinate, to belong to the "in-group," that is, to have a privileged relationship with his or her supervisor, would lead to better career advancement than if he or she belonged to the "out-group," where there would be only a formal relationship with the supervisor. Indeed, for "in-groups," supervisors are more likely to appear as developers, whereas this role is negligible for those in the "out-group." Supervisors' criteria to decide who is part of the in-group or of the out-group may vary depending on national culture.

In the position of supervisor, an individual can gain support from subordinates for the development of one's own career, particularly from those who are part of the "in-group." Hence, subordinates, in return for help in the advancement of their own careers, may give the supervisor their loyalty. It is likely that they will strive to obtain the best results, which should help to advance their supervisor's career. Subordinates in the "in-group" may also possess crucial information, which they may share with their supervisor. This logic of coalition may be more common in a culture low in power distance than in a culture high in this cultural dimension.

Mentors are individuals with extensive knowledge and experience who provide support and help to other less experienced individuals—their protégés—in order to further their development and career (Kram, 1985). The two main functions clearly emphasized in the literature on mentoring relationships are the career support function and the psychosocial support function (Kram, 1985; Noe, 1988; Scandura, 1992). The first function facilitates the protégé's advancement within the organization. The second function contributes to the personal growth and professional development of the protégé. Nevertheless, these functions, based on Western ideas of what supportive behaviors mentors should engage in, may not be desirable and effective in all cultures (Feldman, Folks, & Turnley, 1999). Moreover, recent literature on mentoring relationships underscores possible dysfunctional mentor behaviors, such as sabotage and manipulation (Eby, Butts, Lockwood, & Simon, 2004; Simon & Eby, 2003; Scandura, 1998). Again, some cultures may allow more dysfunctional mentoring relationships than others. Take nepotism, for example, which is more acceptable in some cultures than others. Some cultures may deem it acceptable to extend nepotistic favors in greater or lesser degree as well as to closer or more extended relations.

Individuals may also obtain career support through networking. Luthans, Hodgetts, and Rosenkrantz (1988), in their study of 450 American managers, found that those managers who had the greatest career success, defined by the number of promotions, spent more time on networking and building relationships than their less successful counterparts. These results demonstrate that social and political abilities play a major role in career advancement in the United States. Researchers need to explore whether networking plays a similarly prominent role in the success of careers in non-U.S. contexts. They also need to explore the extent to which network support is available in other countries or cultural contexts.

It should also be noted that men and women appear to use their networks in different ways. Kanter (1977) calls the promotion decision system, which is regularly favored by men and which is particularly unfavorable to women, a "homosocial reproduction system." Is the glass ceiling, the invisible barrier that separates women from top management positions, a universal phenomenon? In cultures high on gender egalitarianism—the degree to which a society minimizes role differences while promoting gender equality (House & Javidan, 2004)—we would anticipate that a glass ceiling is less likely to occur than in cultures low on this cultural dimension. For example, Corsun and Costen (2001) explain the persistence of this situation in the United States as the result of history, the distribution of capital among individuals, the fact that those who hold power do what is necessary to maintain it, and as the result of the majority of those in power being White males.

Finally, individuals may find career support from their families. For instance, in the United States family structure has been found to have a significant impact on career success (Pfeffer & Ross, 1982; Tharenou, 1999). In a similar vein, the theory that proclaims wife-as-resource sheds light on the link between family structure (e.g., whether individuals are married or not and when married, whether couples are dual- or single-earners) and career advancement (Pfeffer & Ross, 1982). According to this theory, married men have more resources to invest in their careers than single men. The additional resources come from the support provided by the spouse, and are all the more influential if the spouse does not work. Husbands therefore have more time to put into their work, which leads to more successful careers. When both spouses work, husbands do not provide their wives with as much support as wives provide their husbands. Because family structures vary across cultures, further research is needed to understand how these differences may affect careers.

CAREER STAGES AND PLATEAUS

Career stages represent another career-related issue that likely differs between countries. Contrasting career experiences in Japan and the United States, Baba and associates noted that Japanese careers possessed more clearly identifiable stages and distinctive retirement points than their American counterparts (Baba, Granrose, & Bird, 1996). In a similar vein, Bird (1988) found that upper-echelon managers in the United States, on average, attained their positions at a younger age and experienced shorter tenures than did their Japanese equivalents. Differences in structural models may explain these results, as would be indicated by the Japanese model mentioned earlier.

One concept that links to age is that of the career plateau. The concept of career plateaus, including structural, content, and salary plateaus, needs to be examined across cultures. Structural plateaus reflect the point at which the likelihood of additional hierarchical promotion is very low (Ference, Stoner, & Warren, 1977). Veiga (1981) includes lateral movements in one's career as also being characteristic of structural plateaus. Individuals experience content plateau when they do a job that is no longer challenging and that they know too well (Tremblay, Roger, & Toulouse, 1995), and salary plateaus occur when the likelihood of a significant increase is very low. Both objective plateaus, for example, the materialization of organization policies such as an average of three years before getting a promotion, and subjective plateaus, for example, the perception of individuals feeling they are stuck in their careers, need to be compared across cultures. For instance, individuals in cultures high on performance orientation, in which the organization or society encourages and rewards group members for performance improvement and excellence (House & Javidan, 2004), would be expected to suffer more from a career plateau than in a culture low on this dimension.

National comparative studies of career may be useful in providing different perspectives on the way a career may be understood. It is clear that there is an important and distinctive difference in how careers are perceived and structured across cultures. As firms compete in the international arena, they must come to terms with these differences. At the same time, companies must also grapple with issues related to sending people to work in other countries. In the next section we take up the issue of expatriate career experience.

EXPATRIATE CAREER EXPERIENCE

Until very recently, few individuals pursued careers exclusively in the international arena. Far more common was the expatriate experience, which often consisted of a 3- to 5-year assignment outside one's own country after which the individual would return home and not likely work overseas again. In this section, we will discuss the expatriate career experience, viewing it from the vantage point of an individual who follows this traditional expatriate career path. We will consider the motivation to accept such assignments, notions of success, and many of the difficulties associated with the expatriate experience. As we consider expatriate career experiences, we will conceptualize a career in terms of its knowledge component, that is, a career is not an evolving sequence of work experiences over time, but the knowledge acquired and lost through those experiences. In short, careers can be understood as repositories of knowledge. Conceptualizing careers as repositories of knowledge redirects attention away from much of the extant research on expatriates, which has tended to focus overwhelmingly on adjustment, thereby ignoring a host of other career issues.

MOTIVATION TO HAVE AN EXPATRIATE EXPERIENCE

From the inception of research on expatriates, interest in the motivations of people who go abroad has been a central feature. The general argument is that the nature of an overseas assignment is filled with challenge and discretion, and the main reason for expatriates to accept foreign assignment is their internal motivation (Stahl, Miller, & Tung, 2002; Stahl & Cerdin, 2004). Osland (1995) found that the most successful expatriates felt a sense of calling. Certainly, employees with strong internal motivation will demonstrate a high concern for the nature of their jobs. This motivation may also exhibit itself prior to employment in an organization. Inkson, Arthur, Pringle, and Barry (1997) note that it is common for many New Zealanders to pursue international experiences as part of their college or immediate post-collegiate lives. These individuals seek out international experiences prior to entering the workforce. Though not discussed at length, the findings of Inkson and associates raise the question of whether some cultures may encourage international experiences, thereby fostering internal motivations for accepting international assignments among people reared in those cultures.

The notion of career anchors is useful to examine the motivation to have an expatriate experience. Schein (1978) defines five main career anchors that characterize what people consider fundamental in their career choices. The five career anchors are technical-functional competence, managerial competence, security and stability, creativity, and autonomy. Individuals with the technical-functional competence anchor are interested in the technical dimension of their work, whereas individuals with the managerial competence anchor view specialization as a trap. They are interested in management per se. Individuals with the security and stability anchor want to feel safe and secure in their career. They favor predictability. Individuals with the creativity anchor are rather entrepreneurial in their attitude. They need to create something that is entirely their own. Individuals with the autonomy anchor want to be their own boss and work at their own pace. Subsequent research by Schein led to the derivation of three additional career anchors. They are service/dedication to a cause, pure challenge, and lifestyle (Schein, 1990). Individuals with a service/dedication anchor want to improve the world, particularly by helping others. Individuals anchored in pure challenge look forward to overcoming impossible obstacles and solving unsolvable problems. People with lifestyle anchors strive to integrate their career with their total lifestyle. It is likely that some of the anchors are more likely to favor expatriation than others. Individuals with security or quality of life anchors are not favorably predisposed to geographical mobility (Schein, 1990). These anchors tend to inhibit decisions to pursue an expatriate assignment. Other anchors seem more favorable to expatriation. For instance, people anchored in autonomy are likely to be attracted to the opportunities inherent in expatriate experience, as expatriation provides many occasions for greater autonomy (Dunbar, 1992). Following this line of argument, it is reasonable to propose that each career anchor, with the exception of the stability anchor, will probably lead to different types of international careers. For example, people anchored in service/dedication to a cause are probably more likely to be drawn to international careers involving humanitarian work assignments as is found in organizations such as Doctors Without Borders or the Peace Corps.

Another reason individuals may pursue an expatriation experience may be due to their career dissatisfaction. Career plateau is also a useful concept in explaining international adjustment. Borg (1988) argued that motivation to accept an expatriate assignment based simply on attempting to escape such plateaus would negatively influence the degree to which such individuals would ultimately adjust to their new work environment. Career plateaus are still common in organizational structures in which employees are guaranteed employment for life or in which the flexibility of the labor market is low. In such organizations with overseas subsidiaries, some employees may volunteer for expatriate experience, not for the position or the experience itself, but because they may perceive this move as the only way to escape from a career plateau.

Despite long interest and more recent explorations of this area, the motivation to go abroad and the processes surrounding the decision to go abroad remain understudied and not well understood. The rise of the boundaryless career perspective, with its focus on self-management of career, may provide sufficient incentive for future researchers to explore this area in greater depth.

EXPATRIATE CAREER SUCCESS

How should we measure the success of an expatriation in career terms? Based on career theory, psychological contract theory, and agency theory, Yan, Zhu, and Hall (2002) suggest taking into

Benefits

Assignment Stage	Individual	Organizational

Expatriation
(shorter-term)
	Task performance
	Skill building, learning, and
	  growth
	Job satisfaction
		Accomplishment of
		  organizational tasks
		Achievement of key
		  organizational objectives

Repatriation (longer-term)	Continual development Attractive future assignments Promotion Enlargement of responsibility	Retention of repatriated employee Utilization of new expertise Transfer of expertise

FIGURE 11.2

account benefits both for the organization and for the individual, as well as considering the assignment stage of the expatriation in a short-term perspective, and the repatriation stage in a long-term perspective (see Figure 11.2). For individuals, success criteria include skill-building, learning and growth, job satisfaction during expatriation, continual development, and the prospect of attractive future assignments and career advancement upon and during the repatriation phase.

In the integrative approach proffered by Yan et al. (2002), agency theory (Smith, 1937) focuses attention on the tendency of economic agents to act in opportunistic fashion. In other words, the individual employee as "agent," and the organization as "principal," may have disparate interests. Yan et al. (2002) note that both the employee and the organization engage in opportunistic actions and, concomitantly, define the success of an expatriate assignment very differently. Researchers focusing on the success of expatriation should distinguish clearly between organization and individual success, as what might be viewed by the organization as successful may not be a good outcome for the individual and vice versa (Lazarova & Cerdin, 2007).

DIFFICULTIES ASSOCIATED WITH THE EXPATRIATE CAREER EXPERIENCE

Research on repatriation has examined both individuals' career difficulties and the organization practices designed to support expatriates upon return. Repatriation is related to numerous frustrations from a personal and professional standpoint. From a personal standpoint, repatriation encompasses loss of social status and lifestyle changes that are stressor agents for repatriates (e.g, Black & Gregersen, 1991). From a professional standpoint, repatriation is frequently depicted as a "career disaster" (Baruch & Altman, 2002). High turnover rates upon repatriation are neither a positive outcome for the organization nor the individual. Individuals may be reluctant to accept an international assignment when they cannot see any positive connections between the international experience and career advancement (Tung, 1998). Caligiuri and Lazarova (2001) suggest that career planning sessions before repatriation and highly visible indications the company values the international experience are crucial to attracting individuals to expatriate assignments and ensuring career success upon repatriation.

Career anchors should also be considered in relation to international adjustment, as positive adjustment contributes to success in a global career. Studying the link between expatriates' decisions to go abroad and their subsequent international adjustment, Cerdin (2002) found that French expatriates anchored in stability were less adjusted to their work than those not having this career anchor.

Much of the extant research on the expatriate experience has tended to focus overwhelmingly on adjustment, thereby ignoring a host of career issues. In their review of expatriate career research, Stephens, Bird, and Mendenhall (2002) proposed a knowledge perspective as a way of addressing many of those neglected issues. Their proposal is consistent with that of the boundaryless career perspective and the emergence of the international career. This is the subject of our next section.

INTERNATIONAL AND BOUNDARYLESS CAREERS

In this third section, we will start by defining international careers as boundaryless careers. This approach will lead to an examination of the concept of international intelligent career. Both boundaryless careers and intelligent careers focus on the knowledge content of careers. Finally, in order to specify the processes whereby international career experiences contribute to knowledge creation or accumulation, we will examine the international career as a repository of knowledge.

Before moving on to a consideration of global careers, it is useful to make the distinction between the expatriate career experience and a global career. Taking on an international assignment, either as an organization-initiated expatriate, or as a self-initiated expatriate, may impact an individual's career in different ways (Inkson et al., 1997). We suggest that international experience is at the core of this distinction, with the expatriate experience representing a one-time event and the global career reflecting a commitment to work in a highly distinctive environment. For instance, the frequency (how often), the length (how long), and the breadth (extent of interaction with other cultures) might be higher for a global manager than for an expatriate. Global managers may be constantly experiencing an international context, interacting and working with individuals from various cultures, even within their own culture. By contrast, expatriates' careers always involve physical transfers from one country to another. Some expatriates may make the most of the international experience, whereas others may not adjust to their environment and may interact mainly with people from their own culture. At times, global managers can experience expatriation or other kinds of international mobility. Their mobility may be, as well, more psychological than physical, that is, requiring them to adopt a global mindset that is sensitive to and considers multiple contexts, cultures, and contingencies. In this regard, there is a clear need for further research on the relationship between career and international experience. It should be noted that research on cross-cultural adjustment also explores this relationship, including both work and nonwork experience (e.g. Takeuchi, Tesluk, Yun, & Lepak, 2005).

INTERNATIONAL CAREERS AS BOUNDARYLESS CAREERS

In the early 1990s two research streams developed simultaneously. The notion of a boundaryless career emerged in response to a growing realization that, across a wide range of industries, individuals were consciously identifying their own career-related drives and motivations, acting to obtain portable competencies and working through social networks to pursue opportunities outside the structure of single organizations (Arthur & Rousseau, 1996). In a parallel and related stream, DeFillippi and Arthur (1994) proposed the concept of an intelligent career, that is, careers driven by individual understanding and awareness of the knowledge content of a career. Both of these perspectives are couched within a broader framework that might best be characterized as the "resource-based view of the career." First fleshed out by Kanter (1989), the primary thrust of the resourced-based view of the career is that careers can be understood in terms of the resources that accrete to them over time. Because research in this area has been couched primarily in terms of boundarylessness, we invoke that characterization to subsume work on intelligent careers and a resource-based view of careers.

The characteristics of a boundaryless career are:

1. Individuals are aware of their personal career motivations and the way in which those motivations shape their career choices.

2. Individuals accept some measure of personal responsibility for career development and direction.
3. Individuals possess, in varying degrees, capabilities—abilities, skills, and knowledge—which allow them to pursue opportunities outside the bounds of a single organization.
4. As a consequence, individuals come to view the individual-organizational relationship in more calculative, contractual terms, thereby reducing the sway of the psychological contract between the two (DeFillippi & Arthur, 1994).

Recent work applying the concept of boundarylessness to global careers (Suutari & Mäkelä, 2005; Lazarova & Cerdin, in press; Stahl, Chua, Caligiuri, Cerdin, Miller, & Taniguchi, 2005; Stahl et al., 2002) has focused particular attention on the impact of substantial shifts in each of these areas. U.S. managers are coming to view boundarylessness as essential to their career advancement, that is, they can find career success either within their current organization or within other organizations (Stahl et al., 2002). Recent empirical studies based on European samples, such as Finnish, German, or French managers, reach conclusions very similar to the findings of Stahl and his associates (e.g., Suutari & Brewster, 2001; Stahl & Cerdin, 2004). Researchers should investigate further the perceived implications of the international assignment within the framework of the boundaryless career. This research should gain in theoretical depth by integrating knowledge development by expatriates and the concept of the international intelligent career.

INTERNATIONAL INTELLIGENT CAREER

The boundaryless career perspective, and the related consideration of intelligent careers, draws attention to the resources that accrue to individuals within their careers. These resources, as a whole, have come to be known as career capital (Suutari & Mäkelä, 2005). Career capital, in turn, has been broken down into two types—social capital and intellectual capital—which are embodied in three categories of career-related knowledge, namely, knowing how, knowing whom, and knowing why. We consider these three types of knowing within the context of global careers.

Knowing How

International assignments are viewed as an effective means of developing new capabilities or enhancing existing ones (Pucik, 1992; Derr, 1993; Roberts, Kossek, & Ozeki, 1998; Seibert, Hall, & Kram, 1995; Solomon, 1995; Suutari, 2003). Capability enhancement may include such things as developing an understanding of worldwide operations and capabilities (Carpenter, Sanders, & Gregersen, 2000); a range of competencies required for effectiveness in a global environment (Adler, 1981; Antal, 2000; Caligiuri & Di Santo, 2001). Knowing how constitutes a form of intellectual capital (Wiig, 2004). It is important to note that knowing how capital may also dissipate as a consequence of international assignments, with some skills withering as a consequence of lack of use while on assignment or inability to use acquired skills after assignment (Stroh, Gregersen, & Black, 2000).

Knowing Whom

The notion of knowing whom connects directly to the literature on social capital, that is, assets embedded in and available through a network of relationships (Nahapiet & Ghoshal, 1998). The concept of social capital is not unique to research on careers (Adler & Kwon, 2002; Burt, 1997). Two distinguishing characteristics of the global context are that of interdependence and multiple stakeholders (Lane, Maznevski, Mendenhall, & McNett, 2004). Managers with global careers are singularly positioned to span boundaries within and without the organization (Kostova & Roth, 2003), thereby performing an important bridging function (Burt, 1997). In this regard, Antal's (2000) finding that Germans significantly expanded their network of relevant contacts, both in the host country and with senior managers back at headquarters, is noteworthy. In a similar vein,

Mäkelä (in press) contrasted the larger volume of social capital possessed by expatriate managers with that of their purely domestic counterparts. This boundary-spanning ability in social networks has in previous research shown to lead to both information benefits and career opportunities (e.g., Burt, 1997; Granovetter, 1973). The social capital embodied in knowing whom confers several benefits, among them access to more and varied information (Burt, 1997); earlier access to information (Burt, 1997); a better reputation (Burt, 1997; Kanter, 1977, 1989); quicker and more effective information search (Borgatti & Cross, 2003); and improved career outcomes, such as job acquisition (e.g., Granovetter, 1973; Boxman, De Graaf, & Flap, 1991) and job promotion (Kim, 2002).

Knowing Why

The intelligent career perspective incorporates a subjective career perspective (Stephens, 1994), what Suutari and Taka (2004) refer to as an "internal" career. An internal career is defined as an individual's perception of meaning within the career and about the relation of career to larger ideas about what is valued in work and life (Schein & van Maanen, 1977). Knowing why refers to individuals' awareness of what their values, interests, desires, and motivations are relative to a career. As Osland (1995) demonstrated, international assignments and global careers have profoundly transformative potential in terms of knowing why impact. More recently, Stahl et al. (2002) addressed not only the transformative aspects of international assignments, but also how subsequent assignments may constrain exploration of new-found motivations and interests. International assignments have been found to moderate individuals' perception of personal identity (Kohonen, 2005), motivation, and potential, as well as their expectations about what their careers should entail in terms of personal growth and development, particularly at the point of repatriation or immediately thereafter (Stroh, Gregersen, & Black, 1998; Welch, 1998; Suutari & Brewster, 2001). Moreover, numerous authors have drawn attention to the high turnover rates resulting from unmet expectations upon return from an international assignment (Black & Gregersen, 1999; Derr & Oddou, 1991; Suutari & Brewster, 2001). Consequently, it is not surprising to find that career patterns for international managers are moving in the direction of "boundaryless" careers (Stahl & Cerdin, 2004; Tung, 1998).

Motivations for accepting an international assignment are varied, and include pursuit of financial benefits (Miller & Cheng, 1978), personal interest in international experience (Inkson et al., 1997), a search for new experiences and learning possibilities (Ensher & Vance, 2001), and career advancement (Tung, 1998; Stahl et al., 2002). The data on motivations for pursuing a global career are relatively scarce, though interest in this area is clearly rising. Suutari (2003) reported that individuals pursuing global careers acknowledge that they choose to work in a context that, from a career standpoint, is both challenging and risky. Nevertheless, these managers appeared to be strongly committed to their global careers. For instance, Suutari & Taka (2004) found that the most typical career anchors of individuals with global careers were managerial competence and pure challenge. Moreover, Suutari and Taka introduced a new career anchor, internationalism, in which individuals are particularly interested in new experience through getting to know unfamiliar countries and cultures. Persons choosing this anchor prefer to develop their competencies in international environments and primarily like to work internationally. They perceive the international experience as more challenging and developmental than a domestic work experience. The clear majority of Finnish global leaders studied by Suutari & Taka (2004) ranked this anchor as their major anchor or among their most important anchors. Managers choosing this anchor were committed to an international career and perceived international experiences as the primary career driver. Further research is called for to determine whether this anchor is universal or simply reflects a unique aspect of Finnish career factors.

INTERNATIONAL CAREERS AS REPOSITORIES OF KNOWLEDGE

Although notions of boundaryless careers and intelligent careers direct attention to the knowledge content of careers, they fail to specify the processes whereby career experiences generate or accumulate knowledge. The "careers as repositories of knowledge" perspective, first proposed by Bird (1994), focuses attention on the relationship between knowledge creation and career experiences. Bird also sought a means of understanding careers in a boundaryless context through an attempt to firmly ground careers research in the emerging stream of knowledge work and knowledge management. Although much of the early focus was on knowledge workers, for example, on professional careers in engineering, medicine, science, etc., more recently Wiig (2004) has noted that employees and work at every level and in any occupation can be distinguished by the amount of knowledge that is required. One of Bird's (1994) central points was that any relevant perspective on careers cannot be disentangled from the fact that knowledge is created from individual experience (Nonaka, 1991a) and that organizations are knowledge creators (Argote & Ingram, 2000; Inkpen & Dinur, 1998) and rely on individuals' experiences in building their knowledge bases (Nurasimha, 2000).

The knowledge repository perspective posits that careers can be meaningfully understood in terms of the knowledge that is acquired through work experiences. In essence, if careers are the evolving sequence of work experiences over time, then the substance of a career is the knowledge that is acquired as a result of those experiences. Objective measures such as positions held, tenure, and so forth are not inconsequential, but are only outward markers of what knowledge may have been obtained. In that regard, similar experiences may yield significantly different knowledge outcomes. Similarly, subjective measures, as that term is understood in careers research (Stephens, 1994), focus on how people make sense of their careers, but fail to objectively assess how much they may have learned, that is, the type and amount of knowledge they have acquired or lost.

Career experiences are valuable to the extent that they lead to knowledge creation. The knowledge creation process occurs through interaction between tacit and explicit knowledge types (Nonaka, 1991b). Nonaka identifies four types of knowledge creation modes that are enacted through the various interactions of tacit and explicit knowledge. These four categories and the interaction among them are presented in Figure 11.3. The sequencing of knowledge creation modes may be thought of as defining a career path. Different experiences lead to shifts from one mode to another.

Nonaka (1994) uses project team experiences as a basis for illustrating the spiral. Socialization begins when individuals join a project team. Rounds of dialogue and discussion among team members trigger the shift to an articulation mode. Concepts generated by the team are pieced together or joined with existing information and there is another modal shift to the combination mode. Experimentation with various new combinations transitions knowledge creation into the internalization mode, as members of the team engage in "learning by doing." As the sequence of a person's work experiences progresses iteratively the store of knowledge grows. A career, then, can be understood as the path of an individual's work experiences through the various knowledge creation modes, and can be visualized as an outwardly expanding spiral.

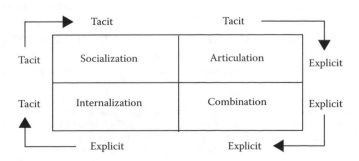

FIGURE 11.3

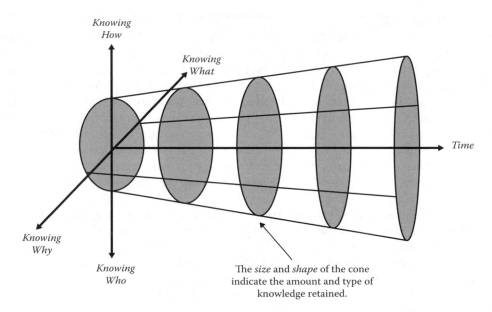

The *size* and *shape* of the cone indicate the amount and type of knowledge retained.

FIGURE 11.4

This leaves open the question as to what types of knowledge are created. Kidd and Teramoto (1995) propose a four-class taxonomy of "knowings" that delineates the knowledge content of a career.* *Know who* refers to a person's social capital, that is, the actual and potential resources embedded within, available through, and derived from the network of relationships an individual possesses. *Know how* relates to a person's set of skills and knowledge about how to accomplish tasks or how to do work. *Know what* relates to the nature and extent of a person's understanding about specific projects, products, services, or organizational arrangements. *Know why* relates to the nature and extent of a person's identification with the firm's culture and strategy. Knowing why gives meaning and purpose to individual action in an organizational context. For example, knowing why the firm chose to set up an overseas operation in Lithuania rather than Estonia can provide direction to subsequent managerial actions. The value, in terms of relevance and utility, as well as the volume of each type of knowing, may shift through time. The term "repository" conveys the acceptance that specific types of knowledge may be acquired, lost, and recovered over the course of a career (Bird, 2001). Figure 11.4 presents a graphic depiction of an idealized career developing over time in terms of the four types of knowing.

The repository perspective seems particularly well suited for analyzing international careers given that a recurring theme of research on international careers has been the dramatic impact that the wealth of new experiences, both work and nonwork, has on people's understanding. In their discussion of the development of global leaders, Osland, Bird, Osland, and Mendenhall (2006) note three critical components of transformational experience: novelty, complexity, and intensity. All three tend to be found in larger measure in international assignments as opposed to purely

---

* The typology proposed by Kidd and Teramoto (1995) overlaps to some extent the typology proposed by DeFillippi and Arthur (1994). There are, however, several important distinctions. First, the Kidd and Teramoto typology is focused on types of knowledge acquired *through* career experiences as opposed to DeFillippi and Arthur's focus on knowledge types to define how individuals *view* their careers. In doing so, the latter incorporate subjective considerations that are missing from the former. Additionally, Kidd and Teramoto incorporate a fourth type—know what—which addresses the factual/informational knowledge dimension of a career.

domestic ones. A consequence of these novel, complex, and intense experiences is that the quality of experiences is richer and deeper, suggesting greater knowledge acquisition (Nonaka, 1994). Stephens et al. (2002) hypothesize that international job changes are likely to lead to extraordinary knowledge acquisition. Osland's (1995) findings, based on extensive interviews with repatriates, lend support to this position.

When understood within the context of knowledge creation, international careers possess unique properties. This section considers those distinctive properties and explores their implications for career theory and research.

If international assignments (IAs) have the potential to lead to significant knowledge creation beneficial to the firm, then career scholars should seek to understand the factors and processes that affect knowledge creation, as these should also impact careers. Two factors seem relevant, duration and sequence. Nonaka (1991a) notes that the cyclical process of knowledge creation requires time to pass through the various phases; however, the duration of IAs tends to be arbitrarily established (Black, Gregersen, Mendenhall, & Stroh, 1999) with little regard for the impact on knowledge acquisition or dissemination. Moreover, cultural distance may impede progress through the learning cycle, leading to differences in knowledge creation and career experiences (Stephens et al., 2002). For example, a common language, and similar cultures and legal systems make it likely that a U.S. manager in Australia may be able to work through the knowledge creation cycle more quickly than a U.S. counterpart in China, where language, culture, and legal system differ significantly. These contextual differences create variations in the speed and extent to which managers may acquire the right sorts of experiences through which useful new knowledge can be created. Similarly, the method of knowledge creation, tacit or explicit, may be influenced by whether a particular culture is characterized by high- or low-context communication preferences (Dulek & Fielden, 1991).

Sequence is an important issue when considering the impact of international assignments on careers. Gunz's work (1989) suggests that many large organizations carry out career planning to identify logical sequencing of positions and promotions for managerial personnel, but it is unlikely corporate career planning adequately addresses the knowledge creation component. Disruption in the knowledge creation process is also likely to occur when managers are brought back from international assignments without attention to impact on knowledge creation (Gupta & Govindarajan, 1991; Black, Gregersen, & Mendenhall, 1992; Stroh, 1995).

When viewed from a repository of knowledge perspective, the role of mentoring in career development also takes on a different cast. One of the key factors enhancing knowledge acquisition is the development of "priming memory," which Wiig (2004, p. 322) describes as "the major repository of context-dependent cues, and hence contributes heavily to our capability to perform and exercise our expertise as part of our daily work." Priming memory, because its central function is to provide associative links to past experience and the current situation, is particularly important for understanding knowledge-centric career phenomena in a global setting because the context is complex and in flux (Lane et al., 2004). Given the vantage point of their more senior position and their more extensive experience, mentors are well positioned to hasten the acquisition of the associative links that comprise priming memory. The role and influence of the mentoring relationship for international careers, particularly as viewed from a knowledge repositories perspective, identify an area where research is clearly needed.

The view of a career as a repository of knowledge has important implications for how scholars address issues of career development activities when considering international job changers (e.g., selection, training, socialization, and mentoring). There is a clear need for additional theoretical work to identify the antecedents, processes, and outcomes of knowledge creation in international assignments and in the broader global context. Current and past research in related domains such as learning theory (Black, Mendenhall, & Oddou, 1991), information technology, and knowledge systems management (Wiig, 2004), to name a few, consider knowledge creation, but not specifically in terms of its effect on careers.

The sequencing of assignments in terms of extending knowledge creation, for example,when is knowledge creation best accomplished at various stages of the international career, pre-assignment, during assignment, and post assignment represents another area of fruitful investigation. Related to issues of sequencing are knowledge retention and loss. Consequently, future research should explore what factors affect knowledge retention and/or loss, that is, international assignments may not only generate knowledge acquisition, but also greater knowledge loss.

Another line of inquiry should address issues of how cultural differences (especially behavioral and assumptive differences) may influence the types of knowing that are developed. For example, might individuals from collectivist cultures (where attention to relationships is considered more important) be more likely to develop larger *knowing who* resources than individuals from individualistic cultures?

Application of the boundaryless career concept raises several additional interesting questions with regard to career plateaus, tangents, and lost careers. For instance, how might different characteristics of international assignments affect the knowledge creation and transfer process (for example assignment length, hierarchical level of the assignee, job characteristics, experience of the expatriate) in ways that moderate the probability of career plateaus? Or, how might nonexpatriate international experiences in knowledge creation (for example, bringing foreign-country nationals to the home-country headquarters) influence career tangents? Conversely, how might experiences with "lost careers," that is, careers of expatriates who have "gone native," be conceptualized from a knowledge standpoint?

CONCLUSION

Perhaps the most significant implication for future research has to do with redirecting the focus of expatriate literature from adjustment to career-centric issues. In the 15 years since Black et al. (1991) put their model of expatriate adjustment forward there has been significant progress in understanding what factors influence adjustment and job performance. At the same time, the overwhelming focus on adjustment has stunted exploration of the larger set of career issues associated with international assignments. Feldman and Thomas (1992) laid out an agenda for future research directions more than 10 years ago, but few have taken up their call. The research that has appeared since then has been disjointed, moving in varying directions with little coherence and no overarching model around which the field might rally and move forward. It may be that the boundaryless career perspective can provide the structure for future explorations. On the other hand, the comparative dearth of international career research may reflect inattention by careers scholars specifically and management scholars more generally. With the advent of increasing research on knowledge management and knowledge organizations, it may be that the boundaryless career perspective also provides an important linking mechanism to those broader fields, thereby increasing the relevance of research on international careers.

Significant further effort is called for in addressing the following aspects of international careers research. First, further construct development—what does "international career" mean?—may lead to the elaboration of the distinctive characteristics of the global context that set the international career apart from a purely domestic one. For example, Lane et al. (2004) posit that the key differentiating factors are multiplicity, interdependence, ambiguity, and flux. How do these factors influence career-related phenomena? One line of reasoning is provided by Lichtenstein & Mendenhall (2002), who suggest that careers under such conditions may best be understood using concepts drawn from nonlinear dynamics. This line of inquiry deserves further attention.

Identification of different types of international assignments may also lead to interesting insights in the evolving nature of international careers. Some initial categorizations, for example, long-term expatriate (more than 3 years); regular expatriate (2 to 3 years); short-term expatriate (1 year or less); headquarters-based international assignees (managers based at headquarters but who spend much of their time on the road); and regionally based international assignees (managers based abroad at regional headquarters, but who spend much of their time outside of the regional office) point to the possibility of significant differences in career paths and wide variation in defining career success.

Just as we have seen the emergence of different types of international assignments, it also seems likely that we will see an expanding variety of international career types. The old dichotomy between a domestic career and a career as a long-term expatriate is increasingly obsolete as companies have become global and concomitantly no longer impose national boundaries on staffing policies. Black et al. (1999) have previously identified four types of international assignees based on their commitment to the parent and/or subsidiary organization. Their categorizations of "hired guns," "gone natives," "hearts at home," and "dual citizens" contain within them the seeds of a rudimentary international careers typology. The increasing and rapidly evolving global labor and global job markets suggest the need for a much more fine-grained and sophisticated framing.

Exploration of the motivations behind international careers represents yet another area worthy of examination. Previously, international careers tended to be driven by the organization. With the rise of boundaryless, person-driven careers, there is a need to better understand the motivations of individuals for an international career. Early research by Inkson et al. (1997) and Osland (1995) suggests that people who pursue international careers may have distinctive motivational profiles.

Last, but certainly not least, there is a need to better understand the relationship between family and international careers. Given the centrality of the family's impact on an international assignee's career outcomes, it is essential current research streams on dual careers and work–family balance be extended to incorporate aspects and issues related to international careers. Again, prior research (e.g., Osland, 1995; Tung, 1998) has provided some initial direction, but there is clearly a need for more.

It seems clear that the domain of careers in a global context offers significant research opportunities as scholars strive to keep pace with those managers whose careers they seek to understand.

REFERENCES

Adler, N. J. (1981). Re-entry: Managing cross-cultural transitions. *Group and Organization Studies. 6:* 341–356.

Adler, P., & Kwon, S. (2002). Social capital: Prospects for a new concept. *Academy of Management Review,* 27: 17–40.

Antal, B. (2000). Types of knowledge gained by expatriate managers, *Journal of General Management, 26:* 32–51.

Argote, L., & Ingram, P. (2000). Knowledge transfer: A basis for competitive advantage in firms. *Organizational Behavior and Human Decision Processes, 82:* 150–169.

Arthur, M. B., Hall, D. T., & Lawrence, B. S. (1989). *Handbook of career theory.* New York: Cambridge University Press.

Arthur, M. B., & Rousseau, D. (1996). *Boundaryless careers: Work, mobility and learning in the new organizational era.* New York: Oxford University Press.

Baba, M., Granrose, C., & Bird, A. (1996). Career planning and development of managers employed in Japanese firms and U.S. subsidiaries in Japan. *Journal of Asian Business, 11:* 71–96.

Baruch, Y., & Altman, Y. (2002). Expatriation and repatriation in MNCs: A taxonomy. *Human Resource Management, 41(2):* 239–259.

Bird, A. (1988). *Nihon kigyo no executive no kenkyu* [Research on Japanese executives]. Tokyo: Sangyo Noritsu Daigaku.

Bird, A. (1994). Careers as repositories of knowledge: A new perspective on boundaryless careers. *Journal of Organizational Behavior, 15:* 325–344.

Bird, A. (2001). International assignments and careers as repositories of knowledge. In M. Mendenhall, T. Kuehlmann, & G. Stahl (Eds.), *Developing global business leaders: Policies, processes and innovations* (pp. 19–36). Westview, CT: Quorum Books.

Black, J. S., & Gregersen, H. B. (1991). When Yankee comes home: Factors related to expatriate and spouse repatriation adjustment. *Journal of International Business Studies, 22(4):* 671–694.

Black, J. S., & Gregersen, H. B. (1999). The right way to manage expats. *Harvard Business Review, March/ April,* 52–61.

Black, J. S., Gregersen, H. B., & Mendenhall, M. E. (1992). Toward a theoretical framework of repatriation adjustment. *Journal of International Business Studies, 23*(1): 737–760.

Black, J. S., Gregersen, H. B., Mendenhall, M. E., & Stroh, L. (1999). *Globalizing people through international assignments.* New York: Addison-Wesley.

Black, J. S., Mendenhall, M. E., & Oddou, G. (1991). Toward a comprehensive model of international adjustment: An integration of multiple theoretical perspectives. *Academy of Management Review, 16*(2): 291–317.

Borg, M. (1988). *International transfers of managers in multinational corporations.* Uppsala: Acta Universitatis Upsaliensis.

Borgatti, S., & Cross, R. (2003). A relational view of information seeking and learning in social networks. *Management Science, 49:* 432–445.

Boxman, E., De Graaf, P., & Flap, H. (1991). The impact of social and human capital on the income attainment of Dutch managers. *Social Networks, 13,* 51–73.

Brewster, C. (1999). Different paradigms in strategic HRM: Questions raised by comparative research. In P. Wright, L. Dyer, J. Boudreau, and G. Milkovich (Eds.), *Research in personnel and HRM* (pp. 213–238). Greenwich, CT: JAI Press.

Burt, R. S. (1997). The contingent value of social capital. *Administrative Science Quarterly, 42,* 339–365.

Caligiuri, P., & Di Santo, V. (2001). Global competence: What is it, and can it be developed through global assignments? *Human Resource Planning, 24*(3), 27–35.

Caligiuri, P., & Lazarova, M. (2001). Strategic repatriation policies to enhance global leadership development. pp. 243–256. In M. E. Mendenhall, T. M. Kuhlmann, & G. K. Stahl (Eds.), *Developing global business leaders: Policies, processes, and innovations.* Westport, CT: Quorum Books.

Carpenter, M., Sanders, W., & Gregersen, H. (2000). International assignment experience at the top can make a bottom-line difference. *Human Resource Management, 39,* 147–157.

Cerdin, J.-L. (2000). *Gérer les carrières.* Caen: Editions Management et Société.

Cerdin, J.-L. (2002). *L'expatriation* (2nd ed.). Paris: Editions d'Organisation.

Cerdin, J.-L. (2004). Les carrières dans un contexte global. *Revue Management & Avenir; 1,* 155–175.

Corsun, D. L., & Costen, W. M. (2001). Is the glass ceiling unbreakable? Habits, fields, and the stalling of women and minorities in management. *Journal of Management Inquiry, 10*(1), 16–25.

DeFillippi, R. J., & Arthur, M. B. (1994). The boundaryless career: A competency-based perspective. *Journal of Organizational Behavior, 15,* 307–324.

Derr, B. (1993). Internationalizing managers: Speeding up the process. *European Management Journal, 11,* 435–442.

Derr, B., & Oddou, G. (1991). Are U.S. multinationals adequately preparing future American leaders for global competition? *International Journal of Human Resource Management, 2,* 227–244.

Dulek, R. E., & Fielden, J. S. (1991). International communication: An executive primer. *Business Horizons, 34*(1), 20–29.

Dunbar, E. (1992). Adjustment and satisfaction of expatriate U.S. personnel. *International Journal of Intercultural Relations, 16,* 1–16.

Eby, L., Butts, M., Lockwood, A., & Simon, S. A. (2004). Protégés' negative mentoring experiences: Construct development and nomological validation. *Personnel Psychology, 57,* 411–447.

Evans, P., Lank, E., & Farquhar, A. (1989). Managing human resource management in international firm: Lessons from practice. pp. 113–143. In P. Evans, Y. Doz, & A. Laurent (Eds.), *Human resource management in international firms.* Hampshire: Macmillan.

Evans, P., Pucik, V., & Barsoux, J.-L. (2002). *The global challenge: Frameworks for international human resource management.* London: McGraw-Hill.

Feldman, D. C., Folks, W. R., & Turnley, W. H. (1999). Mentor-protégé diversity and its impact on international internship experiences. Journal of Organizational Behavior, 20, 597–611.

Feldman, D. C., & Thomas, D. C. (1992). Career management issues facing expatriates. *Journal of International Business Studies, 2,* 271–292.

Ference, T. P., Stoner, J. A. F., & Warren, E. K. (1977). Managing the career plateau. *Academy of Management Review, 2,* 602–612.

Gomez-Mejia, L., & Balkin, D. (1987). The determinants of managerial satisfaction with the expatriation and repatriation process. *Journal of Management Development, 6*(1), 7–17.

Granovetter, M. (1973). The strength of weak ties. *American Journal of Sociology, 78,* 1360–1380.

Granrose, C. (1997). *Careers in Asia.* New York: Quorum.

Gunz, H. (1989). The dual meaning of managerial careers. *Journal of Management Studies, 26,* 225–250.

Gupta, A., & Govindarajan, V. (1991). Knowledge flows and the structure of control within multinational corporations. *Academy of Management Review, 16,* 768–792.

Hill, L., & Kamprath, N. (1995). *Beyond the myth of the perfect mentor: Building a network of developmental relationship* [Case]. Harvard Business School.

House, R. J., & Javidan, M. (2004). Overview of GLOBE. In R. J. House, P. J. Hanges, M. Javidan, P. W. Dorfman, & V. Gupta (Eds.), *Culture, leadership, and organizations: The GLOBE study of 60 societies* (pp. 9–28). Beverly Hills, CA: Sage Publications.

Inkpen, A. C., & Dinur, A. (1998). Knowledge management processes and international joint ventures. *Organization Science, 9,* 454–468.

Inkson, K., Arthur, M. B., Pringle, J., & Barry, S. (1997). Expatriate assignment versus overseas experience: Contrasting models of international human resource development. *Journal of World Business, 32*(4), 351–368.

Kanter, R. M. (1977). *Men and women of the corporation.* New York, Basic Books.

Kanter, R. M. (1989). *When giants learn to dance.* London: Simon & Schuster.

Kidd, J. B., & Teramoto, Y. (1995). The learning organization: The case of the Japanese RHQs in Europe [Special issue]. *Management International Review, 35*(2), 39–56.

Kim, Y. (2002). Executive social capital and its impact on job promotion. *2002 Academy of Management Proceedings* BPS: J1 J6.

Kohonen, E. (in press). Developing global leaders through international assignments: An identity construction perspective. *Personnel Review, 34,* 22–36.

Kostova, T., & Roth, K. (2003). Social capital in multinational corporations: A micro-macro model of its formation. *Academy of Management Journal, 45,* 215–233.

Lane, H. W., Maznevski, M. L., Mendenhall, M. E., & McNett, J. (2004). *The handbook of global management: A guide to managing complexity.* London: Blackwell.

Lazarova, M., & Cerdin, J.-L. (2007). Revisiting repatriation concerns: Organizational support vs. career and contextual influences. *Journal of International Business Studies, 38,* 404–429.

Lichtenstein, B., & Mendenhall, M. (2002). Non-linear dynamics and career response-ibility. *M@n@gement, 5,* 1.

Liden, R. C., & Graen, G. (1980). Generalizability of the vertical dyad linkage model of leadership. *Academy of Management Journal, 23,* 451–465.

Lin, R. Y. (1995). How individualism-collectivism influences Asian and U.S. managers in choosing their career goals and tactics. *Journal of Asian Business, 11*(3), 97–113.

Luthans, F., Hodgetts, R. M., & Rosenkrantz, S. A. (1988). *Real managers.* Cambridge, MA: Ballinger.

Mäkelä, K. (in press). Knowledge sharing through expatriate relationships: A social capital perspective. *International Studies of Management and Organization.*

Miller, E., & Cheng, J. (1978). A closer look at the decision to accept an overseas position. *Management International Review, 3,* 25–33.

Nahapiet, J., & Ghoshal, S. (1998). Social capital, intellectual capital and the organizational advantage. *Academy of Management Review, 23,* 242–266.

Noe, R. A. (1988). An investigation of the determinants of successful assigned mentoring relationships. *Personnel Psychology, 41,* 457–479.

Nonaka, I. (1990). Managing innovation as a knowledge-creation process: A new model for a knowledge-creating organization. Paper presented at New York University, Stern School of Business, International Business Colloquium.

Nonaka, I. (1991a). Managing the firm as an information creation process. *Advances in Information Processing in Organizations, 4*: 239–275.

Nonaka, I. (1991b). The knowledge-creating company. *Harvard Business Review, 69*(6), 96–104.

Nonaka, I. (1994). A dynamic theory of organizational knowledge creation. *Organization Science, 5,* 14–37.

Kram, K. E. (1985). *Mentoring at work: Developmental relationships in organizational life.* Glenview, IL: Scott, Foresman.

Nurasimha, S. (2000). Organizational knowledge, human resource management, and sustained competitive advantage: Toward a framework. *Competitiveness Review, 10,* 123–135.

Osland, J. S. (1995). *The adventure of working abroad: Hero tales from the global frontier.* San Francisco: Jossey-Bass.

Osland, J. S., Bird, A., Osland, A., & Mendenhall, M. (2006). Developing global leadership capabilities and global mindset: A review. pp. 197–22. In G. Stahl & I. Bjorkman (Eds.), *Handbook of international human resource management.* London: Blackwell.

Pfeffer, J. P., & Ross, J. (1982). The effects of marriage and a working wife on occupational and wage attainment. *Administrative Science Quarterly, 27,* 66–80.

Pucik, V. (1992). Globalization and human resource management. pp. 61–81. In V. Pucik, N. Tichy, & C. Barnett (Eds.), *Globalizing management: Creating and leading the competitive organization.* New York: John Wiley & Sons.

Roberts, K., Kossek, E., & Ozeki, C. (1998). Managing the global workforce: Challenges and strategies. *Academy of Management Executive, 12*(4), 93–119.

Rosenbaum, J. E. (1993). Organization career systems and employee misperceptions. In M. B. Arthur, D. T. Hall, & B. S. Lawrence (Eds.), *Handbook of career theory* (pp. 329–353). Cambridge: Cambridge University Press.

Scandura, T. A. (1992). Mentorship and career mobility: An empirical investigation. *Journal of Organizational Behavior, 13,* 169–174.

Scandura, T. A. (1998). Dysfunctional mentoring relationships and outcomes. *Journal of Management, 24*(3), 449–467.

Schein, E. H. (1978). *Career dynamics: Matching individual and organizational needs.* Reading, MA: Addison-Wesley.

Schein, E. H. (1990). *Career anchors: Discovering your real values.* San Diego, CA: Pfeiffer and Company.

Schein, E. H., & van Maanen, J. (1977). Career development. In J. Hackman & J. Suttle (Eds.), *Improving life at work: Behavioral science approaches to organizational change.* (pp. 30–95). Santa Monica, CA: Goodyear.

Seibert, K., Hall, D., & Kram, K. (1995). Strengthening the weak link in strategic executive development: Integrating individual development and global business strategy. *Human Resource Management, 34,* 549–567.

Simon, S. A., & Eby, L. T. (2003). A typology of negative mentoring experiences: A multidimensional scaling study. *Human Relations, 56*(9), 1083–1106.

Smith, A. (1937). *The wealth of nations.* New York: Modern Library.

Solomon, C. (1995). Repatriation: Up, down or out? *Personnel Journal, 74,* 28–37.

Stahl, G. K., & Cerdin, J.-L. (2004). Global careers in French and German multinational corporations. *Journal of Management Development, 23*(9), 885–902.

Stahl, G. K., Chua, C. H., Caligiuri, P. M., Cerdin, J.-L., Miller, E. L. & Taniguchi, M. (2005). *Global careers: European, North American and Asian perspectives.* Paper presented at the 2005 Academy of Management Meetings. Honolulu, HI.

Stahl, G. K., Miller, E., & Tung, R. (2002). Toward the boundaryless career: A closer look at the expatriate career concept and the perceived implications of an international assignment. *Journal of World Business, 37,* 216–227.

Stephens, G. K. (1994). Crossing internal career boundaries: The state of research on subjective career transitions. *Journal of Management, 20,* 479–501.

Stephens, G., Bird, A., & Mendenhall, M. E. (2002). International careers as repositories of knowledge: A new look at expatriation. In D. Feldman (Ed.), *Work careers: A developmental perspective.* (pp. 294–322). San Francisco, CA: Jossey-Bass.

Stroh, L. K. (1995). Predicting turnover among repatriates: Can organizations affect retention rates? *International Journal of Human Resource Management, 6,* 443–456.

Stroh, L. K., Gregersen, H. B., & Black, J. S. (1998). Closing the gap: Expectations versus reality among expatriates. *Journal of World Business, 33,* 111–124.

Stroh, L. K., Gregersen, H. B., & Black, J. S. (2000). Triumphs and tragedies: Expectations and commitments upon repatriation. *Journal of Human Resource Management, 11,* 681–697.

Suutari, V. (2003). Global managers: Career orientation, career tracks, life-style implications and career commitment. *Journal of Managerial Psychology, 18*(3), 185–207.

Suutari, V., & Brewster, C. (2001). Expatriate management practices and perceived relevance. *Personnel Review, 30*(5/6), 554–577.

Suutari, V., & Mäkelä, K. (2005). *The career capital of managers with global careers.* Paper presented at the 2005 Academy of Management Meeting. Honolulu, HI.

Suutari V., & Taka, M. (2004). Career anchors of managers with global careers. *Journal of Management Development, 23*(9), 833–847.

Takeuchi, R., Tesluk, P. E., Yun, S., & Lepak, D. P. (2005). An integrative view of international experience. *Academy of Management Journal, 48*(1), 85–100.

Tharenou, P. (1999). Is there a link between family structures and women's and men's managerial career advancement? *Journal of Organizational Behavior, 20,* 837–863.

Tremblay, M., Roger, A., & Toulouse, J. M. (1995). Career plateau and work attitudes: An empirical study of managers. *Human Relations, 48*(3), 221–237.

Tung, R. L. (1998). American expatriates abroad: From neophytes to cosmopolitans. *Journal of World Business, 33,* 125–144.

Veiga, J. F. (1981). Plateaued versus non-plateaued managers career patterns, attitudes and path potential. *Academy of Management Journal, 24,* 566–578.

Wayne, S. J., Liden, R. C., Kraimer, M. L., & Graf, I. K. (1999). The role of human capital, motivation and supervisor sponsorship in predicting career success. *Journal of Organizational Behavior, 20*(5), 577–595.

Welch, D. (1998). *The psychological contract and expatriation: A disturbing issue for IHRM?* Paper presented at the 6th Conference on International Human Resource Management. Paderborn, Germany.

Wiig, K. M. (2004). *People-focused knowledge management.* London: Elsevier.

Yan, A., Zhu, G., & Hall, D. T. (2002). International assignment for career building: A model of agency relationships and psychological contracts. *Academy of Management Review, 27*(3), 373–391.

12 Summary and Conclusions

Michael M. Harris

CONTENTS

A fundamental assumption of this volume is that culture has a major effect on human resource management (HRM) practices. Indeed, this is probably a cardinal principle of international HRM (IHRM). As noted in the Introduction, some scholars have argued that we need to pay more attention to cultural similarities, as well as cultural differences. Lawler and his colleagues point out several different cultural frameworks have been developed (e.g., Hofstede, Trompenaars, GLOBE). Given the importance of measuring culture in understanding IHRM, it is somewhat surprising that so little research has attempted to compare these frameworks to determine their similarities and differences. Nevertheless, some of these frameworks seem to overlap. As explained by Lawler and his colleagues, Trompenaars' dimensions of universalism and particularism are subsumed under Hofstede's individualism-collectivism dimension, although the former approach retains them as separate dimensions. It would be of great interest to determine whether the different cultural frameworks are empirically highly correlated. Furthermore, it would be of interest to determine whether some of the frameworks lack dimensions that another framework includes and whether those dimensions make a difference in relationships with other variables. For example, are there dimensions in Trompenaars' framework, which are not present in Hofstede's model, that have important relationships with IHRM variables? More research is clearly needed to answer these kinds of questions.

Cultural distance may be a useful construct for IHRM as well. For example, cultural distance may be an important factor in understanding how well expatriates adjust to their assignment country; the larger the cultural distance between their home country and the assignment country, the more difficult the adjustment seems likely to be. Researchers in international management (e.g., Kogut & Singh, 1988) created a measure referred to as "cultural distance," which reflects the difference between two cultures. The typical way in which this variable has been measured is based on a composite of the differences between the ratings on Hofstede's dimensions for, say, an expatriate's home country and the ratings on Hofstede's dimensions for the expatriate's assignment country. Although Shenkar (2001) has raised concerns about cultural distance as it has been measured, a major advantage is that it is measured objectively, in that the dimensional ratings are taken from prior research studies. Researchers should also consider using the other culture frameworks for assessing cultural distance (e.g., the GLOBE measure). Tihanyi, Griffeth, and Russell (2005) suggested other measures that might be used to assess cultural differences, including "language (e.g., membership in language families), family structures, religion, and wealth (measured by GNP per capita)" (p. 279).

Another potentially important issue in studying cultural values concerns the correct analytic model to use. Some have argued that a multilevel model is needed to properly assess the effects of culture on employee behavior (see also Chan's chapter in this handbook), as culture is assumed to be the same within each country and therefore the measures are not independent (Dyer, Hanges, &

Hall, 2005). What effect the issue of the appropriate measurement model for culture has on relationships with other variables remains to be seen. As Lawler et al. point out in their chapter, employees belong to a hierarchy of cultures (e.g., unit, occupational, etc.). Sophisticated models, such as hierarchical linear models (HLM; Bryk & Raudenbush, 1992), may be necessary to properly determine what proportions of variance are accounted for by each of these "cultures."

Gephart and Richardson address qualitative methodologies, while Chan addresses quantitative methodologies. Together, these two chapters provide a number of interesting contrasts and similarities. Gephart and Richardson begin with a useful definition of qualitative research, noting that a research project involves two basic steps: data collection and data analysis. Each of these steps can be either qualitative or quantitative in nature, thus creating four possible combinations (e.g., a project may involve qualitative data collection and quantitative data analysis). To simplify matters, Gephart and Richardson state that their chapter addresses the qualitative analysis of data collected qualitatively. They then proceed to discuss three different research paradigms, urging researchers to "understand the paradigmatic assumptions in their research processes and in the theoretical perspectives they are seeking to advance." Specifically, they discuss positivism (and postpositivism), interpretive research, and critical postmodernism as major paradigms in IHRM. Table 3.1 in their chapter summarizes the nature of reality, key goals, methodological orientation, and implications of each of these three paradigms. Positivism (and postpositivism) is most closely associated with quantitative approaches, where there is an emphasis on precise measurement of the relevant variables and rigorous hypothesis testing. Although Gephart and Richardson provide many examples of qualitative research, the field of IHRM has been dominated by quantitative research. By way of comparison, the interpretive research paradigm focuses on understanding, with an orientation towards "thick" descriptions of members' meanings of reality. The emphasis here is on meaning and sense-making by the actors (e.g., employees of an organization).

Another interesting difference between the positivistic (and postpositivistic) paradigm and the interpretative research paradigm concerns the degree of structure used. On the one hand, Gephart and Richardson describe the positivistic approach as consisting of discrete and separate stages. Typically, a literature review is conducted, hypotheses are developed, measures are constructed, data are collected, and statistical analyses are performed. In contrast, the interpretative research paradigm (which is more closely associated with qualitative research) may not have discrete stages. Therefore, the research question may change over time, as well as the nature of the data that are collected. Scholars subscribing to one paradigm may question the value of research conducted by scholars subscribing to a different paradigm. However, in my opinion, both approaches have much to offer to increase our understanding of IHRM.

Gephart and Richardson proceed by describing four general qualitative methods that they suggest are particularly appropriate for IHRM research. Beginning first with the case study method, Gephart and Richardson assert that the case study methodology is particularly helpful in understanding how a particular phenomenon changes over time and the causal processes that affect it. I believe that the case study method has much to offer IHRM and therefore researchers should make greater use of this approach.

Gephart and Richardson discuss the use of various observational methods, including participant observation and ethnography, in IHRM research. They tie these concepts together using grounded theory, which they define as an "analytical methodology developed in participant observation taken in the interpretive tradition." Grounded theory uses an inductive approach to develop theories from data, but also enables one to integrate major theories. Grounded theory, according to Gephart and Richardson, has specific stages, including comparing incidents applicable to each situation, integrating concepts, and delimiting the theory.

Gephart and Richardson's discussion of interviewing and focus group methods is perhaps one of the most useful sections of their chapter. They identify several types of interviews, including the conventional interview, the active interview, the life story interview, the ethnographic interview, and the long interview. As suggested by the name, the conventional interview follows the positivistic tradition, wherein the interviewer is perceived as a passive recipient of subjects' responses, which provide the true facts. Essentially, the conventional interview would be viewed as an orally administered survey. Active interviews, on the other hand, are more closely associated with interpretive research and the critical postmodernism approach. This approach assumes that the interviewer plays a more active role; as stated by Gephart and Richardson, the active interview "captures the discursive, interactional, meaning-making process," with a focus on how meaning is ascribed to events and processes. The active interview is particularly useful when the goal is to understand others' *interpretations* of events and processes.

The "long" interview comprises another approach to collecting qualitative data. As described by Gephart and Richardson, the long interview is an extended form of the structured interview containing a mix of demographic, factual, and open-ended questions for the purpose of understanding the respondent's mental world. The long interview involves less prolonged involvement on the part of the researcher and focuses on cultural categories and shared meanings. Gephart and Richardson also provide a list of common steps in using the long interview, as well as a description of the five steps involved in the data analysis process used for the long interview. These steps provide a degree of structure to the long interview, which in turn should help standardize the technique. Finally, they describe a number of strengths of the long interview, including its use in cases where the research topic requires "rich and abundant but manageable data." In addition, the long interview enables researchers to study key themes in some detail, even with limited time or relatively few participants. These factors, as well as others described by Gephart and Richardson, suggest that the long interview is well suited for IHRM research.

Gephart and Richardson's chapter provides valuable comments regarding the use of focus groups. After emphasizing that focus groups can be used in different ways, including as a self-contained method and a source of data, Gephart and Richardson note that focus groups may be used to supplement other research methods and to provide preliminary data for the purpose of generating survey questionnaires or other purposes. After providing some general suggestions for focus groups (e.g., each group should have 6 to 10 participants), Gephart and Richardson caution that their guidelines depend much on the specific research project.

Gephart and Richardson offer a number of advantages of the focus group method, including the ability to control the discussion, easier access to groups than other methods (e.g., direct observation), data on variables that may be difficult to observe (e.g., attitudes), and potentially richer information than individuals alone will produce. Despite having a number of strengths, Gephart and Richardson acknowledge that the focus group technique also has its limitations and challenges. Of particular concern is the issue that the group may affect what individuals say, thus producing either a drive towards conformity in opinion, or possibly, towards polarization. Moreover, questions may be raised about the accuracy of the data. This is probably particularly true for topics of a sensitive nature, where participants are concerned about the confidentiality of their responses. Finally, it is unclear whether culture will affect participant responses to focus groups. In some cultures, for example, respondents may be more reluctant to share their feelings and perceptions with others present. Participants from collectivistic cultures may perceive the need for conformity in opinion, while participants from highly individualistic cultures may be more likely to believe that polarized opinions are more appropriate. As described in Chan's chapter on quantitative research, however, all data collection methods are susceptible to cultural effects.

Chan's chapter addresses quantitative research methods and raises a number of questions that should concern IHRM researchers. His chapter is divided into three relatively independent sections, including research methodology, measurement, and data analysis.

One of Chan's major points is that IHRM researchers need to be cautious that they do not inadvertently design their research methodology to confirm their expectations about the outcomes. (Similar challenges, but also raising ethical concerns, have recently been brought to light regarding medical research, where it has been claimed that researchers' connections with drug companies may affect their conclusions; see Scott, 2006). Chan proceeds to discuss key points in research methodology, including study design, method of data collection, and sampling procedure, where investigators' expectations about results may drive their decisions. Chan provides numerous examples; some of the more interesting ones are noted below.

For example, Chan argues that researchers need to be careful in designing role-plays; subjects who are nonsupervisors from high-power-distance cultures may be less comfortable and more unfamiliar with assuming the role of higher authority (e.g., a supervisor) than subjects from low-power-distance cultures. In reviewing the long-debated tension between correlational field studies and experimental laboratory studies, Chan notes that additional concerns may be raised by their respective critics when it comes to IHRM research. For example, critics of the laboratory approach may argue that the contrived nature of the laboratory may affect subjects from one culture more than subjects from other cultures. Supporters of the laboratory approach may critique IHRM correlational field research designs on the grounds that the presence of various cultural differences may increase the number of alternative explanations for results found. Given the relative strengths inherent in laboratory studies (e.g., greater internal validity) versus field studies (e.g., greater external validity), Chan calls for the complementary use of both designs.

Chan raises similar concerns with regard to the method of data collection used. Chan observes in passing a variety of potential problems (e.g., cultural differences in response sets, familiarity with response formats, and respondent motivation) in cross-cultural research when using what is probably the most common method of data collection in IHRM, namely, the self-report questionnaire. However, Chan is quick to point out that other methods of data collection are also likely to be prone to the same problems that may plague the self-report questionnaire and argues that "reactions to the use of a data collection method are essentially a construct contamination issue," which in turn requires the researcher to separate out methods and constructs in analyzing results.

A recent study by Heine, Lehman, Peng, and Greenholtz (2002) indicates just how insidious the effect of culture on data collection may be. Using expert opinions, Heine et al. documented the widely held belief that Japanese were far more collectivistic compared to North Americans. However, when they performed a meta-analysis of past research, they reported a lack of cultural differences on the individualism-collectivism scale. They argued that the difference between experts' judgments and empirical evidence may be explained by the effect of reference groups. That is, in rating themselves on any given construct, North American respondents implicitly compare themselves to other North Americans; Japanese respondents implicitly compare themselves to other Japanese. Thus, although on an absolute scale, Japanese may act in a more collectivistic way than their North American counterparts and North Americans may act in a more individualistic way then their Japanese counterparts, these differences are obscured when using the typical self-rating scales. Indeed, only when using scales that instructed subjects to explicitly compare themselves to another culture (i.e., Japanese subjects were instructed to compare themselves to North Americans; North American subjects were instructed to compare themselves to Japanese) did the assumed differences appear regarding collectivism-individualism.

Chan also raises particularly interesting issues regarding sampling procedures in IHRM research methodology. Specifically, Chan divides sampling issues into two broad categories, sampling across cultures and sampling within cultures. Chan points out that the variation in the selected cultures' scores on a particular construct should reflect the variation in the population of cultures of interest. I think that it is particularly important for IHRM researchers to consider this issue, as sampling cultures that reflect varying degrees of the full variation present in a particular culture may affect the results obtained. Another concern involves the use of only two countries in many IHRM studies. Besides the fact that there is unlikely to be sufficient variation and appropriate cross-cultural representativeness, Chan raises the concern that specific but unmeasured factors such as language may affect the results.

In the second section of the chapter, Chan discusses measurement issues that are pertinent to IHRM. He offers a number of important cautionary statements, such as assuming the reliability coefficients obtained in one culture will be applicable in another culture. Chan also warns that items that are representative of a domain content in one culture may not be representative of the same construct in another culture. He also raises several red flags regarding the translation of questionnaires for use in IHRM research. In particular, he cautions IHRM researchers that translation equivalence is *not* the same as construct equivalence, and warns that various response sets (e.g., socially desirable responding) may be more prevalent in some cultures than others. Certainly, there are sufficient measurement issues that IHRM researchers need to consider these challenges more carefully. For example, measures of social desirability might be added to a questionnaire study across cultures to eliminate differences in that construct as an alternative explanation for results that are found.

The final section in Chan's chapter addresses data analytic issues. The focus there is on using measurement invariance models of increasing complexity. Whether these increasingly sophisticated analytical models will become necessary for IHRM researchers remains to be seen. Clearly, the approaches used by qualitative and quantitative IHRM researchers will continue to diverge. We need to keep in mind, however, that there is much to learn from both approaches.

Whereas the vast majority of this handbook addresses micro-level issues in IHRM, Sparrow and Braun review the role of strategy in IHRM, which refers to HRM policies and practices that are affected by the strategic activities of multinational companies and that, in turn, affect the international concerns and goals of those companies. Presumably, HRM policies and practices affect micro-level behaviors on the part of employees, which in turn impact organizational-level outcomes, such as profitability, innovation, and so forth. Read carefully, it is clear that there is a close interplay between macro-level (i.e., company decisions about HR practices) and micro-level behavior (i.e., employee behavior; see also Schneider, Hanges, Smith, & Salvaggio, 2003). Another underlying theme throughout Sparrow and Braun's chapter is the need to simultaneously create global integration within the organization while at the same time allowing for local differences (which Sparrow and Braun refer to as the integration–differentiation dilemma).

Sparrow and Braun provide an overview of different strategic IHRM models, which they present in historical order. They begin with life-cycle models, focusing on a model that relates headquarter management's attitudes regarding globalization and staffing decisions. Other life-cycle models link organizational stages (e.g., birth, growth, maturity, and revival) to the levels of external and internal fit between and within HRM activities. Sparrow and Braun, however, critique life cycle models on several grounds, including the focus on one independent variable (i.e., product life or organizational life cycle), without taking into account a myriad of other factors that are likely to influence strategic IHRM. Such models appear to have been replaced by more sophisticated frameworks in recent years.

A relatively larger part of Sparrow and Braun's chapter is devoted to organization design models, which focus on the match between strategy and organization structure. Sparrow and Braun assert that information-processing theory underlies many of the subsequent theories of how best to design organizations, where information processing refers to the gathering of data, the processing and transformation of data into useable information, and the subsequent communication and storage of this information. Accordingly, effective organizations match their information-processing needs with their information-processing requirements. Sparrow and Braun further distinguish between traditional organization design models, which date as early as the 1960s and 1970s, and more contemporary change models, which they identify as appearing in the late 1980s. In keeping with current trends, Sparrow and Braun devote relatively more space to the contemporary change models, while noting two major changes in thinking about multinational corporations during the mid-1980s. Specifically, Sparrow and Braun note that there was a shift away from emphasizing the role of the multinational headquarters as the center of attention to viewing the multinational affiliate (i.e., local facilities) as the major unit of analysis. In addition, they observe a shift from early assumptions of a "steady state" form of organization where one can establish and maintain a match or fit between the organization's structure and environment to the assumption of a constantly changing environment, which in turn requires rapidly changing organizational responses. As a result of these two key changes, contemporary change models have emphasized that managing the integration–differentiation dilemma must be less reliant on the organizational structure, and more reliant on "informal, people-based coordination and control mechanisms." The solution, referred to as a "matrix in the minds" of multinational corporation managers, shifts the focus from a formal structure to creating shared values via corporate culture and other mechanisms. This, in turn, is said to increase the importance of HRM policies and practices, though the key practices and policies may differ from those traditionally emphasized in domestic HRM research. Examples provided by Sparrow and Braun include an emphasis on the socialization of employees to ensure they adopt the corporate culture, mechanisms to help facilitate informal, horizontal communication, and formalized cross-departmental relationships. Essential to these models is the assumption that organizations must progress through a series of stages or strains, which enable them to build capability in this regard. Interestingly, these stages are reminiscent of the life cycle models discussed above, and thus similar questions may be raised regarding these contemporary change models (e.g., Sparrow and Braun question whether organizations must proceed through each stage in a linear fashion or whether some stages might by passed).

Contingency models represent the third approach to the strategic IHRM literature addressed by Sparrow and Braun. As explained by Sparrow and Braun, contingency models are quite extensive in terms of the number of independent variables that they include. Given the complexity of strategic IHRM, it is hardly surprising that these models include a large variety of independent variables. Among the interesting features of the more recent contingency model of strategic IHRM (Taylor et al., 1996) is the emphasis on different organizational levels—including the corporate level, the affiliate level, and individual employee groups—and how different variables influence each level. Despite their enthusiasm for the relatively new contingency models, Sparrow and Braun point out several criticisms, including the finding that a great deal of variance in the dependent variable remains unexplained, which is particularly troubling given that these models include increasingly large numbers of independent variables.

Next, Sparrow and Braun address the question of whether a firm's strategy *should* help determine HRM practices in other cultures. To answer this question, they offer four perspectives, including resource dependence theory, the resource-based view (RBV), the knowledge-based view, and the relational/social capital theory. The RBV assumes that organizations are bundles of tangible (e.g., real estate) and intangible (e.g., learning capabilities) resources, which hold the potential for competitive advantage if those resources are valuable, rare, not easily imitable, and nonsubstitutable. As noted by Sparrow and Braun, RBV theory provides the clearest argument for why organizations should transfer capabilities on a global basis, namely, because they benefit from having diverse, global workforces with diverse capabilities. A strategic resource that has competitive advantage to the organization should be transferred to other global facilities to make full use of its capabilities. Sparrow and Braun note, however, that RBV has been challenged recently and provide interesting research questions in regards to this theory.

Knowledge-based theory provides a related perspective, but one that differs from RBV in that the former focuses more on *tacit knowledge* as a resource. Knowledge-based theory considers both source transfer capacity (i.e., the ability of an organization to transmit knowledge to other facilities) and recipient transfer capacity (i.e., the ability of the transferee to receive the information). Organizational learning models are particularly relevant for knowledge-based theory. The notion of organizational simplicity, which refers to a tendency for organizations to overuse routines, is another important concept. Specifically, some scholars have suggested that acquiring international operations may help override tendencies toward organizational simplicity.

Social and relational capital theories presuppose that organizations acquire various forms of capital. Social capital assumes that goodwill helps form trust between organizations. Sparrow and Braun link recent research on interorganizational trust with these theories. Relational capital theory assumes that organizations gain advantage through several means, including reduced cost of transactions between relational network members and the increased ability for partners to learn from each other.

Sparrow and Braun go so far as to argue that the management of social capital is now viewed as a critical organizational competence. Specifically, they assert that while human capital theory views individuals, groups, and organizations as doing better because of their traits or characteristics (e.g., education), social capital theory views people, groups, or organizations as performing better due to their "connections," which might be based on trust, obligation, or dependency. Sparrow and Braun also introduce the notion of "structural holes," which are gaps that reflect a lack of attention to certain parties in a social network. Ultimately, they relate social capital theory to their theme of integration–differentiation, wherein social capital enables an organization to take advantage of diversity, while reconciling differences. They offer several interesting research questions in regard to social capital, including which specific IHRM policies and practices shape aspects and elements of social capital and how those policies influence a multinational organization's ability to learn, despite cultural differences. Clearly, construct definition issues remain as well, as one of the research questions posed by Sparrow and Braun is whether social capital is separate from human capital. They also note that recent theorists have begun to propose more sophisticated theories of social capital. For example, Sparrow and Braun suggest that the level of social capital needed to be successful may depend on the types of interdependencies, where higher levels of social capital are needed as the degree and complexity of interdependence between headquarters and international facilities increases.

To understand whether Western HRM strategies can be more effectively applied in other countries, Sparrow and Braun examine institutional theory in greater depth, noting that institutional theory views organizations' decisions as being less the consequence of strategic choices, and more the result of various isomorphic pulls from external (e.g., legal requirements, decisions by outside consultants) and internal (e.g., shared values) sources. Thus, they assume that there is a relatively weak linkage between strategy and managerial decisions regarding IHRM practices and policies. Sparrow and Braun's chapter introduces some important linkages between macro-level and micro-level behavior that need further addressing. It is clear that both perspectives would gain from reading each other's literature.

Lievens framed his chapter on international selection in terms of three basic questions. First, are there differences in the *use* of common selection procedures (e.g., interviews, cognitive ability tests) from country to country? Second, are commonly used selection procedures *perceived* differently across countries? Third, does the criterion-related validity of selection procedures *generalize* across countries?

The answer to the first question, in terms of whether the use of selection procedures varies from country to country is, simply put, yes. More interesting, then, is what factors determine which selection procedures will be used. Although some research has shown that culture is related to the use of certain selection procedures, Lievens concludes that much more research is needed to determine the combined and individual effects of culture, legal requirements, technology, and so forth on the use of selection procedures.

With regard to the second question, there has been a flurry of recent research, across several different countries (e.g., South Africa, Belgium) examining applicant perceptions of different selection tools. As reported by Lievens, these studies consistently show that interviews, resumes, and work samples are highly regarded; cognitive ability and personality tests are rated somewhere in the middle of the scale. Furthermore, job-relatedness was the major determinant of favorable perceptions. Lievens notes, however, that the countries studied to date are European or share a European heritage. Whether similar results are found in Asian countries is unknown. Finally, Lievens suggested incorporating perceptions of privacy in studying applicant reactions to testing. Although there has been only limited research on privacy, the growing use of the Internet for recruitment and testing, and concerns about data theft, appears to have spurred renewed interest in this construct.

The remainder of Lievens' chapter focuses on the third question, namely, whether the criterion-related validity of tests generalizes across countries. Lievens reports on the results of several meta-analyses indicating that cognitive ability and personality tests appear to be as valid in European countries as they are in North America. Like applicant perceptions, however, there appears to be almost no research on the validity of tests in Asian or African countries. Thus, the question of test validity generalization has not been completely answered.

Lievens offers a theoretical basis for predicting whether validity will generalize across countries by introducing the notion of within-country and across-country applications. In the former setting, criteria data and selection procedures are designed and used in the same country. In the latter situation, selection data and criteria data are collected in different countries. Stated somewhat differently, Lievens argues that it is critical that selection procedures used in one culture are matched with the definition of performance used by that same culture. Thus, Lievens calls for selection researchers in the IHRM area to carefully examine the criterion domain.

Lievens also addresses the notion that different selection procedures may be weighted differently in different countries. Culture therefore may affect the importance attached to different predictors (e.g., the importance of work experience), which in turn could affect the outcome of selection decisions and the validity of a selection battery across cultures.

Much work needs to be done when it comes to studying selection decisions on a global basis. Although there appear to be some similarities across countries in terms of how tests are perceived and the degree to which they are valid, much research needs to be conducted to examine whether these conclusions hold in other cultures, particularly Asia and Africa, which appear to be underrepresented in selection research.

Finally, no mention is made in Lievens' chapter regarding cultural intelligence. The standard definition of cultural intelligence is that it refers to one's ability to adapt to new cultural environments. Cultural intelligence has been described as being conceptually separate from emotional intelligence, in that the latter construct does not take into account different cultural contexts. As such, cultural intelligence has been described as "a multi-faceted structure that includes metacognitive, cognitive, motivational, and behavioral factors" (Harris & Lievens, 2005). Unlike many other constructs, the measurement of cultural intelligence has been the focus of little attention. Harris and Lievens described some existing approaches to measuring cultural intelligence, ranging from self-report questionnaires to simulation exercises (e.g., Lievens, Harris, Van Keer, & Bisqueret, 2003). Harris (2006) described structured interviews as yet another possible method for measuring cultural intelligence.

Harris and Lievens (2005) raised the issue of whether cultural intelligence generalizes across cultures or whether it is more specific to the situation. In other words, they asked whether an individual might adapt well in certain cultures, but not others. Noting that there are various typologies of culture (e.g., Hofstede), Harris and Lievens asserted that using measures of culture might be a reasonable way to assess the context and to determine whether cultural intelligence varies by the situation or not. Thus, the context and the degree of cultural intelligence may interact to determine success. Stated somewhat differently, the "fit" between the culture and cultural intelligence may also be important. Alternatively, it may be the case that cultural intelligence generalizes across cultures; individuals who are culturally skilled in one context will be similarly skilled in another, different context. To date, there has been relatively little application of what is called the "person-situation" approach in social psychology (Mischel, 2004) to selection and training (Harris & Lievens, 2005).

Because they involve communication between supervisors and subordinates, as well as assumptions about how performance is measured (e.g., on an individual basis or group basis), performance appraisal processes probably reflect a great deal about the culture in which they are embedded. As described in Bailey and Fletcher's chapter, much of the research concerning performance appraisal processes has a distinctly North American flavor. North American culture reflects relatively low power distance and high individualism. The growth of 360-degree feedback, for example, probably exemplifies this to a large extent by virtue of the collection of ratings from various parties, including peers and even subordinates, thus reflecting low power differences. Similarly, the focus of the 360-degree feedback is on the individual, rather than on group performance.

Bailey and Fletcher note a number of basic findings gleaned from predominantly North American sources that may not necessarily generalize to other cultures. Several studies, for example, have examined the relationship between self-ratings and ratings from other sources (e.g., peers). As Bailey and Fletcher assert, most research shows that high congruence between self- and other-ratings is associated with higher performance on independent measures. Whether this finding will hold up in other cultures, where modesty in self-ratings may be more prevalent, remains to be seen.

Despite the paucity of research on performance appraisal processes in regions other than North America and Western Europe, Bailey and Fletcher identify some potentially interesting findings from global research that are worthy of further investigation. As an example, they noted a study that reported Hong Kong employees were more accepting of their supervisor's ratings as compared to British employees. Moreover, Hong Kong employees were more supportive of the use of personality constructs in the performance appraisal process than were British employees. Such findings are particularly interesting because, as pointed out by Bailey and Fletcher, in the United States, performance appraisal is considered a "necessary evil" and there is much evidence that the performance appraisal is affected by many factors other than the employee's actual performance (Gioia & Longenecker, 1994).

One of the challenging questions in conducting global research on performance appraisal may be the lack of standardization of practices within a given country, let alone a given culture. As observed by Bailey and Fletcher, a study in India indicated that there were major differences in performance appraisal processes across different types of organizations. Thus, the nature of the organization (e.g., joint venture versus family-owned) may have a considerable impact on the purpose of the appraisal, as well as other features. Clearly, the type of organization will be important to consider in studying performance appraisal systems across cultures and will need to be measured if cross-cultural comparisons are to be made.

As explained by Bailey and Fletcher, economic changes in Japan offer some interesting opportunities to observe performance appraisal processes in transition. As discussed in their chapter, Japanese performance appraisal systems may adopt one of three approaches in reaction to economic changes, ranging from retention of current practices (which appear to be "subjective, disorganized, and closed") to the adoption of Western practices, or some kind of hybrid form of performance appraisal system. While it remains to be seen what kind of transformation will take place, this offers the opportunity to best understand what factors drive the kind of performance appraisal system that is established. If, for example, a Japanese firm is attempting to change its culture to a more individualistic system and to lower uncertainty avoidance, the firm may choose to use its performance appraisal system to help introduce organizational change. Alternatively, a firm might perceive that country culture needs to be preserved to some degree, and therefore utilize a hybrid approach to the new performance appraisal system. This may also tie into various strategic IHRM issues discussed in Sparrow and Braun's chapter on strategic international HRM in this volume.

Despite the lack of existing cross-cultural theories of performance appraisal systems, Bailey and Fletcher offer several promising directions for international researchers in this area. For instance, they noted a theoretical model developed by Flint (1999), which describes the factors influencing the perceived fairness of 360-degree feedback ratings. As observed by Bailey and Fletcher, although Flint's model does not explicitly include cultural issues, one can imagine building in cultural variables (such as power distance) into this model. Of course, culture may not simply have main effects on the variables of interest; culture may also interact with other variables. For example, procedural justice may be less important in predicting the overall fairness of outcomes in some cultures compared to other cultures.

In discussing the role of new technologies in performance appraisal practices, Bailey and Fletcher note that a couple of studies have compared 360-degree feedback ratings obtained via the Internet versus paper-and-pencil administration. These studies apparently do not show psychometric differences; Bailey and Fletcher suggest, however, that the type of administration used (i.e., Internet versus paper-and-pencil) may affect employees' or appraisers' reactions to the performance ratings. What is needed, however, is a model or theory of how the type of administration affects reactions, especially in a cultural context. For instance, Bailey and Fletcher refer to other research indicating that cultural differences exist regarding privacy concerns.

Bailey and Fletcher also describe the advantages, as well as the problems, that may arise from having a global "rollout" of a Web-based 360-degree feedback process. More research looking at the same organization, using a similar policy or practice, across different cultures would produce some interesting findings regarding the effect of culture on performance appraisal practices.

Harris and Park's chapter examines global research on compensation. Their chapter is divided into two major sections: research on the *direct* effects that culture may have on pay practices and research on the *indirect* effects that culture may have on pay practices. In terms of direct effects of culture, Harris and Park report existing research studies addressing two topics. Specifically, they located several studies examining how managers from different cultures differentially weight various factors in making pay decisions. Thus, at a micro-behavior level, culture does appear to affect pay practices. The second topic where research was found concerns the type of pay practices used (e.g., the use of pay-for-performance programs) and culture. Several studies using macro-level designs found significant relationships between culture and certain pay practices. Thus, at least for some pay practices, culture does seem to have a direct effect.

However, Harris and Park also describe many areas where the direct effect of culture on pay practices is unknown. Specifically, for many of the basic compensation practices, such as job evaluation, salary surveys, and pay structures, there is almost a complete absence of global research. Nevertheless, Harris and Park develop a number of hypotheses linking culture to the likely practice of these compensation techniques.

Regarding the second major section of their chapter, Harris and Park discuss the ways in which culture may indirectly affect pay practices. Most of this discussion involves the moderating role of culture on compensation. Focusing on pay level and pay for performance, Harris and Park point to a dearth of global research, but offer a ray of hope in that some motivation theories have begun to include international considerations. They also summarize a stream of research that has looked at the relationship between pay levels and pay and life satisfaction on a country-by-country basis. While that research has produced some interesting findings, no specific model or framework has been established that links culture to the income–pay satisfaction relationship. In general, then, there is a dearth of research addressing culture as a moderator of either employee perceptions of pay or organizational pay practices.

Another area addressed by Harris and Park is the role of culture on motivation in general, and on the motivational effects of pay in specific. Pay may serve as a motivator in many different international contexts. For example, Harris and Park reviewed a conceptual framework that focuses on host-country nationals (HCNs) and the cultural factors that are likely to affect their choice of comparison to others in judging pay fairness. Compensation may also be a motivating factor for expatriates, though no research appears to have been done in this area. Questions, such as the degree to which compensation can help support strategic IHRM goals (see Sparrow and Braun's chapter), need to be considered. Basic questions, including whether money is equally motivating across different cultures, have also not been addressed.

Finally, Harris and Park do not address the role of benefits in compensation. The role of benefits in compensation has not been researched widely in the domestic HR area either, and therefore it is not surprising that there is little global research here. To some extent, this is a function of how benefits are defined; in the United States, benefits may vary considerably from organization to organization because many of them (e.g., pension, health insurance) are discretionary and not required by the law. In other countries, however, what are optional benefits in the United States (e.g., health coverage) are provided universally to all citizens. Thus, researchers must be careful to clarify what a benefit means in a particular culture.

Hundley and Marett's chapter, which addresses unions and collective bargaining, provides a different perspective on the effects of culture. Specifically, they observe that despite the fact that by the cultural measures used by Hofstede that Western Europeans and Americans are quite similar (e.g., individualistically oriented), their labor relationships have evolved quite differently. For example, Hundley and Marett point out that in regions of the world such as northern Europe, unions represent a major component of national life, whereas in other regions, including the private sector in the United States, unions are actively discouraged. Likewise, the union membership density varies widely from country to country; Sweden, for instance, had a union membership rate of 79% in 2000, while France's union density rate was only 10% in that same year. Hundley and Marett therefore argue that a more "fine-grained approach" to national differences in labor relations is needed, given that traditional measures of culture may not correlate with union-related variables.

Another interesting aspect of international labor relations discussed by Hundley and Marett is the rapid change that has marked unions and labor relations in many parts of the world. One example mentioned by Hundley and Marett is Poland, where union membership has declined from nearly 50% of the workforce in 1989 to less than 20% of the workforce 10 years later. Hundley and Marett's chapter also covers some of the many differences between countries in terms of such things as union structure, approaches to collective bargaining, and effects of unionization on key outcomes. In terms of approaches to collective bargaining, for example, Hundley and Marett note that in countries such as the United States and Japan, negotiations occur at the level of the individual firm. In many countries in Europe, however, negotiations typically occur at the industry level. In countries such as Finland, agreements may cover all industries.

Of particular interest is that countries appear to differ in terms of the effects of unionization on outcomes such as productivity. Hundley and Marett note that although unions are associated with higher productivity in the United States, unionized firms in the United Kingdom and Australia were less productive until the 1980s when this effect began to diminish. Hundley and Marett conclude that when unions and management are compelled to work together, union presence does not reduce productivity. Another finding observed by Hundley and Marett is that unions in the United States have a negative effect on innovation, whereas no such effect is found in Europe. These findings deserve more further investigation.

Hundley and Marett briefly review several theories that have been offered to explain how unionization and labor relations processes have evolved, including those proposed by Dunlop (1958), Kerr and colleagues (1960), and more recently, Poole (1986). Most recently, Locke, Kochan, and Piore (1995) have examined unionization from a strategic perspective, arguing that responses to global competition vary considerably as a result of strategic choices made by various parties (e.g., managers, unions, and government). The strategic choices made by the different parties are said to produce various tensions, including management's choice between cost-cutting strategies versus strategies that add value (e.g., new training programs); having a core of full-time, highly trained employees as well as groups of contingent workers; and providing alternative means for employee voice and representation in the absence of unions. Again, there appears to be relatively little investigation as to how culture or politics affect these decisions.

The effects of globalization and the rapidly changing social and economic situation create interesting questions regarding labor relations and union strength. One of the most interesting questions is whether labor unions will be able to serve as a counterweight against global competition. Noting that unions appear to have weakened in terms of their power in the last 20 years, Hundley and Marett question the future of organized labor. They note, however, that others tend to see this period of reduced power as episodic in nature, in that union power has natural periods of decline and growth. The alternative view presented by Hundley and Marett is that the earlier growth of unions was due to a set of structural forces that is unlikely to be repeated in the near future.

In sum, there are major differences from country to country in terms of the structure and power of and degree to which workers belong to unions. Most of the explanations for these differences have not considered culture, at least in the way in which that term has been used in this volume. Although Hundley and Marett remain skeptical, it may be time for investigating whether culture, as measured in the ways discussed by Lawler et al., can help explain variance in various aspects of unions and collective bargaining. Even if culture is not a direct factor, culture may interact with other factors, such as the political context, to predict union structure or union–management relations. Or, perhaps culture is a distal factor, which in turn affects other more proximal factors that in turn affect these outcomes.

Mesmer-Magnus and Viswesvaran's chapter covers considerable ground in examining research on expatriate selection, training, and repatriation. Beginning with the criteria for success, it is noteworthy that "family situation" is one of the factors discussed; indeed, unlike domestic HR, where family issues have been given scant attention in terms of selection, this factor seems to play a much greater role in global HR. In this light, it would be interesting to examine employee beliefs about privacy in regards to assessing family situation. Would employees consider it to be an invasion of privacy, for example, for the company to review whether there are marital problems in determining whether to offer an expatriate assignment? Although many people are likely to feel uncomfortable with that kind of investigation in making a domestic job offer, why may they feel more comfortable with it if an overseas job move is being considered?

In terms of predictors of expatriate success, Mesmer-Magnus and Viswesvaran suggest that personality factors have been the most widely studied, and conclude that personality factors seem to have some validity in expatriate selection. Although there appears to be far less research on cognitive ability, Mesmer-Magnus and Viswesvaran assert that this predictor is likely to be the most predictive of expatriate success. Research is needed to test this hypothesis. Mesmer-Magnus and Viswesvaran note other predictors that may be relevant, including prior experience as an expatriate. They also discuss possible criteria to assess expatriate success.

Mesmer-Magnus and Viswesvaran also review expatriate training programs. Noting that most expatriate training programs do not appear to be well designed or to be considered of much value by companies, they identify several taxonomies used to classify such programs. Interestingly, one of the more effective techniques appears to be the culture assimilator, which consists of 75 to 100 episodes depicting cross-cultural encounters, and an instrument that was initially designed for circumstances where there was limited time for development and delivery. Mesmer-Magnus and Viswesvaran speculate that the more rigorous an expatriate training program is, the more effective it will be in preparing expatriates, although there is limited empirical research on such training programs.

One factor that appears to be somewhat ignored in the literature on expatriates is the different types of expatriate assignments that exist. Roberts, Kossek, and Ozeki (1998) provided a typology with four kinds of expatriate assignments, including aspatial, awareness building, SWAT teams, and virtual assignments. Briefly, an aspatial career involves several long-term assignments, in which the expatriate works in a variety of countries over the course of his or her career. From an organization's perspective, the purpose of an aspatial career is to create an in-depth understanding of global business, as well as an international set of contacts.

The focus of an awareness-building assignment is to enhance expatriates' understanding of cross-cultural issues within a short time frame (e.g., no longer than one year). A company may also use the awareness-building assignment as a means of assessing expatriates' cross-cultural skills. Families usually do not move with the expatriate in an awareness-building assignment, which reduces costs and minimizes other problems often associated with relocation (e.g., where will children attend school).

SWAT team assignments involve "highly mobile teams of experts, deployed on a short-term basis..." (Roberts et al., 1998, p. 98) to solve specific problems (e.g., a labor relations problem) or to work on well-defined projects (e.g., a new plant start-up). Typically, a SWAT team assignment lasts for three months or less. One major difference between the SWAT team assignment and the awareness-building assignment is the emphasis on employee development; in the former assignment, employee development is not a major concern (although it may occur indirectly). In an awareness-building assignment, employee development is the major goal.

The final type of international assignment is referred to as the "virtual solution." The virtual solution involves using a variety of technological tools (e.g., e-mail, instant messaging, videoconferencing) to enable interactions with individuals in other countries. Of the four kinds of assignments described here, the virtual solution probably provides the least amount of cross-cultural experience, as the "expatriate" in a virtual solution is not living in another country, and interactions with people from another culture are somewhat limited in scope. In addition, it may be more difficult to forge networks if all of the interactions are achieved through technology, with minimal face-to-face contact.

It is clear from the examination of these four kinds of international assignments that the selection tools, training programs, and other HR practices may differ considerably across them. For example, the knowledge, skills, abilities, and other requirements (KSAOs) to be successful in an aspatial assignment, for example, may be much different from the KSAOs needed for a SWAT team assignment. Indeed, the notion of the awareness-building assignment is to provide cross-cultural experience to employees who currently lack that kind of experience. Given the short-term nature and presumably relatively "safe" nature of the projects that would be assigned to an expatriate in this kind of assignment, motivation to participate may be more important than having high levels of cross-cultural skills. Likewise, the KSAOs for a SWAT assignment are likely to be far different from those required for an aspatial assignment, given that the SWAT assignment involves a much shorter time frame.

The type and amount of training is also likely to differ considerably, depending on the nature of the assignment. Expatriates preparing for aspatial assignments should receive much more intensive training, geared towards development of strong cross-cultural skills, probably highly focused on the country they will first work in. Employees involved in an awareness-building assignment are likely to need much different kinds of training. Their training is likely to be shorter, more cursory, and more focused on basic facts and information regarding the country in which they will be located, because the majority of the training will probably occur in the assignment itself.

The type of assignment also has significant implications for how expatriate performance should be measured. An aspatial career assignment would focus more on traditional performance measurement issues. Specifically, the performance evaluation would assess the degree to which expatriates are successful in achieving the organizational goals that have been determined to be important for this assignment. Some weight may also be given to cross-cultural skills acquisition, as this may be an important part of an aspatial career assignment. For an awareness-building assignment, where the purpose is to develop the employee, performance should be measured in terms of the degree to which the expatriate has acquired cross-cultural awareness and skills. For a SWAT team assignment, the performance measurement approach would focus almost exclusively on the accomplishment of specific organizational goals, without reference to cross-cultural skills per se. Moreover, because this kind of assignment does not directly address developmental aspects, cross-cultural skills are unlikely to be a central part of the performance evaluation.

Finally, the virtual assignment involves cross-cultural interactions, but mainly through technology, as opposed to face-to-face interactions. Given the difficulties associated with the lack of face-to-face interactions, an important aspect of this type of assignment may be learning how to communicate effectively in a virtual environment. Note that I am not suggesting that cross-cultural communication is unimportant in other assignments; rather, this dimension may take on much greater importance in a virtual assignment. Clearly, this is an area for more research.

Several other factors may also affect the context of the assignment. Mesmer-Magnus and Viswesvaran mention factors such as cultural toughness and job toughness. Like the nature of the assignment, these factors are also likely to affect the KSAOs needed. High levels of flexibility, for example, would appear to be much more important for an assignment in a culturally tough country compared to a country that is not culturally tough.

In general, then, I submit that more attention should be paid to the context of the expatriate assignment than has been the case so far. To date, discussion of what KSAOs should be necessary has assumed certain notions about expatriate assignments, rather than first analyzing the tasks or functions to be performed in an expatriate assignment and then determining the needed KSAOs (for an exception, see Lievens et al., 2003). Determination of the tasks or functions that will be performed in an expatriate assignment demands that a closer examination be performed of the specific assignment.

The final section in Mesmer-Magnus and Viswesvaran's chapter addresses repatriation issues. Repatriation apparently is a significant problem for many organizations; Mesmer-Magnus and Viswesvaran cite figures indicating that some two thirds of returning expatriates perceive the assignment to have had a negative effect on their career, and fewer than half receive a promotion upon return from the organization. Problems associated with repatriation seem to be due to failure on the part of organizations to properly prepare for the return of expatriates. Thus, the causes of, and presumably solutions to, repatriation problems are much different from the problems experienced by expatriates in their assignments.

Cerdin and Bird's chapter addresses careers from an employee perspective. Throughout their chapter, they address the definition of a career and distinguish between different types of career patterns, as well as the potential influence of culture on careers. Clearly, even a definition of the term "career" is not simple; various definitions have been developed in a variety of disciplines. They conclude that a common denominator in a career is an evolving sequence of work experiences over time. Another perspective is to view a career from a resource-based perspective, where a career is viewed in terms of the resources that accrue over time. Cerdin and Bird link this approach to the concept of the boundaryless career, which essentially views careers from an employee-focused perspective, rather than a company orientation.

There are clearly different kinds of careers, however. Cerdin and Bird identify at least four common career models, ranging from the Japanese or elite cohort approach to the multinational corporation model. At a different level, Cerdin and Bird argue that there is a significant difference between a global career and an expatriate experience. Clearly, what seems needed here is a grand theory of careers to pull together the many approaches that have been taken, as well as the changes in how careers develop as the work world becomes increasingly global.

Having discussed different definitions of careers, Cerdin and Bird proceed by examining both determinants and outcomes of careers. In terms of determinants of careers, for example, Cerdin and Bird discuss the motivation to have an expatriate experience, including the notion that certain cultures may promote that kind of experience. The focus appears to be on factors that might *encourage* one to have such experiences; another approach may be to consider the factors that *inhibit* one's motivation to have an expatriate experience. In this regard, there may be personality factors (e.g., openness to new experience) as well as perceived costs associated with expatriate experiences that discourage individuals from seeking them out.

Cerdin and Bird also address the outcomes of having international career experiences. In this regard, Cerdin and Bird emphasize a career capital approach, including both social and intellectual capital, as positive outcomes of such experiences. Specifically, they suggest that what can be learned includes knowing who (e.g, becoming acquainted with appropriate contacts), knowing how (e.g., learning how to do new tasks), knowing what (e.g., the nature and extent of understanding of projects and products), and knowing why (e.g., the nature and extent of one's knowledge of why a project or office was established in one country rather than another country). In light of this approach, Cerdin and Bird argue that the role and purpose of mentoring, and perhaps other career-related processes such as socialization, may be rather different from has heretofore been described in the literature. That is, if the purpose of international experiences is to acquire knowledge, the role of these activities should be to enhance knowledge acquisition and to inhibit the loss of knowledge. Clearly, much more theorizing and research is needed to build and test models of knowledge acquisition and related processes.

Finally, it should be noted that there are numerous linkages between Sparrow and Braun's chapter and Cerdin and Bird's chapter in terms of resource-based views of careers and organizations. Although the former chapter addresses similar concepts from a macro-level approach and Cerdin and Bird's chapter addresses these concepts from a more micro-level approach, there is clearly an opportunity for both perspectives to benefit from the other. Multilevel theories have become increasingly popular in the literature and there appears to be opportunities in this area to build similar models.

CONCLUSIONS

In sum, there is much we do not know about IHRM; many of the topics covered in this volume suffer from a lack of research. Even the basic question of how to measure culture is not completely answered; we do not know whether some measures of culture are more useful than others. The good news is that IHRM is likely to remain a fruitful area for future researchers for years to come. In addition to the need for empirical research, there is a shortage of good theories in many areas of IHRM. I conclude with two major points. First, I urge scholars to carefully consider their methodologies in studying IHRM to ensure that they are using the most appropriate approaches to answer their questions. Second, I encourage investigators to develop and test well-developed theories and avoid relying on dust-bowl empiricism to explain their findings.

REFERENCES

Bryk, A. S., & Raudenbush, S. W. (1992). *Hierarchical linear models: Applications and data analysis methods*. Newbury Park, CA: Sage.

Dunlop, J. T. (1958). *Industrial Relations Systems*. New York: Holt, Rinehart & Winston.

Dyer, N. G., Hanges, P. J., & Hall, R. (2005). Applying multilevel confirmatory factor analysis techniques to the study of leadership. Leadership Quarterly, 16, 149–167.

Flint, D. (1999). The role of organizational justice in multi-source performance appraisal: Theory-based applications and directions for research. *Human Resource Management Review, 9,* 1–20.

Gioia, D., & Longenecker, C. O. (1994). Delving into the dark side: The politics of executive appraisal. *Organizational Dynamics, 22*(3), 47–58.

Harris, M. (2006). Cultural skill: An emerging construct for the 21st century. *Industrial-Organizational Psychologist, 43*(1), 43–47.

Harris, M., & Lievens, F. (2005). Selecting employees for global assignments: Can assessment centers measure cultural intelligence? pp. 221–240. In A. Rahim & R. Golembiewski (Eds.), *Current topics in management (Vol. 10)*. Somerset, NJ: Transaction Publishers.

Heine, S., Lehman, D., Peng, K., & Greenholtz, J. (2002). What's wrong with cross-cultural comparisons of subjective Likert scales? The reference-group effect. *Journal of Personality and Social Psychology, 82,* 903–918.

Kerr, C., Dunlop, J. T., Harbison, F. H. & Myers, C. A. (1960). *Industrialism and the Industrial Man*. Cambridge, MA: Harvard University Press.

Kogut, B., & Singh, H. (1988). The effect of national culture on the choice of entry mode. *Journal of International Business Studies,* 19, 411–434.

Lievens, F., Harris, M., Van Keer, E., & Bisqueret, C. (2003). Predicting cross-cultural training performance: The validity of personality, cognitive ability, and dimensions measured by an assessment center and a behavior description interview. *Journal of Applied Psychology, 88,* 476–489.

Locke, R., Kochan, T., Piore, M. (1995). Reconceptualizing comparative industrial relations: Lessons from international research. *International Labour Review, 134,* 139–152.

Mischel, W. (2004). Toward an integrative science of the person. *Annual Review of Psychology, 55,* 1–22.

Poole, M. (1986). *Industrial Relations: Origins and Patterns of National Diversity,* London: Routledge and Kegan Paul.

Roberts, K., Kossek, E., & Ozeki, C. (1998). Managing the global workforce: Challenges and strategies. *Academy of Management Executive, 12,* 93–108.

Schneider, B., Hanges, P., Smith, D. B., & Salvaggio, A. N. (2003). Which comes first: Employee attitudes or organizational financial and market performance? *Journal of Applied Psychology, 88,* 836–851.

Scott, I. (2006). On the need for probity when physicians interact with industry. *Internal Medicine Journal, 36,* 265–269.

Shenkar, O. (2001). Cultural distance revisited: Towards a more rigorous conceptualization and measurement of cultural differences. *Journal of International Business Studies, 32,* 519–537.

Taylor, S., Beechler, S., & Napier, N. (1996). Toward an integrative model of strategic international human resource management. *Academy of Management Review, 21,* 959–985.

Tihanyi, L., Griffith, D. A., & Russell, C. J. (2005). The effect of cultural distance on entry mode choice, international, diversification, and MNE performance: A meta-analysis. *Journal of International Business Studies, 36,* 270–283.

Author Index

A

Abrahamsen, M., methodological problems of earlier studies, 109
Ackerman, P. L., training programs and approaches, 201
Addison, J. T., works councils and productivity, 173
Addison, J. Y.
  financial performance in U.S. and, 173
  workers covered by union agreements, 172
Aditya, R., effectiveness of certain leadership styles, 19
Aditya, R. N., culture and leadership, 18
Adler, N. J.
  competencies required for effectiveness, 217
  decision making and information processing, 117
  female expatriates and adjustment, 188
  influencing factors on IHRM activities of MNCs, 78
  linking HRM policies and practices, 78
  MNCs and progressive series of attitudes, 79
  person-related predictors, 185
  resolving repatriation problems, 23
Adler, P., concept of social capital, 217
Adler, P. S., social capital and, 91
Adsit, D., 360-degree feedback and, 135
Ainsworth, M., "traditional" PA approach, 128
Alderfer, C. P., ERG theory and, 153
Allen, N. J., follower affective commitment and, 22
Allgar, V., positivist approach to documentary analysis, 46
Alliger, G. M., general learning and training principles, 200
Allport, G. W., improving race relations during the 1960s, 187
Almeida, P., "knowledge leveraging" perspective, 96
Almond, P., policies on unions and, 176
Altman, Y., repatriation as "career disaster", 215
Amba-Rao, S., PA practices in India, 131
Anand, J., qualitative case study approach, 31
Anderson, J. R., training programs and approaches, 201
Anderson, N.
  criterion-related validity of cognitive ability tests, 113
  potential variability in terms of selection procedure use, 109
  situational specificity hypothesis, 113
  validity generalization hypothesis, 112
Anderson, S., computer adaptive rating scales (CARS), 137
Antal, B.
  competencies required for effectiveness, 217
  Germans and expanding networks, 217
Argote, L., "careers as repositories of knowledge", 219
Ariga, K., PA practices in Japan, 132
Arnolds, C., ERG theory and, 153
Arthur, M. B.
  "boundaryless careers", 208, 216
  definitions of career, 208
  internal motivation, 214

Arthur, W., Jr.
  emotional intelligence (EI), 199
  expatriate success, 184, 189
  method versus construct distinction, 117
  training programs and approaches, 201
Arvey, R. D.
  Japan and job discrimination, 111
  predictor weighting and, 118
Asai, M., individualism and collectivism study, 15
Ashkanasy, N., Australia's cultural values, 129
Athanassiou, N., "advice networks" and, 96
Austin, J. T., job performance, 188
Autio, E., joint ventures and, 90
Avolio, B. J.
  culture and leadership, 18
  reward leadership behaviors and, 17
Awasthi, V. N., teamwork and, 20
Aycan, Z., expatriate assignments, 184
Ayres, H., development-oriented PA schemes, 130

B

Baba, M., career stages and plateaus, 213
Bae, J., MNCs from different countries and, 94
Bailey, C.
  feedback and PA ratings, 128, 135
  responsiveness to feedback, 129
  self-assessments to external raters, 139
Bailey, J. R., self-identity and, 18
Baker, T., participant observation and, 37
Baldry, C., multisource assessments and, 128
Baldwin, T. T., training programs and approaches, 201
Bamber, G. J.
  collective bargaining relationship, 178
  union activism and, 170
Banai, M., expatriate selection process, 186
Bar-On, R., emotional intelligence (EI), 199
Barbeite, F. G., off-the-job development activities, 129
Barkema, H. G.
  effects of time and experience on organizational learning, 87
  five cognitive changes and, 89
  international joint ventures and, 88
Barney, J. B., resource-based view (RBV) of the firm, 85
Baron, H.
  national differences and selection practices, 109
  use of selection procedures, 108
Barrett, G. V., matching predictor and criterion domains, 115
Barrick, M. R.
  conscientiousness and job performance, 185
  personality tests and, 113
  predictor weighting and, 118
  salary survey information and, 151
Barry, D., model of HR change in MNCs, 95

Subject Index

CONTENTS

ABOUT THIS BOOK

We know how important it is to look after our bodies, as suggested by the enormous number of diet, exercise and general self-care books available. But it's equally as important to look after your brain. After all, without it you wouldn't be aware of anything at all, and it's important to keep challenging it so that it continues to learn.

This book provides a practical guide to looking after your brain. It isn't a reference book, designed to teach you interesting facts about what's going on upstairs. Instead, it focuses entirely on things that are directly *useful* to you in your everyday life. There are, for example, pages on the importance of sleep for learning, and on methods for solving difficult puzzles through what seems to be guesswork – all presented in a practical way, so you can apply them immediately to your day-to-day life.

The book also integrates a huge amount of fun brain-training material. The pages are packed with puzzles and exercises to try yourself, and most can be solved by writing directly in the book. Due to the wide range of material, there are sure to be many that you have never encountered before – but that's exactly the point. To train your brain you want to provide it with constant *new* challenges, so try everything out and do your best not to skip over anything that looks 'too difficult'. The chances are these are just the puzzles that will help you most of all!

The book is broken up into chapters, each consisting of a small number of separate sections. The sections can be read in any order, so there's no need to go by chapter, or by section within a chapter – everything is designed to be dipped into and dipped out of as you please, and as you have time. All the puzzles have solutions at the back, and you shouldn't be afraid to check them for 'inspiration' if you get stuck.

CAN YOU TRAIN YOUR BRAIN?

Your brain is constantly learning. Every new experience teaches your brain a little more about the world, and so over time you become smarter and smarter, and able to make faster, more sensible decisions. Many of these are not necessarily conscious decisions, but rather the natural result of your brain processing everything it's found out about the world to date. You train your brain every day, just by using your senses to experience the world around you.

So you can certainly train your brain in the general sense. But under the 'brain training' banner, it is often claimed that your brain can learn to make smarter, better decisions about things it hasn't directly experienced, and that this can be done simply by practising other, seemingly unrelated tasks. Some claim that playing the same simple games over and over will lead to a wide range of mental benefits, while others say that this is nonsense. The truth probably lies between the two extremes – exposing your brain to new and novel activities does, indeed, teach it general truths about the world and how to respond to new stimuli, and sometimes these can help your brain with completely unrelated activities. But it's also likely to be the case that once you have played the same, identical game a few dozen times that your iterative mental improvement from each successive play of the game will decrease just as your day-to-day improvement at the game itself also becomes steadily smaller and smaller.

Good brain training, therefore, involves challenging yourself with a constant diet of new and novel tasks. The more variety your brain encounters, the better. It's the new experiences that teach it the most, and so for the greatest mental improvement you should avoid repeating unchanging tasks. If you aren't consciously needing to stop and think, perhaps the subconscious parts of your brain also aren't being sufficiently challenged?

TRAIN YOUR BRAIN WITH THIS BOOK

This book is designed to provide just such a challenge – an incredibly varied range of puzzles, games and activities to help keep your grey matter in top condition. You could, of course, also find this challenge by traveling the world, learning foreign languages, or taking up a new musical instrument, but these aren't luxuries that all of us have the time – or money – for, and so, for the rest of us, that's where this book comes in.

Chapters two to four cover many of the general behaviours of your brain that you might not be aware of. Some of these can be critically important to know about, so you can make safer, faster choices in high-stress or other unusual situations. Chapter five then introduces you to the creative side of your brain, which is incredibly powerful – whether you consider yourself 'creative' or not. This is then followed by chapters on language skills, math, reasoning and spatial awareness.

Each chapter is broken down into sections, and each section of the book includes both an introduction as well as day-to-day practical tips to help build your brain skills in that area. Most sections also include some specific puzzles that are related to that area, which you can use to test out your new skills right away. Of course, the truth is that you will in reality be using a mixture of skills for every puzzle. For example, every decision you make uses 'reasoning', so these headings are there simply to help classify and break down the material – they shouldn't be taken as a literal description of the only activity that is going on when attempting a particular puzzle. This notwithstanding, each chapter contains puzzles where the primary focus is on the corresponding skills, so if you want to work on your map-reading skills then the spatial awareness chapter would be the one to turn to.

PUZZLES FOR FUN BRAIN TRAINING

Moments of high emotion can be very memorable, but your brain generally learns best when it is relaxed and not under stress. It stands to reason, therefore, that the best brain-training activities should also minimize stress. It's good to challenge yourself but, once it turns into frustration, your brain will start to learn that the activity you are engaged in should be avoided where possible. Positive reinforcement, through fun and entertaining brain training, is therefore beneficial.

All of the puzzles and challenges in this book have been designed to be fun. You won't find any long lists of sums to complete, or the same type of puzzle repeated over and over again, but rather a variety of tasks designed to make you think but without causing any deep frustration. If this ever ceases to be the case, you should put the puzzle aside and try another. Come back to it later and see if you can make progress, or turn to the solutions at the back and write in part of the solution to make it easier. In some cases, you could also think about *why* the solution at the back must be correct – although this isn't helpful for all puzzles. This same advice also works if you aren't sure about the rules – check the solved puzzle to see what the instructions mean, then pop back to the actual puzzle and give it a go yourself.

RELAXATION

It's important to try to relax while you work through the puzzles. Of course, simply *wishing* to be relaxed is unlikely to work and may even have the opposite effect, but there are various techniques you can try to help you get there. Any activity you enjoy in your free time is often a good start, whether that's sports, arts, games or even just reading. Laughter is a great relaxant too, so a favourite sitcom can even be a useful tool for helping you to prepare for better brain training.

Other methods of relaxation include trying to calm your breathing by taking longer, deeper breaths, although this should be done only in moderation and it should be stopped immediately if you start to feel light-headed or have any other side effects.

Light physical exercise, even as simple as just getting up and walking around a room while attempting to use as many muscles as possible, can also help you relax. A change of position can help you relax both physically *and* mentally.

Perhaps surprisingly, simply forcing yourself to smile can also help relax you – there is such a strong link between happiness and smiling, that just the act of smiling can help you to feel happy.

THE MOZART EFFECT

Good relaxation techniques for brain training can also help get your brain in a suitable state for learning. A particularly effective one for many people is simply to listen to music. Indeed, the effect of music on helping to put people into a state where they demonstrate better use of their mental faculties is known popularly as the 'Mozart Effect'.

Despite the name, music for priming your brain does not need to be by Mozart, but simply any kind of music that helps you to feel relaxed and yet doesn't send you to sleep. Just as many people find upbeat music helps them to work out physically, so positive and uplifting music helps your brain to work to the best of its ability too. It's important to note, however, that the 'Mozart Effect' does not mean that listening to music just by itself will make you any smarter.

FOCUS – AND DISTRACTIONS

A distracted brain does not learn as well as a brain that is concentrating on the task in hand. Although your brain carries on many different thought processes simultaneously, it is impossible to *consciously* think about multiple things – although we may think we do, in reality we are simply switching between different thoughts in quick succession. Studies have shown that even those people who think they are 'good multitaskers' do not work as well when they do multiple things at once as when they properly concentrate.

DISTRACTIONS

Distractions come in many different forms. There are audible distractions, such as chatter, noise, alarms or even just the click of a computer keyboard. There are physical distractions, such as an uncomfortable chair or desk, a breeze from an open window or even a room that is too hot or too cold. There can be distracting smells, for example from food or drinks, and there can even be distracting tastes that linger on from previous consumption. And then of course there are visual distractions, which run the gamut from email notifications through to people waving for your attention! Of course you cannot control all of these things, but even so when you are trying to 'get things done' you should do what you can reasonably and safely do to minimize them. Shut the door and turn off email or social media alerts, if you can, and find a comfortable position to work from.

FOCUS

Even if we eliminate most distractions, we still need to focus. It's very easy for our minds to drift, and indeed many of us find ourselves perfectly capable of spending a day doing 'work' without actually getting any real work done – if we have the opportunity. It's amazing how many distracting activities we can find to spend time on, whether it's reading news, chatting online with friends or simply doing easy, unimportant work while avoiding what really needs to get done.

Often the hardest part of a task seems to be the getting started, because, typically, once we have overcome the initial inertia against beginning something new, keeping going seems much easier. If this is a problem for you, there are various methods that can help avoid this problem, such as deliberately jumping right into the middle of a task. While it may make logical sense to begin at the start of a report, essay or other project, often the mental pressure of having the 'entire thing' to do feels too overwhelming, leading us to put off any attempts to actually get going. It's much better to do *something*, and then, having got past the 'getting started' hurdle, it's considerably easier to jump back and work on the beginning section of a task, if it's necessary to do so. From this point, maintaining focus often proves easier.

GETTING THINGS DONE
If you find it hard to avoid distractions and get focused, try these tips:

- Make a prioritized list of things you have to do, and put deadlines on it – then display the list somewhere where you can hold yourself, or have someone else hold you, to account for those deadlines.

- Break complex tasks down into a series of much smaller targets, the same way a company would distribute work among many employees. It's much easier to tackle a small, discrete problem than worry about the whole thing at once.

- Try to set aside enough time to complete each individual task you work on, rather than leaving them half-finished – sometimes it can be tricky to pick up exactly where you left off, leading to frustration.

- If you can, complete one project before starting the next.

FOCUS PUZZLES

These puzzles will require your full attention to solve.

1. Place digits from 1 to 9 into each white square so that no number repeats in any row, column or bold-lined 3×3 box. Shaded squares should remain empty, and can therefore represent different digits depending if they are considered as part of a row, column or box.

						6		2
		3	7				8	9
	4		9	6			7	
8			3		2	5		1
	3			7			9	
1		6	8		4	2		
	5				8		2	
3					7	4		
4		7						

2. Place an 'X' or an 'O' into each box so that no lines of four or more 'X's or 'O's are formed – not even diagonally.

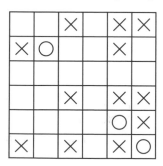

3. Draw solid lines to divide the grid to form a complete set of standard dominoes, with exactly one of each domino. A '0' represents a blank on a traditional domino. Use the check-off chart to keep track of the dominoes you have already placed.

1	4	4	1	1	3	0	5
1	3	6	3	3	2	2	6
6	5	0	3	2	3	1	5
6	6	4	1	4	6	0	2
0	2	1	2	2	5	5	0
2	4	3	3	6	4	4	0
1	5	5	4	5	0	6	0

0	1	2	3	4	5	6	
							0
							1
							2
							3
							4
							5
							6

4. Place a 0 or 1 in each empty square, so that there are an equal number of each digit in every row and column. Reading along a row or column, there may be no more than two of the same digit in succession. For example, 10011001 would be a valid row, but 10001101 would not be valid due to the three '0's in succession.

					0		0
		1		0	0	1	
			1				
0			0		0		
		1		0			1
			0				
	1	1	0		1		
1		0					

5. In the completed puzzle above, how many times does the sequence '010' appear, either horizontally or vertically?

SLEEP – AND CONSCIOUS THOUGHT

If we don't get enough sleep then of course we get tired, but the effects of this can be far more serious than just an urge to close our eyes. Studies have shown that sleep deprivation can have a similar effect to being drunk, and what's more, just as with inebriation, we might not even be aware of it at the time. Those with safety critical jobs usually have mandated rest periods for this very reason, since our bodies physically require sleep to maintain full mental competence.

At a lesser level, lack of sleep can have a range of lesser debilitating effects. It makes it harder to concentrate, and we are rarely at our sharpest. It also means we are less likely to spot mistakes we make, so often, if we slept for even a short while and then continued, we'd actually make faster progress than simply plodding on. And, of course, it is much less pleasant to be doing most things while tired.

MANAGING SLEEP

Maintaining a good sleep pattern is important, and even if it isn't always possible it should still be something you continually aspire to. Sleep also doesn't just need to be overnight – studies have shown that it is perfectly natural to have two separate sleeping periods during each 24-hour period, as for example some societies in hotter countries do with their afternoon siestas, although they have also shown that *more* than two periods of sleep won't work for most people.

Sleeping to a regular schedule also makes it easier to fall asleep quickly, since your body gets into a natural rhythm, and sometimes to wake feeling fresher too. Minimizing disturbances at sleep time is also wise, as is allowing yourself a brief period of time before closing your eyes when you are winding down a little. Otherwise, sometimes you'll find your mind full of thoughts about whatever you have just been dealing with, which can make it hard to get to sleep. Some people find that meditation, which can take the form of prayers if appropriate to your beliefs, also helps in this regard.

If you regularly have trouble sleeping you should consult an expert, since an accumulated lack of sleep can lead to significant mental health issues, quite apart from also being extremely frustrating!

YOUR UNCONSCIOUS MIND

Sleep also has some less obvious tricks up its cerebral sleeve. Firstly, it forms a key part of the process of storing memories. During sleep, your brain rehearses and re-examines the events of the day, learns from them and files away both the memories and the lessons it can take from the memories. If your sleep is impaired, you literally are less able to learn, and less able to remember what you have tried to learn.

Another amazing feature of sleep is that your brain will carry on processing the things you have thought about during the day – *without* your conscious knowledge of this. So if you are stuck on a particularly thorny problem, or have run short of ideas for how to make progress on a task, then try sleeping on it. It's genuinely good advice, because your unconscious mind is entirely capable of coming up with new solutions, which you will then find seemingly magically popping into your mind at hopefully opportune moments.

Indeed, much of our thought is inevitably completely unconscious – we can of course perform complex activities, such as driving, without consciously thinking about every manoeuvre, but our brains can do more than just apply learned procedures. Helping ensure that your brain gets enough sleep, has minimal distractions, and is in a relaxed state, all go a significant way to helping you think genuinely smarter thoughts.

SLEEP PUZZLES

If you get stuck on one of the following puzzles, try sleeping on it. They are all the type of puzzle where an insight might arrive when you least expect it to do so.

6. The day before yesterday I was 8 years old. Next year I'm going to be 11 years old. How can this be?

7. If Cowboy Bill rode into town on Friday, and rode out two days later on Friday, how can that possibly be true?

8. I have a bottle of lemonade that I have started drinking. There's more than half left but it isn't full. I've promised to leave exactly half a bottle for my friend. How can I be sure to do this, without making use of any other item to help measure it?

9. I'm holding a horse race but I want there to be a twist on the usual proceedings: the horse that comes in last will win. I don't want the race to last forever, so what can I do to persuade the jockeys to ride normally?

10. My pet hamster has got stuck in a hole in the ground, and I can't reach in to get it out. Can you think of a simple and safe way to get it out without hurting it?

11. It's pitch dark and you have a wooden splint, a candle and an oil lamp. There is only one match, so what do you light first?

12. If you pick up a scarf, how can you tie a knot in it without letting go of either end?

13. How do you put your left hand into the right pocket, and your right hand into the left pocket, of a pair of jeans without crossing your arms?

14. Between sunset and sunrise, I got out of bed 120 times, and yet I managed to sleep more than 8 hours between each and every one of the times that I got up. How can this be true?

15. If I tell you that I know someone who predicts the future, how can it possibly be the case that I am telling the truth?

16. A father gave his son a family heirloom, and a different father gave his son two family heirlooms. Yet there were only two heirlooms in total – how can this be true?

17. We can all agree that one comes before two, but how can two come after three and four before one?

18. How can you stand over a bare concrete floor and drop an uncooked egg for a metre without it breaking? You cannot modify the egg in any way.

19. When you add these to a box, the lighter it becomes – and yet the box stays empty. What are they?

20. If I go for a walk into a forest, what is the furthest distance I can get from the edge of the forest, expressed as a fraction of the entire width of the forest?

21. You are in a house with fantastic southern views from all four sides, and see a bear. What colour is the bear?

22. You have four identical coins on the table in front of you. How can you arrange them so that every coin is simultaneously touching all of the other coins?

DEALING WITH STRESS

We all experience stress in our lives from time to time, and it can be an important biological cue to help us focus on a pressing problem. However, in many cases it can also devolve into an ongoing source of anxiety which starts to corrode many aspects of our lives, making it hard to get anything done, and damaging important relationships.

If stress starts to take over your life then it is essential to do something about it. This can either take the form of tackling the source of the stress, if possible, or learning to manage the stress itself. The one thing you should never do is to ignore it – if you are continually under stress, your brain is less able to learn and you are far more susceptible to both physical and mental illness.

SIMPLE METHODS TO LESSEN STRESS

Laughter really is a great medicine, at least in terms of making you feel better. It has been proven to alleviate stress, and so if you are feeling stressed then you could do worse than watch something that will make you laugh.

Another great way of relieving stress is physical exercise. Just going for a walk can help, as can more strenuous physical exercise such as working out in a gym, or going swimming. Even just the change of scene can help, since it forces you to refocus, at least briefly, on the physical world around you.

Social contact is also an amazingly powerful tonic. Humans are social animals, and the vast majority of us are much happier in the company of others than on our own. Social media can provide some of this feeling of connectedness, but nothing beats physical contact with other humans.

Ironically, stress, particularly the work-based type, often leads to us working longer hours and having less social time, which in turn increases our stress and makes us less effective at our job. Just as with sleep, taking a break can often lead to faster, better work than simply trying to always power through.

Perversely, deliberately slowing down can sometimes also help with certain sources of stress. Feelings of constant pressure can sometimes be reduced by the act of simply managing your time. Avoid doing everything at breakneck speed, or packing too much into each day. This creates a feeling of control which can help you feel more empowered and less stressed. Just gently slowing your breathing for a minute can be enough, even, to reduce stress – giving your addled brain a moment to escape from the stressful thoughts circulating inside it.

Some people fall back on drugs such as alcohol to help them relax, but while these chemical 'solutions' can in some cases provide short-term escape from stress they are certainly not long-term solutions, and those who come to rely on them will typically end up with significant health problems – both mentally and physically.

CREATING AN ANTI-STRESS STRATEGY

For longer-term methods of avoiding stress, try to restructure your time, if you can, to minimize the stressful periods:

- Set aside 'relaxation' time, or decide that when you are relaxing you will definitely *not* think about your sources of stress, whether they be work deadlines or family-related issues. No matter your responsibilities to others, if you don't look after yourself then you won't be able to help them. You can't be on 24-hour call every day.

- Set a schedule so you know when you will be dealing with the stress-related issues, and try to avoid thinking about them at any other time.

- If you're worrying you might forget to do things, unload them from your brain and make a written list – this simple act can really help.

THE SCIENCE OF GUESSING

Young children have little or no fear of failure, which is an important tool for learning to handle the world. They'd never learn to walk if they were afraid of falling. This childhood fearlessness extends far beyond the toddler years – for example, learning to ride a bicycle as a child is much less nerve-racking than as an adult, where the fear of falling typically becomes much more dominant.

In life in general, fear of failure often holds people back from trying new things. This doesn't just apply to physical fear, but to conscious thought too, limiting what we feel we can do. We *think* we can't do things, and so we don't try. How many times have you heard someone say, 'I can't do that', when perhaps they actually could if they really tried?

As many people age they start to develop a learned helplessness in the face of unfamiliar tasks. This instinctive avoidance of the new shows up in the logical inconsistency of someone who claims they 'can't do maths' while knowing exactly how much they have in the bank, or the pensioner who avoids learning how to send email while continuing to solve complex daily crosswords.

Children learn through experimentation and guesswork, and a limited fear of failure. Children don't yet know what they can and can't do, so give a child a puzzle book and he or she will happily try any puzzle they turn to, whereas an adult will look for the puzzles they already know how to do and will often skip those that are less familiar.

MAKING PROGRESS BY GUESSING

Next time you're stuck on a puzzle, or aren't sure how to handle a situation, try just guessing. When you guess on a puzzle you are usually making a choice without any good reason, and in life in general you may have no idea if something is a sensible choice or not. But, simply by trying out the guess, you are likely to learn more than you knew before. Even if the guess proves itself wrong, or not good in some way, you gain knowledge that will often help make your *next* guess a better one. And in some cases, such as with puzzles, finding out what definitely is *not* correct also moves you a step to the actual solution, plus it can help you to spot patterns that you hadn't previously seen.

An experimental approach works for many aspects of life. If you're a writer unable to put down the first paragraph, or come up with a plot, then make a guess at what will work, even if you feel sure you won't stick with it, and get going. It's a better option than never writing anything. Or if you're looking to move to a new place, or change jobs, but have no idea where to begin, try exploring new options by looking at random places on a map, or arbitrary job listings. When you overthink big decisions, they can feel overwhelming. Making a small start at them, no matter how insignificant or pointless it may seem, will help you begin to narrow down your options – and will get your brain ticking over too. You might find that your brain comes up with new ideas without any extra help, once you get it thinking more positively about a subject.

LEARNING THROUGH GUESSING

The secret to guessing is not to worry about whether your guess will prove to be 'right' or not, or otherwise you will be back at the same problem you had before. The key thing is to just do it – it's only through trying a guess, and possibly 'failing', that you will make progress. But that word, 'failing', is a negative word from a previous mindset – when you guess deliberately then any guess that proves ultimately not to be the way forward is in fact simply a new way of learning. Or, rather, the old way of learning that you once used as a small child.

PUZZLES – TAKE A GUESS!

All of these puzzles can be solved by making guesses and experimenting.

23. The classic guessing puzzle. Solve this maze by finding a route from the entrance at the top to the exit at the bottom.

24. Join *all* of the dots using horizontal and vertical lines to form a single loop. The loop must not cross over or touch itself in any way.

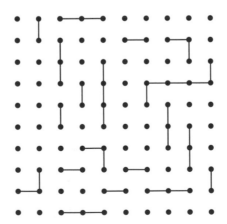

25. Draw a series of separate paths, each connecting a pair of identical numbers. No more than one path can enter any grid square, and a path cannot re-enter a square. Paths can travel horizontally and vertically, but never diagonally.

1	2														
3	4													4	
		2													
	5		6	7											6
											7		8		
	5		1	9					9				10		
11		10													
	12		13									12			
			3	14			14	13							
	15								8	15					
				16							16				
		11													

26. Draw borders along some grid lines to divide the grid into a set of rectangles, so that each rectangle contains exactly one number. The number inside each rectangle must be precisely equal to the number of grid squares that the rectangle contains. Note that the term 'rectangle' also includes squares.

			4			2			
								4	2
			3						
					8			8	
		12	2						
	4		16					12	
							15		
	3			2			3		

FRESH THINKING

From time to time, most of us get stuck in a rut in our thinking. Usually this results in assumptions we aren't aware we're making, which end up limiting the scope of the solutions we are able to come up with.

An outside perspective is often useful in challenging assumptions, although there is an associated challenge in *accepting* that outside view when it contradicts our own. Many people will instinctively cling to what they already believe, even if another person's point is entirely valid. It's good advice to avoid jumping to conclusions, and take time to let your brain digest any points before dismissing them.

Ideas that seem ridiculous or useless do themselves sometimes lead to fresh perspectives on existing problems. Even if you don't bring in an external view, it's useful to come up with solutions that you *don't* think will work – even just explaining to yourself out loud why you 'know' they won't work can help you make breakthroughs in your thinking.

Indeed, talking out loud is a great way of moving on your thought process. When you vocalize thoughts you make your brain think in a different way, and it's amazing how often the very act of explaining something – even to yourself – can lead to moments of revelation. In fact, if you can't explain something clearly then you perhaps don't understand it clearly either, so testing yourself in this way is a good method for discovering weaknesses in your thinking.

THE WISDOM OF CROWDS

Aristotle wrote about the wisdom of crowds in *Politics*, around 2,500 years ago. So it's not a new notion that two heads are better than one, and certainly it's the case that groups can be more creative and bring far more experience to a situation than any one individual can hope to do. In the best situations, individuals can bounce ideas off each other, iteratively improving them. So it's always good to seek a second opinion, so long as you don't let these opinions unduly sway you, unless of course you know they are backed up by far more expertize than you have.

There's a danger with groups, however, that people will be afraid to speak up in front of certain others, or that those who are most ignorant may not realize their ignorance and come to dominate the discussion – or even may do so deliberately. So group discussions need to be carefully managed.

THE WISDOM OF YOU

If you are knowledgeable about a subject area, try not to doubt yourself too much. It's fine to challenge your own assumptions, but when presenting your thoughts or conclusions to others then it is best to appear as confident as possible. You might feel that you need to explain all of the pros and cons of a proposal, and perhaps in some contexts you truly might need to, but in very many cases you will sadly do yourself a disservice by being too intellectually rigorous in a presentation.

As social creatures, we instinctively trust other people who *seem* trustworthy, and who appear to know what they are doing. Ironically, if you explain potential pitfalls you will be less convincing to non-experts than a person who does not. The confident, ignorant person appears more capable – look, their idea has *no* potential pitfalls, says the instinctive part of our brain. Don't give a detailed explanation to people who will be perfectly happy with a simplified version – if they don't follow they will judge you as less competent, and adding unnecessary details only invites potential objections that could otherwise have been avoided.

It's also important to note that usually we don't need a *perfect* solution, but simply a *good enough* solution. This is not to say that aiming for excellence is a bad idea, but that overcomplicating things rarely helps in the long run. Often you will convince someone more with a simple, slightly flawed argument than a complex, flawless one.

NEW EXPERIENCES

The more we challenge our brains, the wiser we get. It's easy to get into a routine where one day is very similar to another, but the more we can mix in variety then the better we will feel and the happier our brains will be.

Introducing variety can be as simple as taking a different route on a regular journey. Leave a few minutes earlier and go a slightly different way, or if you like to walk then even just try walking in the opposite direction to normal on a familiar route.

When you are out and about, try to look around you and take in the sights – don't let familiarity with an area blind you to what's right in front of you. It might be surprising what you see that you've never noticed before. And even if you're a particularly observant person, you probably don't look up very much. In older towns and cities there can often be interesting features higher up on buildings which are well worth discovering.

Of course, the more you can mix up your routine the better. Even if you work during the day, perhaps there are things you can change, whether it's going somewhere else for lunch, reading a different newspaper or website, or listening to a different radio station or music as you travel.

FOREIGN LANGUAGES

Many languages have been developed by communities in sometimes very different parts of the world to our own, and so those languages often include concepts and thoughts that can be quite alien to someone who has had no exposure to those peoples. Just by learning another language, ideally one not very closely related to our own, we are exposed to these other concepts. As we become more fluent, we can then discover new ways of thinking that are facilitated by those other languages. Even if you only learn the basics of a foreign language, it can still act as a gateway to becoming familiar with a range of ideas that help open you up to a raft of new experiences. And it's also a great new challenge for your brain.

TRAVEL TO UNFAMILIAR PLACES

You don't necessarily need to travel far to visit somewhere that can seem very different, but if you have the time and money to visit somewhere distant and exotic then your brain will certainly enjoy the trip. Taking in entirely new sights, sounds and situations will provide a significant mental stimulus – not to mention challenge – that can benefit you for the rest of your life. The more you experience the world around you, whether that's on a local or more distant level, the better you will be able to cope with new experiences when they come at you unexpectedly.

LEARN TO PLAY A MUSICAL INSTRUMENT

Learning to play a musical instrument can be one of the greatest pleasures in life. Perhaps not everyone who listens to you in the early stages may agree with this, but the mental benefit to you can be profound, both in terms of the learning you will engage in and also the relaxation it can bring. Even if you already play an instrument, you could learn one that's very different – for example, if you play the guitar then try the piano, and vice versa. Or even just challenge yourself to play in new ways on an instrument you already play, such as trying to 'play by ear' if you normally read music, or try improvising if you have never done so.

TAKE UP A NEW HOBBY

There are so many activities in the world to choose from that it can be overwhelming to choose one, but if you feel you could benefit from more social contact then why not look locally to see what nearby groups offer, and get involved? Even if you aren't sure you'll enjoy something, there's usually little harm in giving it a go, especially if the costs are minimal.

Whatever it is you decide to do, the important thing is that if you are not enjoying it then you should move on to something else. Remember that a stressed or unhappy brain does not learn well, so if you aren't sufficiently motivated then there is likely to be minimal benefit from the activity.

NEW CHALLENGES

Try these new types of puzzle, and see how you get on with something
that you aren't already familiar with.

27. Draw 1x2 and 1x3 rectangular blocks along the grid lines such that
each number is contained in exactly one block. The number in each
block reveals the total count of white spaces the block can slide into.
Shapes that are wider than they are tall slide horizontally left and
right, and shapes that are taller than they are wide slide vertically up
and down.

See the example solution to the right to
understand how this works. For example
consider the 2 in the top row – it can move
into 2 spaces. Meanwhile, the 0 at the
bottom-right cannot move into any spaces;
the spaces above it do not count because it
does not slide this way.

28. What is the simplest change you can make to this equation in order to make it correct?

29. Draw a fence to protect the sheep ('S') from the wolves ('W') by joining dots with a single continuous line so that all sheep are inside the area and all wolves outside it. Use only horizontal or vertical lines, and the fence cannot touch, cross or overlap itself in any way. The numbers 1, 2 and 3 indicate that the fence must run along 1, 2 or 3 sides of the square formed by the 4 dots around the number.

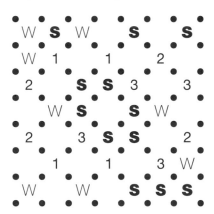

30. Place 1 to 9 once each into this grid. Black dots indicate pairs of squares where one digit is exactly twice the value of the other, such as 3 and 6. White dots indicate consecutive digits, such as 3 and 4. No dot means neither applies. If both a black *and* white dot could be used, only one is given.

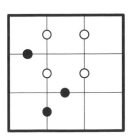

31. Complete this spiral crossword, where the clues read both inwards *and* outwards simultaneously.

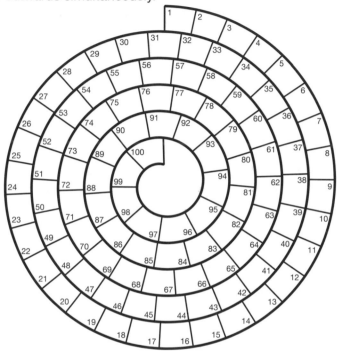

Inward

1-6	Gilded
7-9	Pump an accelerator
10-14	Gawks at
15-18	Possible hair infection
19-22	Dispatched
23-27	Chat-show group
28-30	Prune
31-37	Sweet course
38-42	Allied
43-46	Devotional painting
47-51	Type of heron
52-57	Claim
58-60	Cattle chew this
61-65	Wear down
66-73	Accepted etiquette
74-78	Raw vegetable dish
79-81	Tennis-court divider
82-86	Jobs
87-91	Angry
92-96	Old photo colour
97-100	Elitist

Outward

100-95	Dwarf tree
94-89	Former Spanish currency
88-84	Dangers
83-78	Be present at
77-74	Sadly
73-70	Railway train
69-63	Underwater missile
62-57	Lessen
56-54	Hairstyling substance
53-49	Afterwards
48-41	Racial extermination
40-31	Suffering from great anxiety
30-25	Powder from flowers
24-18	Relevance
17-12	Glittery Christmas material
11-4	Ruled
3-1	Captain's journal

32. Find a route from the lowest to the highest number, visiting all numbers in increasing numerical order. The route can only travel horizontally and vertically between squares, and it can't revisit any square. It can only cross itself on the marked bridges. All squares must be visited, and all bridges must be used in both directions. A small example is given.

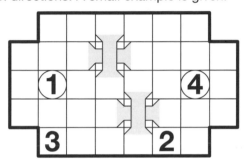

33. Shade some squares, so that no two shaded squares are adjacent, except diagonally, and all unshaded squares form a single continuous area. Any single horizontal or vertical row of unshaded cells cannot cross more than one bold line. Numbered squares may or may not be shaded, but always give the precise amount of shaded squares in a bold-lined region.

A VERY SOCIAL BRAIN

One of the most fundamental desires of most of us is to fit in with the people around us. We worry about embarrassing ourselves in front of others, we worry about appearing strange, and we worry that we are not as good as other people in a whole myriad of ways.

Social media, while allowing some people to feel more connected with others than they might previously have done, also brings with it a whole host of new pressures. The vast majority of people will create a sanitized, polished version of themselves online, whether they do this consciously or not. They will appear to be happier, prettier, richer, more organized, better travelled, more educated and generally wiser than they probably are in reality – and that's just the honest ones! Some people go further and invent a fantasy version of themselves, whether it's through editing photos to remove wrinkles, claiming to be places they aren't, or making claims of happiness they don't truly feel. This doesn't make these people terrible human beings, but what it *does* mean is that when we compare *ourselves* it can lead us to feel inferior or inadequate – even though we are not.

When reviewing stories about others online, whether of celebrities in the press or of friends on social media, we need to remind ourselves that these are sanitized, selected snippets from their lives, and we should never judge ourselves by comparison with these misleading excerpts.

THE JUDGEMENT OF OTHERS

We spend our lives worrying about what others think of us, when in reality the honest truth is that most people – even those reasonably close to us – notice a lot less about us than we might think, or even hope. Most people are so wrapped up in their own thoughts, worries and preoccupations that they devote little time to thinking about those of others. When you consider that this applies to those we know well, just consider how little those who don't know us at all will typically notice about us.

When out in public it is possible to be self-conscious about a whole host of body and other issues, when in reality most people will be paying you very little direct attention. They are probably wrapped up in their own thoughts, and more concerned about themselves. Of course there are occasional exceptions to this rule but, more often than not, from the point of view of strangers you are neither as interesting or as remarkable as you think – even though in reality we are *all* interesting and remarkable.

Studies have shown that people can do all manner of strange things while standing in view of sitting strangers, who then mostly remain entirely oblivious. So next time you think you have embarrassed yourself, try not to worry about it too much – the chances are that most people haven't even noticed. The *worst* thing you can do is draw attention to it – so *don't* apologize, unless you are absolutely certain it is necessary, and be sure not to apologize more than is needed.

BE POSITIVE

Apologizing in general is something many of us get wrong. If you think you have made a mistake, own up to it quickly and say so only briefly. Then move on, *and never mention it again*. If you keep apologizing you will simply make your action memorable, whereas if you handle it and then immediately carry on as if nothing had happened it will almost certainly be forgotten before long.

Be positive whenever you can. *Don't* talk yourself down – in most cases if you are able to self-criticize then you have already considered the pros and cons of an argument; there's no need to weaken your position in front of anyone else. They can think about it themselves if they wish, and people have an inherent tendency to trust those who appear most self-confident – even if they are entirely ignorant. Don't let too much knowledge about a subject make you appear less confident, through your knowledge of the risks, than someone who is broadly ignorant and just ploughs on blindly.

HIDDEN IN PLAIN SIGHT

These puzzles are all based on the concept of things being less obvious than you'd expect.

34. Can you find this plus shape hidden inside this network of lines? It can be rotated or at a different size, but in every other way its shape will be identical.

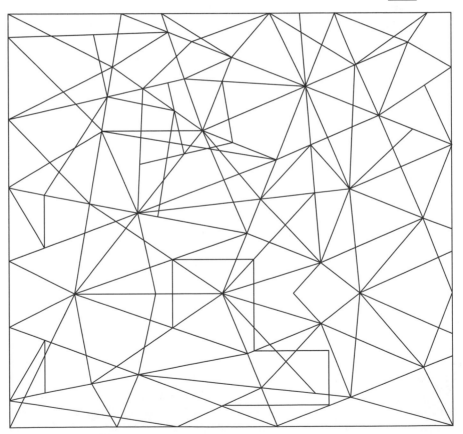

35. Each of the following sentences contains a hidden flower. Can you find them all?

- Never a big fan of synth-pop, Pythagoras preferred to theorize
- After paying in his gyros, Euclid came up with some maths stuff
- The ballerina wore a tutu, lipstick and not much else
- Bengali lychees taste better than average, or so they claim
- The Yugoslav end erased much Eastern European progress
- Scrape onyx from a mine seam and you might get rich

36. How many times does the sequence 121 appear in this string of numbers?

12121222121221212212122112121221211212121111221

37. How quickly can you find each of the two patterns in the overall grid?

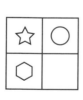

THE CERTAINTY OF BEING WRONG

We all jump to conclusions from time to time, but it isn't always our fault. Our brains are wired to make certain decisions as fast as possible, since they could be critical to our survival. But there's just one problem – in our modern lives, usually we aren't in any immediate danger, and these snap decisions can actually lead to problems.

FALSE LEARNING

We learn by spotting patterns, associating certain events with certain outcomes. This is true all life long. As children we learn to walk by experimenting and sometimes falling – but along the way, our brains connect the dots between action and outcome, until it becomes entirely effortless. Unfortunately, this ability for our brains to spot patterns is so powerful that it can lead to us being 'sure' of things that are entirely false.

One example of false learning is casinos. Many people convince themselves they have spotted patterns in game outcomes and bet accordingly, even when those outcomes are in truth essentially random and therefore are unpredictable.

Historically, people would look for – and think they had found – patterns and secret codes in all kinds of places. Isaac Newton devoted much of his life not to his lasting achievements in maths and physics but rather to searching for the hidden code that he was sure ran throughout the Bible. The fact is that the brain will tend to spot patterns if you look for them, even if those patterns are nothing more than random chance. Out of the infinite number of *possible* patterns, one or more of them are likely to be present in almost any material. Finding those patterns, therefore, is entirely a matter of searching long enough – their presence is not in any way meaningful.

EXPECTATION BIAS

Just as with patterns, we often see the things we expect to see. If you believe in ghosts and the wind blows a curtain, you may take it as evidence of a spiritual presence. Inaudible deep bass sounds can make candles flicker even in the absence of air currents, but this is just a physical phenomenon. It is very easy to work from a conclusion back to a start point, when in fact it would only be meaningful to work the other way. Although lemons are yellow, not everything that is yellow is a lemon.

One particularly problematic area for expectation bias is medical procedures. For many more minor ailments we will usually get better by ourselves, especially if we think positively about them. This means that people unknowingly given placebo drugs, such as sugar pills, are often absolutely certain they have got better due to the pill, when in fact it had no effect.

This unwitting bias forms the basis of most alternative medicine practices, and while these can sometimes be mentally beneficial, due to the belief that we will get better, they sadly cannot help in more complex situations. People who undergo medical treatment, but stop to try alternative medicines, might associate any belated benefits from the medical treatment with the alternative techniques instead. This 'false learning' is just part of your brain's natural learning abilities – but it's important to remember that correlation is not causation. Just because one thing follows another, it doesn't mean it caused it.

SELECTION BIAS

Similarly, our brains love to cherry-pick results from the past. We remember when things turned out the way we expected, and forget about the times when we were wrong. It's important to be aware of this effect, so we know to challenge our own assumptions.

CHALLENGING EXPECTATIONS

Each of these puzzles will require you to challenge your assumptions.

38. One hundred prisoners are lined up all in a row, facing the same direction. Each prisoner is wearing a hat, which is either red or blue. Each prisoner can only see the people in front of them, and which colour hat each of them is wearing. They cannot see their own hat, or anyone behind them.

A prison officer enters the room, goes up to the prisoner at the back of the line, and asks them to say out loud either 'red' or 'blue', to predict whether they are wearing a red or blue hat. If they answer correctly, they will be released from prison. If they answer incorrectly, they will be confined for life. In either case, they must stay in line and the officer will not confirm whether they are correct or incorrect but will simply move onto the next person in line, carrying on down the line until they reach the front of the line.

The prisoners are told in advance what will happen, and have time to discuss and agree a strategy. By using an optimal strategy, what is the maximum number of prisoners that can be *guaranteed* to be released?

39. A waiter gives out 100 glasses of water, but when he collects them back in he is able to combine the remains of the water in 10 glasses to make 1 full glass. How many glasses of water can he make from the 100 glasses he has collected back in?

40. A blind man is marooned on a desert island without any outside contact. He has two green pills and two yellow pills, and needs to take exactly one of each pill. How can he do this, even though he can't see the pills? The pills have no other perceptible differences.

41. Three friends are in a room, and each makes a contradictory statement:

- **Dave**: Exactly one of us is lying

- **Samuel:** Exactly two of us are lying
- **Diana**: Exactly three of us are lying

Which of the three friends is actually telling the truth?

42. A dog fastened via a long leash to a tree is preventing me returning to my car. The dog blocks my every move when I try to step within the radius of the leash. What can I do, without hurting the dog, to reach my car?

43. It looks like you could create a circle by drawing a continuous line through the centres of these eight dots, but is it possible to join them all while making a square?

UNHELPFUL BRAIN RESPONSES

Due to our evolutionary history as prey for larger animals, we have some unhelpful primitive responses. From time to time we need to consciously override these using the more modern parts of our brain.

EXPECT THE UNEXPECTED

One primitive behaviour is the tendency to freeze, both physically and mentally, in moments of extreme pressure. This might be panic in the face of an imminent collision, a sudden painful realization, or extreme challenge in other ways. This behaviour made sense when we were trying to avoid detection, but it is almost entirely useless in a modern context – and indeed can be extremely dangerous when physical peril is the trigger.

It may seem a very pessimistic thing to do, but it is actually a very good idea to consciously think through what you would do in various stressful situations – from threats of physical harm, such as a nearby fire or a rapidly approaching vehicle, through to sudden accusations against us made by others that may not have our best interests at heart. Our immediate instinctive responses are usually unhelpful, but rehearsing in advance what we might do helps us avoid and override the instinctive, primitive response, and better handle these critical situations – should they ever occur, of course, which hopefully they will not.

THINK FOR YOURSELF

Countless evidence exists to show that people will do very surprising things so as not to stand out from the crowd. When asked everyday trivia questions, such as for example whether London is the capital of England, most people would answer correctly in the positive. But put them in a group of actors where the ten people before them all answer 'no', and amazingly the majority of people will then *also* answer 'no'. So strong is the desire to conform, and act as the majority does, that we will start to question our own fundamental beliefs and knowledge.

It's especially important to be aware of this effect in potentially hazardous situations. For example, even if other people stay put when a fire alarm sounds, that doesn't mean you should too. If you think there's a chance it might be a real alarm, then you should act on it – what does it really matter that no one else does? You may be afraid of feeling 'stupid' if you act differently to others, but in a life-and-death situation you owe it to yourself to act as *you* think best, not as others think best. This doesn't mean you shouldn't try to help other people, if appropriate, but simply that it isn't safe to *assume* that others know any better – they don't, unless you have good reason to believe otherwise.

The opposite situation can also arise, where a mass outbreak of panic is caused by something trivial. We instinctively assume that 'the crowd' must be correct, when in reality this is not necessarily the case. This instinct derives from primitive behaviour that benefits a herd animal with less capable mental abilities than we possess. Once you know that in any stressful or hazardous situation your instinct will always be to copy others, you can learn to take a moment to override it – and think for yourself.

FALSE SENSE OF URGENCY

Many times in life we are presented with a false sense of urgency. Whether it's our brain falsely telling us we'd better eat that cake while we still have access to that wonderfully fatty food supply, or a sales person pretending that the apparent bargain in front of us won't still be there if we come back later, our brains are easily rushed into making decisions that they don't have to make. Our primitive fear of losing out on some vital resource outweighs the more considered approach that we should probably take instead. Even if we do occasionally lose out on something, it will probably be more than balanced for by the many times we avoid making a decision we later regret.

UNLEASH YOUR CREATIVITY

Maybe you are an accomplished artist, but there are many people who think that they 'aren't creative'. While it is true that not everyone can paint like Monet, or sculpt like Michelangelo, we are still all capable of being creative. Every time we work out a route from A to B, or indeed think of a solution to any problem, we are being creative. So there is no reason at all why we can't also channel this creativity into more artistic areas – in fact, the Oxford Dictionary of English defines 'artistic' as 'having natural creative skill', which in this sense covers everyone!

A significant problem many of us face in our attempts to be creative is overcoming the initial inertia of the blank page. Faced with the infinite scope of all that is possible, it's no surprise that we can find it hard to write the initial words, or draw the first lines. Luckily, there are a wide range of techniques that can be used to help, all of which are based on the idea of 'just getting going'. Once we have *something* on the page it can help trigger related ideas, or suggest the basis of a framework on which to build the rest. The reason we find these first steps so painful is that we often expect ourselves to decide what we are going to create in advance, but the truth in most creative situations is that the work will develop and evolve as it progresses – and even head off in completely unexpected directions. Trying to have a complete vision before you even begin is putting an unnecessary pressure on yourself.

ART
Art is anything you say it is, so the great thing about creative activities is that it's impossible to 'go wrong'. Many of us are our own harshest critics,

but if we can learn to relax and not worry too much about the end result then even if we don't like where we end up, we can still enjoy the journey to get there. Giving your brain a chance to metaphorically breathe can help you relax, can lessen stress and can also make you feel good about yourself – especially if you discover a skill that you thought you didn't have.

Almost any activity could be classed as art, but the easiest way to get going is just to grab a pencil, scribble a few random lines on a page and then step back to see what it looks like. Our brains are so accomplished at spotting patterns that there's a good chance you'll think it looks a bit like *something* – and then you can either carry on building from that new idea, or draw a few more random lines and take a fresh look. Or of course you could deliberately create a patterned drawing, by repeating the same design continually across a page. If you do this then it doesn't really matter what the repeated pattern is, because the very act of repetition tends to lend an image a visually pleasing quality.

Other types of art to consider include:

- Origami – paper folding can be very therapeutic, and it's an easy way to end up with a rewarding 3D model that feels pretty substantial.

- Sculpting – not with stone, but with modelling clay or plasticine. Start by making abstract structures, or create a range of cartoon figures.

- Paper cutting – taking a sheet of paper, folding it up and then cutting sections out can result in various patterned pieces of paper. It's easy to do and the results can be surprisingly beautiful.

- Guided arts, such as colouring books or dot-to-dots. Even if the outlines are provided for you, there's still a lot of creative freedom to colour as you please. Or if even that feels a bit too much like hard work, you could try a colour-by-number book – the satisfaction from creating your own picture can be remarkable, especially if you haven't felt it since you were a child!

IT'S ALL IN THE DOTS

44. Start by joining the dots in increasing numerical order in this classic puzzle. An image will slowly emerge as you do so. You can then colour it in with your choice of colours if you so wish.

45. What if there are no numbers next to the dots? Give this puzzle a go even if you don't think it seems worth it – you might be surprised at what comes out of it. All you have to do is join the dots – but however you like, and not necessarily all together. Take a moment after you've drawn a few lines to see what the image is starting to look like – a face, or a monster, or a leaf, perhaps, and then if you wish you can start adding lines that build on that existing image. Or you could just join lines randomly, and colour the resulting areas.

CREATIVE WRITING

Many people feel that they 'have a novel inside them', but how many actually put pen to paper, or finger to keyboard, and get writing? Like most creative endeavours, it's typically the getting going that causes the greatest problems. This can either result in not getting started on a piece of writing at all, or it can mean that once you take a break you find it very hard to continue.

Writing is inherently a creative process, even if you are writing fact rather than fiction. The way that you choose to express ideas, and the words you use for that expression, are critical parts of how a reader will experience your message – and understand it, remember it and perhaps also be swayed by it, if you are aiming to convince a reader of a particular point.

GETTING GOING

In many forms of creative endeavour, one method of breaking a creative block is simply to do literally anything, and see if you are inspired. For factual writing this can work particularly well, because you usually know at least the general area that you want to write about. This means that even if you jump into the middle at a bit that's particularly easy to write, that's okay because at least you are working towards your end goal. You don't necessarily need to keep the text you write first, but it will help you decide how to structure and present your ideas.

For long-form creative writing, you will probably need to start at a higher level by deciding on the basics of a plot. But even when you do this, all the same principles apply. Rather than writing finished pieces of prose, you will be noting down characters or events, but the same tactic of starting at an arbitrary point and then fleshing it out as inspiration hits will still work. You should also not be afraid to be inspired by other creative works. After all, there are very few truly fresh novels, and there's no point in setting a goal so lofty that it becomes almost unattainable. Indeed, you could even start by using existing characters, settings or even basic plots and then write your own version of them – the novel *Fifty Shades of Grey* was first written as *Twilight* fan fiction, then modified for publication to remove any direct references. Whatever it takes to get you going is fair game – it is much easier to amend something you have already written than it is to fill in a completely blank page.

DON'T EXPECT PERFECTION

It's unreasonable to expect your early written works to be masterpieces. Maybe they will be, but most people improve with practice, just as we all do with respect to any other skill. Certainly, if you reread text you wrote some time ago you may well be surprised at the difference between your earlier work and your current level of writing.

So another key part of creative writing is simply to just keep trying. Each time you do you'll get better and better, and you'll learn from previous mistakes – such as a plot that was too restrictive, or a piece of factual text that was too broad in its ambition.

WRITE FOR YOURSELF

Creative activities, or at least those performed principally for the purpose of relaxation and fun, are most enjoyable when not taken too seriously. Try not to worry too much about what other people will think, so you can relax and let your brain be truly creative. If you write for yourself, you needn't care about anyone else's opinion – when it's your own creation, no one else can tell you you're wrong. Art is in any case purely in the eye of the beholder.

There are some simple creative writing activities on the following two pages, which should help ease you into the process. If you can handle these, you'll be ready to get started on the real thing!

CREATIVE WRITING ACTIVITIES

Write a second, rhyming line for each of these given lines. For example, you could rhyme 'The light of day awakes in me' with 'A craving for a cup of tea'.

46. From dawn to dusk on every day,

_____

47. The fallen leaves float gently down,

_____

48. The scent of summer wafting wide,

_____

49. The twin-hulled ship of fate was holed,

_____

Now try coming up with some punchlines for these jokes.

50. Why did the aardvark cross the road?

_____

51. What's the difference between a paper fastener and a horse stall?

_____

52. What do you call a one-eyed giant?

_____

53. Write a very short story that uses each of the following items:

Location: The south of France

Person: The king of Spain

Item: A diamond necklace

_____

_____

_____

_____

_____

_____

54. Invent your own place name for an imaginary island, located just off the coast of the equally imaginary continent of Austraferica:

_____

55. Create an imaginary monster. Give it a really evocative name, then go on to describe its features. What does it look like? Is it fearsome or friendly? Does it have any supernatural abilities, such as fire-breathing?

_____

_____

_____

_____

BUILDING CREATIVITY

Blank pages and canvases can present a challenge with getting started, so an alternative option is to pick a creative activity where you start with a set of pieces and then rearrange them. Even a small box of building bricks, for example, can be assembled into an incredibly large number of different structures, so this is nowhere near as restrictive as it may sound. This can also make it easier to experiment, and help avoid the creative block which can stem from an empty page.

One of the simplest of creative activities is to take a small number of flat pieces and arrange them into shapes, such as with tangram pieces. You can easily create your own set of tangrams by simply cutting up a square of paper as shown here. You can also trace the diagram if you prefer, and colour in each piece. Just colour the top side, and avoid flipping them over.

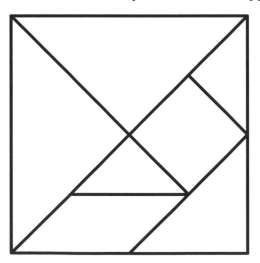

Once you've made your tangrams, try arranging them on a table or other surface to make various silhouettes. Can you make a house, or a goose, or a silhouette of a person?

BUILDING BLOCKS

With even more pieces you can make even more things, and if you step up from two dimensions to three dimensions then the possibilities literally expand in all directions. Manufacturers of interlocking toy blocks, such as LEGO®, provide sets of basic bricks that can be bought for free-form construction, and these provide both a fun and easy method of simply and quickly 'being creative'. And if you think you might be 'too old' for things such as this, it's worth noting that sales of LEGO® to adults account for a significant proportion of their revenue.

Adult versions of activities previously engaged in primarily by children have expanded enormously in recent years, with large numbers of colouring-in, dot-to-dot and other books of this type aimed specifically at adults now widely available. What these trends reveal is that it's simply societal conventions that have previously held back many adults from engaging in the things they enjoyed while growing up – which is a shame, because relaxing in these relatively simple ways is good for your brain.

CREATIVE PUZZLE-SOLVING

All around the world, 'escape rooms' have opened where adults can go and rush about for an hour trying to solve as many puzzles as they can, and in most cases 'escape' from the room before time is up. These are brilliant for your brain, combining creative thinking, physical exercise, social contact and novel exploration into a single activity. The possible downside is that they do tend to be quite expensive.

You don't have to head out to play challenging, sociable, thought-based games, however. There are many open-ended board games, where you must think creatively and strategically to win – popular modern examples include *Settlers of Catan®*, *Carcasonne®*, *Ticket to Ride®* and *Pandemic®*, but if you want something a bit more old-school then you could also consider classic board games such as chess, draughts, go and many others.

Using your tangram pieces, and remembering not to flip any of them over, see if you can work out how to make each of the following shapes:

56. Boat

57. House

In addition to the suggestions at the top of the previous page, can you also make pictures that look like the following:

58. A chair

59. A dog

60. Use your creative imagination to visualize what would happen if you were to combine these two grids. The white squares in one should be replaced with the content squares from the other to form a complete picture.

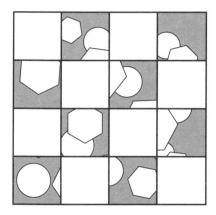 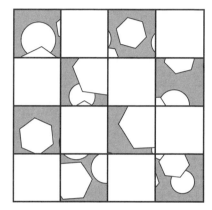

Now answer these questions about the combined image:

- How many hexagons are there?

- How many circles are partially overlapped by hexagons?

- How many circles do not overlap with any other shape?

61. Can you find all six differences between these two images? They are rotated to make it more of a challenge.

QUALITY COMMUNICATION

Learning to express yourself clearly and compactly is useful not just in terms of coming across well when speaking to others, but it also helps you to think with greater clarity. If you are able to represent concepts with fewer words, then you may be better able to manage thoughts related to those concepts in your head – there is less to remember, meaning you can hold more in your memory as you think things through.

Building a good vocabulary is a lifelong task, as well as indeed hopefully a pleasure, and working towards this can be as simple as reading widely. Any reading is probably good for you, but if you are able to read more broadly than a single genre then it's likely to be even *better* for you. Your brain likes to be exposed to new concepts and new situations, and also you are more likely to encounter a wider range of vocabulary.

Another great tip is to do a good crossword puzzle regularly. The 'quick' puzzle from the back page of a daily newspaper is a good start – 'quick' simply means that it is a synonym-based puzzle, rather than the more elaborate cryptic crossword found elsewhere in British newspapers. These are also a good thing to try, but require somewhat more persistence to get started with, since the structure of the various clue types they employ takes time to learn. So 'quick', synonym-based crosswords are great for building vocabulary, although it stands to reason that to learn any new words that are placed in the *grid*, as opposed to the clues, that you will need to check the solutions – or use a crossword solver tool.

VOCABULARY PUZZLES

Start with this 'quick' crossword puzzle, then try the vocabulary puzzles that follow.

62.

Across
1 Plans, as in a course (6)
4 Burrowing marsupial (6)
9 Providing facts (9)
10 Birth name (3)
11 Internet address (inits) (3)
12 Servant (9)
13 Biblical priests' garment (5)
15 Waste from a carcass (5)
20 Long, stringy pasta (9)
22 Become deceased (3)
23 Aardvark's dinner (3)
24 Is more significant than (9)
25 Forgive (6)
26 'Finally!' (2,4)

Down
1 Coterie (6)
2 Really terrible (5)
3 Whirlwind (7)
5 Type of keyboard instrument (5)
6 Fabric square worn around the neck (7)
7 Result of a negotiation (6)
8 Little song (5)
14 Artificial; unnatural (7)
16 Most beautiful (7)
17 Elude (6)
18 Declare (5)
19 One-room apartment (6)
21 Head coverings (5)
22 Doctrine (5)

How many words of three or more letters can you find in each of these word circles? Each word must use the centre letter, plus two or more of the other letters. No letter can be used more than once in a single word. Each has one nine-letter word to find.

63.

H K M
L A L
S R A

_____
_____
_____
_____

64.

N N I
C O T
S N E

_____
_____
_____
_____

65.

S R A
N E U
M R D

_____
_____
_____
_____

66.

A D Q
U O S
N S R

_____
_____
_____
_____

Can you find the 16-letter word hidden in each of these word rectangles? Find words by moving horizontally or vertically from letter to touching letter, but not diagonally, and without revisiting a square in a single word. Also, how many other words of three or more letters can you find?

67.

O	N	T	L
C	N	I	A
S	E	N	T
N	A	R	T

70.

O	G	R	A
I	B	H	P
T	O	I	C
U	A	L	A

68.

T	N	I	S
E	R	O	N
O	C	I	T
N	N	E	C

71.

N	O	I	T
A	L	E	U
I	I	Z	T
N	S	T	I

69.

T	I	E	S
I	L	I	B
S	E	R	I
P	O	N	S

72.

O	N	A	L
I	M	S	I
T	I	N	T
A	N	R	E

ON THE TIP OF YOUR TONGUE

How often have you struggled to remember a word, or the name of a person or place? You often feel as if you can *almost* remember it, and sometimes you are even sure you know the first letter.

In fact, the first letter of a word is a critically important part of our ability to identify it, so when we think we can remember a first letter but no more then there's a good chance we are actually correct. In this respect your brain is very much like the alphabetic index in a book, where words are stored under their initial letter.

So strong is this connection that even when the letters of a word are jumbled, it is often still relatively easy to read so long as the first and last letters remain in the same position, and the words aren't too long. For example, can you read the following phrase?

Tihs sowhs taht it wrkos

It reads 'This shows that it works.' The effect is not quite as remarkable as it is sometimes claimed, however, for when the words get longer it becomes much harder to read them:

Smoe sldpdileny csniunogf wdsro

This reads 'Some splendidly confusing words.' Nonetheless, anagrams are much easier to solve, and words are easier to think of, when we know the first letter. Regular crossword solvers will already be familiar with this.

THE POWER OF WORDS

Words, especially names, carry considerable meaning for us. If we know someone with a particular name and then meet a new person with the same name, our brains will associate some of the characteristics of the existing person with the new person – *based solely on their matching name*. Rationally, of course, we know that this doesn't make any real sense. Despite this, so heavily loaded is the label for that person in our head that when we hear the same label again we recall some of what we have previously learned for the existing person.

Words in turn sometimes have subtle, or perhaps not-so-subtle, variations in meaning to different people, based on our prior experiences – where we grew up, who we spend time with, what films or books we are exposed to, our educational background and so on. Indeed, we all effectively have our own individual private language, since the vocabulary of one person will rarely exactly match that of another, and even if it did then what one person understood by many words would still differ in some respects from what another person understood by them. This is why it's important to always be as clear and explicit as we can when writing or speaking about particularly important matters. Implications that may seem obvious to us may be very *non*-obvious to others. This need to be precise is one reason why many lawyers have their jobs, although it could be argued that many times legal language is so overly precise that it becomes almost impossible for a lay reader to understand what it *really* says!

VOCABULARY SIZE

The single-volume *Oxford Dictionary of English* contains over 350,000 word and phrase definitions. Even if you accept the upper bound of published estimates, which is that a well-educated college graduate might be able to recognize around 60,000 different words, that still leaves a lot of words that most of us won't be familiar with. While it may not always be useful to know many of these words, being exposed to them can help enrich our brains with new concepts in the same way that learning a foreign language can. Online sites such as OED.com and dictionary.com provide 'word of the day' features to help you learn new words, or find out more about words you already know.

VOCABULARY POWER PUZZLES

Use the power of your vocabulary to solve each of these challenges.

Every other letter has been deleted from each of the following sports. How quickly can you find them all?

73. _E_N_S

74. _O_T_A_L

75. _U_B_

76. S_I_M_N_

77. _A_K_T_A_L

78. _O_K_Y

79. _A_M_N_O_

Now try these colours:

80. _U_P_E

81. _R_N_E

82. T_R_U_I_E

83. _O_P_R

84. _H_T_

85. C_I_S_N

86. R_B_

All of the vowels have been deleted from the following films, and then the spacing changed. Can you find all the original titles?

87. FG HTC LB

88. NC PTN

89. CSB LN CA

90. N TRS TL LR

91. MM NT

92. WLL

93. DHR D

94. NS DT

The same letter has been deleted from the start and end of each of these words. Can you recover all the original words?

95. _OPCOA_

96. _RMAD_

97. _YNI_

98. _MOEB_

99. _EURO_

100. _ULA_

101. _AU_

Each of the following letter jumbles can be anagrammed to reveal the name of a country of the world. How many of them can you solve?

102. MEG RYAN

103. THIN AS A FANG

104. AGE GIRO

105. MR NAKED

106. A GREAT INN

107. ARC IGUANA

108. THANK AZ ASK

109. MAD CAR SAGA

Now try the same with these US states:

110. IF A LORD

111. OZ IN AIR

112. CHEATS AS MUSTS

113. WE MIX ONCE

114. SEEN TENSE

115. A LOUTISH ACORN

116. ON HIS LADDER

Given just the initial letters of each of the following classic novels, as well as their authors, can you work out which book each line corresponds to?

117. R C by D D

118. T J by H F

119. E by J A

120. T C O M C by A D

121. D C by C D

122. J E by C B

123. V F by W M T

124. A A I W by L C

Each of the following letter sequences corresponds to a real-world sequence, so for example M T W T F would correspond to Monday, Tuesday, Wednesday, Thursday, Friday. Can you explain all of the following sequences too?

125. F S T F F S

126. A M J J A S

127. M V E M J S

128. H T Q F S S

129. H H L B B C

REASONING WITH LANGUAGE

How do you think? No, really, how *do* you think? When you're trying to explicitly puzzle something out, you talk to yourself with a silent inner monologue, which you use to form your conscious thoughts. Even when the conclusions we reach come to us via a mechanism that we are not consciously aware of, we still think about them in words. So while language may exist as a learned layer on *top* of our ability to reason, it is certainly at the very *core* of our conscious awareness of it.

It's good, therefore, to try word-based games and puzzles where we build our language-based reasoning skills, since our ability to make broad and good use of our vocabulary is so key to our conscious reason.

LANGUAGE REASONING PUZZLES
What connects all four words in each of the following lists?

130. Rite, Right, Write, Wright

131. Parse, Spear, Pears, Spare

132. Madam, Racecar, Kayak, Noon

133. Gouge, False, Eighth, Orange

134. Spy, Rhythm, Lynx, Tryst

Based on your general knowledge, what connects all four items in each of the following lists?

135. Mike, Oscar, Kilo, Hotel

136. Body, Hinting, Finial, Point

137. Powder, Electric, Cambridge, Sky

138. Nonsense, Noisy, Mean, Bounce

139. Blade, Oyster, Skirt, Chuck

140. Caesar, Alberti, Substitution, Hill

141. Nancy, Roger, Susan, John

142. Barron, Eric, Tiffany, Donald

143. Inky, Pinky, Blinky, Clyde

144. West, Clooney, Arnett, Bale

145. Loot, Pyjamas, Avatar, Dinghy

146. Utah, Gold, Sword, Juno

147. Green, Drive, Suspender, Seat

148. Buckeye, Mesa, Glendale, Phoenix

149. Dust, Oversight, Sanction, Clip

150. Snowden, Ritchie, Butler, Jenkins

151. Books, Maps, Play, Santa Tracker

MATHS IS FOR LIFE

Numbers are all around us, from store prices through to recipe quantities, arrival times, currency comparisons and so on. Despite this, there are many who claim that they 'can't do maths', when in fact the truth is usually that they could do it perfectly well if they really wanted to. Many people associate maths with distant memories of school tests, but in reality day-to-day maths requires only basic skills that we all have.

MENTAL ARITHMETIC

When you first try to do sums 'in your head' it can feel a bit stressful. You need to remember both the numbers you're working with *and* the result so far, plus perhaps some partial results too. We make such poor conscious use of our memories that this process of marshalling multiple values can be surprisingly challenging. But what's perhaps even more surprising is that this really does start to get a lot easier with a surprisingly small amount of practice.

When you're out and about, keep a rough reckoning of the amount you're spending in a shop. Don't try to add up every penny, but just try to have a rough idea – and then see how close you were when you check out.

You can challenge yourself in all kinds of other ways too. When you see a date of birth written down, work out how old the person is – although maybe keep the result to yourself! When you have a deadline, work out how many days away it is. And next time you pay with cash, have an idea of how much change you expect.

MULTIPLICATION

Children learn – or are supposed to learn – their 'times tables', so they can rapidly multiply numbers without conscious thought. The problem is that most of us never fully learned those tables, so many people can't instantly tell you the answer to 6 × 7. Being able to rapidly multiply is such a useful skill that it's entirely worth sitting down to try to memorize those sections you missed learning as a kid, if there any.

Multiplication is for example necessary every time you buy more than one of an item and want to have an idea what you're spending. Its close counterpart, division, is essential when working out the effect of a percentage discount, or the per-item or unit price of something bought in bulk. Without these skills we face so many parts of life at a disadvantage.

There are many tricks that can be learned to make multiplication easier, and division has its tricks too – for example, you can find out if a number is divisible by three simply by summing its digits. If these are a multiple of three, then so is the original number. And if it's a multiple of three *and* even, then it is a multiple of six.

NATURAL TALENTS

Take a handful of raisins or nuts, or even cards or pebbles, and sprinkle them over a surface. Divide them into two sections with a sweep of your hand, then quickly look at both sides. The chances are that you will have a good idea which side has the most items. Count and check – you're probably right. Your brain has a natural ability to rapidly compare quantities of items, which was useful on an evolutionary timescale to allow it to rapidly pick the lesser of two threats. With a bit of practice, your brain can extend this ability to a 'feel' for whether one calculated quantity is likely to be higher or lower than another – although this works best when they aren't too close in value.

Take several scraps of paper and write a number on each one. Then randomly place them into two piles and quickly flick through and estimate which pile has the highest sum. Were you correct? Even if you weren't, with a bit of practice you will become much better at this task. If you envisage each number as a weight, and then imagine comparing the weight of each pile, this can help.

MENTAL ARITHMETIC PUZZLES

Solve all of the following mental arithmetic puzzles without making any written notes – that is, just in your head.

For each of the following brain chains, follow each step from the given number until you calculate the final result.

152. | **31** | +14 | -29 | ×1/2 | ÷4 | +21 | RESULT |

153. | **43** | -18 | √ | +50 | -35 | +50% | RESULT |

154. | **24** | ÷6 | ×7 | +25% | -23 | +50% | RESULT |

155. | **20** | -1 | ×2 | +43 | ×2/3 | ÷9 | RESULT |

156. | **26** | -50% | +28 | ×2 | +17 | ×1/3 | RESULT |

157. | **34** | ×1/2 | +58 | -52 | ×4 | -6 | RESULT |

158. | **20** | ×5 | -29 | +13 | -50% | +22 | RESULT |

159. | **60** | -34 | +104 | -42 | ×1/4 | +50% | RESULT |

160. | **67** | -36 | +161 | -75% | ×7/8 | +50% | RESULT |

161. | **110** | -60% | ×1/2 | +50% | ×2 | -3 | RESULT |

Can you hit every one of the totals given below each number dartboard? Choose one number from each of the three rings of the dartboard so that they sum to one of the given numbers. Each dartboard has three separate totals to try to reach. There is only one way to form each total.

162.

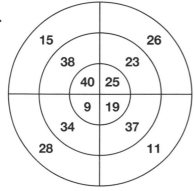

Totals: 63   75   84

164.

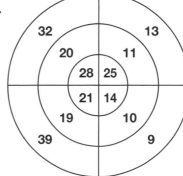

Totals: 52   66   76

163.

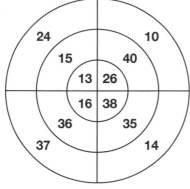

Totals: 61   70   78

165.

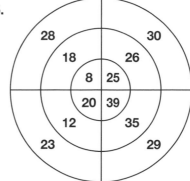

Totals: 57   68   76

ESTIMATING NUMBERS

In most real-life situations you only really need to know the approximate result of a maths calculation, whether it's to check that a discount price is a good deal or to make sure you aren't getting conned in a financial deal.

The great advantage of estimating a number, rather than calculating it exactly, is that if we do it smartly then we can get to our answer much faster than we could via a more precise series of calculations.

ADDING UP A LIST OF NUMBERS

When you're expecting the receipt in a restaurant, you might want to have an idea of what you're likely to owe before it arrives. In situations like this, where you no longer have the exact prices from the menu, your brain will estimate for you without you even consciously asking it to. You'll remember that the side dish cost about £5, and the starter was around £6, without worrying about the exact prices. And in your memory of the menu you will probably round down prices ending in a number less than 50p, and round up those ending in a number greater than 50p. Congratulations, you are using a great technique to estimate the total!

You can consciously use an estimation technique to add up a long list of numbers too, such as a store till receipt. Add up only the amounts in pounds on the list, and apply a few simple rules to the pence:

- If the amount is very close to the next whole number of pounds – for example, ending in .95 or similar – then round up the number of pounds, so £11.95 becomes £12.

- If the amount is very close to the previous whole number of pounds, such as ending in .07 or similar, then round down the number of pounds, so £23.07 becomes £23.

- For all other amounts, keep a rough tally in your head of the total of the pence, and when you feel it has added up to around 100p, add £1 to your mental tally of the number of pounds. It's important that you don't actually *add up* the pence, because this will make the maths much harder – you can consider them as a mental jar of coins that fills up as you throw the spare pence in, and then when you think it's about to overflow you empty it, claim the pound, and start again.

It might take a little practice before you can estimate the total of numbers in this way without too much conscious thought about the pence, but once you can it is sure to prove really useful. The same basic method works whether you are adding or subtracting, too.

RAPID COUNTING

On page 67 we talked about visually comparing two item counts, to decide at a glance which was the most numerous. This also works for estimating actual quantities too, so long as items are not *too* numerous – or partially hidden from vision, such as in a container or in a pile.

Take a handful of small objects of your choice, and drop them on a surface. Small food items, such as nuts or seeds, are one possible option. Spread them out, if necessary, and make a quick estimate of how many there are. Then split them quickly into groups of roughly five or ten items each, and see if you still agree with your estimate. Then you could go ahead and count the exact number, if feasible, but the chances are you can already see you weren't too far from the right total.

As you have just demonstrated, your brain has some impressive built-in reckoning skills when it comes to numbers and quantities, and the more you practise using them the better you will become.

NUMBER CHALLENGES

166. Estimate the result of 8 × 7 × 6 × 5 × 4 × 3 × 2 × 1

167. Now estimate the result of 1 × 2 × 3 × 4 × 5 × 6 × 7 × 8

168. The previous two calculations should of course give the same result, but did you feel that the value of the first product should be higher, because it started with a higher number? Now estimate
19 × 11 × 18 × 12 × 17 × 13 × 16 × 14 × 15

In each of the following puzzles, see how quickly you can spot which of the numbers in the given list can be selected to add up to the totals below. For example, given 2 5 8 9 **you could achieve a total of 14 by choosing 5 and 9; or form 19 using 2, 8 and 9.**

169.   **22   10   19   25   9   21   7**

Totals to form: 34   55   68   92

170.   **9   23   17   6   25   22   18**

Totals to form: 35   52   77   85

171.   **20   12   25   21   16   24   22**

Totals to form: 40   60   80   100

172. By using all of the given mathematical operators, and all of the numbers, can you form both of the given totals for each set?

7   3   6   4   8   +   +   -   ×

Results to obtain: 82   47

173.   **9   10   3   8   5   +   -   ×   ×**

Results to obtain: 97   441

Complete these number pyramids by filling in all of the empty bricks. Each brick should contain a total equal to the sum of the two bricks immediately beneath it.

174.

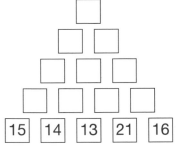

175.

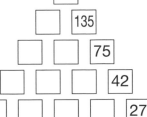

176.

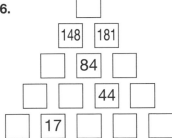

177.

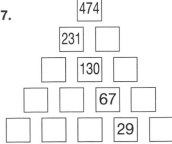

PROBABILITY

Humans have some great innate number skills – but our ability to estimate probabilities is not one of them. Very often we overestimate the likelihood of success, and very much underestimate the probability of failure. It's possible that without this trait we'd be too scared to do or try anything, so it's not necessarily a failing – but when it comes to the numbers game, our instincts aren't always correct.

An inability to grasp the intricacies of probability is one reason why casinos exist. If we properly understood our chances of winning on many of the games then there'd be no takers at all. Even on a simple game like roulette, it's human nature to discount the seemingly 'very unlikely' bank-wins slots, marked '0', and sometimes also '00', on the roulette wheel, and think of all the red/black, odds/even and other two-way bets as being a 50:50 chance. But those 'very unlikely' slots will on average appear 1 in 37 times, or 1 in 19 times in a double-zero casino, meaning that the casino typically retains *all* of the bets on those spins. On the rest it will, on average, break even. Clearly, then, the players betting on the wheel can't also win – if they spin enough times, *every* player will eventually lose all of their money; it's just maths. But it's maths that most people find hard to grasp.

COIN TOSSES AND DICE ROLLS
If you toss a coin then there's a 50:50 chance of either heads or tails, ignoring the extremely unlikely chance that it ends up on its narrow-edged side. So what is the likelihood of tossing heads eight times in a row? It doesn't seem that unlikely, but the actual odds are 1 in $2 \times 2 \times 2 \times 2 \times 2 \times 2 \times 2 \times 2 = 1$ in 256. That's because the probabilities of sequential events *multiply* together. If I was rolling a 6-sided dice, the probability of six '3's in a row, which doesn't seem *too* unlikely at a guess, is actually 1 in $6 \times 6 \times$

6 × 6 × 6 × 6 = 1 in 46,656. That's probably far less likely than you would guess!

THE MONTY HALL PROBLEM

Written probability puzzles can be extremely confusing, because they often go against our natural intuition. To be fair, this is sometimes because the question is asked in a way that is contrary to your natural expectations, but even when the question is very simple our innate expectations are often confounded.

In the 'Monty Hall Problem', there is a game show host and there are three closed doors. Between one of the doors is a luxury car, and behind the other two is nothing. The host – and this is key to note – *knows which door the car is behind*.

You are a contestant, and you are asked to choose one of the three doors. You do this at random, so you have a 1 in 3 chance of winning. The host then opens one of the two doors that you didn't choose that he *knows* does not conceal the car. Do you now switch doors, to the closed door you *didn't* pick, or do you stick with the original door – or does it not matter?

Intuitively, most people who encounter this problem think it either doesn't matter, or they say they would prefer to stick with their original choice. They assume that the likelihood of either closed door winning is now 1 in 2, since there are two closed doors and either could win.

But this is a mistake. It's true that if you *started* the game with two closed doors, there'd be a 1 in 2 chance of either, but this is *not* what happened.

PROBABILITY PUZZLES

178. Should you switch doors in the situation described in the Monty Hall Problem, above, or does it not matter? What are the odds of winning in either case?

179. In a particular country the rulers decide that they want there to be fewer boys than girls in the country, so they come up with the following rule:

Each couple can keep having children while they continue to have girls, but as soon as they have a boy they can no longer have any further children.

The rulers assume that this rule will mean there will soon be many more girls, since families can have as many girls as they want, but no more than one boy. Are they correct?

180. In a different country, a couple have five sons, and each son has a sister. How many children do they have overall?

181. In yet another country, there is a father who has two children, at least one of whom is a girl. You don't know the gender of the other child, but given what you *do* know then what is the probability that the father has two girls? Just to clarify, you're not being asked the probability of *a* father having two girls, but rather the chance that *this* father has two girls, *given what you already know*.

182. A couple, Andrea and Bob, host a party and invite four other couples. Each person on arrival gives a business card to every other person they haven't met before.

Andrea notices that all eight people out of the four couples attending, as well as Bob, has received a different number of business cards to each other.

How many business cards does Bob now have?

183. At a roulette wheel with numbers 1 to 36 plus a single 0 for the bank, what is the likelihood that I will win if I place chips on every multiple of five on the board?

184. If I roll five six-sided dice, what is the likelihood that I roll five identical numbers?

185. If I toss a coin eight times, how likely am I to have all tails or all heads?

186. If the likelihood of winning the lottery is one in ten, and I play twice this year, how likely am I to win this year?

187. Now test your maths *and* logic skills with this calcudoku puzzle. Place the numbers 1 to 6 once each into every row and column of each grid, while obeying the region clues.

The value at the top left of each bold-lined region must be obtained when all of the numbers in that region have the given operation (+, -, ×, ÷) applied between them. For - and ÷ operations, begin with the largest number in the region and then subtract or divide by the other numbers in the region in any order.

24×			15+		2−
12×		6+			
10×	3×	3−		2÷	20×
		24×			
4×	12+	8×		3−	
			10+		

CONSIDER THE EVIDENCE

You don't require any special genius to be able to think logically. Simply take note of what you're looking at, or considering, then take the time to think it through. Maybe describe it to yourself and then draw some preliminary conclusions. Look for connections between parts – if one thing changes does it influence anything else? If that influence isn't what I want, what could I do differently?

Take what you know for sure and call it 'evidence', and see if you can come up with a theory that explains that evidence. Do the facts fit it? What about other, related events? Can the same theory work there too? If not, why not, and what can be done to amend it?

In life in general, a good theory will work over many events, and be able to successfully predict outcomes for events *not* known about when creating the theory. The test of any theory is not how well it works on the information used to create the theory, since it is always possible to find a theory to explain known data, but to see if it works for any previously unknown data. Politicians and others in public view frequently make predictions based on very limited past data, or even mere supposition, without any rigorous logical analysis of what has gone before. There is also a tendency to cherry-pick facts, which at a single stroke will instantly invalidate any conclusions drawn from those facts.

SAFETY IN NUMBERS

Spending just a few moments thinking about the real meaning of information can be extremely helpful. For example, it is very common to read in the press about a so-called 'scientific' study which looks at the impact of a medical treatment on a few dozen people. Before you even consider the many ways it is possible for these studies to be flawed, the fact is that such numbers are generally too small to draw firm conclusions – the results could be simply down to chance. What's more, not all studies are reported in the press so we are making things worse by selecting the 'interesting' outliers, which typically means the most sensational ones.

Imagine I toss a coin ten times and get five heads and five tails, but then I drop it instead and get eight heads and two tails. I *could* then conclude that this method makes me more likely to get heads, but because I have taken very few samples my *confidence* should be relatively low. In this instance, we happen to know for sure that if we took a much larger sample set the apparent benefit of dropping would turn out to have been an illusion.

It's this 'confidence', or statistical significance to give it another name, that should be used to judge any data-based analysis. Our human brains love finding patterns, so we lend them greater credence than they deserve.

FUZZY CONCLUSIONS

Although firm conclusions may not be able to be reached from small sample sizes, this doesn't always mean that nothing useful can be gained. Particularly when considering our own day-to-day lives, the sum of our experience to date often provides a solid grounding for considering specific events, even if we don't consciously evaluate them in that way.

For example, why did the person you were talking to get upset? You have no way of being certain, and perhaps they were just having a bad day, but what was the trigger? Has that trigger ever caused the same effect before? And why didn't the car salesman give you a discount? Was it already discounted, or did you appear too keen to buy? It's sometimes worth taking a moment to analyse an event, but not to *over*-analyse or worry about what happened – remember that you need a huge amount of data to start to reach any firm conclusions! People act randomly outside of our control, and their behaviours can have many possible explanations.

LOGICAL IMPLICATIONS

How do you go about solving a sudoku, or any other logic-based puzzle? Sudoku is a particularly simple puzzle, but despite this simplicity it can still require complex logic to solve. With more complex puzzles, the logic can be even more involved.

Logical reasoning can be presented as a successive series of 'what if' questions. In a sudoku puzzle, if I don't place a 1 in this square then is there anywhere else in this row/column/box it can go? Or, perhaps, if I don't place a 1 in this square, is there any other number that can fit in this square? These may seem similar steps, but they are typically very different to apply – scanning a region for a missing number is fairly straightforward, but spotting that there is a square where *only* one number can fit is much harder! But nonetheless, coming up with these strategies in the first place is an important part of solving the puzzle.

Well-designed logic puzzles are usually crafted so that you can make each successive deduction by careful observation of the puzzle, without requiring any guesses. An experimental guess, however, that can be undone if it proves to be wrong, is still a perfectly valid logical step. If I place this here and carry on solving, is the puzzle still possible or do I reach a contradiction? If I reach a contradiction, I undo all of the deductions from the guess onwards, and try a different option. Sensible choices of place to guess mean that, even when you reach a contradiction, you learn something else useful. Guessing in this way can work well with a heavily constrained puzzle, such as a sudoku, especially if you have narrowed a square down to two options in an almost-complete puzzle.

Especially if a puzzle is nearly complete, it may well be that guessing and looking for a contradiction is the fastest way to finish it. If you don't find one quickly, however, it may be best to stop exploring that particular option and try another.

PROVING A CONTRADICTION

If you feel fairly sure a particular deduction is *false* then it can be useful to pretend it is *true* and then look for a resulting contradiction. Sometimes the inverse of an option is much easier to analyse than its positive version. This same advice can be applied to many situations. Thinking about the opposite of a situation can often be very informative. What are the reasons for doing something, but also what are the reasons for *not* doing it?

PATTERN SPOTTING

The longer you spend on many types of puzzle, the more you learn to spot patterns in those puzzles. You may even spot patterns based on the way the puzzles are set – for example, there may be certain clue arrangements in a logic puzzle that recur time and again. Once you have learned to make sense of these patterns the first time, you know to apply similar logic in future. It's the same general method your brain uses in day-to-day life, whereby your experience with tackling life's many real-world challenges allows you to better handle similar tasks in the future.

The more you solve different types of puzzle, the better you will get at finding logic that can help you make progress as your brain learns to ask more and more sensible 'what if' questions earlier in the solving process. You'll also get better at considering the options in your head, such as the way that skilled sudoku players can 'see' at a glance which numbers are missing from a region, without having to run through them one by one.

You'll also find general rules that can be applied across multiple puzzles – for example, in any loop puzzle, such as the one at the top of the following page, there must always be an *even* number of loop segments travelling in and out of an area, so if a move will make that impossible then it must be wrong. If not, there would be a part of the loop that couldn't connect.

LOGIC PUZZLES

188. Draw a single loop by connecting some dots with horizontal and vertical lines, so that each numbered square has the specified number of adjacent line segments. The loop cannot cross or touch itself.

189. Join dots with horizontal and vertical lines to form a single path which does not touch or cross itself, or any of the solid blocks, at any point. The start and end of the path are given. Numbers outside the grid specify the exact number of dots in their row or column that are visited by the path.

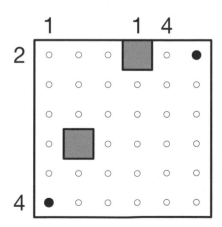

190. Place A to G once each into every row, column and bold-lined region.

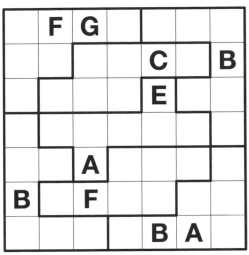

191. Draw a horizontal or vertical line across the full width or height of each empty square. Numbers on shaded squares reveal the total length of all lines touching them, measured in square lengths.

192. Write a number into each of the empty squares, so that the grid contains every number from 1 to 81 exactly once. Place the numbers so that there is a route from 1 to 81 that visits every grid square exactly once in increasing numerical order, moving only left, right, up or down – but not diagonally – between touching squares.

	23						53	
		25				49		
			35		47			
			39		59			
		17				61		
	15						63	

193. Place 1 to 5 once each into every row and column of this grid. Place digits in the grid in such a way that each given clue number outside the grid represents the number of digits that are 'visible' from that point, looking along that clue's row or column.

A digit is visible unless there is a higher digit preceding it, reading in order along that row or column. For example, if a row was '21435' then the 2, 4 and 5 would be visible (giving a clue of '3' visible digits), since 1 is obscured by the preceding higher 2, and 3 is obscured by the preceding higher 4.

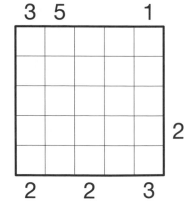

194. Join circled numbers with horizontal or vertical lines. Each number must have as many lines connected to it as specified by its value. No more than two lines may join any pair of numbers, and no lines may cross. The finished layout must connect all numbers, so you can travel between any pair of numbers by following one or more lines.

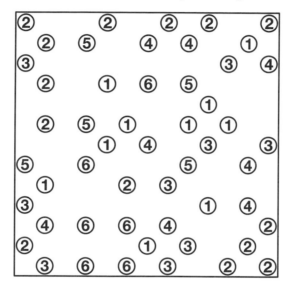

195. Place the letters A, B and C exactly once each into every row and column of squares inside the grid. Two squares in each row or column will therefore be empty. Letters outside the grid indicate which letter appears closest to that end in the clue's row or column.

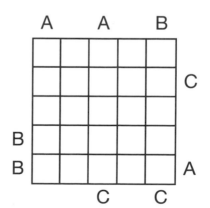

196. Place 1 to 7 once each into every row and column while obeying the inequality signs. Greater than (>) signs between some squares indicate that the value in one square is greater than that in another as indicated by the sign. The sign always points towards the smaller number.

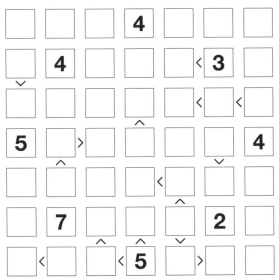

197. Place 1 to 6 once each into every row and column of the grid. Some intersections contain 4 digits, which are to be placed into the touching 4 squares in some order.

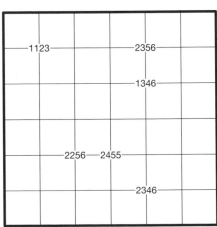

198. Place a digit from 1 to 9 into each white square. Each horizontal run of white squares adds up to the total above the diagonal line to the left of the run, and each vertical run of white squares adds up to the total below the diagonal line above the run. No digit can be used more than once in any run.

199. Draw a single loop through some empty squares, made up of horizontal and vertical lines between square centres. The loop does not cross or overlap itself, and can only pass through empty grid squares. Squares with numbers indicate how many touching squares the loop passes through, including diagonally touching squares.

2							3
					7		
4		8					
						6	
	8			6			
				5			
		5					
							2

WORKING BACKWARDS

It's often instructive, when tackling new types of puzzle, to try deconstructing a solution. A well-designed logic puzzle will have only one unique solution. If it didn't then there would always be a point in the solution where you *had* to guess, since multiple options would be equally valid and there would be no reason to choose between them. When it comes to printed puzzles this is generally considered unfair, and in a book it would mean that the solution at the back wouldn't always match your own solution. All of the logic puzzles in this book have unique solutions.

BEING AT THE END

In day-to-day life you don't have the luxury of beginning at the end, but with a printed puzzle you do. Look at the solution and consider the various given clues, and experiment to see what would happen if the clue wasn't there. Would there be an alternative solution, and if so what might that be? Not all clues are necessarily needed in logic puzzles, however, since they may be there for visual balance – such as a pleasing clue symmetry in a sudoku – or in order to make the puzzle easier to solve. But even so, it's often instructive to examine a solution and see how the various components fit together, and what has resulted from each clue. This is particularly true for more complex puzzles, where the connection between a given clue and its effect may be less directly obvious.

Another use for a solution is to create an easier puzzle. Keep adding parts of the solution to the puzzle until you are able to make a new deduction. You can also use them to check your solve as you go, and perhaps alert you to false assumptions you didn't realize you had made. Especially when learning to solve new puzzles, there's nothing wrong with getting a helping hand in this way. You could try it with some of the puzzles on the following pages, if you wish.

COUNTER-INTUITIVE STEPS

Sometimes the solution to a puzzle requires a counter-intuitive step. In the classic fox, goose and grain puzzle, you must escort all three across a river using a single boat. Unfortunately only two will fit in the boat at any one time, and if you leave the fox alone with the goose it will kill it, or if you leave the goose alone with the grain it will eat it. So how do you cross the river? Can you work it out?

The reason this puzzle is often found hard to solve is that solving it requires you to *reverse* a step you have already made. You must bring one of the three across the river with you, and then bring it *back* too. Reversing a step we have already made seems counter-intuitive.

The solution is to cross with the fox and goose (or goose and grain), then leave the goose on the opposite side *but return with the other* (the fox or the grain). Then you can pick up the remaining item and return to the far side.

SMART REASONING PUZZLES

Try this puzzle, which works in a similar way.

200. Four tourists reach a rickety old bridge late at night, which they need to cross to get to their hotel. They only have one torch between them, but the battery is about to go and so they want to cross the bridge as fast as possible.

Unfortunately, a sign warns them that the bridge can't hold the weight of more than two people at any one time. And they'll need the torch to cross, since it's clearly damaged and they don't want to plunge into the icy waters far below!

The tourists all move at different speeds and will each take a different amount of time to cross the bridge.

(continued overleaf...)

Here's how long each tourist will take to cross the bridge:

- Zeus will take eight minutes to cross

- Yolanda will take five minutes to cross

- Xavier will take two minutes to cross

- Walder will take one minute to cross

When the tourists cross the bridge, they'll always need to have the torch with them and so they'll have to cross at the speed of the slowest person in each pair.

The bridge is too long to be able to throw the torch back to the other side, so each time a pair crosses then one of the pair will have to come back to the original side with the torch.

It turns out that the battery of the torch will last for just 15 minutes – find a strategy that allows all four of the tourists to reach the other side in this exact amount of time.

201. Solve this 'backwards' puzzle where the clues are written outside the grid. Place a single digit from 1 to 6 into every square, so that each digit appears once in every row and column *inside* the grid. Some digits are given outside the grid. These digits must be placed in the nearest two squares in their row or column. If there is one digit, it is up to you to work out which of the two squares to place it into. If there are two digits, they may be placed in either order.

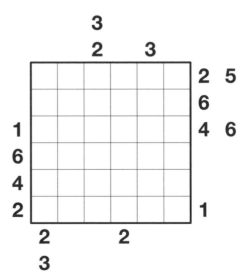

202. In this skeleton crossword most of the grid is missing. Work backwards from the clues to fill in not just the answers but also the grid itself. The grid has rotational symmetry, just like the crossword on page 55, so you can shade in a few squares immediately.

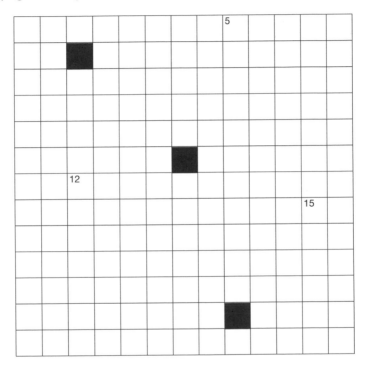

Across
1 Etch (7)
5 Declare (5)
9 Physical convulsion due to the flow of current (8,5)
10 Something that calms (8)
11 Foremost (4)
12 Smoker's need (9)
16 Chinese dynasty (4)
17 Efficient (8)
19 Absolute (13)
21 Age (5)
22 Christmas or Easter (4,3)

Down
2 Neckband (6)
3 Storing records (9)
4 Welsh breed of dog (5)
6 Royal family members (inits) (3)
7 Ploy (6)
8 Meagre; unusual (6)
11 A set of foundation stories (9)
13 Plan (6)
14 Enrol (4,2)
15 Noisy grass insect (6)
18 Exceed (5)
20 Ogre (3)

VISUAL AND SPATIAL AWARENESS

The human brain has the remarkable ability to make easy sense of the visual world around us. We don't usually need to devote much conscious thought to working out what we are looking at, because our brains do it all for us. As babies we learn to recognize objects, shapes and movement, and then as adults these skills are so deeply learned that we rarely give them a moment's thought. Some of our visual learning does have weaknesses, however, and it's good to be aware of them.

PERCEPTION OF SPEED

We aren't very good at judging speeds of objects. Have you ever looked out from a building directly alongside a motorway, such as a service station, and been surprised at just how fast the cars are passing by? And yet when you are in a car on the very same motorway, your perception of speed feels very different. Perhaps if we were all able to sit outside and watch ourselves drive by, there would be fewer dangerous speeding incidents.

When it comes to natural sources of movement, such as someone sprinting or throwing a ball, our judgements are far more accurate. Unfortunately, both our development as a baby – children don't sit by motorways, or learn to drive – and our evolutionary history have not prepared us well for judging high speeds. When driving, most people hugely underestimate how quickly they will reach a vehicle in front should it suddenly brake, nor have any accurate perception of the distance they will require to come to a standstill should they need to brake suddenly. If we come upon a slower vehicle on a fast road, we find ourselves catching up with it much faster than we anticipate – a potentially dangerous lesson that most new drivers experience at some point. The problem is that we don't *know* how bad we are at these judgements, so we consistently overestimate our own abilities.

Perception of speed isn't just important when driving, but also when travelling in any way near objects moving at high speed. Children have even less idea than adults how quickly a vehicle can close on them, so often make very poor judgements in terms of attempting to cross the road, or head out into a road to retrieve a ball, or avoid a barking dog. This is why it's essential to educate about road safety from an early age.

MIRRORS

Although we become familiar with mirrors from an early age, the chances are that you will still need to consciously think whether something is on your right or left when looking at a reflection. Keep in mind, however, that many people have trouble with this concept even when *not* reflected!

Try placing a tray of objects in front of a mirror, and see how well you can pick up and manipulate those objects using just the mirror as your guide. You might be surprised at how tricky this is. It's good to practise using mirrors in complete safety, like this, rather than when driving a car and facing a potentially dangerous situation.

PERCEPTION OF HEIGHTS

We are astonishingly poor at judging heights. If you have ever been to a city with many very tall buildings, such as Manhattan, you will find that if you look upwards from road level that many of the tall buildings all look identical in height. And yet if you climb to the top of a skyscraper such as the Empire State Building, you will be astonished to look down and see just how much they vary in height.

This same weakness exists with much smaller heights too. If you are asked to judge the width and height of a tree, you will typically underestimate the height relative to the width. The taller the item, the greater the disparity between your judgement and the reality.

VISUAL AND SPATIAL AWARENESS PUZZLES

203. Even on a printed page, it can be tricky to judge heights. Looking at the diagram below, make a quick, snap decision on which of the lines on the right is the continuation of the line on the left. Many people get this wrong – use a straight-edged object, such as a ruler, to find out if you were correct.

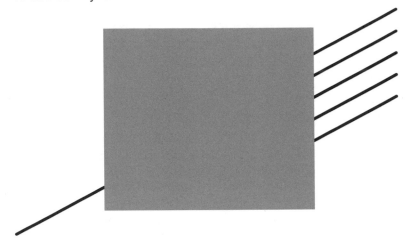

204. Draw borders along the grid lines in this image to divide it into four identical shapes, with no unused squares. The shapes can be rotated relative to one another, but cannot be reflected.

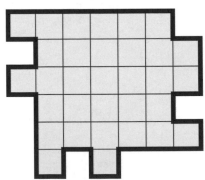

205. Draw exactly three straight lines to divide up this image so that there is exactly one of each size of circle in each resulting area.

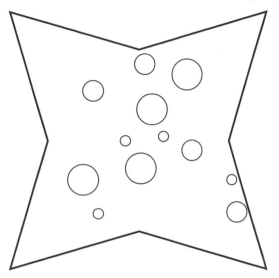

206. Draw exactly three straight lines to divide up this image so that there is exactly one of each type of shape in each resulting area.

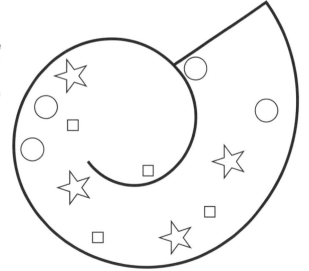

THINKING IN THREE DIMENSIONS

The world around us is constructed in three dimensions, with objects positioned not just left/right or up/down from us, but also with depth near/far from us. However, much of the time information is presented to us on a flat, two-dimensional page or screen – without depth. Being able to readily transform that flat representation into an accurate concept of its three-dimensional representation is therefore a key skill. In some circumstances, such as reading a map when travelling at speed, it can even be critically important.

When it comes to navigating our way from A to B, we are able to do this with relative ease when traveling at walking pace. But as soon as we are moving much faster, as when driving, we need to make more pressurized, quicker decisions. We need to judge the curve and width of a road, as well as the width, length, direction and speed of the vehicle we are driving. Not just this, but the gap between us and the car in front, and the impact of obstacles that we are passing, such as parked cars and traffic coming the other way. At night, we need to infer some of this from even less visual information, and ignore significant distractions such as glare. And when it's raining or misty, there's even more visual confusion. Given all these issues, it's incredible that we are able to manage this process at all, but clearly the faster we travel the less time we are giving ourselves to make corrections should any of these instantaneous calculations be wrong.

Being able to read a map allows us to prepare in advance for some of the decisions we face when driving, or indeed navigating in any way. Learning to understand how our current direction corresponds to what we see on a map, and to translate a series of twists and turns into a rough idea in our head of which direction we should be heading, means that we can be better prepared to handle the road ahead. In many cases map information will be provided dynamically via a GPS-based system, meaning that the ability to immediately interpret the map drawings, or simulated 3D projection on-screen, can be critical to safe driving.

It's useful, therefore, to practise these skills. If you find translating a map into reality tricky, then obtain a map of your local area – or use a smart device with one on and disable auto-rotation – and go outside and walk around until it starts to make more sense. Even if this takes many walks over many weeks, it's a skill well worth learning. Over time you may develop a better sense of direction, allowing you to instinctively know which direction is 'home', at least when walking relatively short distances.

PACKING
Another three-dimensionally based skill is packing, whether it's loading a box for posting or fitting several sets of luggage into a car boot. Some may seem to have an instinctive concept of how things will fit, but in reality it's mostly a mix of experience and common sense. Starting with the largest objects usually works best, and then using small objects to fill gaps around them so as not to waste space. Lots of practice as a child, or indeed adult, with building bricks of various shapes and sizes no doubt helps, but as with many things in life a small pause to think before beginning is often the real key.

THREE-DIMENSIONAL MANIPULATION
Many people find it tricky to imagine rotating three-dimensional objects in their head, especially if rotating them to unusual angles. If you're imagining manipulating the object at the same time as well, for example by folding it, it can even feel mentally overwhelming when you try to picture it. But like many things that seem extremely hard when you first try them, it becomes easier with practice. Most of us lack much direct experience with this kind of deliberate manipulation, so even just a little practice can be surprisingly useful. There are some suitable exercises on the following two pages.

THREE-DIMENSIONAL VISUALIZATION

207. You're holding a spherical object in your hand, such as a football for example, and you mark three points on it at random. What is the chance that all three marks end up all on the same half of the sphere?

208. All but three of the following shape nets could be folded up to form a perfect six-sided cube – which three are the ones that could not?

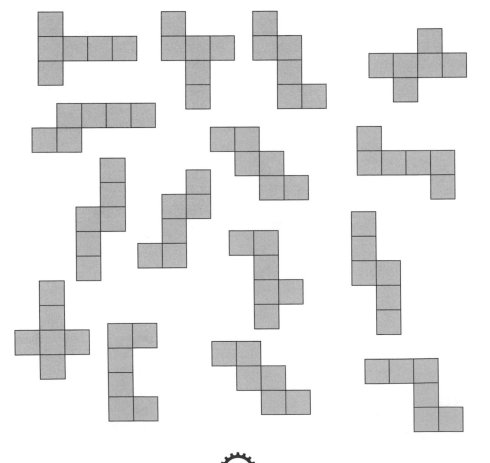

209. Three of these cube nets will fold up to form identical cubes, but one will be slightly different. Which is the odd one out?

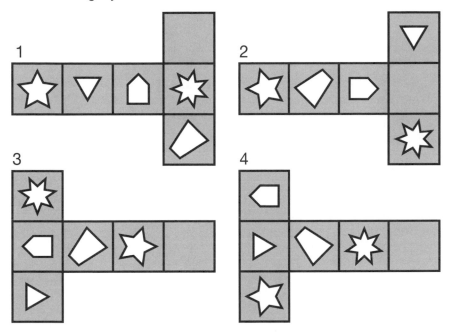

210. Which of the three pyramids below does this shape net make?

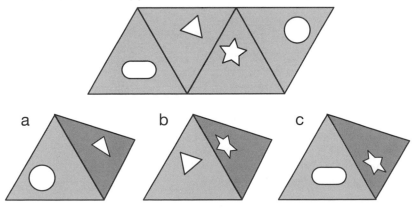

211. Which of the following shape nets could be folded up to make a perfect four-sided triangular-based pyramid?

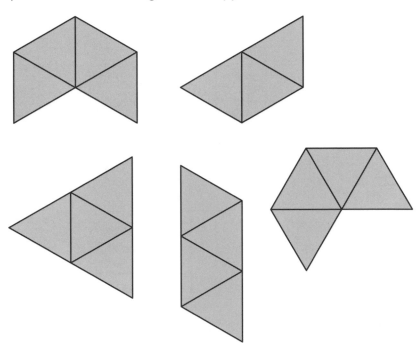

Now imagine that you have a set of cubes arranged as shown to the right. This cuboid is five wide by four deep by four high. Imagine that you remove some cubes. Given that every cube that isn't on the bottom level has to be supported by another and cannot be floating in space, how many cubes are there in each of the following images?

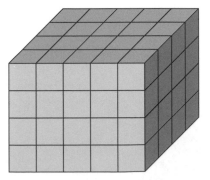

212.

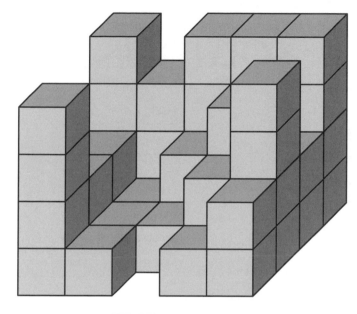

213.

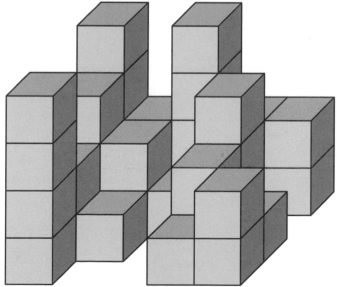

SOLUTIONS

PUZZLE 1

	1	9	5	8	3	6	4	2
6	2	3	7	4		1	8	9
5	4	8	9	6	1		7	3
8	7		3	9	2	5	6	1
2	3	5		7	6	8	9	4
1	9	6	8	5	4	2	3	
9	5	1	4		8	3	2	7
3		2	6	1	7	4	5	8
4	8	7	2	3	5	9		6

PUZZLE 2

O	X	X	O	X	X
X	O	O	X	X	X
X	O	X	O	O	O
X	O	X	O	X	X
O	X	O	X	O	X
X	X	X	O	X	O

PUZZLE 3

1	4	4	1	1	3	0	5
1	3	6	3	3	2	2	6
6	5	0	3	2	3	1	5
6	6	4	1	4	6	0	2
0	2	1	2	2	5	5	0
2	4	3	3	6	4	4	0
1	5	5	4	5	0	6	0

PUZZLE 4

1	1	0	0	1	0	1	0
0	0	1	1	0	0	1	1
1	0	0	1	0	1	0	1
0	1	1	0	1	0	1	0
0	0	1	1	0	1	0	1
1	0	0	1	0	0	1	1
0	1	1	0	1	1	0	0
1	1	0	0	1	1	0	0

PUZZLE 5

Horizontally: 8   Vertically: 10
Total: 18 times

PUZZLE 6

It's the 1st of January today, and my birthday is on the 31st of December

PUZZLE 7

Friday is the name of his horse

PUZZLE 8

Put it down on its side. It will be easy to see if it is half full or not

PUZZLE 9

One way is to get every jockey to swap horses with another

PUZZLE 10

One method is to slowly pour sand into the hole, so the hamster can climb up bit by bit

PUZZLE 11

The match

PUZZLE 12

Fold your arms before you pick up the scarf. When you fold them, make sure that one hand is on top of the other arm, and the other hand is sitting under the remaining arm. Then unfold them.

PUZZLE 13

Put your jeans on backwards or inside out

PUZZLE 14

I live near the poles, where during winter there is no sunrise

PUZZLE 15

They may predict it; they may well not be accurate, however!

PUZZLE 16

One of the fathers was the son of the other

father, who passed on the first heirloom

PUZZLE 17
In a dictionary

PUZZLE 18
Just catch it!

PUZZLE 19
Holes

PUZZLE 20
Half way

PUZZLE 21
White – I'm at the North Pole

PUZZLE 22

PUZZLE 23

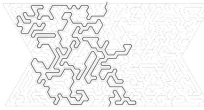

PUZZLE 24

PUZZLE 25

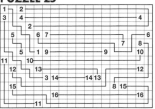

PUZZLE 26

PUZZLE 27

PUZZLE 28
Simply view it in a mirror:

PUZZLE 29

PUZZLE 30

PUZZLE 31

Inward		Outward	
1-6	GOLDEN	100-95	BONSAI
7-9	REV	94-89	PESETA
10-14	OGLES	88-84	RISKS
15-18	NITS	83-78	ATTEND
19-22	SENT	77-74	ALAS
23-27	PANEL	73-70	LOCO
28-30	LOP	69-63	TORPEDO
31-37	DESSERT	62-57	REDUCE
38-42	SIDED	56-54	GEL
43-46	ICON	53-49	LATER
47-51	EGRET	48-41	GENOCIDE
52-57	ALLEGE	40-31	DISTRESSED
58-60	CUD	30-25	POLLEN
61-65	ERODE	24-18	APTNESS
66-73	PROTOCOL	17-12	TINSEL
74-78	SALAD	11-4	GOVERNED
79-81	NET	3-1	LOG
82-86	TASKS		
87-91	IRATE		
92-96	SEPIA		
97-100	SNOB		

PUZZLE 32

PUZZLE 33

PUZZLE 34

PUZZLE 35

Poppy, rose, tulip, lily, lavender, peony

PUZZLE 36

11 times

PUZZLE 37

PUZZLE 38

99 of them can definitely survive, and all 100 might with a 50:50 chance. The prisoners at the back can agree that the first prisoner, who can see everyone, calls out 'red' if he sees an odd number of red hats, and 'blue' if he sees an even number of red hats. Now the person in front of him can simply count how many hats he can see – if he is expecting an odd number of red hats but sees an even number, he *knows* he is wearing a red hat since the difference must be accounted for by him. If, however, he is expecting an odd number of red hats and *sees* an odd number of red hats, then he must be wearing blue. The prisoner in front can then update his expectations appropriately – if the guy behind him calls out 'red', he will change his expectation of red hats from odd to even, or from even to odd. If he calls out 'blue', he won't change it. And so on down the line, with all prisoners now able to answer correctly.

PUZZLE 39

11 glasses. He can make 10 glasses initially, then pour the remains of these together to make one more.

PUZZLE 40

The man breaks each pill in half, discarding one half and consuming the other. By the time he is done he will have eaten a total of one green pill and one yellow pill.

PUZZLE 41

Samuel is telling the truth. If Diana was telling the truth she'd contradict herself, and Dave can't be telling the truth since none of the three agree.

PUZZLE 42

Walk in circles around and around the tree, with the dog following as described, until the leash becomes short enough that you can reach the car. The dog would have to race back around to free itself, even if it was smart enough, during which time you could get inside the car.

PUZZLE 43

PUZZLE 44

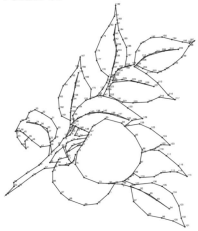

PUZZLE 50

How about 'It was a crazy ant-tic'?!

PUZZLE 51

Maybe 'One is a staple and the other is a stable'?

PUZZLE 52

'It depends on his name', perhaps!

PUZZLE 56

PUZZLE 57

PUZZLE 60

11 hexagons
9 circles
2 non-overlapping circles

PUZZLE 61

PUZZLE 62

PUZZLE 63

Nine-letter word: hallmarks

PUZZLE 64

Nine-letter word: innocents

PUZZLE 65

Nine-letter word: underarms

PUZZLE 66

Nine-letter word: squadrons

PUZZLE 67
Sixteen-letter word: transcontinental

PUZZLE 68
Sixteen-letter word: interconnections

PUZZLE 69
Sixteen-letter word: responsibilities

PUZZLE 70
Sixteen-letter word: autobiographical

PUZZLE 71
Sixteen-letter word: institutionalize

PUZZLE 72
Sixteen-letter word: internationalism

PUZZLE 73
TENNIS

PUZZLE 74
FOOTBALL

PUZZLE 75
RUGBY

PUZZLE 76
SWIMMING

PUZZLE 77
BASKETBALL

PUZZLE 78
HOCKEY

PUZZLE 79
BADMINTON

PUZZLE 80
PURPLE

PUZZLE 81
ORANGE

PUZZLE 82
TURQUOISE

PUZZLE 83
COPPER

PUZZLE 84
WHITE

PUZZLE 85
CRIMSON

PUZZLE 86
RUBY

PUZZLE 87
Fight Club

PUZZLE 88
Inception

PUZZLE 89
Casablanca

PUZZLE 90
Interstellar

PUZZLE 91
Memento

PUZZLE 92
WALL-E

PUZZLE 93
Die Hard

PUZZLE 94
Inside Out

PUZZLE 95
TOPCOAT

PUZZLE 96
ARMADA

PUZZLE 97
CYNIC

PUZZLE 98
AMOEBA

PUZZLE 99
NEURON

PUZZLE 100
GULAG

PUZZLE 101
TAUT

PUZZLE 102
Germany

PUZZLE 103
Afghanistan

PUZZLE 104
Georgia

PUZZLE 105
Denmark

PUZZLE 106
Argentina

PUZZLE 107
Nicaragua

PUZZLE 108
Kazakhstan

PUZZLE 109
Madagascar

PUZZLE 110
Florida

PUZZLE 111
Arizona

PUZZLE 112
Massachusetts

PUZZLE 113
New Mexico

PUZZLE 114
Tennessee

PUZZLE 115
South Carolina

PUZZLE 116
Rhode Island

PUZZLE 117
Robinson Crusoe by Daniel Defoe

PUZZLE 118
Tom Jones by Henry Fielding

PUZZLE 119
Emma by Jane Austen

PUZZLE 120
The Count of Monte Cristo by Alexandre Dumas

PUZZLE 121
David Copperfield by Charles Dickens

PUZZLE 122
Jane Eyre by Charlotte Brontë

PUZZLE 123
Vanity Fair by William Makepeace Thackeray

PUZZLE 124
Alice's Adventures In Wonderland by Lewis Carroll

PUZZLE 125
Ordinal numbers: First second third fourth fifth sixth

PUZZLE 126
Months: April May June July August September

PUZZLE 127
Planets: Mercury Venus Earth Mars Jupiter Saturn

PUZZLE 128
Fractions: Half third quarter fifth sixth seventh

PUZZLE 129
Periodic table elements: Hydrogen helium lithium beryllium boron carbon

PUZZLE 130
Homophones

PUZZLE 131
Anagrams of one another

PUZZLE 132
Palindromic words

PUZZLE 133
Words that have no perfect rhymes in English

PUZZLE 134
Vowelless words

PUZZLE 135
Phonetic alphabet letters

PUZZLE 136
Font terms

PUZZLE 137
Blues

PUZZLE 138
Mr. Men

PUZZLE 139
Cuts of beef

PUZZLE 140
Cypher codes

PUZZLE 141
Characters in *Swallows and Amazons*

PUZZLE 142
Donald Trump's children

PUZZLE 143
Pac-Man® ghosts

PUZZLE 144
Batman actors

PUZZLE 145
English words of Indian origin

PUZZLE 146
D-Day landing beaches

PUZZLE 147
Belts

PUZZLE 148
Cities in Arizona

PUZZLE 149
Words that can mean their own opposite

PUZZLE 150
20th century UK Chancellors of the Exchequer

PUZZLE 151
Google products

PUZZLE 152
31 > 45 > 16 > 8 > 2 > 23

PUZZLE 153
43 > 25 > 5 > 55 > 20 > 30

PUZZLE 154
24 > 4 > 28 > 35 > 12 > 18

PUZZLE 155
20 > 19 > 38 > 81 > 54 > 6

PUZZLE 156
26 > 13 > 41 > 82 > 99 > 33

PUZZLE 157
34 > 17 > 75 > 23 > 92 > 86

PUZZLE 158
20 > 100 > 71 > 84 > 42 > 64

PUZZLE 159
60 > 26 > 130 > 88 > 22 > 33

PUZZLE 160
67 > 31 > 192 > 48 > 42 > 63

PUZZLE 161
110 > 44 > 22 > 33 > 66 > 63

PUZZLE 162
63 = 25 + 23 + 15
75 = 9 + 38 + 28
84 = 19 + 37 + 28

PUZZLE 163
61 = 16 + 35 + 10

70 = 16 + 40 + 14
78 = 26 + 15 + 37

PUZZLE 164
52 = 28 + 11 + 13
66 = 14 + 20 + 32
76 = 25 + 19 + 32

PUZZLE 165
57 = 8 + 26 + 23
68 = 20 + 18 + 30
76 = 20 + 26 + 30

PUZZLE 166
The actual answer is 40,320

PUZZLE 167
The actual answer is 40,320

PUZZLE 168
33,522,128,640

PUZZLE 169
34 = 9 + 25
55 = 9 + 21 + 25
68 = 21 + 22 + 25
92 = 7 + 9 + 10 + 19 + 22 + 25

PUZZLE 170
35 = 17 + 18
52 = 9 + 18 + 25
77 = 6 + 9 + 17 + 22 + 23
85 = 6 + 9 + 22 + 23 + 25

PUZZLE 171
40 = 16 + 24
60 = 16 + 20 + 24
80 = 12 + 21 + 22 + 25
100 = 12 + 20 + 21 + 22 + 25

PUZZLE 172
82 = (7 + 3) × 8 + 6 - 4
47 = (8 + 6 + 4) × 3 - 7

PUZZLE 173
97 = 8 × 9 + (10 × 3) - 5
441 = ((9 + 10) × 8 - 5) × 3

PUZZLE 174

```
        249
     117   132
   56   61   71
  29  27  34  37
15  14  13  21  16
```

PUZZLE 175

```
        253
     118   135
   58   60   75
  31  27  33  42
22  9  18  15  27
```

PUZZLE 176

```
        329
     148   181
   64   84   97
  28  40  44  53
11  17  23  21  32
```

PUZZLE 177

```
        474
     231   243
   101   130   113
  38  63  67  46
13  25  38  29  17
```

PUZZLE 178
You should *always* switch doors. Whatever happens *after* you make your original choice doesn't change your chance of winning – so if you stick with that door, you *still* have a 1 in 3 chance of winning.

It therefore stands to reason that if you switch to the other, since probabilities of all possible events must add up to 1, you have a 2 in 3 chance of winning. So you're twice as likely to win if you switch doors.

Essentially, the host is merging the two other doors into one, by opening the one he *knows* has no prize – which is another explanation for why switching to the other door will give you a 2 in 3 chance of winning.

PUZZLE 179

The policy has *no* effect – the likelihood of any child being born a boy or a girl remains constant, no matter what! All that happens is that some families aren't permitted to have so many children.

PUZZLE 180

Six – there is just the one sister!

PUZZLE 181

1 in 3, not 1 in 2 as might be expected. The possibilities for the genders of his children are boy-boy, boy-girl, girl-boy and girl-girl. But we can eliminate boy-boy, since we know he has a girl, so the chance he has *two* girls is 1 in 3.

PUZZLE 182

The couples already know one another, so the options are for each person to exchange anywhere from 0 to 8 cards. Andrea must therefore exchange the same number of cards as someone else, since there are only 9 options in total.

The person who exchanged 8 cards has to be in a couple with the person who exchanged 0 cards, otherwise that person could only have exchanged 7 cards at maximum. Similarly, the person who exchanged 7 cards is with the person who exchanged 1 card, and so on – so the couples exchanged 8 and 0 cards, 7 and 1 cards, 6 and 2 cards, and 5 and 3 cards. So Bob must have received 4 cards.

PUZZLE 183

I bet on 5, 10, 15, 20, 25, 30 and 35, which is 7 out of 37 options. So my odds are 7 in 37.

PUZZLE 184

$1/6 \times 1/6 \times 1/6 \times 1/6 \times 1/6 = 1/7776$

PUZZLE 185

There is a $(1/2)^8 = 1/256$ chance of all heads, and the same for tails, so 1/128 for *either* heads or tails

PUZZLE 186

The winning possibilities are win-win, win-lose and lose-win. So they are $(1/10 \times 1/10) + (1/10 \times 9/10) + (9/10 \times 1/10) = 1/100 + 9/100 + 9/100 = 19/100$

PUZZLE 187

3	4	2	5	6	1
6	2	5	1	4	3
5	1	3	6	2	4
2	3	6	4	1	5
1	5	4	2	3	6
4	6	1	3	5	2

PUZZLE 188

PUZZLE 189

PUZZLE 190

E	F	G	B	D	C	A
D	A	E	G	C	F	B
C	B	D	A	E	G	F
A	G	B	C	F	D	E
F	D	A	E	G	B	C
B	C	F	D	A	E	G
G	E	C	F	B	A	D

PUZZLE 191

PUZZLE 192

3	2	1	28	29	30	51	52	81
4	23	24	27	32	31	50	53	80
5	22	25	26	33	48	49	54	79
6	21	36	35	34	47	46	55	78
7	20	37	38	43	44	45	56	77
8	19	18	39	42	59	58	57	76
9	16	17	40	41	60	61	62	75
10	15	14	67	66	65	64	63	74
11	12	13	68	69	70	71	72	73

PUZZLE 193

```
     3  5        1
   ┌──┬──┬──┬──┬──┐
   │ 3│ 1│ 2│ 4│ 5│
   ├──┼──┼──┼──┼──┤
   │ 4│ 2│ 5│ 3│ 1│
   ├──┼──┼──┼──┼──┤
   │ 5│ 3│ 1│ 2│ 4│
   ├──┼──┼──┼──┼──┤
   │ 1│ 4│ 3│ 5│ 2│ 2
   ├──┼──┼──┼──┼──┤
   │ 2│ 5│ 4│ 1│ 3│
   └──┴──┴──┴──┴──┘
     2     2     3
```

PUZZLE 194

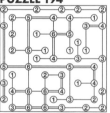

PUZZLE 195

```
      A     A     B
   ┌──┬──┬──┬──┬──┐
   │  │ C│ A│  │ B│
   ├──┼──┼──┼──┼──┤
   │ A│  │ B│ C│  │ C
   ├──┼──┼──┼──┼──┤
   │ C│  │  │ B│ A│
   ├──┼──┼──┼──┼──┤
 B │ B│ A│  │  │  │ C
   ├──┼──┼──┼──┼──┤
 B │  │ B│ C│ A│  │ A
   └──┴──┴──┴──┴──┘
         C     C
```

PUZZLE 196

1	5	2	4	7	6	3
6	4	5	7	1	3	2
2	1	7	3	4	5	6
5	2	1	6	3	7	4
7	3	6	2	5	4	1
4	7	3	1	6	2	5
3	6	4	5	2	1	7

PUZZLE 197

1	3	6	2	5	4
2	1	4	6	3	5
6	5	3	1	4	2
4	6	2	5	1	3
3	2	5	4	6	1
5	4	1	3	2	6

PUZZLE 198

PUZZLE 199

```
 2  ┌─────────┐        3
    │       ┌─┘  7
 4  │  8    │
    │  ┌────┘     6
    │  │  ┌──┐
 8  └──┘  │  │6
       ┌──┘  │5
       │  5  │
       │     └──┐
       │      2 │
```

PUZZLE 200

The secret is to make sure the two slowest people cross together – this involves *both* the initial two people who cross the bridge coming back at some point. So:

Have Xavier and Walder cross the bridge, taking 2 minutes.

Have Walder cross back, taking 1 minute.

Have Zeus and Yolanda cross over, taking 8 minutes.

Have Xavier cross back, taking 2 minutes.

Have Xavier and Walder cross the bridge, taking 2 minutes.